Peg

Edible and Medicinal Plants
of the
Great Lakes Region

Thomas A. Naegele, D.O.

About the Author

Dr. Thomas Naegele spent his youth exploring and studying the flora of Michigan. He earned his B.S. and M.S. in Botany from Michigan Technological University, and his D.O. from Michigan State University. He is also the author of *Edible Wild Plants of the Copper Country* and *Edible and Medicinal Plants of the Great Lakes* (first edition).

Now in private practice in Albuquerque, New Mexico, Dr. Naegele is a pioneer in the study of computerized medical record systems. He has given over 500 hours of workshops and lectures on Clinical Decision Making, Computerized Medical Records, and Total Quality Management.

Tom is pictured above with his wife, Sarah, and their four sons, Zao, Ray, Sun Armando, and Leonard.

Edible and Medicinal Plants
of the
Great Lakes Region

Thomas A. Naegele, D.O.

Bryophytes Section by Janice M. Glime, Ph.D.

Wilderness Adventure Books
Davisburg, Michigan

Copyright © 1996 by Thomas A. Naegele, D.O.

All rights reserved. No part of this book may be reproduced or utilized in any form or by any electronic or mechanical means including photocopying, recording, or by any information storage and retrieval system, without permission in writing from the publisher, except by a reviewer who may quote brief passages in a review.

LCCN: 96-12137
ISBN: 0-923568-37-9

Illustrations by Julie C. Clark, Owen W. Drudge,
Marjorie N. Klein, and Lisa K. Usitalu

Cover Design by BDW Designs, Inc.

 **Wilderness Adventure Books**
P.O. Box 217
Davisburg, MI 48350

Library of Congress Cataloging in Publication Data

Naegele, Thomas A.
    Edible and medicinal plants of the Great Lakes region / Thomas A.
    Naegele. -- (Rev. ed.)
    Includes bibliographical references and index.
    ISBN: 0-923568-37-9
    1. Medicinal plants—Great Lakes Region. 2. Wild plants, Edible—
    Great Lakes Region. 3. Materia medica, Vegetable—Great Lakes
    Region.   I. Title.
    QK99.G73N33   1996
    581.6'3'0977--dc20   96-12137

Manufactured in the United States of America

Acknowledgements: The creation of this book would not have been possible without the Creator Himself, thankyou.

Warning

This manual is only a compendium of literature and folk uses of edible and medicinal plants. Because much of the information is unavailable to this project (information in certain categories is totally lacking), *caution must be exercised when using this manual.*

For instance, the greatest content of the chemical compound, Sanguinarine, in the plant bloodroot occurs in the spring; thus, that is the season it is collected for commercial purposes. Since it is established that the chemical compounds in plants change seasonally, it is quite possible that certain plants are harmless in one season and toxic in another. Seasonal variation is only one consideration; there are many more.

For any health problems, one must consult a health care professional. There are many natural medicine practitioners who are skilled at offering herbal prescriptions.

Any experimental results are welcome. Please send them to:

Thomas A. Naegele, DO
c/o Wilderness Adventure Books
P.O. Box 217
Davisburg, Michigan 48350

Send information in the following format:

LATN	The Latin Name.
FAM	The Family Name.
COMN	The Common Names.
STEM	The Stem Description.
LVS	The Leaf Description.
INFL	The Flower Description.
FRUIT	The Fruit and Seed Description.
ROOT	The Root Description.
GEN	Generalities.
HABT	The Natural Growing Habitat.
WHEN	The Seasons When the Plant is Collected.
WFOR	The Parts of the Plants Collected and How Prepared.
MEDT	Medical Terminology.
SYMP	Symptoms and Folk Lore.
POIS	Poisonous Aspects and Information.
BIOL	Biological and Edible Information.
CHEM	Chemistry and Pharmacognosy.
COMR	Commercial Applications and Products.
PERS	Personal Experimentation and Uses.

Place & date collected, part used, use, how prepared/administered.

Table of Contents

Editor's Note

In 1980 I sold my first book—*Edible and Medicinal Plants of the Great Lakes* by Tom Naegele. My father, Lenny Howarth, paid my sister and me three dollars for every book we sold door-to-door in Davisburg. Since Davisburg is only five blocks long, this first taste of book selling was hardly a profitable venture.

Long after the cases of *Edible and Medicinal Plants* no longer littered our basement, my father again delved into the publishing business. A junior in high school, I had no idea how to pay for college, but had spent the previous three years researching and writing a book. Lenny, remembering the success of Tom Naegele's publishing/tuition endeavor, suggested we publish the book together, sell it, and apply the profits to my tuition. Once again, Lenny had provided the resources and encouraged a student to package research and share it with others in order to continue an education.

Our publishing adventures didn't end when my father died during my freshman year in college. I continued with our plan of owning a small press, and in 1992 purchased Wilderness Adventure Books. Recognizing the incredible resource of *Edible and Medicinal Plants*, I tracked down Tom Naegele, now a doctor in New Mexico, and renewed the Naegele-Howarth publishing partnership.

Len Howarth offered an educational opportunity to a young graduate student in 1976, and gave me the key to an education and career in 1988. It is only fitting that the two beneficiaries of his wisdom, ideas, marketing expertise, and financial backing have come together for this second edition of *Edible and Medicinal Plants of the Great Lakes Region*.

Special thanks to Nancy Howarth, John Bardsley, and Jim Borninski for their invaluable help and advice throughout the creation of this book.

Erin Sims Howarth
Wilderness Adventure Books

Introduction

Every year more people become interested in utilizing the local flora because of its edible and/or medicinal properties. Because medicinal plant information is not passed from generation to generation as it once was, it is hoped that this research of medicinal plants will not only enhance local knowledge, but also inspire new and more thorough investigation into the important field of plant identification and evaluation.

The author obtained the following information through personal interviews and investigation of published material about medicinal plants.

Of all the books written about medicinal plants, there are four that are widely used by people interested in utilizing herbs. Written in short story form, Euel Gibbons' *Stalking the Healthful Herb*[19] emphasizes the importance of personal interviews and self-experimentation in discovering and understanding medicinal plants, as does *Back to Eden*,[35] by J. Kloss. *A Guide to the Medicinal Plants of the United States*,[36] by A. and S. Krochmal, is a valuable manual which presents plant information in easy to use alphabetical and categorical format. *A Modern Herbal*,[22] by M. Grieve, is a thorough history of medicinal plants and their utilization that depicts the vital role medicinal plants have played in the past.

This manual utilizes some of the important aspects of each of the four books mentioned, plus information obtained from personal interviews and experimentation.

I originally wrote this book out of inspiration. Dr. Erbisch and Dr. Glime were my leading teachers and helped me to bring this project to completion and utilize it for a degree in higher learning.

I have been asked by many to update *Edible and Medicinal Plants of the Great Lakes* over the years and have put bits and pieces of time into it. I requested Dr. Glime to write a section on Bryophytes. She is an international expert in her field. Both Dr. Erbisch and Dr. Glime are inspirational lecturers and I highly recommend them for discussions on their topic; they are excellent.

1

Another major assistance, especially financial, was my close friend Len Howarth. He and I spent two weeks out of every year for nearly fifteen years camping and caving all over the United States. He was the financial and business backer of the first edition. He died from cancer on April 20, 1989. This book is in memory of Len Howarth.

◆◆◆

Scurvy, a vitamin C deficiency causing the inability to lay down bone reticulum, hemorrhagic manifestations, delayed healing, loosening teeth, edema, swollen joints, weakness, and eventually death, was a common killer among seamen before the 1800's.[40] During the winter layover of the 1534 Cartier expedition, 25 men died from scurvy.[77] The men that survived drank a tea of northern white cedar leaves, supplied by the Iroquois Indians.[78] Within 6 days, "the distemper relaxed its hold and health and hope began to revisit the hopeless community."[77] Cartier thought this a miracle and introduced the wonder drug to Europe by the name Arborvitae, the tree of life.[78]

There are many everyday ailments which may cause us discomfort and weakness throughout our lives. Teething in children is a common and painful malady for which, generally, little can be done. However, a Baraga, Michigan Ojibwe woman reports that the Ojibwe commonly allow their teething babies to chew gold thread, the root of which alleviates nausea and causes numbness of the gums.[a]

Throughout life, we inevitably incur cuts and scratches. Witch hazel, an understory tree of Michigan's forests, has been utilized as an antiseptic healing agent for cuts, scrapes and scratches. Although Joseph Lister discovered modern antiseptic practice in 1865,[40] the Ojibwe of Upper Michigan have been using witch hazel as an antiseptic for centuries.[76]

The beer we drink is flavored with the stream bank growing hop.[11] While hops are primarily used as flavoring, they have also been an herbal cure for insomnia because of the tiring effect they induce.[b]

---

[a] 47,54,63,70,74,75,76
[b] 5,22,32,73

2

Typha latifolia (the cattail) has sustained Ojibwe life in upper Michigan for generations.[a] The edible qualities of cattails' immature flower spikes, young sprouts, and roots are nearly common knowledge.[b] Though our main encounters may have been at the dinner table, a poultice of the root provided certain relief for a Potawatomi with skin burn.[76]

♦ ♦ ♦

All these plants and many more grow throughout the Great Lakes region. With proper precautions many wild plants can be useful in everyday as well as survival situations. This manual has been designed for people with a sincere interest in the utilization of Great Lakes area indigenous plants.

For proper utilization of this manual it is important to understand its organization. In most cases, it is self explanatory and provides easy access to information. There are six major divisions:

Part One, the introduction, briefly describes how some plants of the Great Lakes area have been used to cure diseases and presents information regarding preparation techniques, which is vital to experimenters.

Part Two, plant information, contains medicinal plant information and is composed of six basic subcategories, making possible the easy locations of desired information. The plants are arranged in alphabetical order by Latin name and both the scientific family name and common names are included for convenience and organization.

Plant Description

Verification with at least three descriptive characteristics should be made to ensure proper identification of any collected medicinal plants. To be positive of identification, each plant should be carefully cross referenced. Although stem and root descriptions are valid year round, the stems and roots of different plants are often similar. The leaves, flowers and fruits of plants are seasonal, but unique qualities between species simplifies identification. With experience, one will soon recognize plants intuitively by general appearance and habitat.

---

[a] 73,74,75,76
[b] 15,18,25,34,47

Seasonal Collection

Collection of medicinal and edible plants is periodic; seasonal gathering can occur once a reasonable quantity of herb is located. Always follow the adage "5 times more than needed, to keep the ground well seeded." Under the heading "Season of Availability," one can find the time of year the herb is collected. Once the plants are collected, they can be used immediately or dried and stored for later use. Since pollutants and automobile exhaust can cause toxic substances on plants, be wary of collecting specimens from roadsides.

Preparation Techniques

The preparation section assumes that one is aware of basic techniques of plant utilization. The techniques are described below and will be referred to by name only in the text. There are two procedures for making herb tea, **infusion** and **decoction**. An **infusion** is made by placing one ounce of plant material in a container, adding one quart of boiling water and allowing the mixture to steep for ten minutes. A **decoction** is prepared by placing the plant parts directly into a container of boiling water, and allowing the mixture to boil for 10-20 minutes. As a general rule of thumb, **steep** leaves, flowers, and stems and **boil** roots, bark, and seeds.

For plant compounds that are insoluble in water, a **tincture** or alcohol **extraction** is used. In this case the plant part is immersed in ethanol for a period of time, usually 48 hours, after which the solution is strained, bottled, and ready for use. In Michigan, ethanol is difficult to purchase; however, vodka serves as an acceptable substitute.

A **poultice** is prepared by applying the crushed or ground plant, usually fresh, to the affected part of the body by binding it with a piece of cloth. A **wash** is a tea that is applied externally to the body with a wash cloth as a healing and cleansing agent.

Since plant collection is seasonal and utilization is not, it is often necessary to dry and store herbs for later use. Drying plants is an art. The best way to dry plants is to place the freshly picked plants on screens that have approximately 25 cm of air space on the top and bottom. The plants should not be layered more than 3 cm thick. The drying screens should be located in a warm, dry, dark room. An attic usually meets these requirements. Darkness is essential to stop chemical breakdown due to photolysis. The warm and dry atmosphere is necessary to insure rapid desiccation of the plant material. Often, the plant material can be ground or powdered for proper utilization.

With freshly picked plant material use the following sequence of steps:

      1) Wash carefully
      2) Cut the plant in small pieces with a sharp knife.
      3) Put the pieces in a mortar.
      4) Add the same volume of water as plant material.
      5) Grind with a pestle.

Because this method is very tedious, using a blender, if available, for steps 2, 3, and 4 is recommended. For dried plant material, the desired consistency may be obtained by crushing with a rolling pin. If a powder form is required, one can grind the dried plant with a mortar and pestle or an electric blender.

Literature Review

Following is a review of literature regarding medical terminology related to a plant's actions, disease symptoms the plant has been used to relieve, and the toxic properties attributed to the herbs. Next, the biological information concerns scientific experimentation involving the species, edibility information, and uses by Native Americans of the Great Lakes.

This section contains dye information and chemical compounds found in the plant. Many of these plants have commercial value and are economically important. This information is found under the commercial heading. There are many botanical companies that buy and sell botanicals from small time collectors. Since this list is constantly changing, consult the *Herb Resource Directory*, which is updated every two years. It is available from The Business of Herbs, Route 2, Box 246, Shevlin, MN, 56676.

The literature review uses scientific notation to cite references, making it easy for the reader to consult the proper reference and ascertain validity should a disagreement or contradiction arise. If one wishes to concentrate on a single species or a portion thereof, that reader is referred to the available literature and thus may eliminate preliminary searching.

An example of scientific notation follows:

The plant is used as an astringent,[12,14] diuretic,[45,48,73] and a sedative.[63,65]

5

The numbers are citation numbers and represent the sequence of articles and books in the bibliography that contain information about the plant involved. Citations 12 and 14 discuss the plant as an astringent; citations 45, 48, and 73 discuss the diuretic and astringent properties of the plant; and citations 63 and 65 concern the plant's applicability as a sedative, a diuretic, and an astringent. If more thorough information regarding any plant is desired, the reader may consult the bibliography and reference the appropriate publications.

Personal Experimentation

The author has experimented with many of the plants discussed in this manual; these experiments are described in the "Personal Experimentation" section, as are discussions of personal encounters with Great Lakes people who use medicinal plants.

Bibliography

There are many references available, but those included here have been chosen for their outstanding reputations, thorough bibliographies, and/or general availability.

Glossaries

If the terminology is too advanced, the reader may consult the two glossaries located near the end of the book. The botanical glossary explains terms used for describing the plants' physical characteristics. The medicinal glossary defines medicinal and scientific terms, diseases, and symptoms.

Appendix

In the appendix, the cross reference tables will be a blessing for the avid collector. The appendix contains tables listing the plants used for many diseases, symptoms, and associated terms. For each category, the plants are listed with symbols describing their habitat and season of availability. This will reduce time spent locating the various herbs.

Following the tables is an index of Latin names versus common names and vice versa. This will familiarize the reader with the uniqueness of Latin names versus common names. This section will also aid the reader in recognizing local plants and provides easy information retrieval.

Although more than one hundred medicinal plants have been included in this work, it is by no means exhaustive. Since the author's purpose is to aid the inspired collector, the emphasis has been placed upon the historically important plants and herbs commonly available throughout the Great Lakes region. Despite recent technological advances, the earth is still, in many ways, a mystery. Every year, new experiments with plants yield increasing success in finding cures for many diseases.[79] The potential is great that a local collector may discover a plant that will make medical history.

ABIES BALSAMEA
Pinaceae
Balsam fir, balsam

Stem: Woody, smooth black-gray bark, up to 25 m, resin blisters common, branching, older trees have scaly bark at the base.

Leaves: Alternate, flat, needle-like, 12 to 25 mm long, whitish green on bottom, dark green on top, distinct mid vein.

Flower Type: Green, cones, monoecious, spring.

Fruit: Brown winged nutlets in a cone that is 5 to 10 cm long, broadly rounded with appressed scales, fall.

Roots: Taproot, with spreading lateral roots.

General Information: Perennial tree, grows in groves.

Habitat: Grows in moist woods and swamps.

Season of Availability: The balsam pitch (resin), needles, and roots can be collected in every season.

Preparation: In an infusion, use fresh needles. The root is used dried or fresh in a decoction. Pitch can be utilized in ointments or infusions.

Medical Terminology: Thought to be rubefacient,[32] stimulant[29] and diuretic in action.[10]

Related Disease Symptoms: The resins have been used to relieve back pain.[36,63] To relieve rheumatic pains, the resin was placed on joints.[a] The resin was applied externally to cuts and sores to heal them.[b] For convulsions, the Chippewa placed the resinous gum on a warm stone and inhaled the vapors.[10] The Ojibwe placed the fresh needles on red hot coals and inhaled the vapors to relieve cold symptoms.[75] An infusion made from the leaves was drunk for colds, coughs[c] and asthma by northern Natives.[40,63] A tea of the leaves was used for consumption.[d] The tea has also been used to cure colic.[64] A tea from the resin was employed for urinary affections.[5,35]

Poisonous Aspects: The resin is known to have caused contact dermatitis.[40]

Biological and Edible: For years the Ojibwe have used the resin to glue and seal their birch bark canoes.[75] Bees utilize this plant for honey.[92]

Chemistry & Pharmacognosy: Resins are a viscid, pale yellow with a terebinthinate odor and an acrid taste.[82] Canada Balsam contains up to 25% volatile oil, consisting chiefly of l-pinene.[82]

---

[a] 5,10,35   [b] 36,63,74,75

[c] 36,74,75,76   [d] 5,40,63

Commercial Products & Uses: Today, the resin's main use is that of a mounting medium for microscopic lenses.[29,82] The sap is an oleoresin commercially known as Canada turpentine.[31]

Personal Experimentation: An Ojibwe woman from L'Anse told me she had gathered the resin when her father was having great back pain.

She heated the pitch in hot water and spread the ointment on his back, which relieved the pain.[47] It is considered common knowledge among northern woodsmen to apply the sap on any kind of cuts or scratches.

Abies balsamea
Balsam fir, balsam

ACHILLEA MILLEFOLIUM, ACHILLEA LANULOSA
Compositae
Yarrow, milfoil, yarroway

Stem: Erect, smooth, up to 1 m, usually branchless, aromatic, stiff.

Leaves: Alternate, pinnately compound, finely dissected, featherlike, 10 to 20 cm, green, aromatic.

Flower Type: White, ray flowers, in a flat topped corymb; corymb 5 to 15 cm across; summer, fall.

Fruit: Small brown achene, papallate; summer, fall.

Roots: Taproot.

General Information: Perennial, aromatic, grows in clumps.

Habitat: Easily found growing in old fields and on roadsides.

Season of Availability: The herb is collected when flowering, during summer and fall.

Preparation: The herb is prepared in an infusion. Make the tea by steeping one ounce of the herb in one pint of boiling water.

Medical Terminology: Yarrow is considered tonic[5,27] and stimulant in action.[a] The infusion has been used for fevers[b] because of its diaphoretic action.[c]

As a wash, it is considered astringent in action.[d]

Related Disease Symptoms: In a poultice or wash, the herb has been utilized in skin affections, such as rash, itch and eczema.[e] Women have drunk yarrow tea to relieve menstrual discomfort.[f] The northwest coast Natives chewed the leaves and swallowed the juice for colds and sore throats.[60] To this day, the tea is commonly used to treat colds.[g] Native Americans chewed the leaves to relieve toothache.[40,52] To cure stomachache and colic, an infusion was administered.[h] The tea has also been used for catarrhal affections.[i] The Chippewa sprinkled the tea on hot stones and inhaled the fumes to treat headaches.[10] The northwest coast Natives soaked and pounded the leaves, then applied them to the head in a poultice to cure headache.[60]

Poisonous Aspects: Rare cases of poisoning by indigestion have been reported.[33]

Biological and Edible: *A. millifolium* inhibited gram + bacteria in antibiotic experiments.[57]

---

[a] 10,22,32,34,36,50,52,58,63,68

[b] 41,64,70,73,74

[c] 22,27,34,36,38,44,50,56,58,63,68

[d] 5,22,27,32,34,41,58,63

[e] 10,36,50,52,70,74   [h] 5,32,36,41

[f] 5,32,38,50   [i] 32,36,50,51

[g] 27,40,52,63,64,68

Chemistry & Pharmacognosy:
Yarrow contains the alkaloid achilleine.[33,58] The flowers contain myristic, palmitic, cerotic, linoleic and oleic acids and cetyl alcohols, sterols, and the hydrocarbon triacontane.[43]

Commercial Products & Uses:
The herb can be collected and sold to drug companies.[37]

Personal Experimentation: I have drunk over a quart of this tea at one sitting and have drunk it periodically over the years and have noticed only a slight diaphoretic effect. Yarrow tea is commonly ingested for winter colds in Michigan's Upper Peninsula.

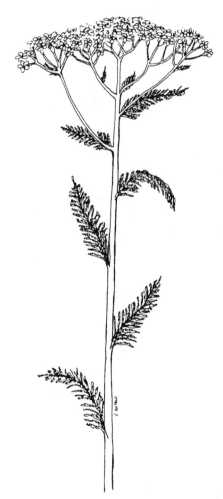

Achillea millefolium, Achillea lanulosa
Yarrow, milfoil, yarroway

ACORUS CALAMUS
Araceae
Sweet flag, calamus

Stem: Green, erect, smooth, 3 angled, up to 1 m, stiff.

Leaves: Alternate, mostly basal, long linear, sharp edges, thickened in the middle, up to 1 m, 6 to 20 mm wide, green.

Flower Type: Yellowish green, in a spadix, cylindric-cone, 7 to 12 cm long, 1 to 2 cm wide, 6 sepals, 6 stamens, solitary ovary, spring, summer.

Fruit: Berry, dry outside, gelatinous on the inside, brown, fall.

Roots: Thick, aromatic rhizome with fibrous roots, creeping.

General Information: Perennial herb, growing in clumps, usually spreading by rhizomes.

Habitat: Grows in marshes, shallow water and wet areas.

Season of Availability: The rhizomes (roots) are collected in the spring and the fall.

Preparation: A cough medicine was made from the combined roots of *Acorus calamus* and *Aralia nudicaulis*.[40] The powdered roots have been used as an abrasive dentifrice.[40]

Medical Terminology: Therapeutically, it is considered a tonic[a] and aromatic stimulant.[b]

It is also considered a carminative[c] and an aromatic bitter.[d] Some Natives considered the rhizome to be a panacea.[18] The rhizome has been considered official in pharmaceutical preparations using 3 grams as an average human dose.[2]

Related Disease Symptoms:
Natives made a root decoction that was drunk to cure pain in the bowels.[e] The dried root was chewed to relieve dyspepsia.[f] For flatulence and colic, the root tea was taken internally.[g] The Chippewa drank the root tea or sniffed the dried pulverized root to treat colds.[10] The tea has been used to stop coughs[36,50] and treat catarrhal affections.[40] The Chippewa chewed the roots to relieve toothaches.[10] Other indications include gastritis, gastric ulcer, and anorexia.[84]

Biological and Edible: The immature leaves are edible.[18,25] In antibiotic studies, *Acorus calamus* inhibited gram + bacteria.[57]

Chemistry & Pharmacognosy: It contains a volatile oil and the bitter principle acorin.[58,84]

---

[a] 35,38,40   [b] 5,10,22,36,51,63,68

[c] 22,35,36,50,51,68,84

[d] 27,40,58,63

---

[e] 23,24,74

[f] 5,18,22,27,35,36,50,55,68,84

[g] 5,22,27,35,36,38,40,55,63,68,73,74,84

The contents of the oil include asamyl alcohol, eugenol, and asarone.[83] Chromatography has been done.[84]

Commercial Products & Uses: The root is used as a flavoring agent in candy.[15,18]

Acorus calamus
Sweet flag, calamus

ACTAEA ALBA, A. RUBRA, A. ARGUTA
Ranunculaceae
Doll's eyes, baneberry

Stem: Smooth, green, branchless, up to 1 m, erect.

Leaves: Alternate, 2 to 3 times pinnately compound; leaflets whitish beneath, ovate, sharply cleft and toothed, smooth, green.

Flower Type: White, 4 to 10 petals, 4 to 5 sepals that are soon falling, 1 pistal, numerous stamens, 3 to 7 mm across, born in a terminal cylindric raceme on thick red pedicels, 5 to 20 cm long, spring.

Fruit: Shiny red or white berries, subglobose, 1 cm long, distinct 'eye spot' which is the persistent stigma, poisonous, summer.

Roots: Creeping lateral roots, poisonous.

General Information: Perennial herb, rarely grows in large clumps.

Habitat: Grows in rich woods and sugar maple forests.

Season of Availability: Collect the roots in any season. The seeds are collected in the fall.

Preparation: The roots and seeds are used fresh or dried, ground or whole in a decoction or mixed with grease in an ointment.

---

[a] 33,40,46

Medical Terminology: The root is considered emetic[33] and purgative in action.[10,51]

Related Disease Symptoms: For stomach trouble, the Penobscots drank a root decoction.[63] The Cheyenne made an infusion from the roots and stems that was administered to women to make the first milk pass off quickly; better results were claimed if *Mertensia ciliata* was boiled with it.[24,70] Chippewa women drank a root tea for excessive menstrual flow.[10] Mixed with grease, the ground root has been rubbed on the body to treat rheumatism.[38]

Poisonous Aspects: The plant is considered poisonous.[a] Kingsbury reports no loss of life has been recorded in the U.S.[33] Muenscher claims there are documented cases of death in children from eating the berries.[46] There are reports that eating six berries is sufficient to produce increased pulse, dizziness, burning in the stomach and colic.[40,46]

Personal Experimentation: I've eaten four of each of the red and white baneberries and felt no effects. The berries are extremely bitter; I doubt anyone would eat more than one.

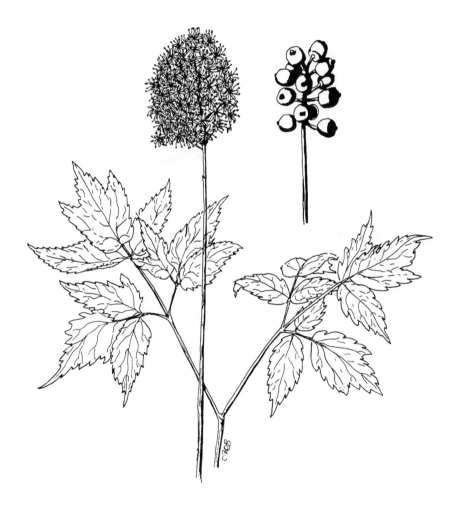

Actaea alba, A. rubra, A. arguta
Doll's eyes, baneberry

ADIANTUM CAPILLUS-VENERIS, ADIANTUM PEDATUM
Polypodiaceae
Maiden hair fern

Stem: An erect stipe, dark distinctive black, lustrous, up to 6 dm, forking, not a real stem.

Leaves: Whorled, pinnately compound, up to 5 dm; short stalked, numerous pinnules, triangular oblong, entire, green membranous.

Flower Type: Gray-brown indusia, on the margin, linear, 2-6 mm long, 1 mm wide, summer.

Fruit: Black microscopic spores.

Roots: Slender black rhizome.

General Information: Perennial, grows in great groups, usually in the hundreds.

Habitat: *Adiantum spp.* grow in rich woods and are commonly found in sugar maple forests in the Northeast.

Season of Availability: Collect the leaves during summer, and the rhizomes in spring, summer, and fall.

Preparation: The leaves are usually used fresh in a poultice. The roots (rhizomes) are used fresh or dried in a decoction.

Medical Terminology: The tea is used for coughs,[a] because of its expectorant properties.[b]

For catarrhal affections,[c] it is used as a pectoral.[d] To relieve hoarseness,[e] the tea was taken for its demulcent action.[f]

Related Disease Symptoms: The Chippewa and Menominee tribes used the entire plant in a tea to relieve menstrual discomfort.[g] Others state its use in alleviating menstrual pains.[h] In Hawaii, the leaves were used to heal skin sores.[48] A poultice of the leaves has been used to relieve pain from rheumatism.[i]

Poisonous Aspects: No mortality has ever been recorded from ingestion of *Adiantum spp.*

Biological and Edible: The fronds are commonly made into a syrup.[32,56]

Commercial Products & Uses: The plant can be gathered and sold to some drug companies.[37]

Personal Experimentation: I have observed *Adiantum spp.* in many states within the U.S. I have dried the leaves successfully, but have not yet ingested the plant in any way.

---

[a] 22,36,74

[b] 27,38,44,56,68

[c] 36,38,44

[d] 22,32,51,58,68

[e] 36,38,44

[f] 22,32,56,58

[g] 63,70,73,74

[h] 22,36,38

[i] 27,36,69

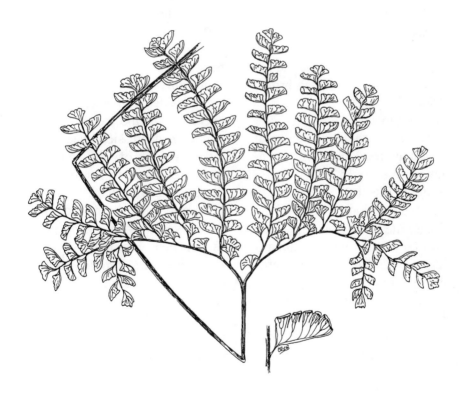

Adiantum capillus-veneris, Adiantum pedatum
Maiden hair fern

AESCULUS HIPPOCASTANUM
Hippocastanaceae
Horse chestnut, buckeye

Stem: Woody, erect tree, dark gray bark, corrugated, branching, up to 25 m.

Leaves: Opposite, palmately compound; 7 wedge-ovate, 10-25 cm irregularly serrate leaflets, green, large resinous buds.

Flower Type: White, 4-5 petals, tubular calyx, terminal racemes with long stout pedicels, cone shaped.

Fruit: Spiny green leathery capsule, round, 4-6 cm in diameter, contains 2 to 3 smooth shiny brown nuts with reddish brown stripes, late summer, fall.

Roots: Taproot.

General Information: Perennial deciduous tree, mostly an ornamental in the area.

Habitat: The tree can grow in forest conditions, but in the Great Lakes region they are usually found where humans have planted them—back yards and cities.

Season of Availability: Collect the flowers in the spring, the nuts during the fall. The bark is collected in any season.

Preparation: The nuts and bark are prepared in a tincture or decoction.

Medical Terminology: Horse chestnut is considered tonic[36,38] and astringent in action.[a] It has been reported that the seeds contain a narcotic principle.[b]

Related Disease Symptoms: The tincture of the seeds has been used to treat hemorrhoids.[c] The seeds have been effective for neuralgia.[36,51] A decoction of the fruit or bark has been used to treat fever.[32,36] A wash, made from the infusion of the bark or nuts, was used for skin sores.[36]

Poisonous Aspects: The seeds are considered poisonous.[d] An overdose of the seeds causes vomiting, depression, weakness, inflammation of the mucous membranes, stupor, loss of coordination, and paralysis.[46,91] Cases of death have been recorded from overdoses of the seeds.[33] Treatment is emesis.[91]

Biological and Edible: In the southern states, the pulped seeds were put in ponds or rivers to stupefy fish.[32] Bees utilize this plant for honey.[92,93]

Chemistry & Pharmacognosy: The plant contains the glucosides aesculin,[32,82] fraxin and tannin.[58] The plant supposedly contains the lactone glucoside esculin[51] and the vasopressor agent, quercitin.[40]

---

[a] 32,51,58   [c] 22,36,38,51

[b] 32,51,58   [d] 33,40,46,58,91

***Commercial Products & Uses*:**
Drug companies sometimes purchase *Aesculus hippocastanum*.[37]

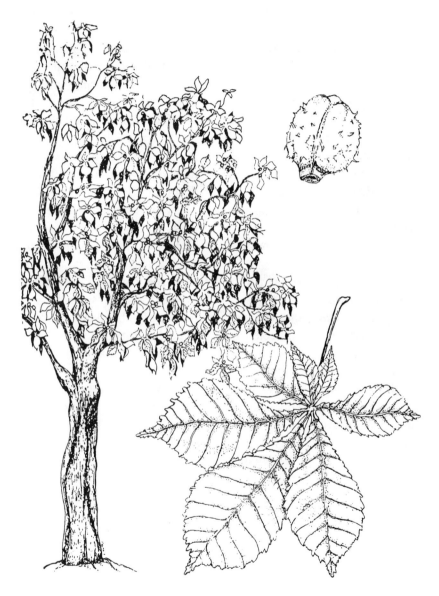

Aesculus hippocastanum
Horse chestnut, buckeye

ALETRIS FARINOSA
Liliaceae
Colic root, star grass, unicorn plant

Stem: Smooth, green, unbranching, practically leafless, 3 to 10 dm tall, erect.

Leaves: Rosette, linear to lanceolate, parallel veined, green, up to 20 cm.

Flower Type: White, 5-8 mm long, in a long (8-25 cm) spiral spike; sepals and petals united into a lobed tube, bracts, 6 stamens, spring, summer.

Fruit: Brown, beaked, ovoid capsule, summer, fall.

Roots: Fibrous.

General Information: Perennial herb.

Habitat: It is found on sandy soil in open woods.

Season of Availability: The rhizomes and roots are collected in the fall.

Preparation: A decoction is prepared from the fresh or dried roots or rhizomes. The dose of the dried rhizome is .3 to .6 grams three times a day.[82] Liquid extract 1:1 in 45% ethanol in .3 to 1 ml dose three times a day.[82]

Medical Terminology: Therapeutically, it is considered tonic,[a] diuretic[51,58] and sedative in action.[b]

The British Herbal Medical Association considers it a bitter, spasmolytic, and a sedative.[83] Johnson believes *A. farinosa* has no medicinal properties other than that of a simple bitter.[32] The dried rhizomes and roots are considered official and are given in 2 gram doses.[2]

Related Disease Symptoms: The most common use of the root decoction is to relieve colic.[c] The Catawaba used the leaves to make a tea to stop diarrhea.[40] The root, mixed with brandy, was drunk to relieve the pain from rheumatism.[36,38] A poultice of the leaves has been used to relieve sore breasts.[36,63] The root treated uterine diseases.[51] It has also been used to treat anorexia and dyspepsia.[82]

Commercial Products & Uses: The root is still purchased by drug companies.[37]

---

[a] 9,22,32,44,68   [c] 9,22,36,38,40,44
[b] 36,38,63   63,68,83

Aletris farinosa
Colic root, star grass, unicorn plant

ALLIUM TRICOCCUM
Liliaceae
Wild onion, leek, wild garlic

Stem: Nearly stemless except for the flowering stem, which is smooth, green, up to 3 dm tall.

Leaves: Basal, usually only 2 leaves, 20 to 30 cm, lance-elliptic, shiny, thick, when bruised they smell like onions, parallel veined.

Flower Type: White, 3 petals, 3 sepals, born on thick pedicels in a terminal umbel, early summer, appearing after leaves have died.

Fruit: Tiny, shiny black capsules, summer.

Roots: White bulb with fibrous rootlets.

General Information: Perennial herb, grows in clumps, common.

Habitat: The leek grows in rich maple and/or beech forests.

Season of Availability: It is collected in the spring.

Preparation: The bulb is used fresh, as a poultice.

Medical Terminology: The bulb has been used as an emetic.[10,63] The Chippewa combined the bulb of *Allium tricoccum* with *Caulophyllum thalictroides* root, and used the tea as an emetic.[10]

Related Disease Symptoms: The bruised wild onion and leek applied to the skin as a poultice was said to relieve the pain from the sting of bees and wasps.[63] Native Americans applied the bulbs and stems as a poultice to carbuncles.[24,40] A tea from the bulbs has been used as a wash for open sores.[40]

Poisonous Aspects: Kingsbury cites cases of toxicity by onions and wild onions but no recorded cases against *A. tricoccum*.[33]

Biological and Edible: In antibiotic experiments, 6 *Allium* species have inhibited gram + and - bacteria.[57] The bulbs are edible.[a] The Menominee, Ojibwe and Potawatomi used the bulbs in stews and soups.[b]

Personal Experimentation: I have eaten the bulbs for years, fresh in salads or on sandwiches, cooked in soups or fried. I have never experienced any harmful effects from wild leeks.

---

[a] 9,15,18,47,79

[b] 74,75,76

Allium tricoccum
Wild onion, leek, wild garlic

23

ALNUS RUGOSA
Betulaceae
Tag alder, swamp alder, speckled alder, alder

Stem: Brown to blackish-gray bark, woody, brittle, branching, up to 5 m.

Leaves: Alternate, oval to ovate, doubly serrate, acute, green, rounded to subcordate at base, 5 to 8 cm long.

Flower Type: Monoecious; staminate, catkins, 2 to 4 cm long; pistillate, small (1 to 2 cm) conelike catkins, green, drying to brown, spring.

Fruit: Small winged nutlets, 5 to 10 mm across.

Roots: Lateral roots.

General Information: Perennial deciduous bushy shrub, prominently lenticilate, always in groups.

Habitat: Commonly found in wet areas such as stream banks.

Season of Availability: The bark is collected in any season.

Preparation: It is prepared in a decoction with either fresh or dried materials.

Medical Terminology: Tag alder has been used as an astringent[10] and alterative.[a]

Related Disease Symptoms:
Natives placed the chewed bark on skin wounds and cuts for a healing poultice.[b] A wash made from the inner bark decoction has been used to heal skin diseases.[c] This same wash has been used to treat poison ivy rash.[36] To stop cramps, Native Americans drank a tea made from the boiled bark.[10,63] Some Natives also used the bark tea as a douche and topically, to cure piles.[63] A poultice from the bark has been used to reduce swelling and inflammation.[10,63] The tea has been used to treat syphilis sores.[d] The bark decoction was taken internally to stop diarrhea.[e] The dried, powdered bark, steeped in water, has been applied to eye infections.[36,38]

Biological and Edible: Bees utilize this plant for honey.[92,93]

Chemistry & Pharmacognosy: The bark has been used for a brown dye.[38] The bark contains tannin.[58]

---

[a] 22,27,32,58,63,68   [d] 22,36,68
[b] 36,38,63   [e] 22,36,68
[c] 22,27,68

Alnus rugosa
Tag alder, swamp alder, speckled alder, alder

AMARANTHUS RETROFLEXUS
Amaranthaceae
Green amaranth, pigweed, wild beet, canne

Stem: Green, coarse, .3 to 2 m high, branching, often reddish at base.

Leaves: Ovate-lanceolate to elliptic or rhombic blades, up to 3 dm long and 1 dm broad, slightly hairy, veined, long petioled, dull green.

Flower Type: Terminal panicles, mostly lobulate, crowded ascending round-tipped lateral spikes, forming a leafy-bracted panicle, bracts about twice as long as calyx, sepals of pistilate flowers about 3 mm long, 5 stamens, dense clusters, bristly green flowers, summer, fall.

Fruit: A black one-seeded utricle, 2 to 3 beaked at the apex, 1 mm broad, small, late summer, fall.

Roots: Tap root, may be slightly reddish.

General Information: Common plant, usually grows in large groups. Farmers usually consider it a pest plant; it is difficult to get rid of.

Habitat: Roadsides, fields, waste places, cultivated ground.

Season of Availability: The plant is collected throughout the summer before flowering.

Related Disease Symptoms: The dried plant, in an infusion, has been used for mouth and throat inflammations, dysentery, and diarrhea. The stems have treated ulcers and profuse menstrual flows. In a wash, the flowers, leaves, and roots have been used as an astringent for wounds and sores, and used as a mouthwash for canker sores and sore gums.[138]

Biological and Edible: This plant is edible as a salad green or pot herb. Boil the soft tops for 10-15 minutes, season and serve. Bees utilize this plant for honey.[92,93]

Amaranthus retroflexus
Green amaranth, pigweed, wild beet, canne

AMELANCHIER SPP
Rosaceae
Serviceberry, sugarplum, juneberry, shadbush

Stem: Woody, up to 4 dm in diameter, smooth striped bark, gray with reddish gray strips, up to 20 m tall.

Leaves: Ovate to slightly obovate, acuminate, rounded at base, 4 to 10 cm long, 2.2 to 5 cm broad, green, alternate, petiolate, doubly serrate, 11 to 17 pairs of primary veins.

Flower Type: White petals, 10 to 14 mm long, in racemes, spring.

Fruit: Purple to black, juicy, sweet, glaucous, diameter up to 2.5 cm, edible, early summer.

Roots: Lateral, stout, woody root.

General Information: Small tree, shrubby, perennial, deciduous, pioneer species.

Habitat: Old fields, burned out or disturbed areas, young forests.

Season of Availability: The dark red berries can be collected in the early summer.

Preparation: The berries can be eaten fresh or made into jams, jellies and/or pies. Because of the numerous seeds, some find it essential to put the jam through a sieve or colander. The berries can be stamped and dried for future use.

Related Disease Symptoms: The Chippewa made a decoction of *Amelanchier spp.* root along with the roots of cherry and young oak, which they drank to treat dysentery.[10] The bark of *Amelanchier spp., Prunus virginiana, Prunus pennsylavanica,* and *Prunus serotina* was prepared in a decoction by the Chippewa and ingested for female weakness.[10] The Cheyenne made a tea from the leaves of sugarplum.[24]

Poisonous Aspects: Wilting leaves of many plants in the *Rosaceae* family contain the deadly poison cyanide. *Amelanchier spp.* may be another.[33]

Biological and Edible: The fruits are edible fresh, dried, and cooked.[a] Natives across the U.S. considered the fruit an important food source.[b] Bees use this plant for honey.[92,93]

Commercial Products & Uses: Presently, there is no commercial processing of sugarplums.

Personal Experimentation: For years I collected sugarplums by the long, tedious hand to bucket method. In 1978, I developed an easier way, making fruit collection fast and easy.

---

[a] 10,15,18,25,47   [b] 10,15,18,25,78

1) Put a large tarp on the ground by the tree.
2) Bend the elastic branches down to the tarp.
3) Shake the branches vigorously.

Using this method, it's easy to collect a gallon of berries within 10-15 minutes. The berries are good fresh, in jams and in pies.

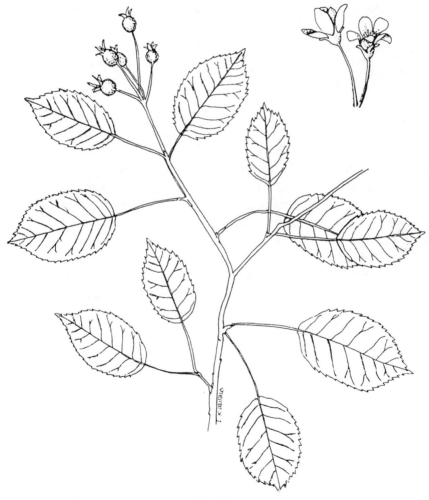

Amelanchier spp.
Serviceberry, sugarplum, juneberry, shadbush

ANAPHALIS MARGARITACEA
Compositae
Pearly everlasting

Stem: White, woolly, branching only at the top, erect, up to 1 m.

Leaves: Alternate, white woolly green, sessile, linear-lanceolate, 4 to 8 cm.

Flower Type: White with yellow centers, in a compound corymb, 1 cm wide; corymb 10 to 15 cm across, thread-like tubular corolla, pappalate, persistent, summer, fall.

Fruit: Tiny light brown achene, fall.

Roots: Taproot.

General Information: Perennial herb, common, usually spread by its rhizome, sometimes confused with *Achillea millifolium*.

Habitat: Grows in groups in open fields and meadows.

Season of Availability: The flowers are gathered in the late summer.

Preparation: The flowers are dried and used in an infusion or powdered. The Cheyenne collected and powdered the flowers.[23,24]

Medical Terminology: The herb decoction was applied to hemorrhoids because of its astringent action.[40]

Related Disease Symptoms: The flower powder was chewed and rubbed on the body before war to keep from getting injured and to make the warrior faster.[23,24] The chewed powder was also put on the warriors' horses' hoofs for speed.[23,24] To aid a patient stricken by paralysis, the Flambeaus spread the pulverized flowers over live coals and let the smoke flow over the affected areas.[63,75] The Chippewa made a tea of pearly everlasting flowers mixed with wild mint, which they sprinkled on hot stones to steam paralyzed areas.[10]

Personal Experimentation: I have often noticed the dried flowers in floral arrangements, probably because they are easy to dry and still appear lifelike.

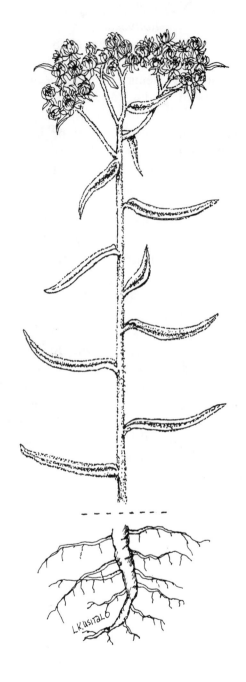

Anaphalis margaritacea
Pearly everlasting

ANEMONE CANADENSIS
Ranunculaceae
Canada anemone, anemone

Stem: 1 to 2 branching stems from rootstock, up to 7 dm, green, villous.

Leaves: Alternate, basal leaves, petiolate; stem leaves sessile; 5 to 7 sharply toothed lobes, divisions acuminate, green.

Flower Type: White, 5 petal-like sepals, numerous stamens, numerous petals, 2 to 5 cm across, solitary on a long peduncle, spring, summer.

Fruit: Flat, brown, winged achene, beaked, summer.

Roots: Fibrous.

General Information: Perennial herb, grows in clumps.

Habitat: The plant is easily found during the spring in open woods in wet areas, like along stream banks (for example, the Salmon Trout river).

Season of Availability: The herb and root are collected in the spring.

Preparation: The herb is used in an infusion, fresh or dried. The root is used in a decoction either fresh or dried.

Related Disease Symptoms: Anemone has been used as a poultice for boils by the Menominee.[63] The Pillager Ojibwe used the herb as a throat lozenge to clear the throat so they could sing better.[63,75] The roots, made into a tea, were used as a wash for eye ailments.[63,73] The root tea was used by local Natives to wash the eyes when they twitched.[73] Rootstocks were crushed and used on wounds and hemorrhages and in infusions for treating infections.[54]

Poisonous Aspects: Kingsbury says that all *Anemone spp.* are on the official poisonous plant list and have been the blame for some reported livestock poisoning.[33]

Anemone canadensis
Canada anemone, anemone

ANGELICA ATROPURPUREA
Umbelliferae
Angelica, purplestem angelica, masterwort

Stem: Purple, ribbed, hollow, stout, up to 2 m, branching.

Leaves: Alternate, 2 to 3 ternately divided compound, 5 to 7 pinnate segments, each oblong-lanceolate to ovate, serrate, smooth, leaflets up to 15 cm long, basal leaves up to 6 dm long, green.

Flower Type: White and greenish petals, in subspherical double umbels, umbel diameter up to 30 cm, summer, early fall.

Fruit: Small (25 to 8 mm) brown, ridged, carpel.

Roots: Taproot, aromatic.

General Information: Perennial herb.

Habitat: It can be found growing in woodland swamps and near forest streams.

Season of Availability: Collect the root in the fall; collect the seeds in the late summer.

Preparation: The roots are used fresh or dried in a decoction.

Medical Terminology: Angelica is considered an aromatic, stimulant, diaphoretic, and in large doses, an emetic.[a]

Related Disease Symptoms: Chewing the root has been thought to relieve stomach gas[b] and colic.[c] The Creek Indians used the root for stomachache, colic, hysterics, worms, and pains in the back.[63] The Menominee used angelica root to reduce swelling and pain by pounding the cooked roots, making a poultice with the pulp, and adding *Artemesia canadensis* leaves.[63,74] It has been used to treat bronchitis, rheumatism, gout and fever.[d] The root tea has also been utilized to promote menstrual flow.[32,36]

Biological and Edible: The dried ground root was mixed with tobacco for smoking.[40]

Chemistry & Pharmacognosy: The root contains a volatile oil and the acrid resin angelicin.[32,58] Chromatography has been done.[83]

Commercial Products & Uses: The root is still purchased by drug companies.[37] The roots are used in making condiments.[e]

---

[a] 27,32,38,41,58,63,66
[b] 35,36,38,63
[c] 27,41,52,83,84
[d] 27,32,35,36,54,83,84
[e] 15,38,66

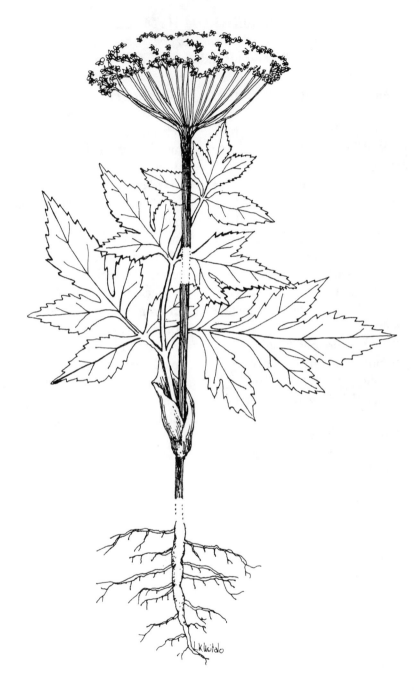

Angelica atropurpurea
Angelica, purplestem angelica, masterwort

APLECTRUM HYMALE
Orchidaceae
Putty-root, adam-and-eve root

Stem: Smooth, usually leafless, green, 20 to 40 cm tall.

Leaves: One elliptic, parallel veined leaf, green, entire, acute, attached to the base of the stem, appears in autumn after flowering.

Flower Type: White lipped, orchid type, marked with purple, 10 to 12 cm across, drooping, 7 to 15 flowers in a spirally terminal spike, spring.

Fruit: Plump reflexed capsules, summer.

Roots: 2 horizontal, subglobose, glutinous corms, connected by stolons.

General Information: Perennial herb, protected, rare.

Habitat: *Aplectrum* can be found in rich woods with lowlands and in peat bogs.

Season of Availability: The corms are collected in the fall.

Preparation: The corms are used fresh or dried, in a decoction.

Medical Terminology: Puttyroot contains a mucilage and is considered as a demulcent pectoral.[58]

Related Disease Symptoms: The corms have been used in treating bronchial illness.[36,38]

Biological and Edible: At one time, the ground corms were mixed with water and used as a paste for pottery.[54]

Commercial Products & Uses: The root is periodically purchased by drug companies.[37]

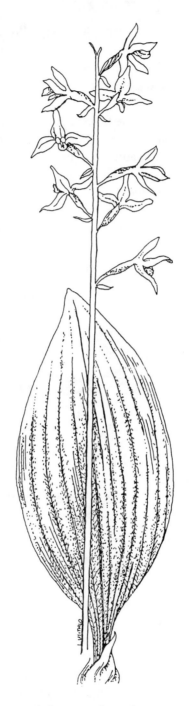

Aplectrum hymale
Putty-root, adam-and-eve root

APOCYNUM ANDROSAEMIFOLIUM, APOCYNUM CANNABINUM
Apocynaceae
Indian hemp, dogbane, milkweed, colicroot, hemp

Stem: Reddish brown, stiff, slender, fibrous, unbranched below, up to 1.2 m, spreading branches above, milky sap.

Leaves: Opposite, petioled, ovate to oblong, entire, acute, smooth, dark green, 2 to 4 cm long.

Flower Type: White to pink, bell shaped, 6 to 9 mm long, 5 lobes, in terminal nodding cymes, summer.

Fruit: Long red slender pods, 7 to 20 cm long, 3 to 10 mm wide, summer, fall.

Roots: Taproot.

General Information: Common perennial herb, grows in clumps.

Habitat: Fields all over MI's Upper Peninsula are good places to find *A. androsaemifolium*. *A. cannabinum* looks very similar and is found in shady fields, such as along forest-field interfaces.

Season of Availability: The roots and rhizomes of both plants are collected in the fall. The immature green fruits are collected in the summer.

Preparation: The roots are usually dried and made into a tincture or decoction. The green fruits are also made into a decoction.

Medical Terminology: *Apocynum* is considered diaphoretic,[40] cathartic[a] and expectorant in action.[b] It is also thought to have the properties of a diuretic[c] and tonic.[d] It acts as an emetic if large doses are ingested.[e] The dried rhizome is considered official with the average dose of 60 milligrams.[2]

Related Disease Symptoms: The root tea has mainly been used to treat dropsy (congestive heart failure).[f] The root decoction is considered a heart tonic or heart stimulant.[g] The Potawatomi drank the decoction of the green fruit as a heart and kidney medicine.[h] The drug from the root possesses a more powerful action on the heart than digitalis, but it is more irritable to the alimentary tract.[1] For headache, the Ojibwe inhaled the smoke of the root.[i]

---

[a] 10,32,36,44,58,63

[b] 22,38,51,68

[c] 10,22,32,51,57,58,63,73,76

[d] 1,38,40,68

[e] 10,32,36,38,40,44,51,58,63,68

[f] 1,22,32,38,40,51,63,68,73

[g] 22,36,37,51,58,68

[h] 36,40,63,76   [i] 36,63,75

The Chippewa sniffed the dry powdered root to cure headaches and treat colds.[10] To ease earaches, the Chippewa poured the cooled root tea into the ear.[10] The root has been used to treat rheumatism.[22,63] The Penobscot tribe drank the root tea to expel worms.[63] Made into a liniment, the roots have been used as a stimulant to sensory nerves.[56]

Poisonous Aspects: Kingsbury cites many articles on laboratory experimentation and separation with the compounds found in both *A. androsaemifolium* and *A. cannabinum*.[33] Only rare cases of death have been attributed by this plant, probably because of its poor taste.[33] The sap has caused contact dermatitis.[40]

Biological and Edible:
The fibers in the stem have been used for weaving, making cloth, thread and rope.[j] In antibiotic experiments, *Apocynum cannabinum* inhibited gram - bacteria.[57]

Chemistry & Pharmacognosy:
The root contains the glucoside apocynein and the toxic resin apocynin.[51,58] The root also contains the cardioactive glucoside cymarin[58] and apocannoside.[40,82] There is also a lactone called cynotoxin.[1] Apocannoside and cyanocannoside have also been isolated.[82] The sap has a rubber-containing latex.[55]

Commercial Products & Uses:
The root is still purchased by drug companies.[37]

---

[j] 29,55,63,73,74,76

Apocynum cannabinum
Indian hemp, dogbane, milkweed, colicroot, hemp

AQUILEGIA CANADENSIS
Ranunculaceae
Columbine, rockbells, meetinghouses

Stem: Green, smooth, branching, up to 1 m tall.

Leaves: Alternate, 2 to 3 times compound, in divisions of 3's, basal leaves long petioled, 10 to 20 cm broad; leaflets, 2 to 5 cm broad, sessile, entire to a lobed or toothed apex.

Flower Type: 5 red to pink spurred petals, 5 petal-like sepals, many long projected yellow stamens, nodding; spring, early summer.

Fruit: Many small black shiny seeds in a brown erect capsule, summer.

Roots: Fibrous.

General Information: Perennial herb.

Habitat: In the Copper Country I have seen this plant many times in open forests and along forest streams.

Season of Availability: The seeds and herb are collected in the summer.

Preparation: The seeds are ground and used in an infusion. The herb is used fresh or dried in an infusion.

Medical Terminology: The entire plant was thought to have diuretic and diaphoretic properties, but it is rarely used.[44]

Related Disease Symptoms: The powdered seeds were put in boiling water and the tea was taken internally for fever and headache.[70] The herb tea was gargled to treat throat and mouth irritations.[27] A root tea was used to stop diarrhea.[52] The seeds were used to hasten childbirth.[52]

Poisonous Aspects: The seeds of *Aquilegia vulgaris* have proven fatal to children, therefore the seeds of this species may also be poisonous.[40]

Biological and Edible: Not much experimentation has been done on the plant.

Aquilegia canadensis
Columbine, rockbells, meetinghouses

41

ARALIA NUDICAULIS, A. HISPIDA, ARALIA RACEMOSA
Araliaceae
Wild sarsaparilla, spignet, bristly sarsaparilla, spikenard, Indian root, sarsaparilla

Stem: (*A. nudicaulis*) single stem, brown, 30-40 cm, branchless, erect; (*A. hispida*) erect, up to 2 m, bristle spines, branching, brown; (*A. racemosa*) erect, up to 2 m, smooth, branching.

Leaves: (*A. nudicaulis*) whorl of 3 pinnately compound, 5 to 7 leaflets, commonly 5, leaflets ovate, acute, serrate, green; (*A. hispida*) alternate, pinnately compound, leaflets, 5 to 7, ovate, acute, serrate, green; (*A. racemosa*) alternate, pinnately compound, leaflets 11 to 15, large, obovate to ovate, acute, serrate, green.

Flower Type: Green, small, 5 petals, in terminal umbels, spring.

Fruit: Blue-black berries, summer.

Roots: Lateral rhizome.

General: Perennial, common.

Habitat: *A. nudicaulis* and *A. racemosa* are easily found in most rich maple hardwood forests in the U.P. *A. hispida* is found in open forests and fields in sandy soil.

---

[a] 10,30,38,44,58,73
[b] 36,38,40
[c] 10,73,74,75,76
[d] 73,74,76
[e] 10,32,75

Season of Availability: The roots of all three are collected in the fall. Collect the berries of all three in late summer.

Preparation: The roots are used fresh or dried in a decoction. The berries are eaten fresh or used in an infusion.

Medical Terminology: It is considered an alterative, stimulant, diaphoretic, and aromatic.[a] The average dose recommended by the National Formulary is 2 gm of ground root.[2]

Related Disease Symptoms: The root tea has been used to cure backache.[b] The Chippewa put the dried and powdered root up the nostrils to stop nose bleeds.[10] The powdered roots, alone or equally mixed with *Acorus calamus*, were utilized as a cough remedy.[40] Natives used the root tea as a carminative and pectoral in coughs and chest pains.[9] The fresh root was pounded, put in cloth, and applied as a poultice for skin sores.[c] Native Americans of this area pounded the roots and used the mash as a poultice to cure burns, sores and swellings.[d] A tea of the roots was used for bad coughs.[e]

Poisonous Aspects: No poisonous aspects have been reported with the above *Aralia* species but Kingsbury reports cases of poisoning by *Aralia spinosa*.[33]

Biological and Edible: For years the root teas have been used for their nutrients.[f] The root is an ingredient in root beer.[15]

Commercial Products & Uses: The roots can be gathered and sold to drug companies.[37]

Personal Experimentation: I have found that the berries of each taste the same and the tea from the berries is also the same. Their taste is that of sweet gin, leaving a dry raspy after-taste if many are eaten. The root tea is bland; I have drunk over a pint at one sitting and noticed no effects.

[f] 10,15,63

Aralia nudicaulis, A. hispida, A. racemosa
Wild sarsaparilla, spignet, bristly sarsaparilla, spikenard, Indian root, sarsaparilla

ARCTIUM LAPPA, ARCTIUM MINUS
Compositae
Burdock, stickers, clotbur, harebur, burrseed, gobo

Stem: Ribbed, hollow, red, stout, branching, up to 2 m, only second year plants have stems.

Leaves: Alternate, heart-shaped, long petioles, rosette the first year, upper leaves ovate, serrate, up to 7 dm, green.

Flower Type: Purple, sessile, born on short terminal peduncles, solitary or in racemes, tubular, green bracts, heads 2 cm wide, summer.

Fruit: Brown spiny fruit, containing many flat rounded achenes, fall.

Roots: Large stout taproot.

General Information: Biennial herb, common.

Habitat: Both species grow side by side in fields and along roadsides.

Season of Availability: The root of the first year plant is collected in the late summer and fall.[84] The official herb is the leaves of the first year growth.[84]

Preparation: The root is used fresh in a poultice or fresh or dried in a decoction. The leaves are used in a poultice for boils and abscess.[84] Dried root dose 2 to 6 grams or by infusion, liquid extract 1:1 in 25% ethanol dose 2 to 8 ml, both t.i.d.[84]

Medical Terminology: Therapeutically, it is diuretic,[52,84] alterative[58] and diaphoretic.[a] It has been considered an aphrodisiac.[18] The first year root has been considered official with the average dose of 2 grams.[2]

Related Disease Symptoms: The root was prescribed as a cure for gonorrhea and syphilis.[b] A salve made from the root was used to heal and soothe burns, wounds and skin irritation.[c] The tea was taken as a blood purifier.[d] It was used by the Meskwaki women as a medicine for labor.[63,73] The tea relieved stomach pain and was a general tonic.[e] The tea was used for pleurisy cough.[f] The British use the root tea and leaf tea for eczema and psoriasis.[84]

Poisonous Aspects: The plant has exhibited hypoglycemic activity.[40] The plant has caused contact dermatitis.[46]

Biological and Edible: In antibiotic experiments, *Arctium minus* has shown gram + bacterial growth inhibition.[57]

---

[a] 10,22,35,38,44,51,55,56,63,66,68
[b] 35,36,38,40
[c] 22,32,35,36,38,44,51,84
[d] 18,27,36,44,57,76
[e] 36,63,75
[f] 10,36,6318,25,34,47

The first year root of the biennial is edible.[g] In the Orient, the edible root is grown commercially and sold by the name of gobo. Bees utilize this plant for honey.[92,93]

Chemistry & Pharmacognosy: The root contains the compound inulin and the glucoside lappin.[58,84]

Commercial Products & Uses: The root has been purchased by drug companies.[37]

Personal Experimentation: I have eaten the first year root many times, either fried or steamed with other vegetables or alone with salt and butter. I've never noticed any strange or harmful effects. I have bought gobo in Yokohama's vegetable markets; it's good to eat. The macrobiotics consider it to be the most yang vegetable.

Arctium lappa, Arctium minus
Burdock, stickers, clotbur, harebur, burrseed, gobo

45

ARCTOSTAPHYLOS UVA-URSI
Ericaceae
Bearberry, kinnikinick, uva-ursi

Stem: Prostrate, reddish brown shredding bark, woody, rarely over 1 dm tall.

Leaves: Alternate, evergreen, spatulate, 1-3 cm long, leathery, brittle, shiny surface, entire, distinct netted veins.

Flower Type: White, terminal racemes, bell-shaped, 5 to 15 mm long, spring.

Fruit: Red mealy berry, 1 cm in diameter, edible, fall.

Roots: Prostrate taproot.

General Information: Perennial shrub, mat forming, dense.

Habitat: This plant is very common in rocky sandy soil in open woods and fields.

Season of Availability: The leaves are gathered in the fall.

Preparation: The leaves are used in an infusion, fresh or dried. The dried leaves are given in 1.5 to 4.0 gram doses three times each day.[83]

Medical Terminology: Therapeutically, it is diuretic,[a] astringent[b] and tonic in action.[c] Some consider the leaves antiseptic.[d]

The National Formulary's recommended dose is 2 gm of ground leaves.[2]

Related Disease Symptoms: Bearberry has been used to heal and relieve back pain and kidney problems.[e] The extract from the leaves has been used for urinary tract infections and problems.[f] The Chippewa smoked the dried pulverized leaves mixed with *Salix spp.* to stop the pain from headaches.[10] It has been used in treating leukorrhea, cystitis,[g] diarrhea, chronic bronchitis and passive hemorrhages.[30,32] Some other indications include urethritis, dysuria, cystitis, pyelitis, and lithuria.[82]

Biological and Edible: The leaves were smoked by many northern tribes of Native Americans.[h] The berries are edible.[i] In antibiotic experiments, kinnikinick inhibited gram + bacteria.[57] Bees use this plant for honey.[92,93]

Chemistry & Pharmacognosy: The leaves contain tannic[22] and gallic acids[51,58] and quercetin.[j] The leaves also contain arbutin,[1,31] ericolin and urson.[k] Corilagin, pyroside, and several esters of arbutin have also been isolated.[82,83]

---

[a] 10,27,31,41

[b] 5,19,22,68,83

[c] 32,44,50,51,58,63,74

[d] 1,10,19,83

[e] 23,24,47,63

[f] 5,19,22,30,32,36,39,40,47,51,63,83

[g] 5,51,74

[h] 10,30,36,40,76

[i] 15,19,25,47

[j] 1,82,83

[k] 51,58,82,83

Commercial Products & Uses:
A commercial product called 'Doans Pills' contains an extract from the leaves of this plant.

Personal Experimentation: I have ingested over 1 quart of the tea made from the leaves of this plant with no ill effects. I have been drinking the tea periodically since 1973. Steeped with *Achillea millefolium* and *Verbascum thapsus*, the tea has helped me to quickly relieve the symptoms of the common cold when administered at 3 to 4 cups every 4 to 6 hours.

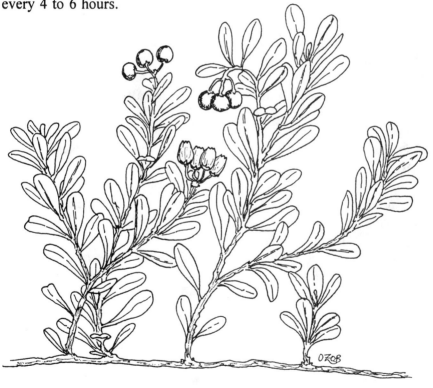

Arctostaphylos uva-ursi
Bearberry, kinnikinick, uva-ursi

ARISAEMA TRIPHYLLUM
Araceae
Jack-in-the-pulpit, dragon root, indian turnip, wake robin, devil's ear, bog onion

Stem: Erect, 30-70 cm, branchless, green.

Leaves: 2 opposite long petioled compound leaves, 3 elliptic to rhombic-ovate green leaflets, 4 to 6 cm long.

Flower Type: Solitary, terminal, purple-green, born on a long peduncle, cup-shaped with one side longer than the other, making an acuminate flap over the spadix, spring.

Fruit: Scarlet berries, in an egg-shaped cluster, easily noticed because they stand alone, fall.

Roots: Bulbous root, corm, it is largest in the fall, 5 to 8 cm in diameter.

General Information: Perennial herb.

Habitat: Jack-in-the-pulpit is commonly found in damp woods and along stream sides.

Season of Availability: Harvest the bulbous root in the fall.

Preparation: The root is used dried in an infusion. Fresh, it is used for special reasons, dealing directly to its calcium oxalate content.

Medical Terminology: Therapeutically, *A. triphyllum* has been considered an expectorant,[32,36] a diaphoretic[27,44] and an irritant.[a]

Related Disease Symptoms: The corms have been grated, boiled in milk, and the infusion was used to treat coughs and tuberculosis.[36] Ground corms were also taken for bowel complaints and constipation.[63] The corms have treated asthma[36,51] and bronchitis.[27,52] The dried corm has been recommended for many catarrhal affections.[27,51] For flatulent colic, a tea from the corms was administered.[b] When sore eyes were encountered, the Chippewa washed them with a root decoction of *Arisaema triphyllum*.[c] The corms have been incorporated in rheumatism treatment.[d]

Poisonous Aspects: The plant has caused contact dermatitis.[40] No known deaths have been caused by *A. triphyllum*.[33] Symptoms include abdominal pain, burning of the mucous membranes, nausea, and vomiting.[91] Treatment is aluminum hydroxide for neutralizing and demulcent effects and symptomatic therapy.[91]

---

[a] 19,22,38,58,63   [b] 32,36,63
[c] 10,74,75   [d] 36,51,52

Biological and Edible: The edible corms, dried for a few months, can be ground into flour or eaten plain.[e]

---

[e] 15,19,76

[f] 19,22,32,33,38,40,58

Chemistry & Pharmacognosy: Calcium oxalate crystals are contained in the plant.[f] The needle-like crystals become embedded in the mucous membranes, provoking intense irritation and a burning sensation.[33,40]

Arisaema triphyllum
Jack-in-the-pulpit, dragon root, indian turnip, wake robin, devil's ear, bog onion

ARMILLARIELLA MELLEA
Agaricaceae
Honey mushroom

Please note: *Mushroom identification can be confusing. Before ingesting, be sure to identify with certainty, and preferably only pick mushrooms with a guide or naturalist.*

Stem: 5 to 15 cm long, .5 to 2 cm thick, fibrous, off-white, discoloration ranges from honey colored to rust brown, usually a ring on top of stalk.

Fruit: Cap is 2.5-10 cm wide, oval to flat, somewhat sticky, yellow to rust brown, sometimes has black, erect tuft-like scales. Gills attached very slightly to stalk.

General Information: Looks very similar to several poisonous mushrooms, **be sure to identify with certainty**.

Habitat: Tree stumps, fields.

Season of Availability: Late summer, fall.

Poisonous Aspects: Some people experience stomach upset.

Biological and Edible: Edible, but must be well cooked.

Personal Experimentation: The honey mushroom is one of my favorites. Besides being good to eat, it nearly always grows in large groups making collection very easy. I tried drying the mushrooms with good results. I put the sliced mushrooms on a piece of newspaper in a hot attic and within 48 hours they were dried. For cooking, just put the dried mushrooms in soups or stews and they will come back to life.

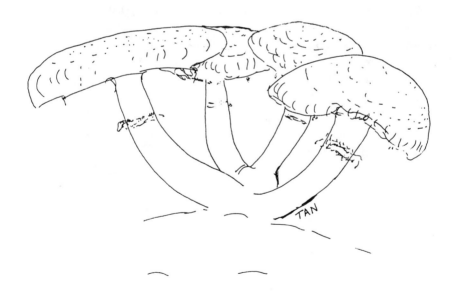

Armillariella mellea
Honey mushroom

51

ARTEMISIA ABSINTHIUM
Compositae
Wormwood, absinthe

Stem: Many branching stalks from the same rootstock, woody at the base, up to 1.5 m, green with white pubescence, persistent for 1 year.

Leaves: Alternate, highly dissected, almost fern-like, green with white pubescence, 5 to 10 cm long.

Flower Type: Yellow discoid flowers, in a terminal spike, 4 to 8 mm across, summer.

Fruit: Brown sliver-like achenes.

Roots: Fibrous.

General Information: Perennial herb, aromatic.

Habitat: The plant grows commonly in fields and roadsides throughout the U.P.

Season of Availability: Collected in late summer and fall.[83]

Preparation: It can be used fresh or dried in an infusion. It is also made into a tincture, either alone or with licorice and mint (absinthe). Dried herb 1 to 2 grams t.i.d.[83] Liquid extract 1:1 in 25% ethanol 1 to 2 ml t.i.d.[83]

Medical Terminology: Therapeutically, *Artemisia absinthium* is considered to be tonic,[32,58] anthelmintic[5] and stomachic in action.[a] It is also considered a stimulant.[b] The oil is a therapeutic component in liniment.[53]

Related Disease Symptoms: The Chippewa of Wisconsin and Minnesota boiled the herb and made a compress with the tea and herb for sprains and strained muscles.[10] It is used as a bitters for indigestion.[c] Indications include anorexia, Enterobius or Ascaris infestation, and atonic dyspepsia.[83]

Poisonous Aspects: *A. absinthium* has no recorded toxicity, but Kingsbury reports on the toxicity of *Artemisia* as a genus and states a few examples using western species.[33] Very large doses are thought to cause death[5] from epileptiform convulsions.[32] The pollen has caused hay fever and the oil has caused contact dermatitis.[40]

Biological and Edible: Incense was made from the herb for spiritual reasons.[24]

Chemistry & Pharmacognosy: The volatile oil contains thujone.[d] The plant contains absinthin[51] and tannin.[58,83] D-isothujone, thujyl alcohol, cadinene, and phellandrene are also present.[82] Chromatography has been done.[83]

---

[a] 10,22,51,63,83 [c] 19,22,32,69

[b] 10,22,32,58,63 [d] 31,82,83

Commercial Products & Uses:
The main production of wormwood is in southern Michigan.[53] The volatile oil is available through steam distillation.[e] It was used as the main flavor in the alcoholic drink absinthe.[f] It has been the main flavoring when making beer.[19]

Personal Experimentation: I have drank 1 quart of the tea at one sitting with no ill effects. The tea is extremely bitter. As I drank it over many months, I acquired a taste for it and found it pleasing.

I have used the tea for bath water. I noticed an exhilarating soothing feeling in my muscles and body. A friend, after hearing of this, repeated the experiment. He also noticed a distinct stimulation feeling. I have used the tincture in around 30 ml doses to bring on hunger when sick, the results were excellent. Using a beer recipe, I substituted *Artemisia absinthium* for *Humulus lupulus*. The beer was extremely bitter and difficult to drink, however the experience was unique.

[e] 22,29,32,58
[f] 22,29,58

Artemisia absinthium
Wormwood, absinthe

ASARUM CANADENSE
Aristolochiaceae
Wild ginger, black snakeroot, coltsfoot, broad-leaved sarabacca, ginger

Stem: Stemless.

Leaves: Whorled, long petioles (10 to 15 cm), roundish heart-shaped leaves, deep green, 6 to 8 cm broad, acuminate.

Flower Type: Reddish brown, bell-shaped with 3 lobes, y-shaped at the base of the leaves, 1 to 3 cm across, early spring.

Fruit: Fleshy globular capsule with thick large seeds, spring, early summer.

Roots: Creeping rhizome, aromatic, ginger-smelling.

General Information: Perennial herb, grows in clumps.

Habitat: I have found the wild ginger along streams in rich moist hardwood stands.

Season of Availability: The roots are harvested in the fall but can be collected anytime as the ginger flavor is always prevalent.

Preparation: The roots are used in a decoction or tincture, fresh or dried. The decoction is made by boiling the roots for 30 minutes.

Medical Terminology: It has been used as an aromatic stimulant[a] and a diaphoretic.[b] For flatulence,[c] it is used as a carminative.[22,58] It is also considered a tonic.[d] The roots and dried rhizomes have been considered official with the average dose of 2 grams.[2]

Related Disease Symptoms: A tea taken internally was used to relieve stomach gas.[e] To relieve aching head and eyes, the powdered root was inhaled like snuff.[36,63] It has been externally applied to wounds to prevent bleeding.[63] It has been utilized for throat trouble, earache, sore ears, lung trouble, and stomach cramps.[63] Canadian Indians drank a root infusion to relieve heart arrhythmia[40] The Catawaba used a ginger remedy to relieve heart pains.[40] To cure ear infections, the Meskwaki steeped the roots and poured the tea directly into the ear.[40,73] For indigestion, the root was eaten.[10] The root has been crushed and used in a poultice for infection and inflammation.[10]

Poisonous Aspects: No recordings of *A. canadense* toxicity have been reported but *A. europaeum*, the species in Europe, is documented as being toxic.[33]

---

[a] 36,51,58 [d] 38,51,58

[b] 22,27,32 [e] 18,30,32,36,

[c] 18,32,44   38,63,74,76

54

Wild ginger has caused contact dermatitis.[46]

Biological and Edible: The Meskwaki used the juices of the root as fish bait.[73] In antibiotic experiments, ginger inhibited gram + bacteria.[57] Two antibiotics have been isolated from this plant.[57,63]

Chemistry & Pharmacognosy: Wild ginger contains aristolochic acid, which has known antimicrobial properties.[40] It contains arasol.[51,58]

Commercial Products & Uses: The roots can be used just like commercial ginger.[f] The roots can be collected and sold to drug companies.[37]

Personal Experimentation: I have ingested one pint of the root decoction at one sitting and noticed no effects. The taste is that of strong ginger. The roots can be boiled a number of times. I have also made ginger candy by adding sugar, making a thick syrup over heat, and letting it cool.

---

[f] 15,25,36,38,63

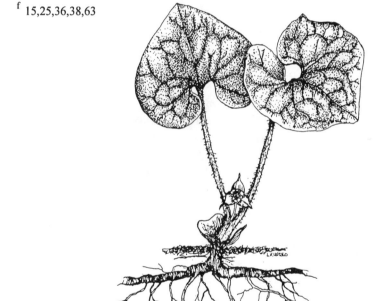

Asarum canadense
Wild ginger, black snakeroot, coltsfoot, broad-leaved sarabacca, ginger

ASCLEPIAS SYRIACA
Asclepiadaceae
Milkweed, silkweed

Stem: Unbranched, stout, downy, grayish-green, erect, milky sap, up to 2 m.

Leaves: Opposite, oblong-ovate to elliptic, acute, thick, fuzzy, entire, green, 8 to 15 cm long.

Flower Type: Pink to white, in globose umbels, originating from the leaf axils, early summer.

Fruit: Ovoid pods, green turning to brown and splitting open, 6 to 8 cm long, inside there are silky white hairs, each connected to a flat round seed, late summer, fall.

Roots: Taproot.

General Information: Perennial herb, grows in clumps.

Habitat: Commonly grows throughout North America in open fields and roadsides.

Season of Availability: The roots are collected in the fall. The herb is collected in the late summer. The milky sap is collected in the late summer. The flowers and young seed pods are collected in July for eating.

Preparation: The roots are used in a decoction, either fresh or dried. The milky sap is used topically, fresh or dried. The flowers and young seed pods are fried in oil, with or without batter.

Medical Terminology: The root is emetic and cathartic in large doses.[a] In average doses it is considered diuretic,[10,36] expectorant and diaphoretic.[b]

Related Disease Symptoms: A root tea was taken for the cure of dropsy (congestive heart failure),[40] dysentery and asthma.[63] The Natchez utilized a root decoction for kidney trouble, including Bright's disease.[63] It was used in the treatment of syphilis.[63] The juice of milkweed was rubbed on warts to make them disappear.[c] The root of *A. syriaca* was used for a female remedy among the Ojibwe.[63] A tea of the root was used by the Chippewa as a remedy to produce the flow of milk.[10,54] The roots have been used to treat rheumatism.[d]

Poisonous Aspects: Kingsbury reports that the *Asclepias* genus has toxic compounds throughout each species.[33] He mentions a paper by Reynard[e] that discusses *A. syriacia*'s toxicity.[33] However, no cases were reported.

---

[a] 10,32,36,52,58

[b] 32,38,58

[c] 36,38,52,63

[d] 30,32,58

[e] Maryland Agr. Expt. Sta. Tech. Bull. A10, 1942

Biological and Edible: The young shoots,[9,15] unopened flower buds and young seed pods are edible.[f] They are usually fried in oil. Bees utilize this plant for honey.[92,93]

Commercial Products & Uses: The Native Americans used the fibers for cloth and thread.[g] The silky hairs on the seeds have been used for stuffing[29] and as a substitute for kapok[6] in the life preserver industry.

[f] 18,25,74,75,76

[g] 6,29,74

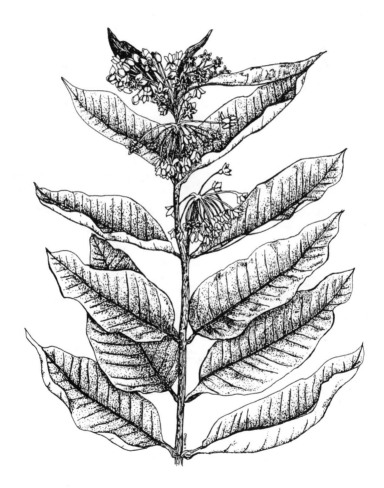

Asclepias syriaca
Milkweed, silkweed

ASCLEPIAS TUBEROSA
Asclepiadiaceae
Butterfly weed, pleurisy root

Stem: Erect, rough, branching only at the top, hairy, up to 1 m, green.

Leaves: Alternate, lanceolate to oblong, 10 to 15 cm long, acute, green.

Flower Type: Orange, in terminal umbels, each flower 5 to 10 mm across, summer.

Fruit: Long slender seed pods, 8 to 12 cm long, green turning brown and splitting open, exposing silky hairs connected to brown, flat, round seeds, summer, fall.

Roots: Taproot. Microscopic descriptions are available.[84]

General: Perennial herb.

Habitat: The plant grows in sandy soils in open fields and roadsides.

Season of Availability: The tuberous roots are collected in the fall.

Preparation: The roots are used in a decoction, fresh or dried. Dried root 1 to 4 grams or by infusion, liquid extract 1:1 in 45% ethanol dose 1 to 4 ml, all t.i.d.[83]

Medical Terminology: Therapeutically, *Asclepias tuberosa* is considered diaphoretic and expectorant.[a] In large doses, its action is emetic[36,38] and purgative.[b]

Related Disease Symptoms: It has been used in pulmonary and bronchial affections,[84] and for rheumatism.[c] The ground roots were used fresh or dry as a poultice for open sores and bruises.[d] As a healing agent, the Omaha placed the chewed roots on wounds and sores.[40] The root tea has been used for pleurisy, thus the name pleurisy root.[e]

Biological and Edible: Bees utilize this plant for honey.[92,93]

Chemistry & Pharmacognosy: The root contains the glucoside asclepiadin.[58,84]

Commercial Products & Uses: The root can be gathered and sold to drug companies.[37]

---

[a] 9,22,32,38,44,51,58,63,72,73,84

[b] 22,32,44,58,63

[c] 30,32,36,58,63,72

[d] 36,40,63,72,74

[e] 9,22,63,72,84

Asclepias tuberosa
Butterfly weed, pleurisy root

ASPARAGUS OFFICINALE
Liliaceae
Wild asparagus, asparagus

Stem: Up to 2 m, stout, smooth, ridged, tapers upward, branched, green, edible.

Leaves: Scale like, needle-like, up to 3 cm, green.

Flower Type: Greenish-yellow, axillary, dioecious, on jointed pedicels, summer.

Fruit: Orange-red, round, 2 cm in diameter, filled with small round seeds, summer.

Roots: Matted, thick, fibrous.

General Information: Looks like a small pine from a distance in the summer, hard to find in the spring when edible, it is better to know a spot or find one the year before.

Habitat: Sandy fields, roadsides, throughout the region.

Season of Availability: Gather the immature succulent stems in the spring.

Medical Terminology: Roots considered diuretic, laxative.

Preparation: The succulent stems are cut into pieces, around 5 cm long, steamed or boiled, and eaten. Some people serve them with butter and/or sauces.

Biological and Edible: Bees utilize this plant for honey.[92,93]

Personal Experimentation: Ever since I can remember, I've collected asparagus for a spring meal. Asparagus usually grows in small clumps, so I usually gather some of the succulent stems, always leaving a stem or two to insure it coming back next year. I cut the stems into bite size pieces, steam them in my vegetable steamer, and eat them with margarine.

Asparagus officinale
Wild asparagus, asparagus

BAPTISIA TINCTORIA
Leguminosae
Wild indigo, indigo, rattleweed, clover bloom, yellow broom

Stem: Branching, slender, smooth, green, up to 1 m.

Leaves: Alternate, compound, 3 obovate leaflets, each 1 to 2 cm long, wedge-shaped at base, stipulate, green.

Flower Type: Yellow, 1 to 3 cm long, 10 stamens, 2 lipped calyx, born in a loose terminal raceme, spring, summer.

Fruit: Papery to woody, inflated pod, 5-15 mm long, summer, fall.

Roots: Taproot.

General: Perennial herb.

Habitat: *B. tinctoria* flowers from late May to September in open fields and roadsides.

Season of Availability: The roots are collected in the fall.

Preparation: The roots are used fresh or dried in an infusion or decoction. Dried root dose .5-1.0 grams, liquid extract 1:1 in 60% ethanol dose .3-1.3 ml all t.i.d.[83]

Medical Terminology: Therapeutically, it has been considered cathartic[38] and emetic in large doses.[a] However, it is mainly used for its antiseptic properties.[b] It is also considered an antimicrobial, antipyretic, and mild cardioactive agent.[83]

Related Disease Symptoms: The roots steeped in water have been applied to cuts and sores as an antiseptic wash.[c] A poultice made from the root was used to treat skin ulcers.[d] A tea of the root was used as a gargle in malignant and scarlatinal sore throat.[32] It has been used in the treatment of typhoid fever.[22,32] Experimentation was done with treating typhoid.[32] It has been used in a fomentation to abate swelling and counteract the poison in rattlesnake bites.[63] Other indications include tonsillitis, pharyngitis, lymphadenitis, furunculosis, aphthous ulcers, stomatitis, and gingivitis.[83]

Poisonous Aspects: *Baptisia* is considered toxic to livestock.[33]

Biological and Edible: Bees utilize this plant for honey.[92,93]

Chemistry & Pharmacognosy: *Baptisia* contains the glucoside babtisin[51] and the alkaloid cystine.[58,83] It also contains some flavonoids and coumarins.[83] Chromatography has been done.[83] It contains the acrid poison, baptisine, and a purgative glucoside, baptin.[51]

---

[a] 22,36,51,58,63

[b] 22,36,38,51,63,83

[c] 22,30,32,36,51,63,83

[d] 22,30,32,36,63,83

Baptisia tinctoria
Wild indigo, indigo, rattleweed, clover bloom, yellow broom

BARBAREA VULGARIS
Cruciferae
Winter-cress, yellow rocket

Stem: Branching, smooth, many-stemmed, leaves alternate, up to 8 dm tall.

Leaves: Pinnately cut, basal rosette, terminal lobe rounded, dark green, glossy, upper leaves broad, toothed.

Flower Type: Yellow, 5 to 7 mm wide, terminal racemes, petals spread above sepals, pistil long and slender.

Habitat: Flowers from April to August in open fields, roadsides, forests, and along streams.

Season of Availability: Spring through summer.

Related Disease Symptoms: Use a tea made of the dried leaves as a cough suppressant or diuretic. The fresh leaves have been used on wounds.

Poisonous Aspects: Has been known to cause kidney malfunctions.

Biological and Edible: Seeds can be sprouted and used as food.[86] The young leaves, gathered in early spring, are fine fresh in salads or cooked. Later in the season, boil the leaves in 2 to 3 changes of water to avoid bitterness. Bees utilize this plant for honey.[92,93]

Barbarea vulgaris
Winter-cress, yellow rocket

BERBERIS VULGARIS
Berberidaceae
Barberry

Stem: Branching, gray to yellowish-gray bark, up to 3 m, spiny, three pointed barbs along stem.

Leaves: Alternate, obovate to oblong-ovate, 2 to 5 cm long, spinulose to denticulate margins, green.

Flower Type: Yellow, 6 petals, 6 sepals, 6 stamens, born in axial, many flowered drooping racemes, spring.

Fruit: Scarlet ellipsoid single seeded berry, 1 to 3 cm across, fall.

Roots: Lateral taproot.

General: Perennial bushy shrub with thorns and red berries.

Habitat: It is commonly found along roadsides in thickets and fence rows in fields.

Season of Availability: The root, root bark, stem, and fruit are collected in the fall.

Preparation: The roots, root bark, and stem bark are dried first for preparations. The stem, root and root bark are used in a decoction. Commercially, the roots are made into a tincture. The berries are used fresh. Dried bark dose 1 to 2 grams or by decoction, liquid extract 1:1 dose is 2 to 3 ml, all t.i.d.[84]

Medical Terminology: The bark has been used as a bitter tonic.[a] The bark is considered a febrifuge.[22,32] It is also considered an antiseptic, laxative, stimulant, and tonic.[30] The British utilize it as a cholagogue, antiemetic, and a tonic to the spleen.[84]

Related Disease Symptoms: A drink of the berries was used to reduce fever.[b] The root bark has been used to treat diarrhea, dysentery, and jaundice.[c] In Europe, a root infusion was used to treat dyspepsia.[d] The berries have been used in treating vitamin C deficiencies.[e] Some British indications include cholecystitis, cholelithiasis, leishmaniasis, and malaria.[84]

Biological and Edible: The fruits are considered edible[15] and are often used in jellies.

Chemistry & Pharmacognosy: The root bark contains the alkaloid berberine.[f] Commercially, the alkaloid is obtained by alcohol extraction.[g] Other compounds include oxyacanthine and chelidonic acid.[84] Chromatography has been done.[84]

---

[a] 1,22,30,51,58

[b] 22,32,36,58   [e] 22,36,38

[c] 30,36,38   [g] 22,30,32

[d] 22,36,38   [f] 22,32,40,51,58,82,84

Berberis vulgaris
Barberry

BETULA ALLEGHANIENSIS
Betulaceae
Yellow birch, bronze birch, birch

Stem: Golden yellow bark, black longitudinal splits, prominent lenticels, young twigs very smooth and red, up to 30 m.

Leaves: Ovate to oblong-ovate, alternate, sharply doubly serrate, petiolate, acute, rounded base, green.

Flower Type: Catkins.

Fruit: Winged samara in a catkin.

Roots: Taproot.

General Information: Perennial deciduous tree, lumber tree used for veneer.

Habitat: The tree grows in sandy loam soils. It is found across the Great Lakes in forests mixed with sugar maples.

Season of Availability: The small twigs are collected in any season.

Preparation: For an infusion, the twigs are steeped fresh. The oil is obtained by steam distillation or alcohol extraction. The twigs were collected by the Potawatomi for a medicinal tea.[63,76]

Medical Terminology: Yellow birch is considered antiseptic[31] and astringent in action.[38,50] In the pharmaceutical preparation, birch tar, it is used as a local stimulant.[31]

Related Disease Symptoms: For stomach pains, the Chippewa used a tea of the black birch, a relative of the yellow birch growing in Minnesota.[10]

Biological and Edible: The yellow birch is used like the sweet birch, *Betula lenta*.[15] The sap, taken in spring, has been used to make birch beer.[36,38] The sap is also used to make a sugar syrup.[15,75] The inner bark of all birch trees can be pulverized into an edible flour.[79]

Chemistry & Pharmacognosy: The bark and twigs contain the volatile oil, methyl salicylate.[a]

Commercial Products & Uses: The twigs have been used in commercial production of wintergreen oil and birch beer.

Personal Experimentation: Many times I have gathered small twigs of the yellow birch, poured boiling water over them, and enjoyed hot cups of the wintergreen-flavored tea. One spot comes to mind on a crisp cool fall morning near the Graveraet river, south of Freda, MI. If you are skeptical, just break off a young twig and start chewing, soon the wintergreen flavor will appear.

---

[a] 15,31,36,38,58,59,82

Betula alleghaniensis
Yellow birch, bronze birch, birch

69

CALTHA PALUSTRIS
Ranunculaceae
Marsh-marigold, cowslip, may-blob

Stem: Hollow, green, furrowed, erect, branching, up to 8 dm.

Leaves: Green, roundish to open reniform, dentate, up to 20 cm across, alternate, edible, spring.

Flower Type: Yellow, 5-9 petal-like sepals, 10-40 stamens, 5-10 pistils, 3 cm across, immature flower buds edible, spring.

Fruit: Green follicle, 1-1.5 cm long, prominent beak, spring.

Roots: Fibrous.

General Information: Grows in large groups, perennial herb.

Habitat: Wet muddy areas, stream banks, marshes.

Season of Availability: The leaves and the immature flower buds are collected in the spring.

Preparation: Boil or steam the leaves in two waters (important). Serve with butter and/or vinegar. The boiled flower buds can be placed in pickle juice and eaten as pickles.[15,19]

Related Disease Symptoms: Marsh-marigold has been used to treat warts, congestive heart failure, and anemia.[19] It has also been used as an expectorant for cough syrups.[10,19] For warts, a drop of the leaf juice was applied daily until the wart disappeared.[19] The Chippewa applied the dried powdered and moistened or fresh root of cowslip twice daily to cure scrofula sores.[10]

Poisonous Aspects: The leaves must be boiled to destroy a bitter toxic substance.[15,47] Symptoms include mouth and skin paresthesias, hypotension, nausea, vomiting, and seizures.[91] Treatment is atropine 2 mg IM, repeat if necessary, maintain vitals.[91]

Biological and Edible: The leaves are edible after boiling in two waters.[a] Young immature green flower buds can be placed in salt water or pickle juice and eaten as pickles.[b]

Chemistry & Pharmacognosy: The plant contains a poisonous glucoside, which is expelled by boiling.[19] The poisonous principle is volatile, thus after drying it is harmless.[33] The plant is known to contain anemonin.[33]

Personal Experimentation: It is extremely important to boil the leaves in two waters, or the taste is so bitter, it renders the leaves inedible. I find it easiest to collect the single leaves, place them in boiling water for 3 to 5 minutes, drain the water, pour in

---

[a] 15,19,25,47,78,88,89

[b] 15,19,25,78

cold water, heat to boiling and boil for 3 to 5 more minutes. Then drain the water and serve with margarine and vinegar or with tomato sauce and cheese.

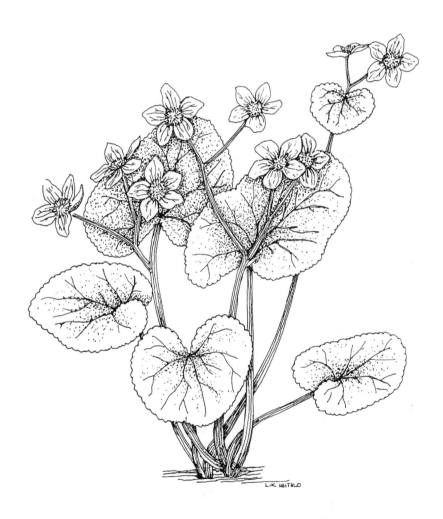

Caltha palustris
Marsh-marigold, cowslip, may-blob

CANNABIS SATIVA
Cannabinaceae
Hemp, marijuana, reefer, pot

Stem: Branching only at the top, scabrous, green, up to 3 m, fibrous.

Leaves: Alternate, palmately compound, 3-15 linear-lanceolate coarsely toothed leaflets, green.

Flower Type: Green, dioecious; staminate in axillary compound racemes, 5 sepals, 5 stamens; pistillate in spikes along the branches, late summer.

Fruit: Hard round achene, 2 to 5 mm in diameter, brown, shiny, edible, fall.

Roots: Taproot.

General Information: Annual herb, not common, brought to this area through cultivation.

Habitat: The plant has been found growing in fields and roadsides in the Great Lakes region. Introduced by man, it does not grow naturally. It is illegal to cultivate in the U.S.

Season of Availability: The plant is collected in the late fall. It is then dried by various techniques to achieve color and quality. The leaves and flowers are collected in October.

Preparation: The flowers and leaves are dried and used by smoking or in an infusion. The plant is smoked, made into a tea, and/or cooked and eaten.[a]

Medical Terminology: People use this plant to achieve euphoric sensations.[b] It is thought to be an anodyne, hypnotic, and antispasmodic.[c] It has been thought to possess aphrodisiac properties.[40] *Cannabis* is considered an intoxicant.[d] The dose for smoking is 200 to 250 micrograms per 1 kilogram of body weight and 300 to 480 micrograms per kilogram of body weight for ingesting.[40] According to a pulmonary specialist at Lansing General Hospital, *Cannabis* appears to be recognized as a bronchodilator.

Related Disease Symptoms: It has been employed to treat glaucoma.[40] Marijuana has been used as a sedative in cases of sleeplessness due to acute neuralgia or nervous exhaustion.[e]

Poisonous Aspects: The drug produces a pleasurable sensation, loss of time, difficulty in concentration and can cause vomiting.[26] The leaves and flowers have caused dermatitis.[46] The pollen is a cause of hay fever.[40]

---

[a] 1,29,68

[b] 1,4,8,29,32,33

[c] 5,29,36,68

[d] 1,5,8,32,33,36,40,51,56

[e] 1,29,32,36,68

Kingsbury reports one case of animal poisoning in Greece.[33]

Biological and Edible: In antibiotic experiments, *Cannabis* has inhibited gram + bacteria.[40] The drug produces physiological activity.[26,33]

Chemistry & Pharmacognosy: *Cannabis* contains tetrahydrocannabinol[4,82] and cannabidiol.[f] The concentrations of cannabidiol and tetrahydrocannabinol are inversely related;[82] cannabidiol concentration is highest in the early growing season and as it declines tetrahydrocannabinol increases.[82]

---

[f] 1,31,33,82
[g] 3,29,82
[h] 1,29,33,68

Commercial Products & Uses: The stems of the male plant have been collected and used commercially for fiber.[g] Other compounds from the resins include cannabinol, cannabidiolic acid, cannabichromene, and cannabigerol.[82] Hempseed contains around 20% fixed oil which is used for the manufacture of soaps and paints while the cake meal is used for cattle food.[82] In the United States, there are legal restrictions for possession, use, and trade of reefer.[h] However, it is presently legal in Michigan as a prescription drug.

Personal Experimentation: I met a person who smoked marijuana and said that he hid it in his shower curtain rod.

Cannabis sativa
Hemp, marijuana, reefer, pot

CAPSELLA BURSA-PASTORIS
Cruciferae
Shepherd's purse, case weed, shovel weed

Stem: Smooth, 1 to 6 dm tall, few branches, green.

Leaves: Alternate, basal leaves in a rosette; basal leaves toothed, linear-lanceolate, 5 to 10 cm long; cauline leaves progressively smaller, sagitate, sessile, green.

Flower Type: White, 4 petals, 2 to 4 mm long, 4 sepals, in a terminal raceme, spring, summer, fall.

Fruit: Green, later turning brown, heart-shaped silicle, 5 to 10 mm long, spring, summer, fall.

Roots: Taproot.

General Information: Annual herb, common, lacy looking.

Habitat: *Capsella* is found along roadsides, in lawns, and in many open fields.

Season of Availability: The herb is collected throughout the spring, summer, and fall.

Preparation: The herb is used fresh or dried in an infusion. Dried herb dose 1 to 4 grams, liquid extract 1:1 in 25% ethanol dose is 1 to 4 ml both t.i.d.[83]

---

[a] 30,32,35,58,68
[b] 27,30,35,36,68
[c] 22,30,68
[d] 22,27,32,36,41,55
[e] 22,35,36,83

Medical Terminology: Thought to be a tonic, ascorbutic, and astringent.[a] Others attribute the herb's action as diuretic.[b] In Europe it is considered an antihemorrhagic and urinary antiseptic.[83]

Related Disease Symptoms: The Cheyenne made an infusion of the leaves and stem, cooled it, and used it to treat headaches.[24,70] To cure earaches, a strong decoction of the herb was used as ear drops.[c] For stomach cramps, the Chippewa used a tea from the herb.[10] *Capsella* has been used to stop bleeding from the kidneys.[d] The tea has been utilized to check profuse menstruation.[e] For poison ivy rash the Menominee steeped the herb and used the tea as a wash.[70] A specific indication is for uterine hemorrhage.[83]

Poisonous Aspects: I couldn't find any cases of poisoning of any sort on *Capsella*.

Biological and Edible: Experiments on animals have shown that the extract has a marked tonic effect on the uterine muscles similar to that of ergot.[7]

Chemistry & Pharmacognosy: It contains luteolin 7-rutinoside and quercetin 3-rutinoside.[83] Chromatography has been done.[83]

Personal Experimentation: The seed pods have a slight peppery taste. The spring leaves are crisp and bland like lettuce. I recommend trying them.

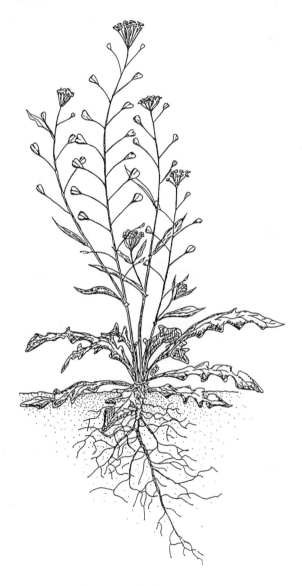

Capsella bursa-pastoris
Shepherd's purse, case weed, shovel weed

CAULOPHYLLUM THALICTROIDES
Berberidaceae
Blue cohosh, cohosh, papoose root, blueberry

Stem: Branchless, up to 1 m, usually about 6 dm, green.

Leaves: Usually only 2 leaves, terminal, 2-3 times compound in groups of 3's, the main divisions petioled, leaflets 2-3 lobed, obovate, wedged-shaped at the base, pale green.

Flower Type: Yellow to green, 6 petals, 6 sepals, 1 to 2 cm across, born in a loose terminal raceme, spring.

Fruit: Round blue drupes, persistent, looks similar to a blueberry, summer.

Roots: Lateral taproot.

General Information: Perennial herb.

Habitat: *Caulophyllum* grows in rich moist hardwood forests and along streams in hardwood stands.

Season of Availability: The roots are collected in the fall and allowed to dry.

Preparation: The roots are used in a decoction. A tea is made from the plant's root and rhizome.[a] Dried rhizome and roots dose .3 to 1 gram, liquid extract 1:1 in 70% ethanol dose .5 to 1 ml, both t.i.d.[83]

Medical Terminology: The rhizomes and root of blue cohosh are said to have sedative properties.[10] It is considered a diuretic and emmenagogue.[b] The dried rhizome and roots have been considered official with the average dose of .5 grams. The British find it to be a spasmolytic, emmenagogue, uterine tonic, and antirheumatic.[83]

Related Disease Symptoms: Many Native American tribes used the root tea to facilitate childbirth.[c] Blue cohosh has been employed to treat rheumatism, bronchitis[51] and colic.[d] The root decoction has been used to promote menstruation.[e] A root tea was used by the Chippewa for lung trouble.[10] The same root tea, mixed with the root of *Rudbeckia laciniata*, was used for indigestion.[10]

Poisonous Aspects: The rootstocks have caused dermatitis.[46] Children have been poisoned by eating the blue berries.[40] Poisoning is treated with gastric lavage or emesis and followed by supportive therapy.[96]

---

[a] 30,36,44,63

[b] 10,30,32,35,44,51,58,96

[c] 9,30,32,35,36,38,63,76

[d] 30,32,35,36,38,96

[e] 35,36,40,63,73,74,75,76,83,96

Biological and Edible: Heating the seeds denatures the poisonous aspect and these roasted seeds have been ground and used as a coffee substitute.[96]

Chemistry & Pharmacognosy: The leaves and seeds contain the alkaloid methylcystine.[f] It also contains a glucoside called leontin.[1] Other compounds include magnoflorine, laburine, cytisine, caulophylline, and caulosapogenin.[83,96] Chromatography has been done.[83]

Low doses of *Caulophyllum* extracts given to rats have inhibited ovulation.[96]

Commercial Products & Uses: The roots can be sold commercially.[37]

Personal Experimentation: I dug up one root along the Firesteel river, let it dry for 3 weeks, boiled it in 2 quarts of water, and drank the decoction. No ill effects came about, though it was slightly bitter.

---

[f] 40,58,96

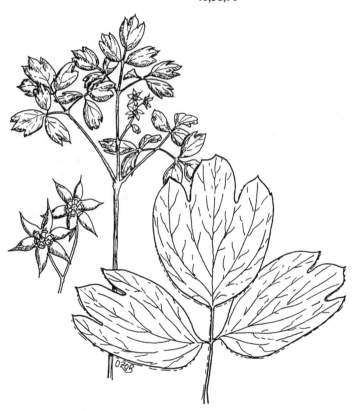

Caulophyllum thalictroides
Blue cohosh, cohosh, papoose root, blueberry

CEANOTHUS AMERICANUS
Rhamnaceae
Red root, New Jersey tea

Stem: Branching, erect, grayish-green, up to 1 m.

Leaves: Alternate, ovate, 3 to 8 cm long, serrate edges, acute, dark green top, pale green bottom.

Flower Type: White, 5 lobed calyx, hooded petals, terminal umbel corymbs, spring, summer.

Fruit: 3 lobed brown carpel, summer.

Roots: Red taproot.

General Information: Perennial herb, bushy in appearance.

Habitat: *Ceanothus* grows in dry upland woods and open fields.

Season of Availability: The root is collected in the fall. The leaves are collected in summer and fall.

Preparation: The root is used dried or fresh in a decoction. The leaves are usually dried, but may be used fresh, in an infusion. Native Americans and the early colonists drank a tea made from *Ceanothus*.[a]

Medical Terminology: The root was used as an astringent, stimulant, sedative, antispasmodic, and expectorant.[b]

Both the leaves and the root have been employed internally and externally as an astringent.[c] It is considered a hemostatic and blood coagulant.[82]

Related Disease Symptoms: A tea of the root was utilized to reduce high blood pressure[38] and treat enlarged spleen.[d] It has been used against syphilis and gonorrhea.[e] The Chippewa grated and boiled five inches of the root in one quart of water to stop coughs.[10] For mouth sores, the tea was gargled.[f] Supposedly, it was used for bronchitis, asthma, and pulmonary complaints.[35,68] The drug has been shown to have marked blood coagulative powers.[82]

Biological and Edible: Bees utilize this plant for honey.[92,93]

Chemistry & Pharmacognosy: As an organic dye, the roots impart a cinnamon color to wool.[22,27] *Ceanothus* roots contain tannin and the active principle ceanothin,[51] which tends to increase the rate of blood clotting.[g] Other compounds include succinic, oxalic, malonic, malic, orthophosphoric, and pyrophosphoric acids.[82]

---

[a] 9,15,18,25,32,36,38,62,70

[b] 30,35,38,44,68

[c] 32,51,73,74,82

---

[d] 30,35,38   [f] 35,36,44,68

[e] 22,30,36   [g] 22,27,58,82

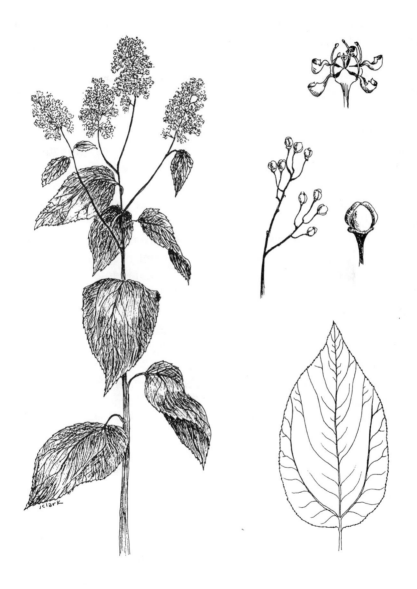

Ceanothus americanus
Red root, New Jersey tea

CELASTRUS SCANDENS
Celastraceae
Climbing bittersweet, bittersweet, climbing orange root, waxwork

Stem: Twining shrub, up to 18 m long, trunks up to 2.5 cm thick, woody.

Leaves: Alternate, oblong to ovate, acuminate, serrulate, 5 to 10 cm long, green.

Flower Type: Green, polygamodioecious, crenulate petals, 5 stamens, in terminal panicles, spring.

Fruit: Orange subglobose capsule.

Roots: Taproot.

General Information: Climbing vine, perennial, deciduous.

Habitat: The twining plant is found in thickets along roadsides and in old fields.

Season of Availability: The bark of the root is collected in the fall.

Preparation: In a decoction or infusion, the bark can be utilized fresh or dried.

Medical Terminology: Medicinally, it is considered a diaphoretic, diuretic, and alterative.[a] The root is thought to be a mild narcotic.[32,58] The tea was used for babies as a physic.[10]

Related Disease Symptoms: The root bark tea was used in liver affections,[51] rheumatism, and obstructed menstruation.[68] The plant has treated leukorrhea.[40,68] It has been taken internally to induce vomiting, to quiet disturbed people, to treat venereal disease, and to increase urine flow.[36] Mixed with grease and utilized as an ointment, it was used to treat skin cancers, tumors, burns, and swellings.[36] To treat skin eruptions, the Chippewa used a decoction of the stalk as a wash.[10] Tea from the root bark was used to start menstrual flow.[36]

Poisonous Aspects: There have been cases of horses being poisoned from eating the leaves.[46] This plant is considered poisonous.[40,46]

Biological and Edible: The tender branches and the sweetish bark of bittersweet were boiled and eaten for food by the Chippewa.[b]

Chemistry & Pharmacognosy: The fruits and leaves contain euonymin.[46]

---

[a] 10,32,36,44,58,68
[b] 15,74,76

Celastrus scandens
Climbing bittersweet, bittersweet, climbing orange root, waxwork

81

CHAMAELIRIUM LUTEUM
Liliaceae
Blazing star, helonias, devil's bit, star root, false unicorn

Stem: Single 2 to 12 cm high stem, green.

Leaves: Alternate, flat lanceolate, getting progressively smaller up the stem, entire, green, rosette of basal leaves.

Flower Type: Dioecious; staminate white; pistillate green; 6 narrowly spatulate one nerved sepals, persistent, in a terminal raceme, spring.

Fruit: Ellipsoid, 3 valved capsule, summer.

Roots: Fibrous, bulbous.

General: Perennial herb.

Habitat: *Chamaelirium* is found in moist woods and bogs.

Season of Availability: The roots and rootstocks are collected in the fall.

Preparation: The roots are used, fresh or dried, in a decoction. The dried root may be ground and taken in capsules, made into a tea, or used as an alcohol extract.[72] Dried rhizome and roots 1 to 2 grams or by infusion, liquid extract 1:1 in 45% ethanol dose 1 to 2 ml, both are taken t.i.d.[83]

Medical Terminology: The root has been used as an anthelmintic.[a] It has also been considered a diuretic,[40] tonic[b] and a uterine tonic.[72] The British consider it only a uterine tonic.[72,84]

An interesting use of *Chamaelirium luteum* is that of a spermatorrhea.[68]

Related Disease Symptoms: The powdered roots were used to treat uterine problems, pain in the head, and pain in the side.[36] The rootstock was used to treat intestinal worms.[22,36] Natives chewed the root to relieve coughs.[36] They also chewed the root to check miscarriage.[36,72] Blazing star has been used to cure impotence, as a tonic in genitourinary weakness or irritability, and for liver and kidney diseases.[22] Alice Henkel reports it as being used as a 'tonic in the derangements of women.'[63] History shows its use in cases of amenorrhea, ovarian dysmenorrhea, and leukorrhea.[72,84]

Poisonous Aspects: Large doses may cause vomiting and nausea.[c] Large doses are said to act as a cardiac poison.[22]

Chemistry & Pharmacognosy: The root contains the bitter principle chamaelirin.[d]

---

[a] 22,32,38,51,58

[b] 22,38,51

[c] 15,72,84

[d] 22,58,72,84

Chamaelirium luteum
Blazing star, helonias, devil's bit, star root, false unicorn

CHELONE GLABRA
Scrophulariaceae
Turtle head, balmony, snakehead

Stem: Erect, usually branchless, up to 2 m, green.

Leaves: Opposite, sessile, linear-lanceolate, sharply toothed edges, acute, green, 7 to 12 cm long.

Flower Type: White, tubular, irregular, 2 lipped, arched upper lip, 2 to 4 cm long, in a terminal spike, summer, fall.

Fruit: Small capsule, fall.

Roots: Fibrous.

General: Perennial herb.

Habitat: *Chelone glabra* is found in wet ground, stream banks and swamps.

Season of Availability: The leaves are harvested in the spring. The herb is gathered in the late summer through early fall.

Preparation: In an infusion the herb is used fresh or dried. As a poultice, the fresh herb is utilized. Herb dose 1 to 2 grams or by infusion, liquid extract 1:1 in 25% ethanol dose 2 to 4 ml, both given t.i.d.[84]

Medical Terminology: Balmony has been used in a tea as an anthelmintic and tonic.[a] The herb is also considered a laxative and purgative.[b] Another use is that of a cholagogue and antiemetic.[84]

Related Disease Symptoms: *Chelone* tea is used in consumption, dyspepsia, debility and jaundice, and in diseases of the liver.[c] To reduce inflammation, turtlehead leaves have been used as a poultice.[35,38] An ointment was made from the leaves and used for inflamed tumors, irritable ulcers, inflamed breasts and piles.[22,44] The ointment has been largely used as an external application for many skin diseases.[51] A tea of the leaves has been used for indigestion.[27] Other indications include cholecystitis, anorexia, and intestinal colic.[84]

---

[a] 22,30,35,36,38,44,51,68

[b] 9,22,32,35,36,51,58,68,84

[c] 22,30,35,44,68

Chelone glabra
Turtle head, balmony, snakehead

85

CHENOPODIUM ALBUM
Chenopodiaceae
Pigweed, lamb's-quarters, wild spinach

Stem: Green, erect, up to 2 m, strongly ascending branches.

Leaves: Glaucous, farinose beneath, sinuate-dentate, rhombic to rhombic-ovate, green on top, whitish beneath, alternate, edible, summer.

Flower Type: Green, ball-like in paniculate spikes with white mealiness substance all over spikes, summer.

Fruit: Round, black, 1.3 to 1.5 mm across, summer, fall.

Roots: Taproot.

General Information: Annual herb, common.

Habitat: Roadsides, cultivated ground, waste places, fields.

Season of Availability: The young tops can be collected in the summer and fall. The seeds are collected in the fall.

Preparation: The young tops are eaten steamed or boiled. The seeds are ground into a flour.

Medical Terminology: The leaves are considered mildly laxative.[36]

Related Disease Symptoms: A tea of the herb has been ingested to relieve stomach pains.[36]

Poisonous Aspects: *Chenopodium album* has been found to contain potentially dangerous concentrations of nitrate.[33]

Death due to *Chenopodium album* has not been documented, but there have been cases of livestock poisoning where it was the principal suspect.[33]

Biological and Edible: *Chenopodium album* contains vitamin A and C.[19] The leaves are edible by steaming or boiling.[a] Natives ground the seeds into flour for bread.[b] Seeds can be sprouted and used as food.[86]

Commercial Products & Uses: The commercial product New Zealand Spinach and pigweed are different species in the same genus.

Personal Experimentation: With all the emphasis on edible wild plants, I found many people who eat wild spinach regularly. Just cut up the young immature tops, steam or boil, and serve as you would spinach. I have eaten wild spinach since I was a boy.

---

[a] 18,19,25,47
[b] 18,19,25,78

Chenopodium album
Pigweed, lamb's-quarters, wild spinach

CHIMPAPHILA UMBELLATA
Pyrolaceae
Prince's pine, pipsissewa

Stem: Erect, green, smooth, up to 3 dm tall.

Leaves: Whorled, oblanceolate, wedged-shaped base, thick, upper shiny lustrous green, lower paler, toothed to entire, 5 to 10 cm long.

Flower Type: Pink or white, 5 concave petals, 10 stamens, from 2-5 flowers in a terminal corymb, summer.

Fruit: Brown capsule with many tiny seeds, fall.

Roots: Creeping underground rootstocks.

General Information: Perennial evergreen, grows in small groups, it is a protected plant.

Habitat: Pipsissewa is commonly found on dry sandy soils in coniferous forests and mixed pine, birch and aspen stands.

Season of Availability: The leaves can be collected in the spring, summer, or fall. The fruit is collected in late summer. The herb is preferably collected in late summer, during flowering.

Preparation: The herb is used fresh or dried in an infusion.

Medical Terminology: The fresh leaves, when broken up and applied to the skin, act as vesicants and rubefacients, which are thought to be of great use in cardiac and kidney diseases, scrofula, and chronic rheumatism.[a] It is considered an astringent, tonic, and diuretic.[b] It has been used as an anodyne, diuretic, and sudorific, especially in diseases of the breast, colds, etc.[63] The berries were eaten as a stomachic.[36,63] Two grams of the dried leaf is the official prescribed dose.[2,63]

Related Disease Symptoms: Natives used a hot tea to induce profuse perspiration in the treatment of typhus.[36,63] The Ojibwe used a tea of the herb for upset stomach.[c] As a tea, it was used for rheumatic and nephritic conditions.[36,63] The Mohegans applied the steeped plant, as a healing agent, to blisters.[63] The Menominee considered the plant a valuable remedy in female ailments.[63,74] For eye diseases, the Chippewa boiled the root and dropped the cooled tea in the eye.[10] It has been used to relieve backache.[40] To treat skin eruptions, the dried leaves are used in a wash.[51] A tea of the herb is supposed to retard the excretion of urine.[40]

---

[a] 22,32,68

[b] 22,27,30,32,34,44,63,68

[c] 36,63,75

Poisonous Aspects: The plant shows experimental hypoglycemic activity.[40]

Biological and Edible: The herb is an ingredient in root beer.[15,34] The berries are edible.[15,34] The dried leaf is the official part.[2,63]

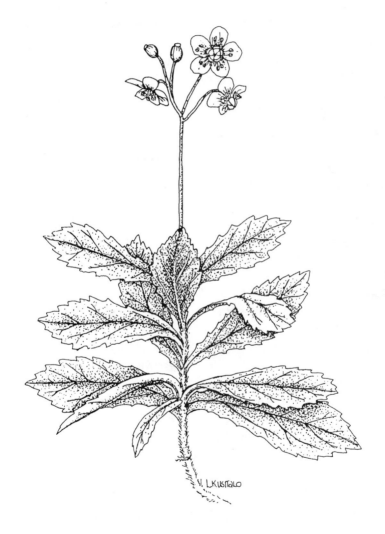

Chimpaphila umbellata
Prince's pine, pipsissewa

CICHORIUM INTYBUS
Compositae
Chicory, succory

Stem: Erect, stiffly branching, milky sap, green, up to 1.2 m.

Leaves: Cauline leaves alternate, lanceolate to spatulate, pinnately cut to serrate; basal leaves in a rosette, larger, 10 to 15 cm, green, prominent main vein.

Flower Type: Blue, sessile heads of ray flowers, 2 to 5 cm across, in leaf axils, many heads to one plant, summer, fall.

Fruit: Small angular achene with a parachute-like pappus, summer, fall.

Roots: Large stout taproot.

General Information: Perennial herb, common.

Habitat: Succory is commonly found in old open fields and along roadsides.

Season of Availability: The root is collected in the spring and the fall. The leaves are collected in the spring, while still in a rosette.

Preparation: The root is used in a decoction, usually dried. The tea is made up of one ounce of root to one pint of boiling water.[68]

Medical Terminology: Medicinally, the root is a tonic, diuretic, and laxative.[a]

Related Disease Symptoms: The root tea is used to increase appetite and aid digestion.[32,58] It also eliminates unwanted phlegm from the stomach that interferes with absorption.[30,41] It is used for upset stomach.[30,41] The tea is active in uratic acid conditions of gout, rheumatic, and joint stiffness.[30,68] Chicory is effective in disorders of the kidneys, stomach, liver, urinary canal, and spleen.[35,41] It is good for jaundice.[35,68] The French made a chicory medicine that acted as a sedative in consumption.[41] Old herbalists considered a poultice of the bruised leaves effective for swellings, inflammations, and inflamed eyes.[22]

Poisonous Aspects: If used in excess as a medicine it is said to cause the loss of visual power in the retina.[22]

Biological and Edible: The ground roasted root is used as an adulterant of coffee and as a coffee substitute.[b] The leaves are eaten as salad greens.[c] It is reported to produce an undesirable flavor in cow's milk.[46] Bees use it for honey.[92,93]

---

[a] 22,56,68

[b] 15,18,22,25,29,32,34,35,41,55,58,68,79

[c] 15,18,22,25,30,34,55,68,79

Personal Experimentation: I have eaten the spring leaves many times in salads. They look like dandelion leaves and are just as edible.

Cichorium intybus
Chicory, succory

CICUTA MACULATA, CICUTA BULBIFERA
Umbelliferae
Water hemlock, hemlock, spotted cowbane, cowbane

Stem: Erect, many branches, up to 2.3 m. tall, bottom often purple.

Leaves: Lower long-petioled, bright green, often tinged with red, sharply toothed, pinnate veins. Upper leaves have distinct blades. *C. bulbifera* has small clustered bulbs in the axils of upper leaves.

Flower Type: Tiny, white, flat topped terminal or axillary umbels. June to September.

Fruit: Oval, alternating ribs and furrows.

Roots: Fleshy, white, branching.

Habitat: Swamps, along streams.

Poisonous Aspects: Cicutoxin works directly on the central nervous system and causes violent seizures.[82,91] Other symptoms include GI symptoms and respiratory depression.[84] Treatment is gastric lavage or emesis, symptomatic, and seizure control with parenteral short acting barbiturates.[84]

Chemistry & Pharmacognosy: Cicutoxin, which is a highly toxic unsaturated alcohol, has been isolated.[82]

Personal Experimentation: I have seen *Cicuta* all over the U.S. It looks similar to the plant called Water Parsnip (*Sium suave*). The last poisoning I've read about was on April 26, 1984, when Kenneth Kromer, 22, a river rafter and outfitter guide, picked some *Cicuta* roots mistaking it for *Sium suave* along the Owyhee River in Oregon. Six of the seven people ate the roots; two ate nearly full meals, four had only 1-2 bites and one had none. The two who had full meals started having seizures within 45 minutes, Kromer died in under 2 hours. The other five survived but needed assistance to evacuate the area.

Cicuta maculata, Cicuta bulbifera
Water hemlock, hemlock, spotted cowbane, cowbane

CLAYTONIA VIRGINICA
Portulacaceae
Spring beauty, mayflower

Stem: Simple, green, erect to decumbent, 20 cm tall.

Leaves: Green, 2, opposite, linear to oblanceolate, acute, 4 to 15 cm long, smooth.

Flower Type: White to pink, loose raceme, showy, 2.5 cm across, 5-19 flowers, spring.

Fruit: 1 locular, 3 valved capsule, 3-6 m round seeds, spring.

Roots: Perennial corm, up to 7 cm in diameter, edible, like potatoes, spring.

General Information: Perennial herb, grows in large groups.

Habitat: Hardwood forest floors, well drained sites.

Season of Availability: The tubers are collected in the spring.

Preparation: The tubers are prepared like potatoes: fried, boiled, or steamed and eaten.

-----

[a] 15,18,25,47

Biological and Edible: The tubers are edible raw or cooked.[a] The young succulent leaves may be a pot herb considering that other members of the *Portulacaceae* family are.[15]

Commercial Products & Uses: Presently, there is no commercial production of any kind for *Claytonia* tubers. Someone should look into the feasibility of producing the tubers.

Personal Experimentation: The tubers are difficult to collect. The only time it is profitable to collect them is in a large tightly grouped patch. Use a shovel and start spading the ground, shift the ground through your fingers and after some time one should be able to get a small bucket full of tubers. Eating spring beauty tubers is not a common practice. The tubers taste like potatoes.

Claytonia virginica
Spring beauty, mayflower

95

COMPTONIA PEREGRINA
Myricaceae
Sweet fern, ferngale, canadian sweet gale

Stem: Woody, new branches villous, reddish-brown bark, up to 1.5 m.

Leaves: Alternate, deeply pinnately lobed, linear, 5 to 8 cm long, green, aromatic.

Flower Type: Monoecious or dioecious, catkins, green, spring.

Fruit: Small ellipsoid nuts, 4 or 5 mm across, summer.

Roots: Taproot.

General Information: Perennial deciduous shrub, grows in large groups.

Habitat: Sweet fern grows in dry sandy soil in open fields and under sparse jack pines.

Season of Availability: The leaves are collected in summer and fall. They are usually dried, but can be used fresh.

Preparation: The leaves are used in an infusion.

Medical Terminology: Medicinally, it is an astringent and tonic.[a]

Related Disease Symptoms: To treat poison ivy rash, the tea is used as a wash.[38] The tea has been used for colic.[32,36] The boiled leaves were tied to the cheek for toothache relief.[36,63] To treat diarrhea, one pint of the tea is ingested.[b]

Biological and Edible: The fruit is edible.[15,47]

Personal Experimentation: Since most people get diarrhea, I am no exception. When this happened I took the opportunity to try this tea. By drinking 4 cups of the tea within 2 hours, my case of diarrhea ceased. Many locals drink the tea for its pleasing taste. The largest patch I ever saw was in the Baraga plains just south of Baraga, MI. It seemed as though there was enough to supply the U.S.

---

[a] 32,44,68

[b] 32,36,38,44,68

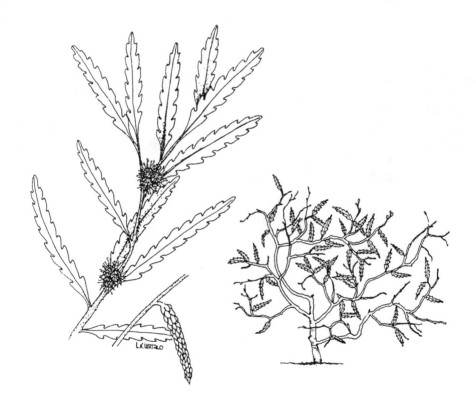

Comptonia peregrina
Sweet fern, ferngale, canadian sweet gale

CONIUM MACULATUM
Umbelliferae
Poison hemlock, hemlock, spotted hemlock

Stem: Hollow, smooth, purple-spotted, up to 2 m tall, hairless leaf stalks.

Leaves: Petioled, alternate, compound 2 to 3 times, leaflets pinnately cut and deeply crenate.

Flower Type: Tiny, white, June through September.

Fruit: Smooth, oval, prominent wavy ribs.

Roots: Carrotlike, white, .6 to 1.8 m.

Habitat: Open areas, roadsides.

Season of Availability: Late spring to early fall.

Medical Terminology: *Conium* has been utilized as an antispasmodic, sedative, and an anodyne.[82]

Poisonous Aspects: Poisonings have occurred with *Conium*; it is thought to be the plant that killed Socrates.[82] The symptoms include GI upset, necrosis, muscular weakness, seizures, and respiratory paralysis.[91] Treatment is emesis or gastric lavage, saline cathartic, keep vitals intact, possibly artificial respiration and seizure precautions.[91]

Biological and Edible: *Conium* alkaloids are thought to act on the peripheral ganglia as a neuro-transmitter.[82]

Chemistry & Pharmacognosy: It contains coniine, N-methylconiine, coniceine, conhydrine, and pseudoconhydrine.[82]

Conium maculatum
Poison hemlock, hemlock, spotted hemlock

COPRINUS COMATUS
Agaricaceae
Shaggymane

Please note: *Mushroom identification can be confusing. Before ingesting, be sure to identify with certainty, and preferably only pick mushrooms with a guide or naturalist.*

Stem: White, often darker at base, cylindrical, hollow with a thin ring at the top, 10-30 cm high.

Fruit: Dome-shaped top spreads with age, white cap has superficial brown or white scales, covered with a downy coat, 3 to 5 cm across.

Habitat: Roadsides, waste areas.

Season of Availability: Late summer, fall.

Biological and Edible: Gather when young and use immediately. Should not be eaten raw.

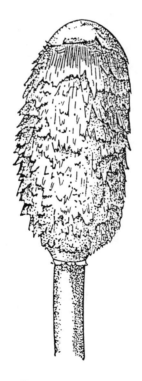

Coprinus comatus
Shaggymane

COPTIS GROENLANDICA
Ranunculaceae
Gold thread, canker root

Stem: Stemless.

Leaves: Basal, compound, 3 foliate shiny leaflets, each 2.5 to 5 cm wide, ovate to round, toothed, green.

Flower Type: White, 5-7 petals, 1 cm across, 5 to 7 petal-like sepals, 15 to 25 stamens, 3 to 9 pistils, spring.

Fruit: Small round seeds.

Roots: Golden-yellow threadlike spreading rootstocks.

General Information: Perennial evergreen, usually grows in small clumps.

Habitat: It grows in forests on acid soils; sometimes found in and around spruce bogs.

Season of Availability: Collection of the yellow root can be done in spring, summer, or fall.

Preparation: The root is chewed fresh or used in a decoction, fresh or dried.

Medical Terminology: Medicinally, it is a tonic and stomachic.[47,63] It is used as a bitters.[a]

Related Disease Symptoms: Local Natives used the golden roots for treating sore gums and lessening the pain in babies while teething.[b]

The tea is used as a mouthwash for canker sores.[c] It was also used as a gargle for sore throat and ulcers of both the stomach and throat.[d] Although hard to believe, a tea made from gold thread and golden seal will supposedly release the driving desire for alcoholic beverages.[e] The tea is used for improving digestion.[f] It is good for dyspepsia.[g] The Montagnais used the boiled tea as a wash for sore eyes, lips, and the interior of the mouth.[36,63] For inflammation of the eyes, the root tea is used as an eye wash.[5]

Chemistry & Pharmacognosy: A bright yellow dye can be made by boiling the yellow roots.[10,54]

Personal Experimentation: Having indigestion one day and being in an area where gold thread was handy, I dug up some roots, washed them off, and chewed them. To my amazement, my indigestion problem went away. To this day, many people use the roots for teething babies and indigestion.

---

[a] 5,22,30,32,44,47,63,68

[b] 47,54,63,70,74,75,76

[c] 5,19,27,30,32,36,44,63,74,75,76

[d] 27,30,35,68,70

[e] 19,22,30,35,44

[f] 19,22,32,35,36,68

[g] 5,22,27,36

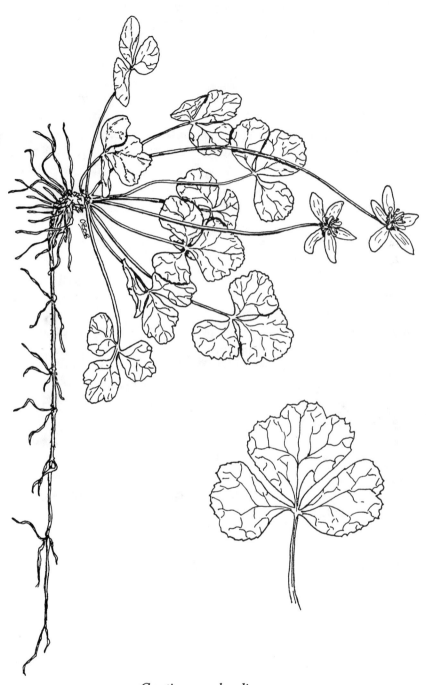

Coptis groenlandica
Gold thread, canker root

CORALLORHIZA MACULATA, CORALLORHIZA ODONTORHIZA
Orchidaceae
Coral root, spotted coral root, crawley

Stem: Erect, unbranching, reddish brown, fleshy, up to 6 dm.
Leaves: Leafless.
Flower Type: Purple to yellowish red, orchid type, spurred, drooping after pollination, 1 to 2 cm across, in a terminal raceme, summer.
Fruit: Small brown capsules, 1 to 2 cm long, summer.
Roots: Rhizome, coral shaped, reddish brown.
General Information: Perennial herb, rare, protected.
Habitat: Coral root is found in hardwood stands, usually on well drained sites.
Season of Availability: The stem and root are collected in the spring, summer, and fall if you are lucky enough to find any.
Preparation: The root is used fresh or dried in an infusion or decoction.

Medical Terminology: Coral root tea is considered a diaphoretic.[a] Some consider the root decoction sedative in action.[b] It is also considered a febrifuge.[22,30]
Related Disease Symptoms: In the treatment of fevers and pleurisy, the root tea was used to bring on perspiration.[35,68] It is a powerful and effective remedy in skin diseases of all kinds: scurvy, scrofula, boils, tumors, fevers, acute erysipelas, night sweats, pleurisy, cramps, and cancer.[35] Combined with blue cohosh, it was used for scanty or painful menstruation.[35] The dried stalks, in a tea, are utilized for strengthening patients suffering from pneumonia.[36]
Commercial Products & Uses: The root is of commercial value.[37]

---

[a] 22,30,32,36,38,58,68
[b] 22,30,36,38,68

Corallorhiza maculata,
Corallorhiza odontorhiza
Coral root, spotted coral root, crawley

CORYLUS CORNUTA
Betulaceae
Hazelnut, beaked hazel, filbert

Stem: Woody, alternate branching, smooth gray bark, golden stretch patterns, up to 10 m.

Leaves: Green, ovate to ovate-oblong, doubly serrate, alternate, 7 to 10 cm.

Flower Type: Monoecious; 8 stamens, single locular anther; short style, 2 red stigmas.

Fruit: Brown nut with green prickly husk, looks like a small bird with a long open beak, 1 to 4 per cluster, edible, fall.

Roots: Woody, lateral.

General Information: Perennial, deciduous, understory tree.

Habitat: Meadows, hardwood forests, well-drained sites.

Season of Availability: The nuts are collected in the fall. One has to be quick because as soon as they are ripe the squirrels start gathering.

Preparation: The nuts can be eaten raw, roasted, or dried and ground into flour.

Biological and Edible: The nuts are edible and choice.[a]

Chemistry & Pharmacognosy: The Chippewa boiled the green immature hazelnut and the butternut to make a black dye.[10]

Commercial Products & Uses: The commercial filbert and the beaked hazel are different species in the same genus.

Personal Experimentation: When collecting the beaked hazel, it is essential to wear gloves because the prickly husks leave painful splinters. After removing the husks, I've found the nuts bitter and prefer them roasted. I have met others who disagree. To grind the nuts into flour, first remove the husk and outer shell, roast the nuts, and grind in a flour mill or table grinder. The roasted nuts can also be ground into a delicious nut butter.

---

[a] 10,15,25,47,79

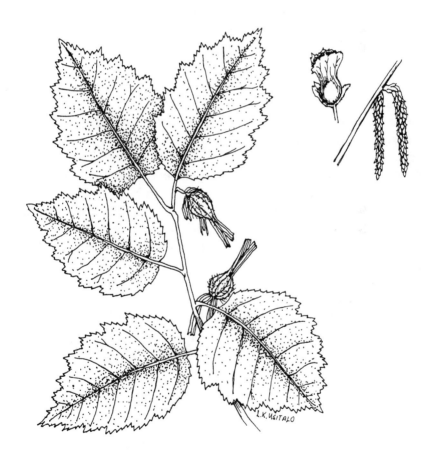

Corylus cornuta
Hazelnut, beaked hazel, filbert

CYNOGLOSSUM OFFICINALE
Boraginaceae
Hound's tongue, stickers

Stem: Erect, hairy, up to 8 dm, green, branching at the top.

Leaves: First year rosette, hairy, lanceolate to spatulate, entire, petioled, 10 to 15 cm; cauline leaves sessile, lanceolate, hairy, green.

Flower Type: Reddish purple, 1 cm across, tubular with 5 rounded lobes, born terminally on a one sided raceme, spring, early summer.

Fruit: 4 nutlets, covered with recurved spines, summer, fall.

Roots: Taproot.

General Information: Biennial herb, common, but rarely in big patches.

Habitat: *Cynoglossum* is commonly found in open fields and along roadsides.

Season of Availability: The leaves are collected and dried in the early summer. The root is collected in the summer or fall.

Preparation: The root is used fresh or dried in a decoction. The leaves are used fresh or dried in an infusion.

Medical Terminology: Medicinally, *Cynoglossum* is considered an anodyne, demulcent, and astringent.[30,68]

Related Disease Symptoms: As a demulcent and mild sedative, it is beneficial for bronchial catarrh, coughs, and pulmonary complaints.[27] In Europe, the root was used in a decoction and as pills for coughs, colds in the head, and shortness of breath.[22] The leaves were boiled in wine as a cure for dysentery.[22] An ointment, made from the leaves mixed with lard, was used to prevent baldness.[22,68] The same ointment was used to relieve pain from burns.[a] As a wash, the tea has been used in the treatment of piles.[22,68] The tea is considered soothing to the digestive organs.[22,68] History records its use in the treatment of coughs, colds, catarrh, diarrhea, and dysentery.[30,68]

Biological and Edible: Bees utilize this plant for honey.[92,93]

---

[a] 22,30,68

Cynoglossum officinale
Hound's tongue, stickers

CYPRIPEDIUM CALCEOLUS
Orchidaceae
Lady's slipper, moccasin flower, nerve root, yellow lady's slipper

Stem: Downy, erect, sometimes more than one stem from the same rootstock, unbranched, 15 to 70 cm tall, green.

Leaves: Alternate, 3 to 6 total, ovate to elliptic, narrowed and clasping at the base, parallel veined, distinctly ribbed, downy, up to 20 cm long, acute, green.

Flower Type: Yellow, 3 petals striped with purple, linear spirally twisted, 1 lip—sac-like, yellow with purple stripes, 3 sepals, colored like the petals, 5 to 6 cm long, solitary, spring, summer.

Fruit: 1-locular 3 valved capsule, summer.

Roots: Coarsely fibrous.

General: Perennial herb.

Habitat: *C. calceolus* is found in swampy, open or shaded ground. In bogs, on wet wooded beaches and in rich woods. It is a protected flower.

Season of Availability: Collect the roots and rhizomes in the spring or the fall.

Preparation: The roots and rhizomes are used fresh or dried in a decoction. The root is powdered and made into a tea or put in capsules.[68]

Medical Terminology: *Cypripedium calceolus* has been used as a sedative, antispasmodic, and in alleviating nervous symptoms.[a]

Related Disease Symptoms: As a home remedy the root was used for nervous conditions in women.[b] A decoction of the root is good for women in pain from childbirth[63,72] Dr. Clapp cited a case of a sleepless hypochondriac who obtained no benefit from opium, but rested soundly after taking the powdered root of *Cypripedium*.[63,72] The Cherokee used the root tea to dispel worms in children.[63,72] The Penobscots steeped the root for a nerve medicine.[63,72] The root tea was used for female disorders.[63,72] It allays pain, gives sleep, and is useful in headache, female weakness, and neuralgia.[c] It is reportedly successful in treating epilepsy, neuralgia, and other nervous diseases.[32] To treat toothaches, the dried powdered root was put on decayed teeth.[10] It is valuable for treating anxiety.[84]

Poisonous Aspects: It has been known to cause dermatitis.[46]

Commercial Products & Uses: The root is salable.[37]

---

[a] 9,22,27,30,32,63,68,72,84

[b] 63,72,84   [c] 27,36,68

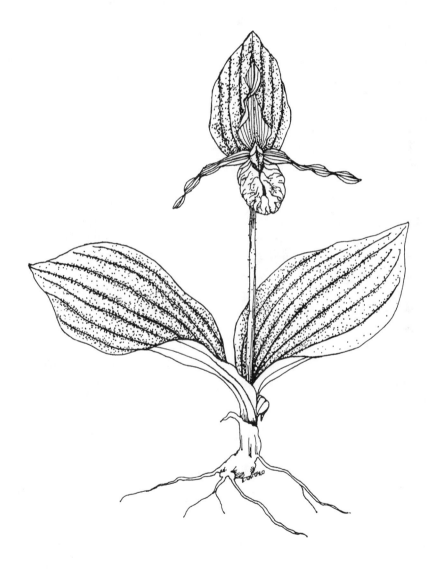

Cypridedium calceolus
Lady's slipper, moccasin flower, nerve root, yellow lady's slipper

DAUCUS CAROTA
Umbelliferae
Wild carrot, carrot, queen anne's lace

Stem: Bristly, branching, 3 to 16 dm tall, green.

Leaves: First year rosette, second year alternate, pinnately decompound, leaflet segments linear, finely dissected like a feather, green, 6 to 12 cm long.

Flower Type: White, small, grouped together in terminal umbels, single center flower is purple, summer, fall.

Fruit: Small, oblong, flattened carpel, 2-3 mm long, summer, fall.

Roots: Taproot, white to orange.

General Information: Biennial herb, common, looks similar to *Conium maculatum*, a deadly mistake.

Habitat: Wild carrot grows in open fields and roadsides.

Season of Availability: The root and mature seeds are collected in the fall. The herb is collected and dried in the summer, while flowering.

Preparation: In a poultice, the fresh ground or mashed roots are used. The seeds and herb are used in an infusion. Dried herb dose 2 to 4 grams or by infusion, liquid extract 1:1 in 25% ethanol dose 2 to 4 ml, both to be used t.i.d.[84]

Medical Terminology: It is considered a diuretic, deobstruent, and stimulant.[a] It has also been considered an antilithic.[84]

Related Disease Symptoms: A tea from the seeds and roots have been used to increase urine flow.[36] The boiled mashed root is used as a curing poultice for bruises and cuts.[b] The seeds have been eaten to stimulate menstruation.[c] The seeds have been employed to treat intestinal worms.[30,36] A tea has been used in the treatment of dropsy (congestive heart failure), retention of urine, affections of the bladder and gravel.[30,68] A decoction of the fruit has been employed in diseases of the kidneys, flatulence, colic, and dropsies.[d] The blossoms of *D. carota*, in a tea, are utilized as a remedy for dropsy.[19,63] The seeds were used in liver disorders and jaundice.[19,27] Specific indications include urinary calculus, cystitis, and the gout.[84]

Poisonous Aspects: Cases of dermatitis have been associated with wild carrot.[46,54]

---

[a] 5,19,32,35,44,55,58,63,68,84

[b] 5,19,32,35,36

[c] 19,30,32,35,36,63

[d] 5,19,30

Kingsbury reports of nervous symptoms caused by *D. carota* in horses and cattle.[33]

Biological and Edible: The first year roots are edible.[e] Milk from cows that forage on *D. carota* becomes tainted with a bitter flavor.[46] Bees utilize this plant for honey.[92,93]

Chemistry & Pharmacognosy: The herb contains a volatile oil and an alkaloid called daucine.[84]

Personal Experimentation: Every summer for years I have eaten carrot roots—in stews and soups and fresh, wild or cultivated. Remember, wild carrots and cultivated carrots are the same plant.

[e] 15,29,47

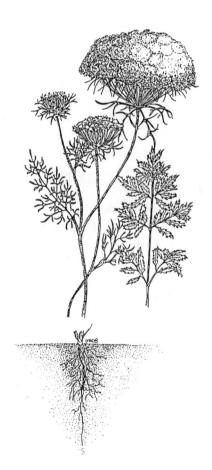

Daucus carota
Wild carrot, carrot, queen anne's lace

DICENTRA CANADENSIS, DICENTRA CUCULLARIA
Fumariaceae
Squirrel corn, dutchman's breeches

Stem: Stemless.

Leaves: Basal, finely dissected, divisions in 3's, fern-like, green on top, silvery pubescent on the bottom, 5 to 8 cm long.

Flower Type: White, heart-shaped, 6 stamens, 1 pistil, on a scape in a terminal raceme, spring.

Fruit: Small crested seeds, spring, early summer.

Roots: Corms, bulbous.

General Information: Perennial herb, usually disappearing by July.

Habitat: *D. canadensis* and *D. cucullaria* grow in rich woods, many times side by side.

Season of Availability: The yellow corms are collected in the spring or fall. If you plan to collect them in the fall you must know where they grow for there are no signs above ground.

Preparation: The bulbs are used fresh or dried in an infusion.

---

[a] 22,32,36,58,63

Medical Terminology: The bulbs are used as a tonic, diuretic, and alterative.[a] The dried tubers have been considered official.[2]

Related Disease Symptoms: Physicians used squirrel corn as a remedy in cutaneous diseases and as a substitute for mercury in venereal diseases.[36,63] It has been utilized as a tonic with syphilis.[22,32] A poultice of the tubers has been employed for skin diseases.[36]

Poisonous Aspects: Death in livestock is recorded, though it seldom occurs because of the plants extreme distastefulness.[33] The symptoms of *D. cucullaria* poisoning in cattle are trembling, nervousness, salivation, and vomiting, leading to the animal falling down with convulsions and pain. Within a few hours complete recovery is obtained unless extreme amounts were ingested.[33]

Dicentra canadensis, Dicentra cucullaria
Squirrel corn, dutchman's breeches

EPIGAEA REPENS
Ericaceae
Trailing arbutus, arbutus, ground laurel, mayflower

Stem: Prostrate, trailing, reddish-brown stem, height up to 10 cm.

Leaves: Alternate, thick, leathery, veined, rusty colored hairs on young leaves, oval to ovate, rounded at the base, petioled, 3 to 6 cm long, entire, green.

Flower Type: White to pink, 5 lobed, 5 sepals, 10 stamens, 1 to 2 cm across, tubular, terminal or axillary clusters, spring.

Fruit: 5 celled many seeded brown capsule, summer.

Roots: Fibrous.

General: Perennial, prostrate shrub, evergreen, protected.

Habitat: *Epigaea repens* grows in sandy or boggy soil in pine or aspen forests.

Season of Availability: The leaves are collected during the spring.

Preparation: The leaves are used in an infusion, fresh or dried. The infusion is made by taking 1 ounce of leaves per 1 pint of boiling water.[22,68]

Medical Terminology: Medicinally, arbutus is diuretic and astringent.[a]

Related Disease Symptoms: The tea has been utilized in gravel, debilitated or relaxed bladder, and in urine containing blood or pus.[b] It is used for urinary tract problems.[c]

Biological and Edible: The leaves are used as a substitute for *Arctostaphylos uva-ursi*.[d] The flowers are edible.[15] Bees utilize this plant for honey.[92,93]

---

[a] 22,27,30,68   [c] 22,27,30,68

[b] 22,30,68   [d] 22,30,32,58,68

Epigaea repens
Trailing arbutus, arbutus, ground laurel, mayflower

ERIGERON CANADENSIS
Compositae
Fleabane, horseweed, butterweed, horsetail fleabane

Stem: Erect, usually branchless, downy, green, up to 1.5 m.

Leaves: Alternate, linear to oblanceolate, margins serrate to entire, 5 to 8 cm long, green.

Flower Type: White, small daisy-like ray flowers, in terminal panicles, summer, fall.

Fruit: Small, brown achene connected to a white pappus.

Roots: Taproot.

General Information: Annual herb, common.

Habitat: Commonly found in fields and along roadsides.

Season of Availability: The herb is collected and dried during the fall. The root is also collected during the fall.

Preparation: The herb is used in an infusion, fresh or dried. The root is used in a decoction, fresh or dried. Natives used the plant as a steaming agent in sweat baths.[63,73]

Medical Terminology: It has the medicinal properties of an astringent, diuretic, and tonic.[a]

Related Disease Symptoms: In a tea, it is used as a remedy for diarrhea and dysentery.[b] The extract has been recommended for gonorrhea.[5] The extract has been employed as an application to inflamed and enlarged tonsils and in inflammations and ulcerations of the throat.[5,36] For stomach pain, the Chippewa drank a tea of *E. canadensis* roots and leaves.[10] For menstrual discomfort the local Natives made a tea of the herb.[10,63] The preparation is said to be useful in pulmonary, uterine, and other internal hemorrhages.[32] The Ojibwe made a tea to stop fever.[63] To cause sneezing and loosen a head cold, the pulverized flowers were snuffed up the nostrils.[63]

Poisonous Aspects: *Erigeron* has been known to cause dermatitis.[46]

Biological and Edible: At one time, fleabane was commonly used to keep fleas away.[55]

Chemistry & Pharmacognosy: It contains a volatile oil that is utilized in pharmaceutical preparations.[c]

Commercial Products & Uses: Fleabane is collected for commercial use in its wild state.[53]

---

[a] 5,10,27,32,35,55,58,63,68
[b] 5,35,36,39,68
[c] 53,55,58

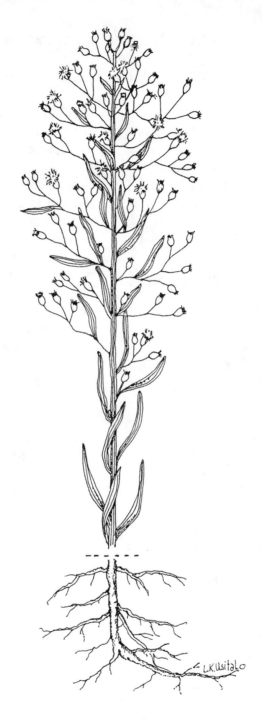

Erigeron canadensis
Fleabane, horseweed, butterweed, horsetail fleabane

117

ERYTHRONIUM AMERICANUM
Liliaceae
Trout lily, dog toothed violet, adder's tongue

Stem: Stemless.

Leaves: Young plants have only 1 elliptic to elliptic-lanceolate mottled fleshy green leaf; mature plants have 2 leaves; both petioled, acute, mottled green, 8 to 10 cm long.

Flower Type: Yellow, solitary, on a long scape (2 to 3 dm), 2 to 4 cm across, lily-like, edible, spring.

Fruit: 3 valved capsule, erect, spring.

Roots: Bulbous rootstock.

General Information: Perennial herb, gone by July, grows in groups.

Habitat: Trout lily is found in rich woods.

Season of Availability: The bulbs are collected in the spring or fall. The leaves are collected and dried in the spring.

Preparation: As a poultice, the fresh leaves and/or bulbs are used. The bulbs are used fresh or dried in a infusion.

Medical Terminology: The corm, when fresh, is an emetic.[a] The root and herb were official in the U.S.P. from 1820 to 1863 as a specific for gout.[63]

Related Disease Symptoms: The leaves were steeped to make an infusion for stomach distress.[54] The fresh leaves are used as a poultice in scrofulous ulcers and tumors.[68] It has been used in dropsy (congestive heart failure), hiccough, and vomiting.[68]

Biological and Edible: The bulbs can be boiled or fried and eaten as food.[b]

Personal Experimentation: I have eaten the corms and the flowers and have never experienced any harmful effects. For salads, I found the yellow flowers to make a great addition in taste and appearance. My experience with the starchy bulb has always been in soups or fried with leeks.

---

[a] 15,32,58,63,68
[b] 15,32,47,63

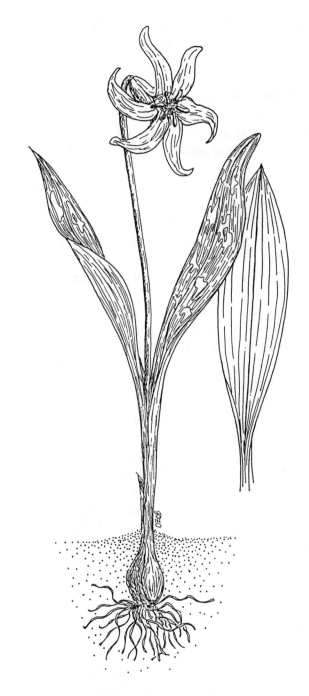

Erythronium americanum
Trout lily, dog toothed violet, adder's tongue

EUPATORIUM PERFOLIATUM
Compositae
Boneset, thoroughwort

Stem: 4 to 5 dm, erect, conspicuously crisp-villous, with long spreading hairs, from a stout rhizome, single, unbranching, green.

Leaves: Opposite, broad-based, strongly connate-perfoliate, tapering gradually to the acuminate tip, crenate-serrate to base, 7 to 20 cm long, 1.5 to 4.5 cm broad, pubescent above, hairy beneath.

Flower Type: Flat topped involucre, 4-6 mm, bracts pubescent, 9 to 22 flowers per head, white, 2.7 to 4 mm across, summer.

Fruit: Small, brown sliver-like achene.

Roots: Rhizome, netted, fibrous.

General Information: Perennial herb, grows in clumps.

Habitat: Moist, wet areas, stream banks, marshes.

Season of Availability: Collect the herb in the early summer; collect the leaves and flowers in the late summer and fall.

Preparation: The herb is used fresh or dried in an infusion. Dried herb dose 1 to 2 grams or by infusion, liquid extract 1:1 in 25% ethanol dose 1 to 2 ml, both are t.i.d. doses.[84]

Medical Terminology: It has been considered a tonic and diaphoretic.[a] In large doses it acts as an emetic and cathartic.[b] It has been used as a laxative[c] and as a purgative.[d] Natives and early settlers considered boneset a panacea.[40] The dried leaves were official with the prescribed dose of two grams.[2]

Related Disease Symptoms: Natives used the tea to combat fevers.[e] The herb tea has been used to treat coughs and consumption.[f] It has also treated rheumatism,[g] arthritis and gout.[63] Chiefly, the tea was used for fevers,[h] colds and flu.[i] Creek women who complained of aches and pains in the hips boiled boneset and steamed the hip area for relief.[36,63] It has been used to treat dyspepsia and general debility.[j] In the late 1700's, it was used for yellow fever.[63] Some Natives used it to heal broken bones.[27]

---

[a] 1,5,9,22,27,32,44,51,58,63,68,73,84

[b] 5,22,32,40,51,58,63,68

[c] 22,38,68

[d] 5,22,63

[e] 5,19,22,27,32,36,51,54,63,74

[f] 27,36,38,84

[g] 1,19,22,27,54

[h] 5,32,36

[i] 1,19,22,27,51,54,63,84

[j] 5,19,22,32,38,68

Poisonous Aspects: *E. perfoliatum* has been known to cause contact dermatitis.[40]

Biological and Edible: Bees utilize this plant for honey.[92,93]

Chemistry & Pharmacognosy: It contains the bitter glucoside eupatorin.[58,84] Recent experiments have shown the presence of four sesquiterpene lactones: euperfolin, euperfolitin, eufoliatin, and eufoliatorin, which have cytotoxic and antitumor activity.[28]

Personal Experimentation: I took one ounce of the dried leaves, poured one quart of boiling water over them and let it steep for ten minutes. I drank the quart within one hour; the taste was very bitter and I noticed a slight diaphoretic effect.

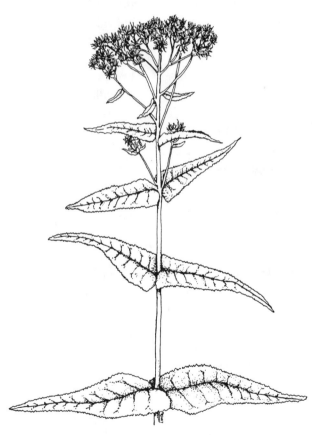

Eupatorium perfoliatum
Boneset, thoroughwort

EUPATORIUM PURPUREUM
Compositae
Joe-pye weed

Stem: 6 to 20 dm tall, speckled or evenly purple, unbranching, erect.

Leaves: Whorled, in 4's or 5's, lance-elliptic to lanceolate, gradually narrowed to the short petiole, 6 to 21 cm long, 2 to 9 cm wide, sharply serrate.

Flower Type: Flat topped, involucre 6-9 mm, imbricate obtuse bracts, prominent midvein, flowers purple, 9 to 22 per head, summer.

Fruit: Small, brown sliver-like achene.

Roots: Fibrous.

General Information: Perennial herb, grows in clumps.

Habitat: Streams, wet areas, marsh.

Season of Availability: The rhizomes are collected in the fall. Collect the leaves and flowering tops in the summer and fall.

Preparation: Joe-pye weed is used fresh or dried. The herb is used in an infusion, the root in a decoction. Dried rhizome and root dose 2 to 4 grams or by decoction, liquid extract 1:1 in 25% ethanol dose 2 to 4 ml, both are used in t.i.d. doses.[84]

Medical Terminology: The roots have been mainly considered diuretic,[a] astringent,[b] and tonic.[9,36] To create profuse perspiration, Joe-pye weed was utilized for its diaphoretic properties.[c] Some considered the plant a nervine.[d] For an aphrodisiac, the Meskwaki made a root decoction.[40] The British consider it an antilithic.[84]

Related Disease Symptoms: The Wisconsin Natives used the fresh leaves as a burn poultice and as a medicine to clear afterbirth.[63,76] It has been employed for gravel in the urinary tract.[e] A decoction of the roots was used for urinary disorders and infections, such as cystitis.[f] It supposedly relieved pains from rheumatism.[g] Some drank the root tea to treat dropsy.[22,27] The Chippewa utilized the root tea as a wash for skin inflammations.[10] Specific indications include urinary calculus, cystitis, urethritis, and prostatitis.[84]

Biological and Edible: Experimentally, it has shown hypoglycemic activity.[40] Bees utilize this plant for honey.[92,93]

---

[a] 27,32,51,58,63,72

[b] 5,18,22,38,44,68,84

[c] 9,10,36,63

[d] 22,35,68

[e] 22,27,40,68,72,84

[f] 22,27,32,38,40,63,68,72,74,84

[g] 22,35,72,84

Chemistry & Pharmacognosy: It
contains a volatile oil, a yellow
flavonoid euparin, and a resin.[84]

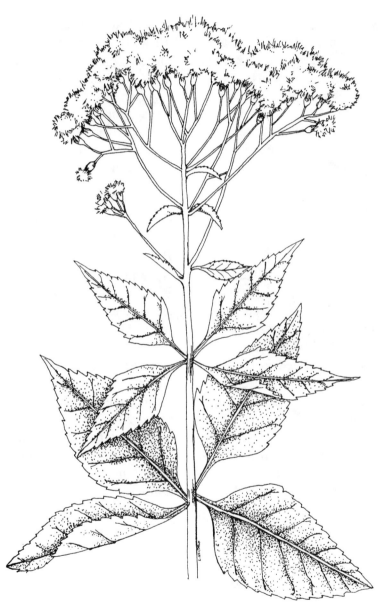

Eupatorium purpureum
Joe-pye weed

FAGUS GRANDIFOLIA, FAGUS AMERICANA
Fagaceae
Beech, beechnut

Stem: Tree to 30 m, smooth gray bark.

Leaves: Short-petioled, ovate to oblong, densely silky when young, later glabrous above, straight veined, vein running to each tooth, 10 to 13 cm long, 4 to 6 cm broad, sharply serrate.

Flower Type: Appearing with the leaves, staminate from the lower axils, pistillate from the upper, spring.

Fruit: Marble-sized spiny capsule, containing edible nuts.

Roots: Taproot.

General Information: Tree, perennial, deciduous.

Habitat: Forest, mixed hardwoods across the Great Lakes.

Season of Availability: The leaves are collected in the summer. The bark is collected in any season. The nuts are collected in the fall.

Preparation: The leaves are used fresh or dried in a decoction. The bark is used fresh or dried in an infusion or decoction. The nuts are eaten fresh, dried, or roasted.

Medical Terminology: Therapeutically, the bark and leaves are thought to be astringent,[35] tonic, and antiseptic.[30]

Related Disease Symptoms: Local Native Americans steeped a handful of the bark in a pint of boiling water for use 3 times a day as a treatment for poison ivy rash.[36,63] A tea was said to be used for improving the conditions of diabetes.[30,35] The leafy twigs, made into a decoction, were used for pains in the lower back.[27] A wash and poultice for burns, scalds and frostbite was made from a decoction of the fresh or dried leaves.[36,76]

Poisonous Aspects: The pollen is a known cause of hay fever.[40]

Biological and Edible: The nuts are edible.[a] The young expanding leaves can be eaten as a pot herb.[15]

Personal Experimentation: I haven't had much luck at collecting these nuts. So far, the nuts are too high in the tree, not every husk contains a nut, and I have not found any good localities. I am open to any information.

---

[a] 9,15,29,74,75,76,79

124

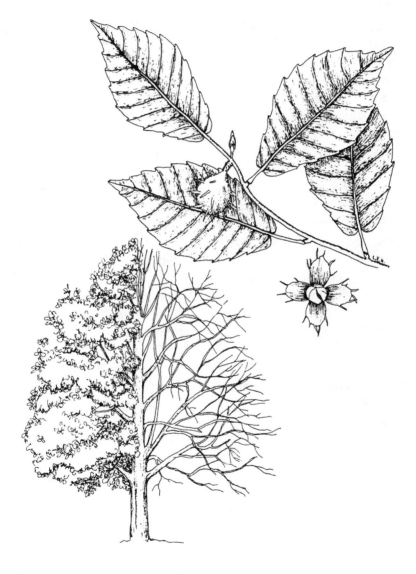

Fagus grandifolia, Fagus americana
Beech, beechnut

FRAGARIA VIRGINIANA
Rosaceae
Strawberry

Stem: Stemless, red runners up to 3 dm.

Leaves: Petiolulate, basal, 3 leaflets per leaf, serrate, ovate to obovate, coarsely toothed, leaflets 2 to 5 cm long, 1.5 to 4 cm broad, green.

Flower Type: Up to 12 flowers on a pedicel, 5 petals, white, obovate, bracts, many pistils, many stamens, 14 to 20 mm across, spring.

Fruit: Red fruit, numerous achenes on a greatly enlarged juicy red receptacle, 1 to 3 cm thick, edible, late spring, early summer.

Roots: Fibrous, stoloniferous.

General: Ground plant, perennial herb, grows in groups.

Habitat: Meadows and open fields, dry sites.

Season of Availability: The leaves are collected in the spring and summer. The fruit is collected in the early summer when ripe. The roots are collected in the fall.

Preparation: The leaves are dried thoroughly and used in an infusion. The fruits are used fresh. The roots are dried and used in a decoction.

Medical Terminology: The berries are considered refrigerant.[38] The leaves have astringent properties.[a] The roots are considered diuretic.[10,36] The berries act as a dentifrice, and remove tartar from teeth.[27,52]

Related Disease Symptoms: The fruit was used as a remedy for gout.[b] In the treatment of diarrhea[36,40] dysentery and dysuria[52] a tea of the leaves was utilized. For sore throat and mouth, a decoction of the root was used as a gargle.[27,52] A root tea was used by the Chippewa to treat cholera infantum.[10,75]

Poisonous Aspects: The wilting leaves contain cyanide.[33]

Biological and Edible: The fruit is edible[c] and sold commercially.[29]

Commercial Products & Uses: The wild herb can be sold to drug companies.[37]

Personal Experimentation: I have picked wild strawberries ever since I can remember to make jam, pies, and strawberry shortcake. For full flavor, the leaves must be dried before making the tea. The Trap Rock river valley produces some of the finest strawberry leaf tea in the Great Lakes area.

---

[a] 10,38,44,52 [c] 15,18,47,54,73,74,75
[b] 27,36,38

Fragaria virginiana
Strawberry

FRAXINUS AMERICANA
Oleaceae
Ash, white ash

Stem: Tree to 40 m, corrugated bark, dark, smooth on young growth.

Leaves: Opposite, pinnately compound, 5 to 9 (usually 7) oblong to ovate leaflets, abruptly acuminate, crenulate to entire, more pale and papillose beneath, wingless petiole, leaf scar on twigs, green.

Flower Type: In dense fascicles, short racemes or panicles, unisexual, sometimes perfect, green, spring.

Fruit: Linear to oblanceolate, 1 to 5 cm long, brown, 1 seeded samara.

Roots: Taproot.

General: Perennial tree, deciduous, valuable timber tree.

Habitat: Forests, rich moist woods.

Season of Availability: The inner bark of the trunk, roots and stem are collected in the spring. The leaves are collected in the summer and fall.

Preparation: The inner bark and leaves are dried and used in an infusion. The Chippewa used the root tea as an enema.[10]

Medical Terminology: The root bark has been used as an emmenagogue.[51] It is also used as a tonic, cathartic and diuretic.[38,58] The seeds were thought to be aperient, diuretic and an aphrodisiac.[36,63]

Related Disease Symptoms: People have chewed the bark and applied the chewed material to skin sores as a healer.[36,38] It is reported that a Native American from the East Coast cured cancer by the internal and external use of the fluid juice of white ash that trickled out the ends of a burning log.[63] The bark was used as a treatment for hemorrhoids.[40] The Meskwaki cured sores and itching skin using a wash of the infused bark.[40,73] Reputedly it is beneficial in dysmenorrhea.[32,58] Aborigines of America carried leaves of *Fraxinus americana* to defend themselves against rattlesnake bites.[a]

Poisonous Aspects: The pollen is a known cause of hay fever and contact dermatitis.[40]

Chemistry & Pharmacognosy: It contains several resins, an alkaloid and the glucoside, fraxin.[58] *Fraxinus* species are known to contain mannitol.[82]

Commercial Products & Uses: The bark is salable to some drug companies.[37]

---

[a] 9,38,63

Fraxinus americana
Ash, white ash

129

GALIUM APARINE
Rubiaceae
Cleavers, clivers, goose grass, bedstraw, stickers

Stem: 1 to 10 dm, weak stems, retrorsely hooked-scabrous on the angles, seldom much branched, green, 4 angled.

Leaves: In whorls of 6 to 8, 1 nerved, cuspidate, 1 to 8 cm long, retrorsely scabro-ciliate on the margins, they tend to cling to clothes and skin, edible, green.

Flower Type: 3 to 5 flowers on axillary peduncles, white, 3 to 8 mm across.

Fruit: Dry, uncinate-hispid, globose carpel, 1.5 to 5 mm in diameter.

Roots: Fibrous.

General Information: Annual, sometimes forms a dense mat.

Habitat: Wet areas, usually shaded, stream banks.

Season of Availability: Collect the herb in spring and summer during flowering. For eating, collect the herb in early June when still succulent.

Preparation: The herb is used fresh or dried in an infusion. The edible herb can be utilized as a pot herb. Dried herb 2 to 4 grams or by infusion, liquid extract 1:1 in 25% ethanol dose 2 to 4 ml, both in t.i.d. doses.[84]

Medical Terminology: The herb has been considered a diuretic,[a] alterative, and aperient.[b] Some consider *Galium* a refrigerant.[c]

Related Disease Symptoms: The a wash of the herb is used to treat psoriasis and other skin inflammations.[d] To ease the pain of sunburn, the cooled tea was applied with a washcloth.[e] The tea was taken internally for urinary troubles, such as stones in the kidney or bladder.[f] Other indications include lymphadenitis, dysuria, and psoriasis.[84]

Biological and Edible: The plant is edible.[g] The roasted seeds can be used as a coffee substitute.[h]

Chemistry & Pharmacognosy: A red dye is obtained from the roots.[i] The plant contains galitannic acid, other organic acids and a bitter principle.[58] *Galium* contains the glycuside asperuloside.[84] Also, coumarin has been isolated from some species of *Galium*.[82]

---

[a] 32,44,56,58,75,84
[b] 19,22,30,35,38,51,68

[c] 27,30,35,44,56,58
[d] 8,22,27,30,32,35,51
[e] 19,22,27,55
[f] 8,19,22,27,30,32,35,38,68,75
[g] 15,19,25,47,68
[h] 15,19,25,34,55
[i] 32,34,39,55

Personal Experimentation: I have eaten at least 200 grams of the freshly cooked plant at one sitting with no ill effects; it tastes like spinach.

Galium aparine
Cleavers, clivers, goose grass, bedstraw, stickers

GAULTHERIA PROCUMBENS
Ericaceae
Wintergreen, teaberry, checkerberry

Stem: 1 to 2 dm tall, erect from a horizontal rhizome, green to red.

Leaves: Leaves crowded near top, petioles 2 to 5 mm, blades elliptic to oblong, 2 to 5 cm long, glabrous, entire to crenulate, alternate, leathery, brittle, waxy, green.

Flower: White, solitary from the leaf axils on reddish drooping pedicels, urn-shaped corolla, 5 sided, 5 toothed, summer.

Fruit: Red berry-like fleshy capsule, persistent, white inside, 1 to 2 cm in diameter, wintergreen flavor, edible, fall.

Roots: Runners, fibrous.

General Information: Ground plant, perennial, evergreen.

Habitat: Open sandy soil, meadows, and on the floor of aspen and conifer forests.

Season of Availability: Collect the herb in the fall. Collect the fruit in the spring and fall.

Preparation: The herb is dried or used fresh in a tincture or infusion. The infusion is difficult to make. Pour boiling water over the leaves and let it sit for two days, then reheat or cool as desired.

The fruit can be eaten fresh, dried, or in jam. For topical use, methyl salicylate is used in 10 to 25% concentrations.[82] Dried leaves dose .5 to 1 gram or by infusion, liquid extract 1:1 in 25% ethanol dose .5 to 1. ml, volatile oil external application only, in t.i.d. doses.[84]

Medical Terminology: The leaves are considered diuretic,[44] stimulant and astringent.[a] It has been used as an emmenagogue,[b] but its virtues are doubtful,[5] It has also been used as a galactagogue.[22,36] The oil is known for its use as a local irritant, antiseptic, and antirheumatic.[82,84]

Related Disease Symptoms: Internally, the tea was used as a carminative to relieve gas and colic pains.[c] The tea has been used to ease rheumatic pains.[d] To treat fevers, one pint of the tea was ingested within one hour.[e] Headaches have been arrested by using the infusion.[19,50] The root was chewed by Native Americans for 6 weeks in the spring to prevent and cure toothaches.[36,40] Specific indications include rheumatoid

---

[a] 5,19,22,51,63,68,84

[b] 22,27,36,52

[c] 36,38,50

[d] 19,22,27,32,36,40,52,63,66 68,70,72,74,75,76,82,84

[e] 19,52,58,63,76

arthritis, myalgia, intercostal neuralgia, and sciatica.[84]

Poisonous Aspects: Overdoses of the pure oil on the skin produce drowsiness, congestion and delirium.[f]

Biological and Edible: The berries are edible.[g] *G. procumbens* has shown lectinic properties.[40] The leaves and berries can be brewed into a palatable tea.[87] Bees use this plant for honey.[92,93]

Chemistry & Pharmacognosy: The plant contains the glucoside gaultherin, tannin and the crystalline principles arbutin, ericolin and ursone.[58,82] It contains methyl salicylate.[h] The oil has been used in the production of aspirin.[80,87]

---

[f] 74,75,76,82

[g] 15,25,47,75,87

[h] 31,58,59,80,82,84

[i] 19,22,36,38,58,66,87

Commercial Products & Uses: The oil is used as a flavoring agent for toothpaste, gum, and candy.[i] Most commercial wintergreen oil production is extracted from wild plants in Pennsylvania.[53] Some drug companies still purchase the plant.[37]

Personal Experimentation: I have eaten a cupful of the berries at one time with no ill effects. I have made a tea by using 1 ounce of the dried leaves steeped in a quart of boiling water, which I let sit for two days to get the full flavor. I drank the whole quart with no ill effects. Obtaining some of the pure oil, I noticed that it is painful to the skin upon application. I suggest diluting the oil in a 10:1 ratio or greater of safflower oil to wintergreen oil.

Gaultheria procumbens
Wintergreen, teaberry, checkerberry

GERANIUM MACULATUM
Geraniaceae
Wild geranium, geranium, alum root, crane's bill

Stem: 3 to 7 dm tall, hairy, erect, green, branched, from a rhizome.

Leaves: A few long petioled basal leaves, pedately cleft into 5-7 cuneately laciniate segments, single pair of short petioled leaves from the stem, 10 to 20 cm across, 3 to 5 lobed palmately cut, segments narrow at base.

Flower Type: Few flowered terminal corymb, peduncles and pedicels, purple, sometimes white, hairy, 5 separate ovate petals, 10 stamens, spring.

Fruit: Elongate capsules, up to 5 cm long, erect, tipped with the persistent style, summer.

Roots: Fibrous, from rhizome.

General Information: Perennial herb, bushy.

Habitat: Rich moist woods and meadows.

Season of Availability: Collect the leaves and rhizomes in the spring before flowering. The rhizome can also be collected in the fall.[84]

Preparation: Dried leaves are used in an infusion. Fresh or dried rhizomes are used in a decoction. Dried rhizome dose 1 to 2 grams or by decoction, liquid extract 1:1 in 45% ethanol dose 1 to 2 ml, both in t.i.d. doses.[84]

Medical Terminology: Because of the rhizome's astringent qualities,[a] it has been used to treat diarrhea.[b]

Related Disease Symptoms: Natives used the decoction as a gargle to cure bleeding gums, sore mouth, sore throat or pyorrhea.[c] The decoction, prepared as a douche, was used to treat leukorrhea.[d] Some consider the dried powdered rhizome a styptic; it arrests bleeding from nose bleeds, cuts, and scratches.[e] The root in a decoction with *Vitis cordifolia* (grape) was used by the Cherokee to cure thrush in children.[63] Natives utilized a poultice of the pounded roots for hemorrhoids.[f] The tea was used for birth control.[50,52] Specific indications include diarrhea, peptic ulcer, hemorrhoids, hematemesis, melena, menorrhagia, and dysentery.[84]

Biological and Edible: The plant has shown hypoglycemic activity.[40] Experiments with *Geranium maculatum* showed

---

[a] 10,27,38,40,51

[b] 5,9,22,30,32,36,44,50, 52,63,68,72,74,75,84

[c] 5,10,27,30,32,36,38,40,44,50,63,73,75

[d] 5,32,50,63,72,84

[e] 5,22,27,30,32,36,38,50,63,68,84

[f] 22,63,72,73

[g] 32,51,84

gram + bacteria inhibition in antibiotic test.[57]

Chemistry & Pharmacognosy:
Contains tannic and gallic acids.[g]

Commercial Products & Uses:
Drug companies still purchase the rhizome.[37]

Geranium maculatum
Wild geranium, geranium, alum root, crane's bill

GEUM RIVALE
Rosaceae
Purple water avens, chocolate root, avens

Stem: 3 to 6 dm, sparsely hirsutulous, green, erect.

Leaves: Basal leaves up to 3 dm, with 3 or 5 principal leaflets, compound, terminal one broadly ovate or subrotound, serrate, 3 lobed; others adjacent, narrowly obovate; cauline leaves much smaller, reduced above, variously toothed to divided, stipulate.

Flower Type: Several yellow subfused and veined with purple, obcordate, about 2 cm wide, 5 petals, constricted at the apex, contracted to a claw at the base; calyx hairy, purple, bell-shaped with 5 erect lobes and a small bract, spring, early summer.

Fruit: Achenes, spreading with decurved styles, summer, fall.

Roots: Netted, fibrous.

General Information: Perennial herb, grows in clumps.

Habitat: Swamps, wet meadows, wet areas.

Season of Availability: The roots are collected in any season. The best place I've found for collecting *Geum rivale* was by the old Cliff Mine near Phoenix, MI.

Preparation: They are used fresh or dried in a decoction or tincture.

Medical Terminology: The root is considered astringent[63] and tonic.[a]

Related Disease Symptoms: As a gargle, Native Americans used the tea to heal sore throats.[63] Many tribes also used the powdered root as a remedy for ague.[9,63] It is chiefly utilized to relax mucous membranes.[32] The roots or herb, in a tea, has been used to treat dyspepsia.[22,36] It has been used to treat hemorrhaging[36] and diarrhea.[22] The root tea was used for heart trouble.[25,34]

Biological and Edible: The root imparts a chocolate flavor when boiled.[b]

Personal Experimentation: I have drank over a quart of this decoction with no ill effects. It has a slightly bitter, blandish chocolate flavor; with sweetener added, the flavor is much more distinctly chocolate.

---

[a] 9,22,32,51
[b] 25,34,47

Geum rivale
Purple water avens, chocolate root, avens

HAMAMELIS VIRGINIANA
Hamamelidaceae
Witch hazel

Stem: Woody, brown-black bark, 3-6 m, erect, branching.

Leaves: Alternate, oval to obovate, 5-15 cm long, margins with many rounded teeth, broadly rounded base, green, stipulate.

Flower Type: Bright yellow petals, 1.5 to 2 cm, fall.

Fruit: Woody capsule, ovoid to ellipsoid, fall.

Roots: Taproot.

General Information: Bushy shrub, understory species.

Habitat: In moist woods.

Season of Availability: The bark, young twigs and leaves are collected in the fall. The bark can also be collected in the early spring.

Preparation: The bark and leaves are usually prepared in an alcohol extract, but a decoction will suffice in all applications. To relieve inflammation and bruises, *Hamamelis* is applied externally by rubbing or fomentation.[82]

Medical Terminology: The extract is used as an astringent,[a] hemostatic,[b] sedative[27] and tonic.[c] The official drug comes from the freshly cut twigs and dried leaves, administered in a 2 gram average dose.[2,83]

Related Disease Symptoms: To this day it is used in lotions for bruises, sprains, burns, cuts and scratches.[d] As a wash, in suppositories or as an enema, it was used to treat hemorrhoids.[e] The decoction, taken internally, has been utilized to check internal bleeding in the stomach or lungs.[f] Native Americans washed the eye with the decoction to treat eye inflammation such as ophthalmia.[g] The Potawatomi used witch hazel in sweat baths, pouring the decoction over the hot rocks, for sore aching muscles.[h] It has been used as an injection for vaginitis.[44,50] As a wash, it was found beneficial for relief from insect stings or bites.[i] Topically, it treated varicose veins.[j] The decoction was gargled for sore gums and mouth irritations.[k] It has been used for colitis.[83]

[a] 38,40,51,66

[b] 1,17,29,32,82,83

[c] 9,19,22,50,63,68

[d] 17,19,22,27,32,36,38,50,51,63,83

[e] 1,17,19,22,27,32,36,40,44,50, 51,58,63,68,83

[f] 17,19,22,32,51,58,63,68

[g] 17,22,27,36,63

[h] 9,36,63,76

[i] 19,22,27,50

[j] 19,22,32

[k] 19,27,36,44,50,83

138

Chemistry & Pharmacognosy:
Witch hazel contains tannic acid.[1] Hamamelis leaf contains the compounds hamamelitannin, tannin, a hexose sugar, a volatile oil, a bitter principle, gallic acid, and calcium oxalate.[82,83] The volatile oil contains 2-hexen-1-al (9.7%), acetaldehyde (3.2%), alpha-ionone (3.5%), beta-ionone (1%), and safrole (.2%). Chromatography has been done.[83]

Commercial Products & Uses:
Some companies are in the market for wild witch hazel from local collectors.[37] Most of the witch hazel production comes from the Blue Ridge Mountains.[82] Most of the U.S. commercial witch hazel production occurs in Connecticut.[53]

---

[1] 32,38,58,83

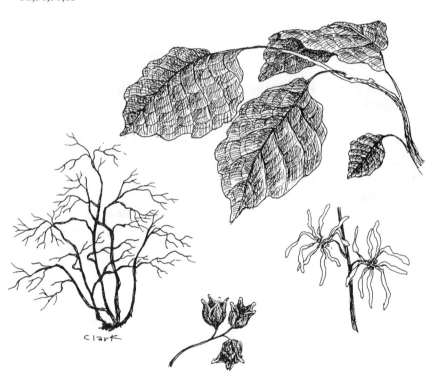

Hamamelis virginiana
Witch hazel

HEDEOMA PULEGIOIDES
Labiatae
American pennyroyal, mock pennyroyal, pennyroyal, pulioll-royall

Stem: Square, branching, green, erect, hairy, 1 to 4 dm tall.

Leaves: Opposite, petioled, lanceolate to oblong-ovate, 1-3 cm long, entire to serrulate, green.

Flower Type: Blue, in whorls in the leaf axils, 2 lipped, erect, tubular calyx, 2 to 5 mm long, 2 stamens, summer, fall.

Fruit: Smooth ovoid nutlets, fall.

Roots: Fibrous.

General: Perennial herb.

Habitat: Forest, dry upland sites.

Season of Availability: Collect the whole herb in the summer.

Preparation: It is used dried or fresh in an infusion.

Medical Terminology: In action, the herb is considered a stimulant,[38] carminative,[27,40] emmenagogue[a] and diaphoretic.[b] At one time the distilled oil was used directly as an emmenagogue.[1,81]

Related Disease Symptoms: An herb tea has been used to ease headaches.[c] A cup of pennyroyal tea supposedly will relieve upset stomach, indigestion, flatulence or nausea.[d] The tea has been used to stimulate suppressed menstruation.[e] In Appalachia, the tea was used as a remedy for pneumonia.[38,63] The oil is sometimes used for its counterirritant action.[29,38] Some Natives believed the topical application of the herb, to pains of any limb, would remove the pain.[40] The crushed green herb has been used to remove the marks of bruises and burns.[81] The plant is good for female disorders, especially when associated with nervous disturbances.[81]

Poisonous Aspects: The oil can cause contact dermatitis.[40] There is a report of abortion and death in livestock attributed to pennyroyal.[63] There are recent reports of women utilizing the oil to induce abortion with lethal results.[77,81] Overdose symptoms include dizziness, nausea, abdominal pain and sometimes death.[77] Pennyroyal oil can cause extensive damage to the liver.[77]

Biological and Edible: Natives utilized the plant as an effective insect repellant and remedy for tikes.[f] The dried herb sewn into sachets has been used to repel moths in drawers with woolen goods.[19] The oil is thought to promote the flow of bile.[81]

---

[a] 32,58,63

[b] 5,19,30,35,44,81

[c] 35,40,63,81

[d] 5,27,32,81

[e] 5,19,30,32,35,36,81

[f] 19,29,35,40,63,81

Chemistry & Pharmacognosy:
The herb contains pulegone[31] and hedeomal in the volatile oil.[51,82] The evaporation rate is 86, the odor intensity is 7.[81] Other compounds include menthone, isomenthone, piperitone, and various terpene hydrocarbons.[82]

Commercial Products & Uses:
Drug companies still buy the herb from small time collectors.[37] Most of the commercial production of pennyroyal oil is from wild plants in the southern states.[53]

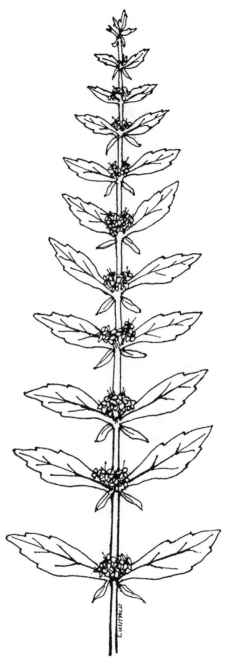

Hedeoma pulegioides
American pennyroyal, mock pennyroyal, pennyroyal, pulioll-royall

HELIANTHUS ANNUUS
Compositae
Common sunflower, sunflower

Stem: 1 to 5 m, simple to branched, hairy, green.

Leaves: Alternate, heart-shaped to elliptic-ovate, petiolate, 3 main nerves, rough, green, toothed, 12 to 25 cm long.

Flower Type: Terminal floral heads, 5 to 8 cm wide, yellow to orange ray flowers, brown to purple disk flowers, summer, fall.

Fruit: Grayish-white achene, obovate, edible, fall.

Roots: Fibrous.

General Information: Annual herb, grows in large groups.

Habitat: Fields, open areas, dry sites.

Season of Availability: Collect the seeds in the fall. Gather the flowers in the summer.

Preparation: The seeds are smashed or broken and put in cold water, where the shells float and are poured off. The seeds are used fresh or dried, though they already are very dry. The flowers are usually used freshly picked.

Medical Terminology: The seeds are considered diuretic[27,50] and expectorant.[a] Johnson believes the seeds have little, if any, medicinal activity.[32]

Related Disease Symptoms: In a tea, the seeds have been used for pulmonary affections, coughs and colds.[b]

Biological and Edible: Experimentally, *Helianthus annuus* has shown hypoglycemic activity.[40] The seeds are edible.[c] An oil is extracted from the seeds and used for cooking.[d] Seeds can be sprouted and used as food.[86] Bees use this plant for honey.[92,93]

Chemistry & Pharmacognosy: A yellow dye is obtained from the flowers.[e] A purple and black dye is obtained from the seeds.[34]

---

[a] 22,32,51,58,68

[b] 22,27,36,50,51,68

[c] 15,18,25,34,47,50

[d] 25,29,58

[e] 22,34,50

Helianthus annuus
Common sunflower, sunflower

HELIANTHUS TUBEROSUS
Compositae
Jerusalem artichoke, sunflower

Stem: Green, coarse, scabrous, up to 3 m, branching above.

Leaves: Green, thick, scabrous above, puberulent large midvein, coarsely toothed, petiolate, alternate, broad, up to 15 cm across.

Flower Type: Yellow, many ray flowers in a circle, black and yellow disk flowers, fall.

Fruit: Gray oval seed in a blackish-purple husk, 1 to 2 cm, edible, fall.

Roots: Fibrous, with large edible white tubers, fall.

General Information: Perennial, grows in groups.

Habitat: Fields, meadows, waste places.

Season of Availability: The seeds and potato-like tubers are collected in the fall.

Preparation: The tubers are usually fried, boiled, or steamed, though they can be eaten raw. Pickle the tubers by putting them in old or new pickle juice. Crush the seeds and put in water so the husks float and can be poured off; the seeds will be left behind. The process is more work than it sounds and may not be worth the trouble. The seeds can be eaten raw, cooked, or ground into flour.

Biological and Edible: The tubers[b] and seeds[a] are edible. The young flower heads can be boiled and eaten.[78] The tubers seem to lack starch and can be eaten by people that are suffering ailments due to starch.[78]

Commercial Products & Uses: Jerusalum artichoke tubers are not commercially available, though many seed companies sell the seeds.

Personal Experimentation: When collecting *Helianthus tuberosus* tubers, a shovel is essential. The plants always grow in large groups and the tubers perpetuate the plant yearly. The tubers are within 1 foot of the ground surface. I find it easiest to spade the ground for a while, then sift the dirt by hand in search of tubers. The tubers are usually plentiful. To me, they are very similar to potatoes, so I prepare them as such.

---

[a] 25,78,85

[b] 10,15,18,25,78,85

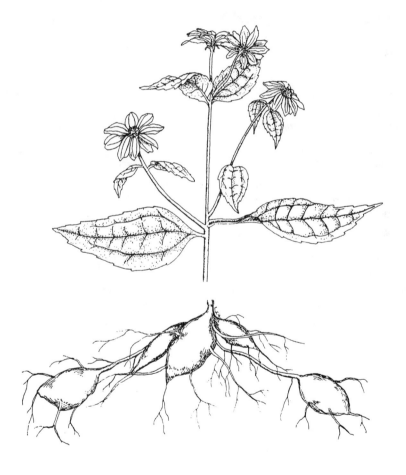

Helianthus tuberosus
Jerusalem artichoke, sunflower

145

HEMEROCALLIS FULVA
Liliaceae
Day lily, orange day lily

Stem: Smooth, 1 to 2 m tall.

Leaves: 3 to 6 dm long, 1 to 1.5 cm wide, basal, tapering to both ends, light green.

Flower Type: Orange, 6 to 10 cm long, 3 to 12 at top of stem, each lasting one day. May to July.

Roots: Thin, long tubers, each .9 to 1.8 m.

Habitat: Roadsides, waste areas.

Season of Availability: May through July.

Medical Terminology: The root tea is considered a diuretic and antibacterial, and the flower buds are considered astringent.

Related Disease Symptoms: The root tea has been used to treat jaundice and leukorrhea. The flower buds have been used for jaundice, or made into a poultice for treating hemorrhoids.

Biological and Edible: The tubers, found in early spring, may be eaten raw or boiled. The shoots may be used in salads, or prepared as a potherb. The flowers may be eaten fresh, or dried and added to soups.

Poisonous Aspects: The roots and very young leaf shoots may be toxic, and are said to cause blindness.

Personal Experimentation: I have eaten the edible flowers fresh off the stalk, in salads, and fried in an egg batter for the last 10 years.

Hemerocallis fulva
Day lily, orange day lily

147

HEPATICA ACUTILOBA
Ranunculaceae
Liverleaf, hepatica, liverwort, sharp-lobed hepatica

Stem: Nearly stemless, 5 to 15 cm tall.

Leaves: All basal, 3 sharp lobes, cordate at the base, 5 to 10 cm long, green, appear after flowers.

Flower Type: Purple, pink, or white, 12 to 20 mm across, 6 or 7 petal-like sepals, pointed bracts, solitary on long scapes from 5 to 15 cm, spring.

Fruit: Pointed oblong, hairy achenes, spring, summer.

Roots: Fibrous.

General Information: Ground floor plant, perennial herb.

Habitat: In forests with rich dry upland sites.

Season of Availability: The leaves and roots are collected in the spring.

Preparation: The roots and leaves are used dried or fresh in a tea or syrup.

Medical Terminology: The herb is thought to have astringent and tonic properties.[a] Reportedly, it also has demulcent activity.[22] Presently, the herb is thought to be inert of medicinal value.[32,58]

Related Disease Symptoms: The Menominees used the roots of *Hepatica* and maiden hair fern for female disorders, such as leukorrhea.[63,74] As a wash, the Meskwakis used it for deformities such as twisted mouth and crossed eyes.[63,73] The roots have been used to treat coughs.[b] Originally, the herb was thought to cure hepatic affections, thus the name liverleaf.[63]

Chemistry & Pharmacognosy: *Hepatica acutiloba* contains tannin, mucilage and sugar.[58]

Commercial Products & Uses: Some drug companies still purchase this herb from small time collectors.[37]

Personal Experimentation: Bill Hill introduced me to this plant in 1972. We gathered the leaves and made an infusion. The tea was slightly bitter and after 3 cups we noticed no effects. I noticed a large patch of hepatica growing in the Sturgeon Gorge wilderness area.

---

[a] 22,38,44

[b] 36,44,63

Hepatica acutiloba
Liverleaf, hepatica, liverwort, sharp-lobed hepatica

HERACLEUM LANATUM
Umbelliferae
Cow parsnip, masterwort

Stem: Stout, ridged, thick at base, 1 to 3 m, unbranched, pubescent, green, hollow stem.

Leaves: Alternate, compound, 3 palmately lobed leaflets, strongly toothed, large, each 3 to 6 dm long, green.

Flower Type: Terminal double umbel, 10 to 20 cm across, small white flowers, summer.

Fruit: Small ridged, 2 seeded carpel.

Roots: Taproot.

General Information: Biennial herb, grows in groups.

Habitat: Wet areas, in forests and meadows.

Season of Availability: The roots are collected in any season.

Preparation: The roots are used fresh or dried as a poultice or in a decoction.

Medical Terminology: Therapeutically, the root is thought to be a carminitive, a stimulant[10,39] and an antispasmodic.[32,35]

---

[a] 35,36,52,63,73

[b] 32,39,40,63,73

Related Disease Symptoms: The Ojibwe pounded the fresh root to a pulp and used it as a poultice on sores.[63,75] The Chippewa tribe used a root tea as a mouthwash for sore throat.[10] The root was taken internally for colic and stomach cramps.[a] A root decoction has been recommended for epilepsy and nervous disorders.[b] The boiled root, pulped, was used in a drawing poultice for boils.[10] The dried powdered roots were put on gums to relieve the discomfort caused by loose teeth.[36,60]

Poisonous Aspects: Fresh leaves and roots in contact with human skin have caused irritation and inflammation.[32] The leaves are a known cause of dermatitis.[46,74]

Biological and Edible: The Vancouver Island Salish Indians roasted and pounded the root, mixed it with dogfish oil and used the concoction as a hair lotion to make the hair grow longer.[60] The first year root is edible.[34] The young sprouts are cooked and eaten as a pot herb.[15]

150

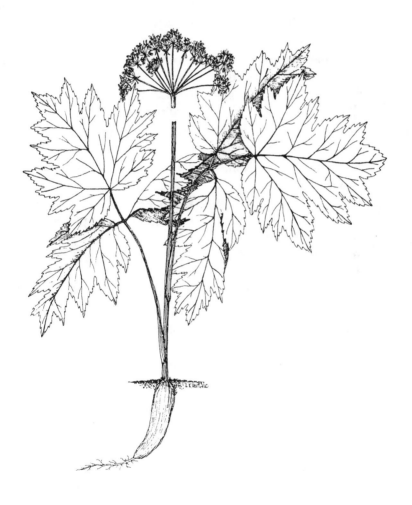

Heracleum lanatum
Cow parsnip, masterwort

151

HUMULUS LUPULUS
Cannabinaceae
Hops

Stem: Vine, 5 to 10 m, rough, green to brown.

Leaves: Opposite, petioled, 3 pointed lobes, cordate at base, upper leaves lobeless, smooth, green.

Flower Type: Dioecious, staminate flowers paniculate, 5 sepals, 5 stamens, numerous pistillate flowers in short spikes, paired, bracts entire, 2 filaform stigmas, green, summer.

Fruit: Achene closed in a peresistant calyx (a strobilus), cone like shape, green to brown, fall.

Roots: Taproot.

General: Perennial vine, usually carpets an area, sometimes climbing fence posts and trees.

Habitat: Open fields, roadsides, fence rows, almost any soil type.

Season of Availability: Collect the fruiting strobili in the fall.[82] It deteriorates upon aging and exposure to the atmosphere.[82]

Preparation: Strobiles are dried and used in a tincture or infusion. Lupulin consists of the glandular trichomes separated from the strobiles.[82]

Dried strobiles dose 1 to 2 grams or as an infusion, liquid extract 1:1 in 45% ethanol dose .5 to 2 ml.

Medical Terminology: It is generally accepted that hops have tonic[a] and sedative properties.[b] Others claim it to be an anodyne[51] and diuretic.[c] It is thought to have mild narcotic properties.[d] Because of its bitter qualities, it is considered a stomachic.[51,63] The herb is thought to be a bitter.[e] The dried strobili are official and administered in 2 gram doses.[2,84]

Related Disease Symptoms: For insomnia, use a pillow stuffed with hop blossoms or tea.[f] Drink an infusion to relieve indigestion and upset stomach.[g] A heated fomentation of hops placed against the painful area was used to treat earaches and toothaches.[35,63] To relieve the stress and pain from painful swellings and inflammation, a fomentation of the strobili has been applied.[h] It has been used to treat the pain of rheumatism.[i] The tea has reduced fever.[j]

---

[a] 5,40,44,51,68

[b] 22,29,30,32,35,36,58,63,73,82,84

[c] 22,30,35,36,52,68

[d] 5,32,51,52

[e] 1,22,31,82

[f] 5,22,30,32,35,44,50,52,63,68,73,84

[g] 5,22,32,40,52

[h] 22,32,36,51

[i] 5,22,36,52

[j] 5,36,50

152

The tea is also used for neuralgia.[k] To improve the appetite, a cup of the infusion was drunk.[22,50] Years ago, the tea was used to relieve the stress from delirium tremors.[l] Some of the more novel indications include priapism, mucous colitis, and topically applied to crural ulcers.[84] Many other claims have been made for hops, but I doubt the validity of the sources that claim these virtues, so they are not mentioned.

Poisonous Aspects: The pollen is known to cause hay fever and the plant has caused contact dermatitis.[40] Depression is a contraindication to its use.[84]

Biological and Edible: The strobili and leaves are used to flavor beer.[m] The young shoots are edible in salads or cooked and eaten as a pot herb.[n]

In antibiotic experiments, hops have known gram + and - bacteria inhibition.[o] Bees use this plant for honey.[92,93]

Chemistry & Pharmacognosy: It contains the vasopressor agent, quercitin.[40] It is known to contain lupulon,[p] humulon, tannin and an essential oil, about .2 to .5 % by weight, which contains the compounds humulene and myrcene.[11,82]

Commercial Products & Uses: The strobili can be bought in herb stores, co-ops, and beer making supply stores.

Personal Experimentation: I have collected the strobiles throughout the Great Lakes area and have made infusions from them. The tea is bitter to the taste.

---

[k] 5,30,35,52,84

[l] 5,22,30,35

[m] 5,15,22,29,34,50,82

[n] 11,15,34

[o] 11,40,57

[p] 31,51,58

Humulus lupulus
Hops

HYDRASTIS CANADENSIS
Ranunculaceae
Golden seal, yellow puccoon, yellowroot, orangeroot

Stem: Single, unbranched, hairy, 3 to 5 dm, green.

Leaves: 2 alternate palmate leaves, sharply toothed, 5 lobes, up to 25 cm across, green.

Flower Type: White, solitary, 3 petal-like sepals falling off during opening; numerous stamens, 12 to 20 pistils, spring.

Fruit: Dark red berries in a head, 2 seeds per berry.

Roots: Knotty, yellow to yellow-orange rhizome with fibrous rootlets.

General: Perennial herb, rare.

Habitat: Rich forests, maple-beech stands, hardwood sites.

Season of Availability: The root is collected in the late fall. The leaves are collected in the summer or fall after the seeds are ripe. It takes 3 to 4 years to produce marketable roots from rhizome buds.[82]

Preparation: The leaves are used fresh or dried. The roots are usually dried and used in a tincture, decoction, or powder. Dried rhizome .5 to 1 gram or by decoction, liquid extract 1:1 in 60% ethanol dose .3 to 1. ml, all in t.i.d. doses.[84]

Medical Terminology: There are many therapeutic values attributed to *Hydrastis*. The main qualities appear to be tonic,[a] laxative[b] and stimulant.[c] The root is also considered diuretic.[d] Others say it has antiperiodic qualities.[e] Because of its astringent qualities,[51] it was used as a hemostatic.[f] One of its actions appears to be that of a uterine hemostatic.[31,72] The dried rhizomes and roots have been considered official.[2]

Related Disease Symptoms: The root decoction has treated gonorrhea[5,63] and leukorrhea.[32] The root decoction has been used beneficially for chronic inflammations of mucous membranes.[g] It was also utilized as a wash to treat eye infections and inflammations.[h] The decoction, chewed root, or tincture was gargled or applied to mouth sores or ulcers such as pyorrhea.[i] To treat catarrhal conditions, a decoction or tincture was used.[j] It is reportedly useful in treating stomach and liver ailments.[k] A cup of the tea supposedly aids digestion.[22,36]

---

[a] 1,9,36,58,66

[b] 5,30,32,35,44,50,68

[c] 22,63,72,84

[d] 5,35,38,63

[e] 5,35,51

[f] 1,38,40,82,84

[g] 5,29,51,58,63,66,82,84

[h] 9,22,27,30,32,35,38,40,50,63,72,84

[i] 30,32,35,36,38,50,63,72

[j] 1,9,29,32,38,44,50,58

[k] 5,8,27,40,50,63,72,84

154

In an enema or tea, it helped relieve the pain of hemorrhoids.[l] The tea was also used to treat constipation.[m] As a wash, the decoction treated skin diseases such as acne, eczema[50,73] and indolent ulcers.[n] As an application, it was used to treat chronic coryza, prolapsus ani and glandular swellings.[32] The powdered roots were applied to wounds to promote scab formation.[35,36]

Poisonous Aspects: When eaten, it produces ulcerations and catarrhal inflammations of any mucous surfaces.[46,91] Pregnancy and hypertension are contraindications to its use.[84] Symptoms include mouth and skin paresthesias, hypotension, nausea, vomiting, and seizures.[91] Treatment is atropine 2 mg IM; repeat if necessary and maintain vitals.[91]

---

[l] 5,22,32
[m] 5,22,44
[n] 22,30,35,63

Biological and Edible: The plant has shown hypoglycemic activity in experiments.[40] Native Americans mixed the roots with bear grease and used the ointment as an insect repellant.[36,63]

Chemistry & Pharmacognosy: From the roots comes a yellow dye.[o] *Hydrastis* contains the three alkaloids hydrastine, berberine[40] and canadine.[p] Berberine has been shown to have antibiotic activity.[40]

Commercial Products & Uses: Roots are easily sold to some drug companies.[37] The product Murine contains hydrastine hydrochloride and berberine hydrochloride.[82]

Personal Experimentation: I have ingested one tablespoon of powdered root for the flu two days in a row. The taste was very bitter and quite unpalatable, nevertheless my health improved within two days.

[o] 5,9,22,27,44,63,82
[p] 1,31,58,82,84

Hydrastis canadensis
Golden seal, yellow puccoon, yellowroot, orangeroot

HYPERICUM PERFORTUM
Hypericaceae
Saint John's wort

Stem: Smooth, branched, up to 1 m, black spots, sometimes runners at base.

Leaves: Opposite, sessile, small, linear-oblong, minute holes that are noticable when held up to light, 2 to 4 cm long.

Flower Type: 5 yellow oblong petals, 10 mm long; 5 sepals, lanceolate; numerous stamens; 1 pistil; compound cyme, summer, fall.

Fruit: Small carpels.

Roots: Fibrous, with runners, numerous, in groups, common.

General Information: Perennial herb, in groups, common.

Habitat: Open fields, meadows, and dry sites.

Season of Availability: The flowering herb is collected during the summer.[84]

Preparation: The herb can be used dried or fresh in an infusion. To make an ointment, the fresh flowers are put in olive oil and let sit in the sunlight for 30 days. Dried herb dose 2 to 4 grams or by infusion, liquid extract 1:1 in 25% ethanol dose 2 to 4 ml, both used t.i.d.[84]

Medical Terminology: Most literature agrees that *Hypericum perforatum* is an astringent,[a] diuretic[b] and stimulant.[51] It has been used as a sedative, and topically as an analgesic and antiseptic.[84]

Related Disease Symptoms: The ointment is mainly used to heal skin cuts, bruises, wounds,[c] and insect bites.[d] As a wash, the herb tea has treated caked breasts and hardened skin.[e] The herb tea was supposedly useful for pulmonary complaints.[f] British indications include sciatica, excitability, neuralgia, and fibrositis.[84]

Poisonous Aspects: Ingestion of the herb has caused photosensitization in livestock,[40,46] resulting in severe itching, increased heart and respiration rate, fever and diarrhea.[33,84] Livestock death resulting from ingestion has been reported.[33] Contraindications to its use include depressive states.[84] The leaves have caused contact dermatitis on humans.[40,46]

Biological and Edible: In antibiotic experiments, it showed gram + and - inhibition.[57]

Chemistry & Pharmacognosy: The herb contains a volatile red oil and the florescent compounds hypericin and hypericum.[58,84]

---

[a] 22,44,84

[b] 30,35,68

[c] 8,27,32,35,44,49,50,58,68,84

[d] 27,44,49

[e] 22,30,35

[f] 22,30,50,68

Hypericin has been recently identified as an antiviral agent.[97]

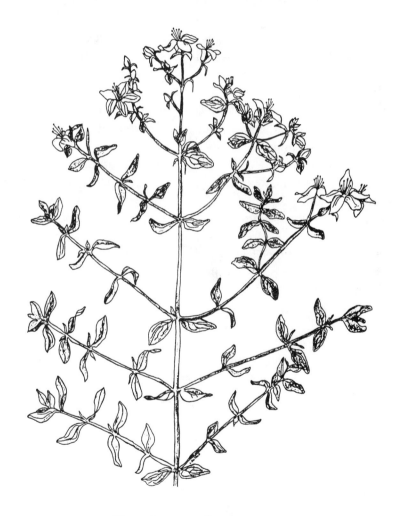

Hypericum perforatum
Saint John's wort

IMPATIENS CAPENSIS
Balsaminaceae
Jewelweed, snapweed, touch-me-not, lady's earrings, celandine

Stem: Up to 2 m tall, smooth, watery, multi-branched.

Leaves: Bright green, wilt quickly, alternate, thin, 3 to 10 cm long.

Flower Type: Ranging from light yellow to orange with red spots, up to 3 cm long, dangling, blossoms look like small snapdragons; bloom from July to September.

General Information: Grows with poison ivy in damp, shaded areas. Also in sunny areas when roots are near water.

Habitat: Swamps, streams; low, damp ground.

Season of Availability: July to frost.

Preparation: Simmer leaves and stems in a large pot of water, which will turn clear to medium dark brown. Bottle or freeze.

Related Disease Symptoms: Use the fresh juice to wash nettle stings, skin rash, and poison ivy. Wipe on areas of the skin exposed to poison ivy for quick relief. The poultice of jewelweed has been used on bruises, burns, cuts, eczema, insect bites, sores, sprains, and ringworm.

Commercial Products & Uses: Apparently jewelweed is available commercially.

Personal Experimentation: One man highly allergic to poison ivy experimented by drinking the decoction one spring. Although the taste was decidedly unpleasant, he did not get poison ivy that year, and plans to drink it every spring before his first exposure.

Impatiens capensis
Jewelweed, snapweed, touch-me-not, lady's earrings, celandine

IRIS VERSICOLOR
Iridaceae
Blue flag, wild iris, fleur-de-lys

Stem: Stiff, erect up to 1 m, smooth, green.

Leaves: Linear, parallel veined, clasping at the base of the stem, crease in the center, up to 1 m, rough, green.

Flower Type: Purple to blue, showy, 3 erect petals; 3 petallike sepals, yellow at the base, purple veins; 8-15 cm across, summer.

Fruit: Green cylindric capsule, 3 valved, 10 cm long, 4 cm across, summer, fall.

Roots: Thick, fleshy rhizome, pink, produces runners.

General Information: Perennial, grows in clumps.

Habitat: Wet areas, marshes, slow streams, ponds.

Season of Availability: Collect the rhizome in the fall.

Preparation: Dry and use in a tincture or decoction.

Medical Terminology: Therapeutically, iris is mainly considered a cathartic,[1,40] diuretic[a] and alterative.[b] Reports claim the rhizome has been used as an emetic.[c] The rhizome reportedly has vermifuge properties.[d]

It has also been utilized as a sialagogue.[e] Two grams of the rhizome is the average official dose.[2,83]

Related Disease Symptoms: The Chippewa applied the mashed root to painful inflammations to quickly reduce the swelling.[10] The boiled mashed root has been applied as a poultice to treat skin infections, bruises, and sores.[f] In earlier years, the decoction was used to treat dropsy (congestive heart failure).[g] The pulverized root mixed with water was used by Missouri Valley Native Americans as an earache remedy.[63]

Poisonous Aspects: Full doses of the rhizome produce violent vomiting, nausea and prostration.[h] Treatment is emesis and keeping vitals stable.[91] The rhizomes have caused dermatitis.[46]

Chemistry & Pharmacognosy: Iris root contains the acrid resinous compound, irisin.[22,58] Other Iris species are known to contain iron and myristic acid.[82] It's also been known to contain isophthalic and salicylic acid.[83]

---

[a] 5,22,27

[b] 30,32,35,44,51,58,63,68,83

[c] 5,22,58,63,73,74,75,83

[d] 30,32,35,58

[e] 30,32,35,44

[f] 9,22,40,63,73,76,83

[g] 30,35,63

[h] 22,32,91

Iridin is the commercial dry extract of the rhizome.[1,22]

Iris versicolor
Blue flag, wild iris, fleur-de-lys

JUGLANS CINEREA
Juglandaceae
Butternut, white walnut

Stem: Woody, grayish-brown smoothly ridged bark, stout twigs, tree up to 30 m.

Leaves: Alternate, pinnately compound, 11 to 17 (always an odd number) oblong to lanceolate leaflets, pointed tips, main vein, green.

Flower Type: Monoecious; staminate flowers in catkins; pistilate flowers terminal on young branches, with a cup-shaped involucre of bracts, green, spring.

Fruit: Green husk, later turning brown, ovoid, 4 to 8 cm, aromatic, 2 or 4 distinct ridges, a ridged shell covering an edible nut inside, fall.

Roots: Large taproot.

General Information: Perennial deciduous tree, fast growing, short lived, intolerant.

Habitat: Forests, along stream banks, well-drained gravel soils, mostly ornamental in this area.

Season of Availability: Collect the inner bark of the root in any season. The leaves and nuts are collected in the fall.

Preparation: The inner root bark is used fresh or dried in a decoction. The leaves are used fresh or dried in an infusion or decoction. Dried bark dose 2 to 6 grams, liquid extract 1:1 in 25% ethanol dose 2 to 6 ml, both t.i.d.[83]

Medical Terminology: Mainly, butternut is used for its cathartic[a] and vermifuge properties.[b] The bark is reputed to have rubefacient properties.[5,38]

Related Disease Symptoms: The decoction of the root bark was taken internally to get rid of tapeworms.[c] As a wash, the decoction was used to treat fungal infections, maculae and other skin affections.[d] The tea has been ingested to treat dysentery[63] and diarrhea.[27,30] The tea has eased constipation.[e]

Poisonous Aspects: The pollen is a known cause of hay fever.[40]

Biological and Edible: The nuts are edible.[f] The spring sap has been tapped for a sweet syrup.[g] Bees use this plant for honey.[92,93]

Chemistry & Pharmacognosy: The husks of the fruit are boiled and used to dye cloth brown.[h]

---

[a] 5,36,38,44,51,63,73,83
[b] 22,30,68   [d] 30,36,38,63,83
[c] 22,30,36,38

[e] 5,32,51,83   [h] 5,22,29,75
[f] 9,15,25,29,75
[g] 15,25,29,74

The dried bark contains juglone, juglandic acid, tannin, and fixed and volatile oils.[83]

Commercial Products & Uses: The inner bark can still be sold commercially.[37]

Personal Experimentation: I have eaten butternuts many times. They taste nearly like black walnuts.

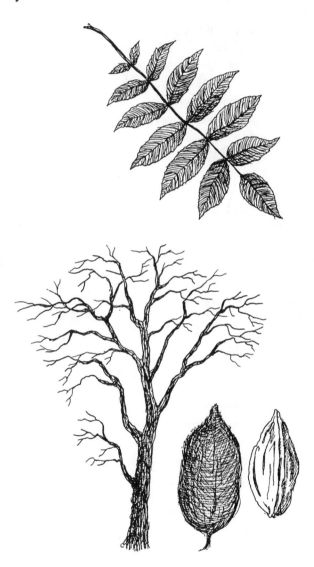

Juglans cinerea
Butternut, white walnut

JUGLANS NIGRA
Juglandaceae
Black walnut

Stem: Woody tree, black bark with rough ridges, up to 40 m, stout twigs.

Leaves: Alternate, pinnately compound, 11 to 23 (always an odd number) oblong to ovate leaflets, acuminate, green.

Flower Type: Staminate flowers in catkins; pistilate flowers terminal on young twigs; Monoecious; cup-shaped involucre of bracts; green, spring.

Fruit: Green husks, later turning brown, subglobose, 5 to 8 cm, ridged, 2 valved, containing a ridged shell around an edible ridged nut, fall.

Roots: Large taproot.

General: Long lived, perennial deciduous tree, fast growing, reproduction depends largely upon rodents, valuable lumber.

Habitat: Forests, fertile, well drained soils.

Season of Availability: Collect the inner bark of the root in the spring or fall. Collect the fruit in the late summer or early fall. Collect the leaves in the spring, summer and fall.

Preparation: Prepare all parts in a decoction or infusion.

---

[a] 36,58,73   [d] 30,36,50
[b] 22,38,44,50   [e] 9,15,25,29,85
[c] 30,36,50

Medical Terminology: Black walnut is used as a cathartic[a] and astringent.[b] It is also thought to be a vermifuge.[c] The plant has lectinic properties.[40]

Related Disease Symptoms: The decoction of the bark has been gargled for sore throats, mouths, tonsils and diphtheria.[d] The inner bark, used in a wash or poultice, is effective against dermatomycosis, for example ringworm.[40,50] The wash also treats skin affections such as eczema.[22,30] To rid worms, the decoction was taken internally.[36]

Poisonous Aspects: The pollen is a cause of hay fever.[40]

Biological and Edible: The nuts are edible.[e] The sap has been boiled to make a sugar syrup.[15,25] Husked nuts seem to keep longer and fresher than unhusked.[85] Bees use this plant for honey.[92,93]

Chemistry & Pharmacognosy: The fresh or dried husks of the fruit can be used for a brown dye.[22] It contains ellagic acid and juglone, which are used in cancer chemotherapeutic drugs.[40]

Commercial Products & Uses: The inner bark of the root can be sold commercially.[37]

Personal Experimentation: I took 50 g of the dried husks, boiled in 2 quarts of water,

strained the mixture and successfully dyed some white linen
brown.

Juglans nigra
Black walnut

JUNIPERUS COMMUNIS
Pinaceae (Cupressaceae)
Juniper

Stem: Many branched, reddish-brown scaly bark, up to 10 m.

Leaves: Whorled, in 3's, scale-like, linear, 6 to 20 mm long, green with a white stripe in the center.

Flower Type: Dioecious; cones, spring.

Fruit: Green, at maturity it turns a deep bluish-black, drupe-like cone, fall.

Roots: Prostrate taproot.

General Information: Shrubby evergreen, perennial.

Habitat: Dry, rocky, open fields and meadows.

Season of Availability: Collect the fruits in the fall and winter. The small twigs and leaves are collected in any season.

Preparation: The berries are usually distilled for their oil, but can be used in an infusion. The oil is usually steam distilled from the unripe fruit.[5] The leaves and twigs are used in an infusion. Dried ripe fruit infusion 1:20 in boiling water dose 100 ml, liquid extract 1:1 in 25% ethanol dose 2 to 4 ml, given t.i.d.[84]

Medical Terminology: It is used as a diuretic,[a] stimulant[44,51] and carminative.[b] One of the oil's major contributions is that of an emmenagogue.[c] Years ago it was considered a urinary antiseptic.[d] Two grams is the average dose of the official dried ripe berries.[2]

Related Disease Symptoms: The berries, eaten or in a tea, have treated colds.[52,70] A tea from the berries or leaves was reputedly beneficial in kidney, bladder and urinary troubles such as stones, catarrhal deposits, leukorrhea, or gonorrhea.[e] A cup of the tea reportedly ceases indigestion.[f] As a poultice, the leaves have treated wounds.[36] Specific indications are cystitis and topically for rheumatic pain in joints or muscles.[84]

Poisonous Aspects: Internal consumption of the tea may cause irritation to the urinary passages[32,44] and usually imparts a violet odor to the urine.[5] Pregnancy and renal disease are contraindications.[84] In large doses, the oil has caused strangury and/or priapism.[81] Overdoses may cause abortion.[34]

---

[a] 27,38,50,52,57,63

[b] 5,22,30,32,36,58,68,81,82,84

[c] 1,32,36,58,63,81

[d] 38,63,76,81,84

[e] 5,22,27,35,36,41,50,52,63,68,81

[f] 22,30,35,36,52,81

Biological and Edible: A study on the diuretic action of *Juniperus* revealed its action enhanced glomerular filtration, and that increased amounts of potassium, sodium, and chlorine are excreted.[81] It is considered effective against meningococcus, staphylococcus, diphtheria bacillus, and Eberth's bacillus.[81] In large doses, the oil has been known to cause strangury and/or priapism.[81]

Chemistry & Pharmacognosy: The plant contains a volatile oil; some of its constituents include pinene, caninene and camphor.[31,82] The evaporation rate is 30, the odor intensity is 5.[81] Chromatography has been done.[84]

Commercial Products & Uses: Juniper berries are most commonly used to flavor gin.[g] The berries can be picked and sold commercially.[37]

Personal Experimentation: I've collected the berries and leaves along the south shore of Lake Superior many times. The tea tastes like gin. I steeped a handful of the leaves in 2 quarts of boiling water. I drank one quart of the tea at one sitting and noticed no physical or psychological effects.

---

[g] 5,22,29,38,41,50,51,67,81,82

Juniperus communis
Juniper

LACTUCA SCARIOLA, LACTUCA SERRIOLA
Compositae
Prickly lettuce, lettuce, milkweed

Stem: Smooth, unbranched, up to 15 dm, green, often prickly, white sap.

Leaves: Alternate, clasping, twisted at the base, pinnately lobed to lobeless, prickly toothed margins, smooth, oblong to oblanceolate, 7 to 30 cm long, 1 to 10 cm wide, prickles on midrib, green.

Flower Type: Yellow flowers with an involucre, bracts, all ray flowers, often drying to blue, 10-15 mm across flower head.

Fruit: Gray achene with a pappus.

Roots: Taproot.

General: Biennial herb.

Habitat: Open fields.

Season of Availability: Gather the leaves in summer or fall. Collect the sap in the summer.

Preparation: The leaves are used in an infusion, fresh or dried. While collecting, the milky sap can be rolled into a ball. An infusion is made from the sap.

Medical Terminology: Therapeutically, lettuce appears to mainly be sedative in action.[a] Secondly, it is a diuretic.[b]

Related Disease Symptoms: A tea from the leaves was prepared by some Natives and given to women in convalescence after childbirth to hasten the flow of milk from the mammary glands.[c] The tea is also noted to induce sleep.[19,52] Gibbons said he noticed a marked relaxing effect from eating the young leaves.[19] It has been used in treating diarrhea and relieving pain from rheumatism, colic, and coughing.[19] A wash from the herb was employed to soothe sore and chapped skin.[36]

Poisonous Aspects: Large quantities ingested by cattle have proven toxic,[40] producing symptoms and lesions of pulmonary emphysema.[33]

Biological and Edible: The young leaves are considered edible.[d] The seeds can be sprouted and used as food.[86]

Chemistry & Pharmacognosy: Flowering plants contain a milky white sap which has a bitter taste and an opiate-like odor.[96] This juice is collected and dried and called lactucarium.[96] Lactucarium contains lactucin, which is a sesquiterpinoid lactone.[96] Also it contains a volatile oil, caoutchouc, and taraxasterol.[96]

---

[a] 27,36,58,63,73   [c] 36,63,73

[b] 36,38,55,63   [d] 15,19,55

Commercial Products & Uses:
In the 1700's, it was thought that *Lactuca* might be used as an opium substitute.[19] There are a number of commercial products of Lettuce Opium, with the resultant intoxicant appearing to be more fiction than fact.[96] Drug companies occasionally purchase the herb from part-time collectors.[37]

Lactuca scariola, Lactuca serriola
Prickly lettuce, lettuce, milkweed

LATHYRUS JAPONICUS
Leguminosae
Beach pea, japanese beach pea, wild pea

Stem: Up to 1.5 m long, heavy, angled stems.

Leaves: 1 to 6 cm long, pinnately compound with curling tendril at the end, leaflets oval, paired or alternate.

Flower Type: 1.4 to 3 cm long, ranging in color from deep red to blue violet, stipules shaped like arrowheads, cling to leafstalks; blooms in July and August.

Fruit: Seed pods look like small garden peas.

Habitat: Along shores and beaches; common along the Great Lakes.

Season of Availability: June through August.

Preparation: Prepare young pods as a green vegetable; boil 15 to 20 minutes.

Biological and Edible: Fresh stalks and young sprouts are edible.

Lathyrus japonicus
Beach pea, japanese beach pea, wild pea

LEDUM GROENLANDICUM
Ericaceae
Labrador tea

Stem: Standing up to 1 m tall.
Leaves: Alternate, up to 2.5 cm long, oblong, underneath covered with dark hair, untoothed, thick, leathery, dark green, with curling rims.
Flower Type: Regular, white with 5 petals, 1 cm wide, in terminal clusters, May and June.
General Information: A low evergreen shrub.
Habitat: Swampy areas, bogs, around lakes and streams.
Season of Availability: May through June.
Preparation: Commonly dried and prepared as a leaf tea.
Medical Terminology: Used as a tonic and febrifuge, the fresh leaves are chewed as a stimulant; supposedly, large quantities are cathartic.[138]

Related Disease Symptoms: The leaf tea is used for treating asthma, colds, kidney ailments, rheumatism, coughs, dysentery, and indigestion. Use the tea externally to ease burns and stings.[138]
Poisonous Aspects: Andromedotoxin is a toxic compound that has been found in honey from bees feeding on these plants.[82] It is said to be poisonous to sheep.[54]
Biological and Edible: Used by colonists to make tea during the Revolutionary War.
Chemistry & Pharmacognosy: All members of the *Ericaceae* contain andromedotoxin, which is a diterpene derivative.[82]

Ledum groenlandicum
Labrador tea

LEONURUS CARDIACA
Labiatae
Motherwort

Stem: Square, erect, sometimes branched, up to 2 m, short hairs, green.

Leaves: Opposite, petioled; bottom leaves palmately lobed, sharply toothed, 5 to 10 cm broad; upper leaves progressively more or less 3 lobed with the toothed margin changing to entire, green.

Flower Type: Purple to pale pink, 2 lipped tubular flower surrounded by stiff spines, in the leaf axils, 5 mm long, 4 stamens, summer, fall.

Fruit: Small nutlet, 2 to 4 mm across.

Roots: Fibrous roots.

General Information: Perennial herb, grows in small groups.

Habitat: Fields, shaded meadows, and waste places.

Season of Availability: Collect the herb in the summer and fall.

Preparation: Used fresh or dried in an infusion. Dried herb dose 2 to 4 grams or by infusion, liquid extract 1:1 in 25% ethanol dose 2 to 4 ml, both in t.i.d. doses.[84]

Medical Terminology: The herb is used as a tonic[a] and stimulant.[36,58] Others believe it is a diaphoretic.[b] Still others say it is a nervine and emmenagogue.[c] The British use it as a sedative and antispasmodic.[84]

Related Disease Symptoms: The herb tea has been used to reduce heart palpitations[d] and as a remedy for asthma.[36,38] One or two cups of the infusion is supposed to calm nervousness and hysteria.[22,40] At one time the herb tea was recommended for amenorrhea.[e] A cup of the tea relieved menstrual cramps.[f] British indications are cardiac debility, sinus tachycardia, and effort syndrome.[84]

Poisonous Aspects: The leaves have caused dermatitis.[46]

Chemistry & Pharmacognosy: *Leonurus* contains alkaloids, bitters, and a volatile oil.[84]

Personal Experimentation: I noticed a marked sedative effect when drinking one quart of the infusion, one ounce of the herb to one quart boiling water. I asked a female friend to drink the tea during menstruation if cramps occurred. She did and replied that it helped to relieve the cramps very well, but it was extremely bitter.

---

[a] 22,51,55 [c] 22,30,35,55

[b] 22,32,55,58

[d] 22,40,84 [f] 22,27,30,35,40,47,55

[e] 27,30,35,84

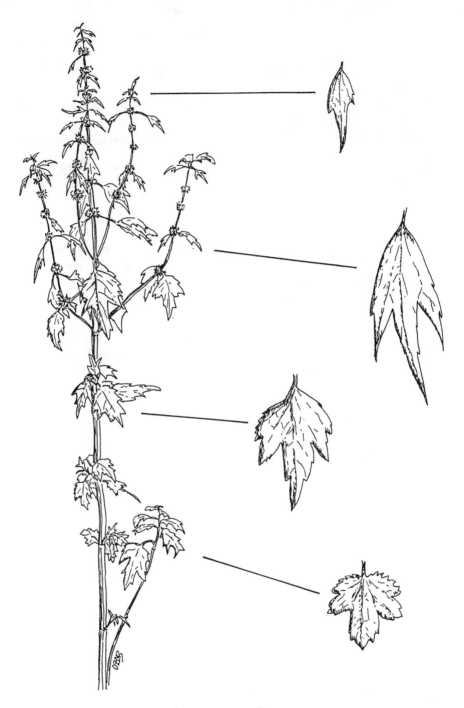

Leonurus cardiaca
Motherwort

LITHOSPERMUM CANESCENS
Boraginaceae
Hoary puccoon, Indian paint

Stem: Erect, hairy, up to 60 cm, often several from the same rootstock, green.

Leaves: Alternate, lanceolate, sessile, 5 cm long, downy, green.

Flower Type: Yellow tubular calyx with 5 lobes, 10 to 20 mm across, in terminal leafy bracted cymes, spring.

Fruit: Smooth, shiny nutlets.

Roots: Thick red taproot.

General Information: Perennial herb.

Habitat: Dry open woods and fields.

Season of Availability: The whole plant is gathered in the spring and summer while flowering.

Preparation: It is dried and ground into a powder and used in a poultice or rubbed on the skin.

Related Disease Symptoms: The leaves, stems and roots were ground into a powder and rubbed on paralyzed parts of the body in hopes of reviving them.[23,24] The ground powder was moistened and used as a poultice on painful areas to relieve rheumatism.[24]

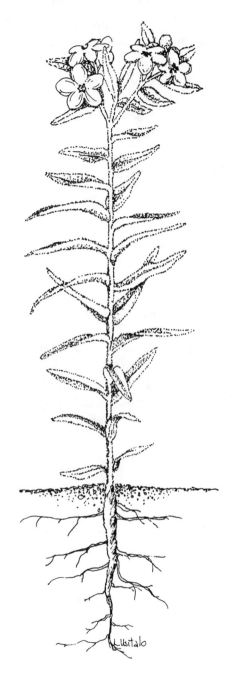

Lithospermum canescens
Hoary puccoon, Indian paint

LOBELIA INFLATA
Campanulaceae
Indian tobacco, lobelia, wild tobacco

Stem: Branched, hairy, up to 1 m, green.

Leaves: Alternate, sessile, ovate to oblong, serrate, 5-8 cm long.

Flower Type: A terminal blue to white lipped corolla, in racemes, bracts, bearded lower lip, fall, summer.

Fruit: Flowers inflate to form a seed capsule, brown, fall.

Roots: Fibrous.

General: Annual herb.

Habitat: Open woods, fields.

Season of Availability: Collect the herb in the summer when flowering. Collect when the capsules are inflated.[82,84]

Preparation: The herb is dried and used in a tincture, infusion or powder form. Dried herb dose .2 to .6 grams or by infusion or decoction, liquid extract 1:1 in 50% ethanol dose .2 to .6 ml, both in t.i.d. doses.[84]

Medical Terminology: Therapeutically, it is an expectorant[a] and antispasmodic.[b] *Lobelia* is considered a violent emetic[c] and diaphoretic in action.[d] The herb stimulates respiration.[e]

The herb tea is considered a cathartic.[40,51] The dried leaves and tops are considered official with the average dose of .1 gram.[2]

Related Disease Symptoms: Many preparations of *Lobelia* are currently used for the treatment of asthma[f] and bronchitis.[g] The herb has been prescribed as a remedy for laryngitis.[h] The tea is recommended for whooping cough.[36,51] Natives used the infusion as a wash or chewed the leaves into a poultice for sore and inflamed eyes.[i] It has been used in an ointment or wash for swellings, sprains and bruises.[22,27] Lobeline has been used to treat asphyxia in the newly born and in accidental overdoses of anesthesia.[31,40]

Poisonous Aspects: Kloss repeatedly states that *Lobelia inflata* has no harmful effects.[35] This is extremely conflicting with others who report that overdoses of the plant are dangerous[57,66] and result in nausea, vomiting, sweating, paralysis, depressed temperature, rapid

---

[a] 5,22,29,38,50,56,63,66,68,72

[b] 1,30,35,58,82,84

[c] 1,9,29,40,58,84

[d] 5,30,35,51,52,63,68,82

[e] 30,38,40,63,68,72,82,84

[f] 1,32,36,46,51,52,58

[g] 22,27,38,50,56,68,72,84

[h] 32,46,58

[i] 9,22,63

but feeble pulse, convulsions, collapse, coma and death in human beings.[j] The plant is considered poisonous.[k] Treatment is emesis, then artificial respiration, give 2 mg of atropine IM, repeat if necessary. The leaves have caused dermatitis.[46] *This plant should be employed with caution.[5]*

---

[j] 5,32,33,40,46,72,91
[k] 33,40,51,91
[l] 1,46,58,80,82,84
[m] 31,36,38,82

Chemistry & Pharmacognosy: *Lobelia* contains the alkaloids lobeline and lobelidine.[l] Lobeline has a physiological action like that of nicotine, it first excites nerves cells and then paralyzes them.[1,80] The plant contains 14 alkaloids.[82]

Commercial Products & Uses: Lobeline is used in many antitobacco therapy drugs.[m] This plant is commercially salable.[37]

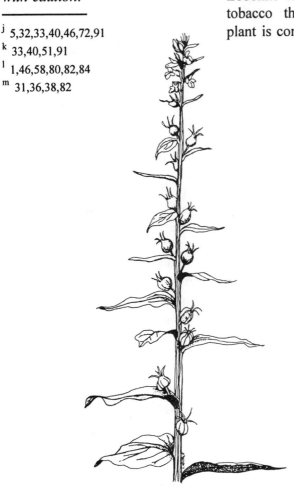

Lobelia inflata
Indian tobacco, lobelia, wild tobacco

LYCOPUS VIRGINICUS
Labiatae
Bugleweed, water-horehound

Stem: Square, smooth, erect, stoloniferous, green.

Leaves: Opposite, serrate, lance-olate to lance-ovate, pointed tip, midvein, smooth, petiolate, green, 5 to 12 cm long.

Flower Type: White, tubular, with bract in leaf axils, 2 to 4 mm long, summer, fall.

Fruit: Small nutlets.

Roots: Fibrous.

General Information: Perennial herb.

Habitat: Wet areas.

Season of Availability: The herb is collected in the summer and fall, during flowering.

Preparation: It is used dried or fresh in an infusion.

---

[a] 32,44,58
[b] 22,27,36,68

Medical Terminology: Thera-peutically, the herb has been considered sedative,[36] astrin-gent,[38,51] mildly narcotic[22,68] and tonic.[a] However, there is great skepticism as to the validity of any of these virtues.[32] Another species of *Lycopus* has been used by the British as a cardiac inotropic drug, antitussive, seda-tive, and thyroxine antagonist.[84]

Related Disease Symptoms: Its main uses appear to be in treat-ing coughs, consumption and bleeding from the lungs.[b] It has been used to treat intermittent fever[32] and diabetes.[36]

Biological and Edible: The herb has experimentally shown hypo-glycemic activity.[40]

Commercial Products & Uses: Drug companies periodically purchase this herb.[37]

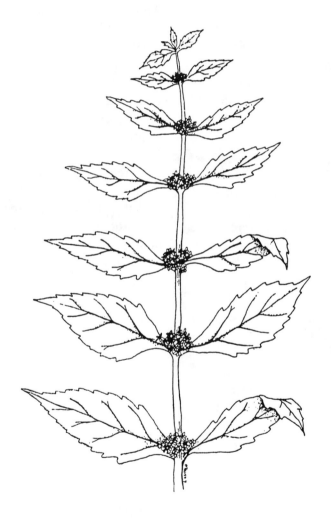

Lycopus virginicus
Bugleweed, water-horehound

MALUS SPP
Rosaceae
Apple

Stem: Woody, up to 1 m in diameter, 10 to 20 m tall, scaly bark, branching, erect.

Leaves: Green, ovate, serrate, acute, petiolate, 5-10 cm long.

Flower Type: White, 5 sepals, aromatic, 5 petals, numerous stamens, 2 to 5 styles, spring.

Fruit: Red, juicy, edible pome, up to 14 cm in diameter.

Roots: Large woody, lateral roots.

General Information: Distinct ragged shape, pioneer species, deciduous tree.

Habitat: Meadows, old fields.

Season of Availability: The round pomes, called apples, are collected in the fall and into winter.

Preparation: Apples can be eaten raw or cooked in jelly, pies, or alone. Apples can be dried easily by slicing them and placing the slices on drying racks.

Poisonous Aspects: Ingestion of large quantities of apples have caused dullness, weakness, staggering, and death in livestock.[33] There is a documented report of a man that died of cyanide poisoning from eating a cupful of apple seeds.[33]

Biological and Edible: Apples are known to be edible raw or cooked.[18,47] Bees utilize this plant for honey.[92,93]

Chemistry & Pharmacognosy: Apple seeds contain cyanide compounds.[33]

Personal Experimentation: It is common among Great Lakes people to gather apples in the fall. Many people, including myself, collect wild apples for canning, pies, jellies, and just for yearly eating. Drying apples is a relatively simple process. Slice the apples in 50 mm slices. Lay the slices on a screen in a hot attic, turn over every 24 hours; in two days they should be dried and ready for eating or storage.

Malus spp.
Apple

MARRUBIUM VULGARE
Labiatae
Horehound

Stem: Square, several stems from the rootstock, prostrate to suberect, whitish-green, woolly, up to 6 dm.

Leaves: Round opposite, round to ovate, crenate, wooly white hairs, soft, 2 to 6 cm long, petiolate, green, aromatic.

Flower Type: Small white tubular flowers in upper leaf axils, bracts, 4 to 6 mm long, 4 stamens, summer.

Fruit: Smooth nutlets, fall.

Roots: Fibrous.

General Information: Aromatic perennial herb.

Habitat: Open fields, roadsides, waste places.

Season of Availability: The leaves and stems are collected in the spring before flowering.

Preparation: The herb is dried and used in an infusion or syrup. Dried herb dose 1 to 2 grams or by infusion, liquid extract 1:1 in 20% ethanol dose 2 to 4 ml, both in t.i.d. doses.

Medical Terminology: Acts as a tonic,[66] expectorative,[a] laxative,[b] and stimulative;[c] known to produce a diaphoretic effect.[d]

Related Disease Symptoms: For coughs[50,66] and colds[e] the herb is made into a cough syrup.[f] To relieve menstrual discomfort and cramps, drink a cup of the tea every hour.[36,38] The infusion is used for pulmonary consumption and affections.[g] Horehound was used to relieve asthma.[h] A cup of the infusion treated dyspepsia.[i] A strong tea was thought to expel worms.[j]

Biological and Edible: The plant contains vitamin C.[84] Bees utilize this plant for honey.[92,93]

Chemistry & Pharmacognosy: The herb contains tannin[1,84] and the bitter principal marrubiin.[k]

Commercial Products & Uses: Horehound is used to flavor candy and throat lozenges,[l] which soothe sore throats.[m] Collecting wild horehound is still profitable in the U.S.[37]

Personal Experimentation: Chip Ranson of Houghton, MI uses horehound tea when he feels a cold coming on. He says the tea is bitter, but relieves the throat tickle that creates a persistent cough.

---

[a] 1,38,40,56,84   [d] 5,19,32,35
[b] 34,35,36,51,52   [e] 8,19,30,35,39,40,44
[c] 5,30,32,44,58
[f] 1,5,18,22,27,32,36,38,84

[g] 1,5,22,30,32,38,51,68,84
[h] 22,35,36   [k] 32,51,58
[i] 27,29,34   [l] 5,19,50,66
[j] 8,30,34,50,55   [m] 27,34,35,39,40,55

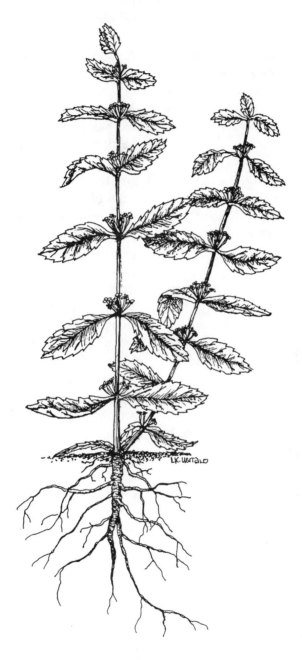

Marrubium vulgare
Horehound

183

MATRICARIA MATRICARIOIDES
Compositae
Pineapple weed, wild chamomile

Stem: Erect, branching, smooth, green, aromatic, 5 to 40 cm tall.

Leaves: Alternate, 2 to 3 times pinnately divided into narrow segments, 1 to 5 cm long, green, aromatic.

Flower Type: Yellow to green disk flowers in terminal heads, sometimes small white petals clinging to the outside, involucre bracts, many flower heads to a plant, summer, fall.

Fruit: Sliver-like achenes, small pappus, 2 to 4 mm, summer, fall.

Roots: Small taproot.

General Information: Annual herb, with a pineapple scent; common.

Habitat: Hard packed ground, open fields, roadsides.

Season of Availability: The herb is collected in the summer and fall.

Preparation: To make an infusion, the herb can be used fresh or dried.

Related Disease Symptoms: The tea has been used to cure indigestion.[47] Local residents of this area use the tea as a beverage and for indigestion.

Biological and Edible: Cheyenne women used the herb as a perfume.[24]

Personal Experimentation: I took an ounce of the herb and steeped it in a quart of boiling water. The flavor is like that of German chamomile. I noticed that it soothed my stomach when I had indigestion. I have drunk the tea many times throughout the year and never noticed any harmful effects.

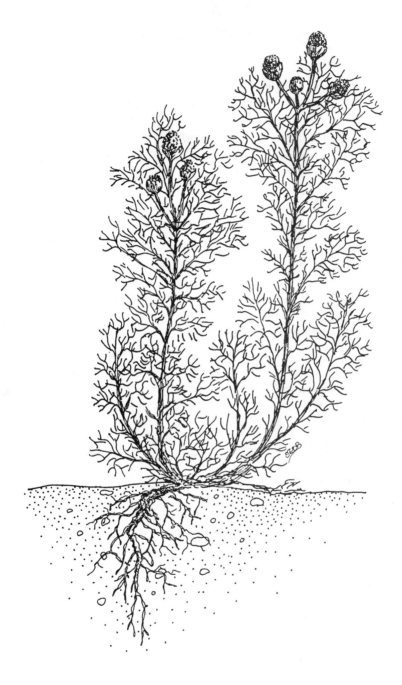

Matricaria matricarioides
Pineapple weed, wild chamomile

185

MEDICAGO SATIVA
Leguminosae
Alfalfa, lucerne

Stem: Erect to decumbent, branched, smooth, green, up to 1 m.

Leaves: Alternate, compound, 3 serrulate leaflets, oblanceolate to obovate, 1.5 to 3 cm long, stipulate, green, smooth.

Flower Type: Blue or white tubular flowers; erect peduncles; flowers in a head; 8 to 12 mm long; sepals 2 to 3 mm, summer, fall.

Fruit: 1 seeded pod, fall.

Roots: Fibrous.

General Information: Perennial herb.

Habitat: Open fields.

Season of Availability: Collect alfalfa in the summer and fall.

Preparation: It can be used fresh or dried, in an infusion or ground into a powder.

Medical Terminology: *Medicago sativa* is mainly considered a nutritive.[a]

Related Disease Symptoms: The tea has been utilized to increase appetite and weight.[b]

Poisonous Aspects: Photosensitization has been reported in cattle from ingesting large quantities of alfalfa.[33,40] There have been rare reports of death in cattle.[33]

Biological and Edible: Seeds can be sprouted and used as food.[86] Bees utilize this plant for honey.[92,93]

Chemistry & Pharmacognosy: The plant contains vitamin K.[30,58] It also contains some triterpine saponins.[40]

Personal Experimentation: I have made a drink of this herb by blending the fresh plant and a small amount of water in a blender for two minutes. I drank over a cup of the thick green liquid with two other friends; it had a strong taste, but was palatable. For years, I have sprouted the seeds and eaten the young sprouts in salads.

---

[a] 8,30,44

[b] 22,50,68

186

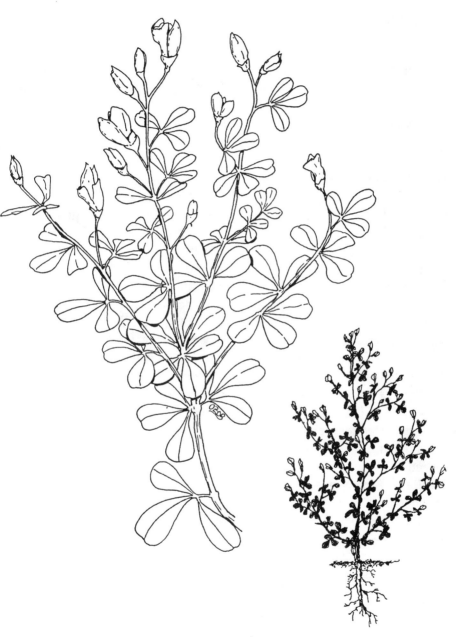

Medicago sativa
Alfalfa, lucerne

MENISPERMUM CANADENSE
Menispermaceae
Canada moonseed, yellow parilla

Stem: Woody vine, climbing, brown, 2 to 4 m.

Leaves: Alternate, suborbicular, 3 to 7 shallow lobed to entire, 10 to 15 cm long, green, smooth, bases not attached to leafstocks, sometimes nearly round with pointed tip.

Flower Type: White to greenish small flowers, 4 to 8 petals, 4 to 8 sepals, in clusters, drooping, summer.

Fruit: Bluish-black drupe, 6 to 10 mm, each contains 1 crescent-shaped seed, fall.

Roots: Taproot.

General Information: Perennial vine, deciduous, twining.

Habitat: Moist forests, thickets.

Season of Availability: Collect the rhizomes, roots in the fall.

Preparation: The roots are usually dried for storage and made into a tincture or decoction when needed.

Medical Terminology: It is considered diuretic,[38] tonic[36,63] and alterative in action.[a]

Related Disease Symptoms: The tincture or decoction has been made into a lotion to treat scrofula[9] and cutaneous, rheumatic, syphlitic or gouty affections of the skin.[b] A cup of the decoction was used to treat dyspepsia.[22,68] For arthritis, this root has been recommended in treatment.[c]

Poisonous Aspects: The fruiting berry contains sharp ridged pits that can cause mechanical damage to intestines.[46,91] There are reports of children dying from eating the berries.[33,40] Treatment is symptomatic.[91]

Chemistry & Pharmacognosy: The root contains the toxic isoquinoline alkaloids,[40] berberine and menispine.[51,58]

Commercial Products & Uses: The collected root can be sold to drug companies.[37]

---

[a] 22,32,51,58

[b] 22,32,36,68

[c] 22,32,38

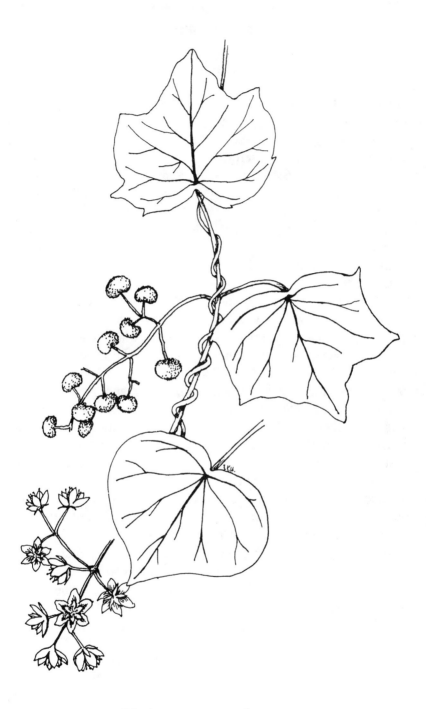

Menispermum canadense
Canada moonseed, yellow parilla

189

MENTHA PIPERITA
Labiatae
Peppermint

Stem: Square, purple, erect, smooth, branched, up to 1 m, aromatic.

Leaves: Opposite, ovate, serrate, acute, green, 3 to 6 cm, petiolate, aromatic.

Flower Type: Purple, terminal spikes, tubular, 2.5 to 4 mm, summer, fall.

Fruit: Small nutlet, 1 to 3 mm, summer, fall.

Roots: Fibrous.

General Information: Grows in clumps, perennial herb, mint flavor, propagates by the spreading roots.

Habitat: Streams and wet areas.

Season of Availability: The herb can be picked in the spring, summer or fall, though it usually has the strongest flavor during flowering. The plant can be propagated by rhizome cuttings.[82]

Preparation: The infusion is made from the fresh or dried plant. The oil is obtained by steam distillation.[82] Dried herb dose 2 to 4 grams or by infusion t.i.d.[83]

---

[a] 27,32,36,38,44,47

[b] 5,19,22,40,44,81,83

[c] 5,22,27,44,81,83

[d] 19,22,27,81

Medical Terminology: The oil is official in pharmaceutical preparations.[59,83] *Mentha piperita* is considered analgesic, antiseptic, and stomachic.[81] It has also been used as a carminative, stimulant, and counterirritant.[82,83]

Related Disease Symptoms: One or two cups of the tea is a common remedy for indigestion, colic[a] and nausea.[b] This tea has also been ingested to cure flatulence,[c] colds and flu.[d] To cure pneumonia, the Menominee made an infusion by combining equal portions of *M. piperita, M. arvensis* and *Nepeta cataria*.[74] The herb has been prescribed for diarrhea[44] and cholera.[22,68] Fresh mint contains high amounts of vitamins A and C, which is probably why it was used to cure scurvy and night blindness.[19] Peppermint oil has been used in an eyewash for inflamed eyes.[12] To ease muscular aches and rheumatic pains, rub the oil on the body.[36] Diluted peppermint oil is effective in treating ringworm, pruritis, and scabies.[81]

Biological and Edible: The leaves are edible and commonly used in salads.[25,47] The oil is considered a vasoconstrictor.[81] Bees utilize it for honey.[92,93]

190

Chemistry & Pharmacognosy: Peppermint oil is colorless or pale yellow.[82] The oil contains from 50 to 78% free menthol and 5 to 20% of other combined esters.[82,83] It also contains acetaldehyde, isovaleraldehyde, acetic acid, valeric acid, pinene, phellandrene, cineole, limonene, menthone, menthyl acetate, menthyl isovalerate, cadinene, amyl alcohol, and dimethyl sulfide.[82] The odor intensity is 7, the evaporation rate is 70.[81] Chromatography has been done.[83]

Commercial Products & Uses: Most people probably recognize peppermint as a flavoring agent in toothpaste, gum and candy.[e] The dried herb is easily sold to local buyers and some drug companies.[37]

Personal Experimentation: The leaves are edible[25,47] and I have eaten them many times in salads or just wandering in the woods. I have ingested over one quart of the infusion at one sitting and have drank this tea at least three times a week for over a year with no harmful effects. For a refreshing cooler, I highly recommend iced mint tea. Mint herb wine was one of my better experiments. Just brew a batch of strong tea, add 1 cup of sweetener per gallon of tea, add yeast, and in two weeks filter, add 10 teaspoons of sweetener, bottle, and it will be ready to drink in 10 days.

---

[e] 19,31,38,56,66,81,82

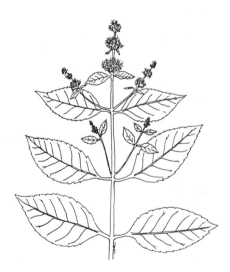

Mentha piperita
Peppermint

MENTHA SPICATA
Labiatae
Spearmint

Stem: Square, erect, smooth, 3 to 10 dm, green, branching.

Leaves: Opposite, ovate to elliptic, serrate, nearly sessile, 2 to 7 cm long, acute.

Flower Type: Pink to white tubular flowers in a terminal spikes, 1.5 to 2 mm long, summer, fall.

Fruit: Small nutlet, 1 to 3 mm, summer, fall.

Roots: Fibrous, spreading.

General: Grows in clumps, perennial herb, mint odor, propagates by the spreading roots.

Habitat: Streams and wet areas.

Season of Availability: Collect the herb in the spring, summer and fall. The strongest flavor occurs during flowering.

Preparation: The herb, dried or fresh, is utilized in an infusion. The oil is obtained by steam distillation. The dose is 4 grams of herb.[82]

Medical Terminology: Spearmint's actions are carminative,[a] stimulative[b] and aromatic.[c] It is also considered antispasmodic by some.[d] The herb and the oil have been considered official.[59]

Related Disease Symptoms: The tea is commonly taken to relieve colic, indigestion,[e] hiccough and flatulence.[22] The oil as an ointment or the tea as a wash can relieve the pain of hemorrhoids.[22] Drink a cup of the tea to prevent vomiting.[36,38] It has been used as a topical application for skin sores.[36]

Poisonous Aspects: The oil has caused contact dermatitis.[40]

Biological and Edible: The fresh leaves are edible alone or in salads.[f] Bees utilize this plant for honey.[92,93]

Chemistry & Pharmacognosy: The volatile oil contains carvone, cineole and limonene.[31,82] Other compounds include phellandrene and pinene.[82]

Commercial Products & Uses: Spearmint's widest appeal is as a flavoring agent in medicine, toothpaste, and candy.[g] Drug companies still buy the herb.[37]

Personal Experimentation: The leaves are edible[h] and I've eaten them many times. I've often made an infusion by steeping one ounce of the dried herb in one pint of water. I have drank up to a quart at one sitting with no ill effects.

---

[a] 27,38,40,51,56,82   [b] 22,32,36,68

[c] 5,32,58   [d] 22,27,51,68

[e] 22,27,32,36,38,47,68   [f] 22,36,47

[g] 38,56,66   [h] 22,36,47

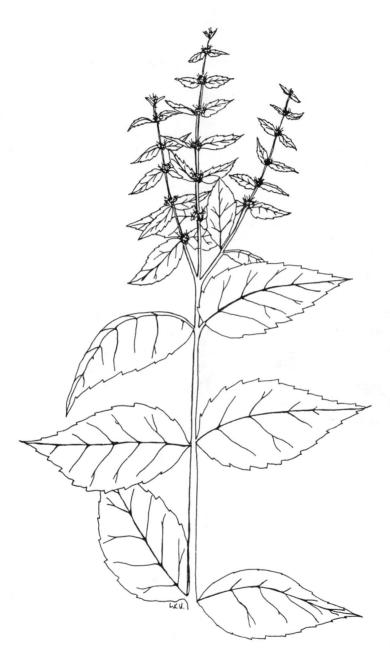

Mentha spicata
Spearmint

MITCHELLA REPENS
Rubiaceae
Partridge berry, squaw berry, squaw plum, squaw vine

Stem: Trailing, freely branching, prostrate, rooting at the nodes, mat forming, never more than 3 dm tall, green.

Leaves: Opposite, round to broadly ovate, small stipules, 1 to 2 cm, petiolate, dark green.

Flower Type: White to violet, united corolla, 4 short lobes hairy within, terminal, 10 to 14 mm across, long style, 4 stigmas, spring, summer.

Fruit: Red to scarlet double berry, crowned with the caylx, fall.

Roots: Fibrous.

General Information: Perennial evergreen, ground cover.

Habitat: Forest floors.

Season of Availability: Collect the herb and fruit in the fall.

Preparation: The herb is used in an infusion, fresh or dried. Dried plant dose 2 to 4 grams, liquid extract 1:1 in 25% ethanol dose 2 to 4 ml, both t.i.d.[83]

Medical Terminology: *Mitchella* has diuretic,[44] astringent[a] and parturifacient properties.[b] It is considered a tonic.[c] The plant was official, prescribing a 2 gram average dose.[2]

Related Disease Symptoms: Native American women drank a tea of partridge berry weeks before their parturition to render safe childbirth.[d] The tea has been taken to cure insomnia.[e] The infusion has been used to curb diarrhea and in the treatment of suppressed urine.[f] Two ounces of the herb steeped in one pint of boiling water and mixed with cream that has been thickened by boiling was used as a lotion for sore nipples.[22,30] The British use the herb to facilitate childbirth.[83]

Biological and Edible: In antibiotic experiments, partridge berry showed gram + and - bacteria inhibition.[57] The berries are edible.[15]

Chemistry & Pharmacognosy: *Mitchella* contains tannin, a bitter principle, and a saponin.[83]

Personal Experimentation: I drank 3 cups of the infusion that was steeped for 15 minutes. The taste was slightly bitter, yet bland. I didn't notice any effects. A friend drank over a quart of the tea at one sitting and said that he noticed a distinct, relaxing, sedative effect.

---

[a] 27,38,51   [b] 22,30,32,58,63,68,83
[c] 22,30,44,51   [d] 9,27,32,36,40,63
[e] 36,40,63,70,74
[f] 22,36,68

Mitchella repens
Partridge berry, squaw berry, squaw plum, squaw vine

195

MONARDA FISTULOSA
Labiatae
Wild bergamont, wild oregano

Stem: Square, often branching above, 5-15 dm tall, upper stem hirsute, green to reddish brown.
Leaves: Deltoid-lanceolate to lanceolate, opposite, serrate-dentate margins, aromatic, 1 to 4 cm broad, petiolate, bracts, green.
Flower Type: Pink, tubular, calyx tube densely bearded, 2 to 3 cm long; terminal head-like clusters, 3 to 7 cm in diameter, summer.
Fruit: Small nutlet, 1 to 3 mm, summer, fall.
Roots: Fibrous.
General: Perennial herb.
Habitat: Open woods, open fields, along forest borders.
Season of Availability: Gather the herb in summer and fall.
Preparation: Dried or fresh, it is used in an infusion. The leaves can be ground into a powder. Thymol is used in lotions, creams, and ointments in .1 to 1.0% concentrations.[82]
Medical Terminology: The main action of *Monarda* is that of a carminative.[a] It may also be considered a diaphoretic[51,55] and diuretic.[b] Thymol is an antifungal and antibacterial agent.[82]

Related Disease Symptoms: The Native Americans of this area used the infusion to relieve colic and pain in the stomach and intestines.[c] The Ojibwe boiled the plant and inhaled the fumes to treat catarrh and bronchial ailments.[d] The tea has been used to treat colds,[55,73] sore throats and fever.[36] The Winnebago drank the infusion for a cardiac stimulant.[40] To relieve headache, the dried and powdered leaves were rubbed on the forehead.[36]
Biological and Edible: Bees use this plant for honey.[92,93]
Chemistry & Pharmacognosy: *Monarda* contains thymol.[82]
Commercial Products & Uses: The leaves were used as a substitute for quinine.[51] *Monarda fistulosa* is sold in Houghton under the name wild oregano.
Personal Experimentation: A local resident from Calumet grinds the dried herb and uses it like oregano. I have drunk the infusion periodically, with no harmful effects. The taste is strong and much like that of oregano. I use the dried herb as a spice in place of oregano.

---

[a] 40,44,50,73   [c] 36,50,55,70
[b] 49,50,73   [d] 9,36,40,70,74,75

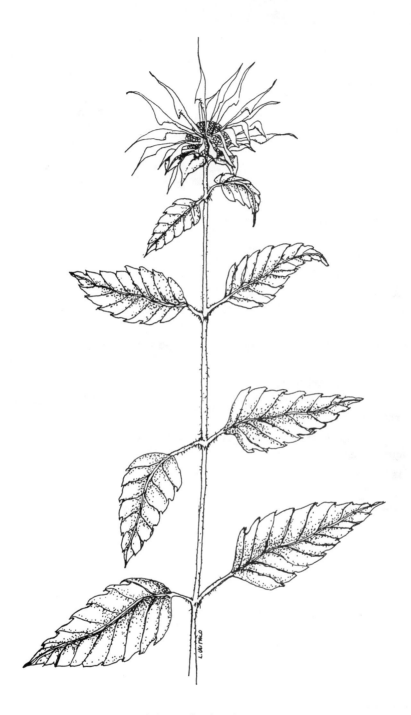

Monarda fistulosa
Wild bergamont, wild oregano

MONOTROPA UNIFLORA
Pyrolaceae (Ericaceae)
Indian pipe, corpse-plant, convulsion-root, fits-root

Stem: White, erect, fleshy, waxy, smooth, turns black when dried, 5 to 30 cm tall.

Leaves: Alternate, scale-like white appendages.

Flower Type: Solitary, fleshy white, nodding, bell-shaped, 10 to 17 mm, summer.

Fruit: Ovoid capsules, tiny, fall.

Roots: Fibrous.

General Information: Parasitic on roots or decomposing vegetable matter, perennial herb.

Habitat: Forest floors.

Season of Availability: The whole plant is collected during the summer.

Preparation: The stem and leaves are usually used fresh, but can be used dried. The root is dried and powdered.

Related Disease Symptoms: The plant was smashed, mixed with water and applied to sore and inflamed eyes as a cure.[a] To treat epilepsy and convulsions in children, the dried powdered root was administered in tea form.[36] Potawatomi women drank a tea made from the roots to alleviate female troubles.[76] *Monotropa* has been used to relieve pain and induce sleep.[36]

Biological and Edible: Indian pipe is edible cooked or raw.[15,34]

Personal Experimentation: I have eaten the plant raw; it is very bland and tasteless. In the forests surrounding Wheal Kate Bluff, outside of South Range, MI, the floor is literally covered with *Monotropa*.

---

[a] 9,36,40,69

Monotropa uniflora
Indian pipe, corpse-plant, convulsion-root, fits-root

MORCHELLA SEMILIBERA, M. ANGUSTICEPS, M. ESCULENTA, M. DELICIOSA

Ascomycetes

Morels, black morel, white morel

Stem: Grows by proliferating hyphae, small white filaments.

Leaves: None.

Flower Type: There is no true flower, the sexual part being the head of the mushroom-like fruit. The head is cone-shaped, composed of ridges and pits, pale tan-gray.

Fruit: The fruit is the stem and head of the fungus. The stem of the fruit is white and the head has ridges and pits. The spores are in the pits of the heads.

Roots: The hyphae is filamentous and long.

General: Perennial.

Habitat: Grows in pioneer forests and meadows.

Season of Availability: The fruiting mushrooms are collected in the spring. **Avoid morel-like mushrooms in the summer and fall**; they are only look-alikes.

Preparation: The fruiting mushrooms are collected and eaten.

Biological and Edible: The mushrooms are edible and considered choice.

Commercial Products & Uses: These mushrooms can be collected and sold to specialty stores such as the American Spoon in Petosky, Michigan.

Personal Experimentation: Many times I have wandered throughout the Great Lakes area in search of morels. The most I've ever come across was one spring out on Government Island in northern Lake Huron. To my surprise, on a meager spring outing I stumbled across a bucket full in a small area around 30 meters in diameter. I like to use them in soups, fried, and occasionally if there is enough, I'll dry what's left for future use.

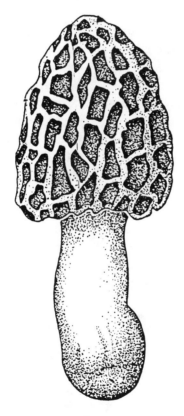

Morchella semilibera, M. angusticeps,
M. esculenta, M. deliciosa
Morels, black morel, white morel

201

MORUS RUBRA
Moraceae
Red mulberry, mulberry

Stem: Hairless.

Leaves: Simple, alternate, fine-toothed, 1.7 to 1.5 cm long, rough above, hairy underneath.

Flower Type: Greenish-white, composed of dense spikes, spring.

Fruit: Blackberry-like fruit, densely clustered, one-seeded drupes, red when unripe, ripening to purple.

General Information: The tree grows 6 to 10 m high, contains milky sap.

Habitat: Open woods.

Season of Availability: Fruit found May through July.

Medical Terminology: Used as a febrifuge and sedative, the juice is a mild narcotic.[138]

Related Disease Symptoms: The inner bark boiled into a syrup or tea is used as a purgative or laxative for children. The Native Americans near the Rappahannock River rubbed the sap on their skin to avoid ringworm. They made an infusion from the outer bark and drank the tea to expel worms.[138]

Poisonous Aspects: The shoots and unripe fruit contain hallucinogens; large doses of the berries may cause vomiting.

Biological and Edible: The berries may be eaten fresh or put in jellies. When the shoots are very young and tender they may be eaten as a green vegetable if boiled for 20 minutes.

Morus rubra
Red mulberry, mulberry

MYRICA GALE
Myricaceae
Sweet gale, gale, bog gale

Stem: Woody

Leaves: Aromatic, thin, wedge-shaped, blunt-tipped, gray-green with spots on underside, tip is toothed, 2.5 to 7.5 cm long.

Fruit: Compact cones of tiny nutlets.

General Information: Deciduous, fern-like perennial bush, 1 m high.

Habitat: Swamps, bogs.

Season of Availability: The fruit can be gathered in the summer, fall, and winter.

Preparation: Prepare in an infusion.

Related Disease Symptoms: The tea is used as a wash for poison ivy, blisters, and sores. A strong tea can be taken internally to relieve cramps and diarrhea. It can be used as a diuretic, or taken at childbirth to ease delivery.[138]

Myrica gale
Sweet gale, gale, bog gale

NASTURTIUM OFFICINALE
Cruciferae
Watercress

Stem: Floating, prostrate stems, freely rooting, succulent, smooth, green, mat forming.

Leaves: Alternate, pinnately compound, 3 to 11 roundish to oblong leaflets, green, entire, 15 to 25 cm long.

Flower Type: White, small, 4 petals, 2 to 5 mm, across, in racemes, spring, summer, fall.

Fruit: Slender silique, 1 to 3 cm long, on a pedicle, green, spring, summer, fall.

Roots: Fibrous.

General Information: Perennial herb, common.

Habitat: In slow moving streams, usually cool water.

Season of Availability: The plant can be collected in any season.

Preparation: The fresh plant is utilized raw in salads or cooked as a potherb.

Medical Terminology: Watercress is considered an antiscorbutic[a] because it is rich in vitamin C[27,58] and vitamin A.[36,38] In Africa, watercress has been thought to be an aphrodisiac.[36]

Related Disease Symptoms: The herb was freshly eaten for kidney and heart ailments.[38,58] The crushed macerated plant put into cold water was a remedy for tuberculosis.[b] The juices of the plant have been used to clear the skin of pimples and spots.[22,50] The herb is used to treat colds, asthma[36] and sore throats.[48] Eating watercress in a salad helps promote the appetite.[22,32]

Poisonous Aspects: Because watercress may cause an abortion, pregnant women are warned not to use it.[38] Interestingly enough, another text said that Native American women ate it during labor.[52]

Biological and Edible: The plant is edible and considered a great salad green.[c]

Personal Experimentation: I have collected and eaten this plant at all times of the year. During the summer it gets to be bitter, but blanching makes it much more palatable.

---

[a] 22,32,58

[b] 22,36,38

[c] 8,18,22,25,32,34,47

Nasturtium officinale
Watercress

NEPETA CATARIA
Labiatae
Catnip, catmint

Stem: Square, erect, whitish-green, downy, branched, up to 1 m.

Leaves: Opposite, round to kidney-shaped, petiolate, crenate, green, whitish downy green on the bottom, 3-8 cm long.

Flower Type: White with purple dots or stripes, in whorls or terminal spikes, tubular corolla, 2 lipped, 2 to 6 mm long, summer, fall.

Fruit: Small nutlet, 1 to 3 mm, summer, fall.

Roots: Fibrous.

General: Grows in small groups, perennial, aromatic.

Habitat: Fields, shaded fields, meadows, waste places.

Season of Availability: The herb is collected in the summer when in flower.

Preparation: The herb is used dried or fresh in an infusion. The oil is obtained by steam distillation. Dried herb dose 2 to 4 grams, liquid extract 1:1 in 25% ethanol dose 2 to 4 ml, both t.i.d.[83]

Medical Terminology: Catnip is used as a carminative,[a] stimulant[51,58] and emmenagogue.[b] It is also considered tonic,[c] diaphoretic[22,51] and antispasmodic.[d] The dried ground leaves have been smoked as an intoxicant.[40] The dried flowering tops are official.[2]

Related Disease Symptoms: Catnip's main use has been to treat colic[e] and flatulence.[f] The tea is highly recommended in infantile colic.[g] Hot catmint tea has induced sleep.[h] The tea of the leaves has been used to reduce fever.[i] For years, the tea has been a cold remedy.[j] The tea is thought to relieve nervous conditions[k] and headaches caused by nervousness.[l] The Menominee used the tea to treat pneumonia[63,74] (see *Mentha piperita*). The Chippewa mixed the leaves with *Tanacetum vulgare* leaves and used the infusion for fever.[10] The tea is used to bring on delayed menstruation.[m] To treat painful swellings, the leaves were crushed and applied as a poultice.[n]

---

[a] 27,35,44,56,83

[b] 5,10,19,22,30,38,68

[c] 5,10,39

[d] 19,30,83

[e] 19,36,55,83

[f] 8,22,27,30,44

[g] 19,32,40,83

[h] 18,19,22,52,55,83

[i] 10,19,55

[j] 22,30,36,38,40, 55,63,83

---

[k] 5,36,38,55

[l] 22,30,35,83

[m] 5,19,32,36,38

[n] 22,36,52,63

To relieve respiratory affections, the leaves were smoked.[36,38] The chewed leaves reportedly relieve toothaches.[5,40] Another remedy applied to aching teeth was catnip leaves mixed with cloves and sassafras and applied in a poultice.[40]

Biological and Edible: Bees use this plant for honey.[92,93]

Chemistry & Pharmacognosy: The volatile oil is about 85% nepetalactone.[31] Other compounds include citral, citronellol, geraniol, a bitter principle, and tannins.[83]

There are cases of using catnip to get "high" by smoking the herb or volatile oil with reports of giddiness and euphoria.[96]

Commercial Products & Uses: The plant is still sold commercially.[37]

Personal Experimentation: I have drunk over a quart of the infusion and noticed no effects, except slight perspiration. It tastes minty with a bitter accent.

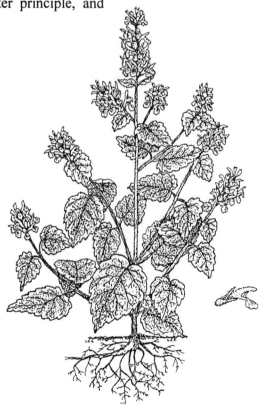

Nepeta cataria
Catnip, catmint

OSMORHIZA LONGISTYLIS
claytoni → *nearly smooth*
Umbelliferae
Anise-root, sweet cicely

Stem: Slender, smooth, erect, green, aromatic, 1 to 1.2 m tall.

Leaves: Alternate, compound, 2 to 3 times ternate, leaflets glabresent beneath, green, stipulate, 4 to 7 cm long.

Flower Type: Tiny white flowers, double umbels, above leaves, styles are longer than the petals, 1 mm across, summer.

Fruit: Ribbed carpel, cylindric, brown, 1.2 to 1.5 cm long, summer, fall.

Roots: Thick fibrous roots, anise flavor.

General Information: Perennial herb, aromatic.

Habitat: Rich forests.

Season of Availability: The roots are collected during the summer and fall.

Preparation: The roots are used in a decoction, either fresh or dried.

Medical Terminology: The roots are considered to have aromatic, carminative and stomachic activity.[10,51]

Related Disease Symptoms: The Cheyenne made a tea from the roots for tight or bloated stomachs.[24] Native Americans used the decoction as a wash for sore and inflamed eyes.[a] Ojibwe women drank a tea from the roots to ease parturition.[75] Local Native Americans used a tea of the roots as a gargle for sore throat.[75] To regain flesh and strength, the Meskwaki drank a tea made from the roots of *Osmorhiza longistylis* and *Gleditsia tricanthes*.[73]

Biological and Edible: The roots are known to have a strong anise flavor.[15,34]

Personal Experimentation: I have made teas from the roots and found the anise flavor weak in the specimen I experimented with. No ill effects were encountered.

---

[a] 24,73,75

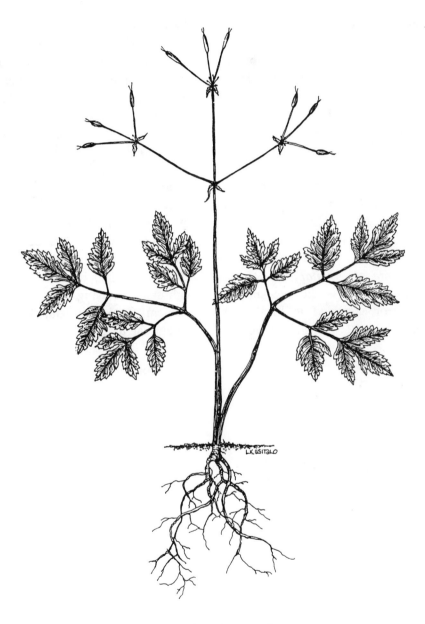

Osmorhiza longistylis
Anise-root, sweet cicely

OSMUNDA CINNAMONEA
Osmundaceae
Cinnamon-fern, buckhorn, fiddle-heads

Stem: Underground rhizomes.

Leaves: Dimorphic fronds, up to 2 m, oblong lanceolate, edible in early spring, while in a fiddle-head.

Flower Type: Fertile frond, reddish-brown, up to 1 m.

Fruit: Microscopic brown spores.

Roots: Lateral off stolons.

General Information: Grows in groups, common, perennial.

Habitat: Stream banks, moist woods.

Season of Availability: These are collected in the late spring. The time period is local and rarely lasts longer than 2 weeks.

Preparation: Only the curled up frond looking like a fiddlehead is collected. Once the frond starts unraveling, it becomes bitter. The fiddle-heads can be eaten raw as a salad green or cooked in stews or soups. They can also be placed in pickle juice for a great pickle.

Biological and Edible: The spring fiddle-heads are edible raw or cooked.[15,47]

Personal Experimentation: I find the raw fiddle-heads leave a strong aftertaste, but in a salad with salad dressing, there is no problem. Cooked in soups, they are similar to asparagus.

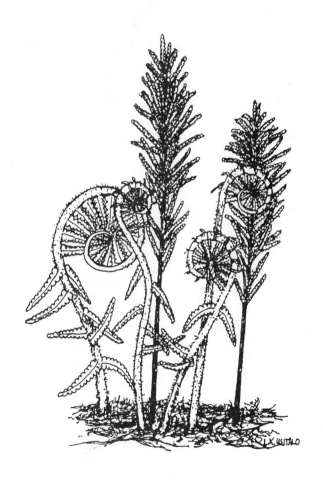

Osmunda cinnamonea
Cinnamon-fern, buckhorn, fiddle-heads

PANAX QUINQUEFOLIUS
Araliaceae
Ginseng, sang

Stem: Unbranched, smooth, 2 to 6 dm tall, green, erect.

Leaves: Whorl of 3 palmately compound leaves, 3-7 (usually 5) oblong-ovate to ovate leaflets, serrate, acuminate, green, leaflets from 6 to 15 cm long, green.

Flower Type: Greenish-white, perfect, terminal umbel, 2 styles, 1 to 2 mm, spring.

Fruit: Bright red berry, 1 cm in diameter, summer.

Roots: Fusiform taproot, 1 to 4 dm long.

General: Perennial herb, lives 20-30 years, though there are stories of thousand-year-old plants;[42] rare in this area.

Habitat: Rich forests.

Season of Availability: Collect the roots in the fall from plants that are over 5 years old.[19,65] Some say that 3 year plants are acceptable.[36,38] Over 220,000 pounds of ginseng are exported from the U.S. yearly.[82]

Preparation: The root is prepared in many different ways. The easiest is in a decoction, either fresh or dried. However, some people eat the dried root daily for health purposes.

Dried root dose 1 to 2 grams or by decoction t.i.d.[83]

Medical Terminology: There is no scientific proof of any of ginseng's therapeutic values.[42,65] However, it is considered a stimulant,[a] stomachic[b] and an aromatic bitter.[c] The Chinese consider ginseng a great aphrodisiac[d] and tonic.[e] Many Asians pay high prices for the root because of its believed panacea properties.[f] Dr. Lo Yu Guang, a cardiologist at Hospital 254 in Tianjin, China, treats Sick Sinus Syndrome, a cardiac dysrhythmia, by having patients chew and swallow 1.5 to 3 grams of ginseng root each day.

Related Disease Symptoms: Prolonged intake of ginseng is said to promote longevity and good health.[g] Ginseng has been used to cure nervous complaints,[22,68] headaches, fevers[36] and cramps.[63] Long use of the tea is thought to promote fertility in women.[63] The tea is also used to relieve menstrual discomfort.[63] The tea was taken internally to stimulate the appetite[40] and aid digestion.[22,68] The tea supposedly relieves consumption, spasmodic

---

[a] 32,36,66

[b] 19,22,35,63,68,74

[c] 58,65,83

[d] 42,50,65

[e] 19,22,36,38,63

[f] 27,38,40,42,44,50,63,66

[g] 19,27,42

212

disorders, and dyspepsia.[h] The Chinese utilize the infusion as a heart tonic.[65] The tea is drunk to stop or prevent vomiting.[i] Chewing the root is supposed to strengthen the stomach against indigestion.[63] It has been used in the treatment of anemia, gastritis, insomnia, diabetes, sexual impotence, and neurasthenia.[82,83]

Biological and Edible: The Meskwaki tribe used the root as a seasoner to make other remedies more powerful.[73]

---

[h] 19,22,63,68

[i] 22,63,68

Chemistry & Pharmacognosy: Ginseng contains a mixture of triterpenoid saponins that are separated into three categories: the panaxosides, the ginsenosides, and the chikusetsusaponins.[82,83]

Commercial Products & Uses: Collectors can easily sell their roots to many drug companies.[37]

Personal Experimentation: I have drunk ginseng tea many times. It is slightly bitter and produces a slight stimulating effect when large quantities are consumed.

Panax quinquefolius
Ginseng, sang

PHYTOLACCA AMERICANA
Phytolaccaceae
Pokeweed, poke, poke salad, scoke, garget, pigeonberry

Stem: Smooth reddish-purple stem; grows up to 4 m tall.

Leaves: Alternate, large, ovate.

Flower Type: White clusters, blooms from July to September.

Fruit: Green when young, berry is glossy, dark purple with a seed in each of 10 cells, red stem.

Roots: Dark, up to 1.5 dm in diameter.

Habitat: Open woods, on roadsides.

Season of Availability: *Phytolacca* is the dried root collected in the fall.[84]

Preparation: Dried root dose .06 to .3 grams or by decoction, liquid extract 1:1 in 45% ethanol dose .1 to .5 ml, both in t.i.d. doses.[84]

Medical Terminology: Actions are thought to be antirheumatic, anticatarrhal, mild anodyne, and in large doses a purgative, parasiticide, emetic, and fungicide.[84]

Related Disease Symptoms: Its indications include chronic rheumatism, tonsillitis, laryngitis, chronic respiratory catarrh, sillitis, adenitis, mastitis, and mumps.[84] Topically it is utilized in scabies, tinea, sycosis, acne, mammary abscess, and mastitis.[84]

Poisonous Aspects: Symptoms of poisoning include a burning and bitter taste in the mouth, persistent vomiting, amblyopia, respiratory depression, dyspnea, seizures, weakness, and tremors. Treatment is gastric lavage or emesis.[91]

Biological and Edible: The plant has immunosuppressive properties.[91] After two boilings, the spring leaves are edible.

Chemistry & Pharmacognosy: *Phytolacca* contains phytolaccine, phytolaccic acid, resins, tannins, and sugars.[84] Chromatography has been done.[84]

214

Phytolacca americana
Pokeweed, poke, poke salad, scoke, garget, pigeonberry

215

PINUS STROBUS
Pinaceae
White pine

Stem: Woody, erect tree, rough furrowed black bark, up to 70 m, young trees have smooth black bark.

Leaves: Alternate, linear needles, 5 needles to a follicle, triangular cross section, 8 to 13 cm long, green.

Flower Type: Monoecious; oval staminate flowers, orange catkin-like cones, 2 to 4 cm long; pistilate flowers in hard bracted, subcylindrical cones, nodding, resinous, 6 to 25 cm long, brown, flowers in the spring.

Fruit: 2 seeded winged nuts per cone bract, fall of second year after fertilization.

Roots: Large taproot.

General Information: Soft wood, perennial evergreen, valuable timber wood.

Habitat: Forests and sandy-loam sites.

Season of Availability: Collect the inner bark and buds in the spring. Collect the sap and needlelike leaves in any season.

Preparation: The inner bark is dried, then it can be boiled and eaten or made into a decoction. The buds and leaves are made into an infusion, usually fresh.

The resinous sap is put in hot water and made into an infusion, liniment or ointment. Pine tar can be made from most *Pinus* species.[82]

Medical Terminology: Everyone seems to agree that the white pine is an expectorant.[a] Pine tar is a local irritant and an antibacterial agent.[82]

Related Disease Symptoms: To relieve headache, the Ojibwe crushed or boiled the leaves and applied them to the forehead.[63,70] The Ojibwe also put the leaves in a small hole in the ground, placed hot stones on top of the leaves and inhaled the rising vapor to cure backache and headache.[63,70] The Menominee steeped the inner bark of the young trees and drank the tea to relieve chest pains.[63,70] To heal wounds and sores[27,70] and as a plaster for burns and scalds, Natives pounded the bark and used it as a poultice.[b] The Chippewa boiled the trunk of the young tree with the inner bark of *Prunus serotina* and *Prunus americana* until it was a mash, then the mash was dried and resoaked in water when needed for a poultice on cuts and skin sores.[10] The bark tea was thought useful in urinary and

---

[a] 22,27,35,36,38,44,51,58,63,68,82

[b] 36,52,63

216

kidney troubles.[64] Some tribes used the inner bark made into a poultice to relieve piles.[63] The needles have a high concentration of vitamin C[19] and were used to cure scurvy.[47] Natives used the male cones or strobili in a liniment for rheumatism.[63] Some utilized a decoction of the gummy sap for sore throats, colds and consumption.[c] The gum has also been used to relieve rheumatic and muscular aches.[35,36]

Biological and Edible: The inner bark is edible.[d] The seeds are also edible.

Chemistry & Pharmacognosy: The volatile oil contains the compounds bornyl acetate, pinene, carene and cadinene.[31,82]

[c] 22,44,52,63,68

[d] 15,19,79

[e] 19,22,27,35,52,68

Commercial Products & Uses: The volatile oil is considered antiseptic[27,38] and is commercially used in inhalants.[31] The dried inner bark is made into a cough syrup[e] that is an official pharmaceutical preparation.[2] The inner bark can be collected and sold to drug companies.[37] The commercial product Prunicodeine contains White Pine extract.[82]

Personal Experimentation: I steeped two ounces of the leaves in one quart of boiling water for 15 minutes. I drank the quart of tea at one sitting, and thought it was a good tea. It has an aftertaste like turpentine. I drank a cup of the tea almost every day for one month and noticed no unusual effects.

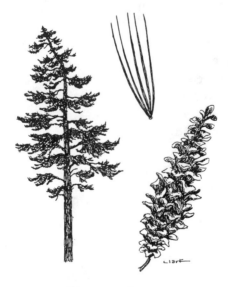

Pinus strobus
White pine

PLANTAGO MAJOR
Plantaginaceae
Plantain, whiteman's foot

Stem: Stemless.

Leaves: Rosette, thick, broadly elliptic to oval, strongly nerved, smooth, entire to undulate, green, 5 to 20 cm long.

Flower Type: White, 4 sepals, small, up to 1 mm; spike heads on a tall scape, conic shape, spring, summer, fall.

Fruit: Brown conic capsule, summer, fall.

Roots: Fibrous.

General: Perennial herb.

Habitat: Fields, yards, roadsides, hard packed ground.

Season of Availability: Collect the leaves in the summer and fall. Collect the seeds in the late summer. The commercial herb *Plantago major* consists of the dried leaves gathered during the flowering season.[84]

Preparation: The leaves are usually used fresh, in a poultice or ground into an ointment. Soak the seeds in water and use in a cold or hot tea. Dried leaves dose 2 to 4 grams or by infusion, liquid extract 1:1 in 25% ethanol dose 2 to 4 ml, both t.i.d.[84]

Medical Terminology: It is considered diuretic in action.[a] It appears to have some properties of a vulnerary[27,38] and tonic.[36] The seeds soaked in water and ingested are used as a laxative.[b]

Related Disease Symptoms: Plantain has mainly been used to treat cuts, scratches and wounds.[c] In these cases a poultice of crushed or macerated leaves is applied to the wound. The fresh leaves rubbed on the skin are supposed to relieve insect bites or stings.[d] The Rappahannock Native Americans bound the bruised leaves to the body to reduce fever.[63] The Menominee heated the leaves and applied them to swellings.[70] The Chippewa took the finely chopped roots of *Asarum canadense*, spread them on a plantain leaf and used it as a poultice on skin inflammations.[10] Plantain leaves have been used as a poultice to stop rectal itch from piles.[e] The fresh roots or leaves were boiled and applied to sore nipples for relief.[36]

Chemistry & Pharmacognosy: *Plantago* contains the glycoside aucubin, a mucilage, ascorbic acid, and protocatechuic acid.[84]

---

[a] 22,30,50,57,58,68,84
[b] 34,36,50,56   [e] 38,44,50,84
[c] 8,22,27,30,36,38,44,50,52
[d] 8,22,27,40,50,68

***Commercial Products & Uses*:**
Seeds of other *Plantago* species
are utilized in commercial laxative products.[82]

***Personal Experimentation*:** I
have used the crushed leaves
many times on scratches and
cuts and amazingly enough they
always got better, never worse.
While hiking on Isle Royale, my
father used the crushed leaves to
help heal his blisters.

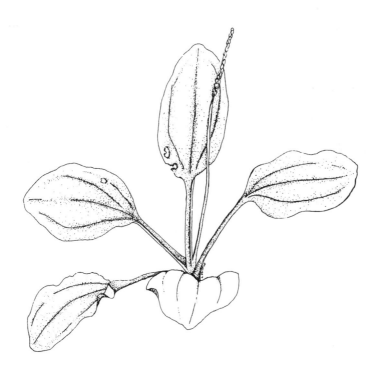

Plantago major
Plantain, whiteman's foot

PODOPHYLLUM PELTATUM
Berberidaceae
May apple, mandrake, wild jalap, jalap

Stem: Smooth, only 3 to 5 dm tall.

Leaves: Large and umbrella-like, deeply 3 to 5 parted, stem attached to the middle.

Flower Type: White to off-white, 6 or 9 petals, 2 to 3 cm long. Blooms from April to early June.

Fruit: 2 to 5 cm long, yellow.

Habitat: Open woods and fields.

Season of Availability: Collect the roots in the fall after the herb has died.[82] Several hundred tons are harvested each year for production.[82] Collect the edible yellow fruits in July.

Preparation: The roots and rhizomes are used in a decoction or the resin is extracted with solvents.[82] The fruits can be eaten fresh off the plant, or cooked into jams, pies, or jellies. Dried rhizome dose .12 to .6 grams, liquid extract 1:1 in 90% ethanol dose .3 to .7 ml, in t.i.d. doses.[84]

Medical Terminology: It has been utilized as a purgative.[82,84] *Podophyllum* resin is used for its caustic properties to destroy papillomas usually caused by wart viruses.[82,84] Other indications include sialogogue and choleretic.[84]

Related Disease Symptoms: *Podophyllum* is used topically for the removal of venereal warts.[82,84]

Poisonous Aspects: The resin is cytotoxic and may be embryopathic.[84] Pregnancy is a contraindication.[84] Symptoms of poisoning include a strong laxative effect.[91] Topically, it may produce contact dermatitis.[91] Treatment is symptomatic.[91]

Chemistry & Pharmacognosy: It contains podophyllotoxin, alpha, and beta peltatin.[82,84] The resin called podophyllin is the widely used drug.[82]

Personal Experimentation: I have accidently dropped *podophyllum* resin on my skin; it burned and destroyed the skin in the local area by the next day. Many times I have eaten the wild yellow fruits with no ill effects. They taste very sweet and are similar to plums in texture.

Podophyllum peltatum
May apple, mandrake, wild jalap, jalap

221

POLYGALA SENEGA
Polygalaceae
Seneca-snakeroot

Stem: Numerous from the rootstock, unbranching, smooth, 1 to 5 dm tall, green.

Leaves: Alternate, numerous, linear-lanceolate to ovate, acuminate, serrulate, 1 to 7 cm long, 2 to 15 mm wide, green.

Flower Type: White, in solitary terminal racemes, winged, 2 to 5 mm long, spring, summer.

Fruit: Rounded capsules, 2.5 to 3.5 mm long, brown.

Roots: Thick crown, stout, rhizome, prostrate main root.

General: Perennial herb.

Habitat: Dry rocky fields.

Season of Availability: The root is collected in the fall.

Preparation: The root is dried and prepared in a tincture or decoction. Dried root dose .5-1 gram or by infusion, liquid extract 1:1 in 60% ethanol dose .3 to 1 ml, both in t.i.d. doses.[84]

Medical Terminology: *Polygala* has many therapeutic actions. It is considered an expectorant,[a] emetic[b] and cathartic.[c] Some other actions attributed to it are diuretic,[38,51] diaphoretic[d] and emmenagogue.[e]

It also has been considered as a sialagogue.[f] Less than 70 years ago, the dried roots were official.[2]

Related Disease Symptoms:
Many Natives thought the root would cure rattlesnake bite[g] by chewing the root and applying it to the bite.[63] However, it appears to be useless for that purpose.[5] The decoction has been used to treat bronchitis and asthma.[h] The decoction was supposedly able to cure gout and pleurisy.[36,63] Because of the emetic and purgative action, it has been found to be useful in treating dropsy (congestive heart failure)[22,68] and rheumatism.[i] The decoction has been utilized as a stimulating expectorant in pulmonary affections.[j] It has also been used for heart trouble.[k] The decoction has removed unwanted catarrhal deposits in the bronchial area.[l] The Ojibwe used a leaf infusion for sore throats and a tea of the roots for coughs and colds.[63] The tea has treated amenorrhea and dysmenorrhea.[5,63]

---

[a] 1,27,30,66
[b] 29,58,63,72,84
[c] 5,32,36,38,44,51
[d] 22,30,32,58,63,72,84
[e] 5,22,36

[f] 5,22,30,72,84
[g] 27,36,40
[h] 5,66,72,84
[i] 5,32,63

[j] 32,36,63
[k] 5,36,63
[l] 22,27,32,68

Poisonous Aspects: The plant is the source of a poisonous irritant drug.[33,66] Overdoses have caused violent vomiting and nausea.[22] There are reports of similar species that have been suspected in poisoning horses.[33]

Biological and Edible: *Polygala senega* appears to affect the heart like digitalis.[51]

Chemistry & Pharmacognosy: The plant contains two saponin glucosides, senegin and polygalic acid[51,58] and a small trace of methyl salicylate.[1,84] Chromatography has been done.[84]

Commercial Products & Uses: Drug companies still buy the root from part-time collectors.[37]

Polygala senega
Seneca-snakeroot

POLYGONATUM BIFLORUM
Liliaceae
Solomon's seal

Stem: Slender, erect, curving or arching, smooth, green, 2-9 dm.

Leaves: Alternate, parallel veined, sessile, narrowly lanceolate to broadly oval, smooth, green, 5 to 15 cm long, 1 to 8 cm wide.

Flower Type: Greenish white, hanging in pairs from the leaf axils, tubular perianth, 14 to 25 mm long, spring.

Fruit: Blue to black several seeded berry, summer.

Roots: Knotty rhizome, prostrate, just below the surface, whitish, rootlets are fibrous, 5 to 10 cm long.

General Information: Perennial herb, grows in small clumps.

Habitat: Rich forest floors.

Season of Availability: The root is gathered in the fall.

Preparation: The root can be used dried or fresh in a decoction or an infusion. Some prefer to powder the root before use.

Medical Terminology: Therapeutically, the root is considered astringent,[50] tonic[38,51] and demulcent.[a]

Related Disease Symptoms: The root has lessened irritation of mucous surfaces.[32,58]

A wash made from the boiled root was used to treat poison ivy.[b] This same wash has been used for erysipelas[22,51] and skin sores.[50] The cut up roots were boiled in water and used as a poultice or wash to heal and relieve pain from hemorrhoids.[c] The root tea was thought to relieve pulmonary consumption and heal bleeding lungs.[22,68] The fresh root has been used as a poultice for bruises[50] and black eyes.[22] The roots were also used to treat pain from arthritis, rheumatism[36] and gout.[51]

Poisonous Aspects: The berries contain an anthraquinone that can cause vomiting and diarrhea.[40]

Biological and Edible: The young shoots are cooked and eaten like asparagus.[15,22] The roots are considered edible.[22,79]

Commercial Products & Uses: Drug companies periodically purchase the roots.[37]

Personal Experimentation: I have made a tea from one ounce of the root to one pint of water. The tea was very bland. I noticed no effects from drinking two cups.

---

[a] 22,30,68

[b] 32,36,50

[c] 22,30,36,50

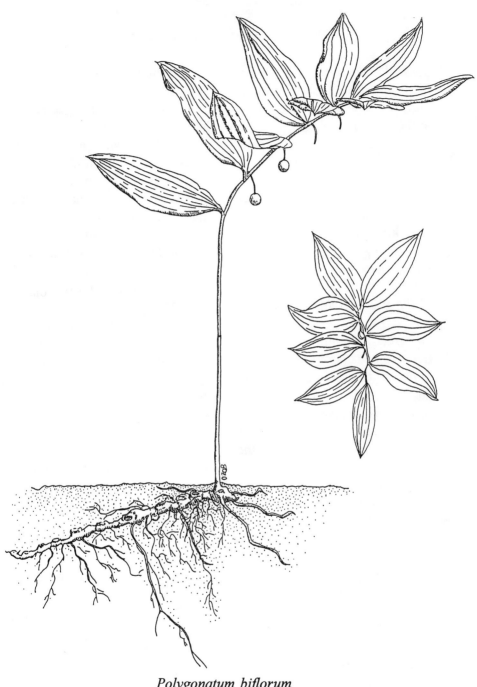

Polygonatum biflorum
Solomon's seal

225

POPULUS BALSAMIFERA
Salicaceae
Balsam poplar, hackmatack

Stem: Woody tree, up to 30 m high, corrugated black bark at the bottom, smooth yellow bark at the top.

Leaves: Alternate, acuminate, broadly lanceolate to ovate, sub-cordate at the base, shiny on the upper surface, petiolate, dark green, over wintering in large resinous buds.

Flower Type: The flowers are dioecious catkins, staminate and pistilate, that appear in spring.

Fruit: Winged capsule, summer.

Roots: Taproot.

General: Perennial deciduous tree, resinous, aromatic.

Habitat: Moist forests, stream and river banks, lake shores.

Season of Availability: Collect the resinous buds in the winter or very early spring.[84] Gather the bark and root in any season.

Preparation: The buds are made into an ointment, tincture or infusion. The bark and root are used in a decoction. Buds dose 4 grams by infusion, liquid extract 1:1 in 90% ethanol dose 4 to 8 ml, both in t.i.d. doses.[84] Here is a salve recipe: heat 1 c. of coconut oil, add 2 tbs of *Populus* buds and simmer for 30 minutes. Add 1 tbs *Hydrastis canadensis* (golden seal) and 3/4 tsp *Commiphoramolmol* (myrrh), simmer for 15 minutes. Strain. Melt a 1 inch cube of beeswax and pour into a container; it is ready for use.[90]

Medical Terminology: *Populus* is reputed to be tonic, stimulant[58] and slightly antiperiodic in action.[32] However, many others highlight its tribute as an expectorant.[a] The resinous buds are known to have analgesic properties.[40] The air dried winter leaf buds are considered official used in 4 gram doses.[2,84]

Related Disease Symptoms: Natives made a salve out of the winter buds and fat and put it in their nostrils to relieve congestion from colds, bronchitis and catarrh.[b] The same salve was rubbed on the skin for muscular aches and pains.[c] The Chippewa mixed the resinous buds of balsam poplar with *Quercus rubra*, *Populus tremuloides* and *Polygala senega* and used the decoction as a heart remedy.[10] For back pain, the Chippewa drank the decoction made from the roots of *Populus balsamifera* and *Cirsium spp.*[10]

---

[a] 10,27,44,58,82,84

[b] 27,38,40,63

[c] 10,63,84,90

In the case of excessive menstrual flow, the Chippewa boiled the roots of balsam poplar and *Populus tremuloides* for a tea that was drunk every hour.[10] Many tribes made a salve from the balsam buds and fat to heal skin sores and infections.[27,63] The bark decoction or tincture has been used to treat pulmonary ailments, gout, and rheumatism.[36,38] Specific indications for the buds include laryngitis, chronic bronchitis, and respiratory affections of children.[84]

Poisonous Aspects: The resinous buds have caused dermatitis.[40]

Chemistry & Pharmacognosy: Poplar buds contain humulene, gallic acid, malic acid, salicin, populin, mannitol, chrysin, fixed oil, and tectochrysin.[82,84]

Populus balsamifera
Balsam poplar, hackmatack

227

PRUNELLA VULGARIS
Labiatae
Self-heal, heal-all, carpenter-weed

Stem: Square, hairy to smooth, sometimes branched, decumbent to erect, 1 to 5 dm tall.

Leaves: Opposite, oblong-ovate to lanceolate, entire, 2 to 9 cm long, petiolate, green.

Flower Type: Purple to white, tubular, in 3 flowered clusters, grouped in a terminal head, definite bracts, spring, summer, fall.

Fruit: Small nutlet, summer, fall.

Roots: Fibrous.

General Information: Perennial herb, common.

Habitat: Open fields, open woods.

Season of Availability: The herb is collected in the spring, summer and fall.

Preparation: It is dried or used fresh in an infusion or poultice.

Medical Terminology: Self-heal is mainly an astringent.[a] It also has some carminative action.[36,38] The Chippewa steeped the root with catnip leaves and used the tea as a physic.[10]

Related Disease Symptoms: Self-heal's main use is as a gargle for sore throat and throat irritations.[b] The fresh leaves or infusion has been used as a styptic to stop hemorrhaging.[c] At one time the bruised leaves were bound to the throats of people suffering with quinsy as a cure.[55] To stop diarrhea, one cup of the infusion is taken every half hour.[d] For hemorrhoids, the herb infusion was used as an enema.[22]

Chemistry & Pharmacognosy: The herb contains a volatile oil.[58]

Commercial Products & Uses: It is on the list of marketable plants.[37]

---

[a] 22,27,35,56,68

[b] 22,27,36,38,68

[c] 36,38,55

[d] 27,36,38,55

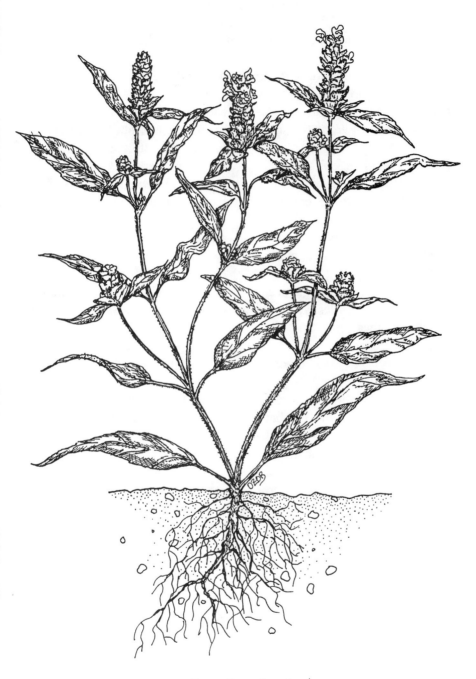

Prunella vulgaris
Self-heal, heal-all, carpenter-weed

229

PRUNUS SEROTINA
Rosaceae
Black cherry, wild cherry, rum cherry

Stem: Woody tree, erect, up to 30 m, black bark, reddish-black bark on branches, gum exudations common, aromatic inner bark.

Leaves: Alternate, oblong-ovate, acute, serrate, main vein, petiolate, green, 3.5 to 15 cm long, lustrous above.

Flower Type: 5 white petals, many stamens, 2 to 4 cm across, fragrant, spring.

Fruit: Red to black single seeded drupe, shiny, fleshy, juicy, edible, summer.

Roots: Taproot.

General Information: Perennial tree, deciduous.

Habitat: Dry woods.

Season of Availability: The bark and the inner bark can be gathered in any season. The fruit is collected in the summer.

Preparation: The bark is prepared in a syrup, decoction or infusion. The fruit is eaten, pressed into a juice, fermented into wine or dried. Powdered bark dose .5 to 2 grams or by infusion, liquid extract 1:1 in 25% ethanol dose 1 to 2 ml, all t.i.d.[83]

Medical Terminology: Wild cherry bark is sedative,[a] tonic,[5,51] astringent[58] and pectoral.[b] Its main use appears to deal with having expectorant[32,36] and flavoring properties.[38,72]

Related Disease Symptoms: The bark decoction or syrup is used to stop coughing,[c] treat colds[36,40] and treat cholera.[38,72] The primary utilization of the bark is with consumption[5,32] from catarrhal and bronchial affections.[d] The Chippewa dried and pounded the root of the black cherry, mixed it with the dried powdered root of *Ledum groenlandicum* and applied the powder directly on the skin ulcers and sores to heal them.[10] The inner bark was boiled with the trunk of a young *Pinus strobus* and the inner bark of *Prunus americana* until it was a mash; then the mash was dried and resoaked when needed as a poultice for cuts.[10] The Ojibwe and Chippewa used the inner bark, boiled, bruised or chewed, as an application to external sores.[10,63] During the first pains of labor, Cherokee women were given a warm infusion of the bark.[36,63] The infusion of the bark was used to relieve pains in the chest.[63] The pounded bark was used by Native Americans

[a] 27,52,63

[b] 10,22,68,83

[c] 22,32,52,68,83

[d] 22,27,68,83

as a poultice on amputated frozen members.[63] The dried fruit or bark tea has been used to stop diarrhea.[e] The bark tea was thought to lower the pulse and lower the temperature in intermittent fever.[5] The Chippewa used the root tea for worms and infantile cholera.[10]

Poisonous Aspects: There is approximately 212 mg hydrocyanic acid per 100 gm of leaves; it is lethal.[33] All types of livestock have been killed by eating black cherry leaves.[33,46] There are documented cases of human death from ingestion of black cherry leaves.[33] However, the dried leaves contain practically no hydrocyanic acid.[33] Symptoms include stupor, vocal cord paralysis, twitching and seizures.[91] The treatment is a Lilly cyanide kit.[91]

Chemistry & Pharmacognosy: The bark contains tannic and gallic acids, hydrocyanic acid and a volatile oil.[g] Wild cherry also contains prunasin, prunase, a cyanogenic glycoside, p-coumaric acid, trimethyl gallic acid, and scopoletin.[82,83] Chromatography has been done.[83]

Commercial Products & Uses: The cough syrup made from the bark is the official preparation.[h] The bark can be collected and sold to drug companies.[37]

Personal Experimentation: For years I have eaten wild black cherries fresh, in pies and jams.

Biological and Edible: The fruit is edible.[f] Bees utilize this plant for honey.[92,93]

---

[e] 36,52,63 [g] 32,58,82,83
[f] 9,15,25 [h] 1,32,44,51,59

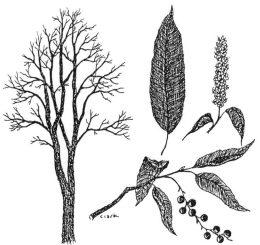

Prunus serotina
Black cherry, wild cherry, rum cherry

PYROLA ROTUNDIFOLIA
Pyrolaceae
Shinleaf, wintergreen, round-leaved pyrola

Stem: Stemless.

Leaves: Rosette, thick, leathery, round to obovate, shiny, margined petiole, crenate, 2 to 5 cm long, green.

Flower Type: White to pink, 5 petals, waxy, concave, 10 stamens; 1 to 2 cm across, raceme stands on a scape that is 1 to 3 dm tall, summer.

Fruit: Minute and innumerable seeds, summer, fall.

Roots: Fibrous.

General: Evergreen perennial herb, grows in small clumps.

Habitat: Sandy soils, bogs, open woods.

---

[a] 22,30,44,63

[b] 22,30,44

Season of Availability: The herb is collected in the spring, summer or fall.

Preparation: The herb is used in an infusion, dried or fresh.

Medical Terminology: *Pyrola rotoundifolia* is considered astringent in action.[a]

Related Disease Symptoms: For cankers and irritations in the mouth and throat, Indians used *Pyrola* tea as a gargle.[44,63] The decoction of the plant was utilized to heal skin wounds and sores.[40,63] To treat sore and inflamed eyes, the decoction was used as a wash.[b] The root tea was used by Natives to treat weakness and back problems.[63]

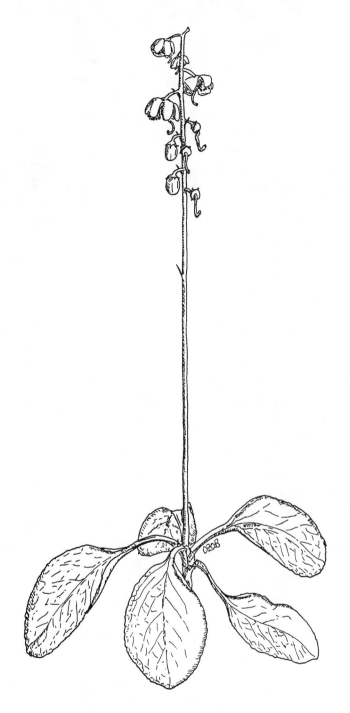

Pyrola rotundifolia
Shinleaf, wintergreen, round-leaved pyrola

RHUS GLABRA, RHUS TYPHINA
Anacardiaceae
Staghorn sumac, sumac, smooth sumac

Stem: *R. glabra*, smooth black-red bark; *R. typhina*, velvety red bark; both have stout branches; branching, orange wood, up to 6 m, but usually only up to 3 m in this area.

Leaves: Alternate, pinnately compound, 11 to 32 leaflets, leaflets oblong-lanceolate, serrate, acuminate, green, 5-10 cm.

Flower Type: Sometimes dioecious, greenish-white terminal spikes, spikes cone-shaped and about 8 cm tall, summer.

Fruit: Red drupes in clusters; *R. typhina*'s are velvety; *R. glabra*'s have small hairs, fall.

Roots: Taproot.

General Information: Perennial deciduous shrub.

Habitat: Dry rocky soils, open fields and meadows.

Season of Availability: Collect the bark of the stem and roots in spring or fall; the ripe fruit in late summer and fall.

Preparation: The fruit is used fresh in an infusion, but can be utilized dried. The bark is dried and used in a decoction.

Medical Terminology: Sumac is considered astringent[a] and refrigerant in action.[b] Sumac also has hemostatic properties.[c]

Related Disease Symptoms: For sore throat, the infusion of the fruit is used as a gargle.[d] To stop bleeding in women after childbirth, a tea made from the fruit was used as a wash.[63] The hot fruit infusion was taken internally to reduce fever.[e] Natives used a wet poultice of the leaves or berries to cure poison ivy.[63] The root bark was used to heal and treat burns.[f] For cuts and sores, use a decoction of the bark.[27,36] The root bark decoction was used to treat piles.[g] The bark decoction was used to halt diarrhea.[h] The Chippewa mixed the flowers with alum root as a remedy for children with sore mouths during teething.[10] Many smoked the leaves as a treatment for asthma.[36,38]

Biological and Edible: Natives mixed the leaves with willow smoked it like tobacco.[63] Antibiotic test have shown sumac to inhibit the growth of gram + and - bacteria.[57]

---

[a] 38,39,44,52,63

[b] 10,22,30,32,35,51,56,58,68

[c] 27,40,52,63

[d] 15,22,25,27,30,32,35,36,40, 44,51,56,58,63

---

[e] 22,27,35,36,52

[f] 27,36,63

[g] 22,30,40,63

[h] 22,36,52,68

Chemistry & Pharmacognosy: The leaves and the bark contain tannic and gallic acids.[i] A yellow dye is made from the roots.[22,70]

Commercial Products & Uses: The dried leaves are a commercial source of tannin.[29] The plant can be collected and sold commercially.[37]

---

[i] 32,58,82

Personal Experimentation: I took three clumps of the ripe fruit, poured 2 quarts of boiling hot water over them and let the mixture steep. I then cooled the tea and drank it. It was extremely astringent, so I added honey. This made it taste almost exactly like lemonade. I drank over a quart of this at one sitting and noticed no effects.

Rhus glabra, Rhus typhina
Staghorn sumac, sumac, smooth sumac

RIBES AMERICANUM
Saxifragaceae
Wild black currant

Stem: Woody, ascending, up to 2 m, sometimes with prickles, branching, shrubby.

Leaves: Green, suborbicular, 3 to 5 lobed, doubly serrate, 10 cm across.

Flower Type: White or yellow, drooping racemes from branch axils, tubular, spring.

Fruit: Black, round, sweet, juicy, edible, summer.

Roots: Woody, lateral.

General Information: Perennial, deciduous.

Habitat: Slopes, undergrowth in forests, meadows.

Season of Availability: Currants are collected in the late summer.

Preparation: The fruit is eaten fresh or cooked into jams, jellies, or pies. Currants can be dried like raisins.

Related Disease Symptoms: For kidney trouble, the Omaha drank a strong decoction of *Ribes* root.[70] Women of the Winnebago tribe drank the strong root decoction for uterine problems.[70] The leaves and stalks of both *Caltha palustris* and *Ribes spp.* were brewed in a decoction and drunk by the Chippewa when urination did not occur.[10]

Poisonous Aspects: Though no experimentation has been done on *Ribes*, other members of the *Saxifragraceae* family are known to be toxic to humans.[33]

Biological and Edible: The berries are edible raw or cooked.[a] Bees use this plant for honey.[92,93]

Personal Experimentation: In my wanderings, only once have I found a large patch of *Ribes*. The patch was near Copper Harbor, Michigan and is presently a parking lot. The berries are great either fresh, dried, or cooked in pies or jellies.

---

[a] 10,15,25

236

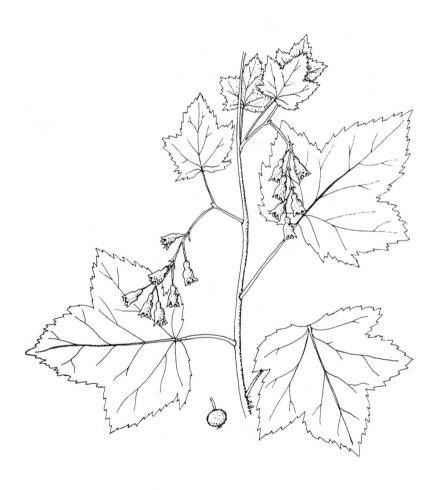

Ribes americanum
Wild black currant

ROSA SPP
Rosaceae
Rose, wild rose, rose hips

Stem: Reddish green, smooth, cane, rounded, thorns, up to 2 m, 3 cm in diameter.

Leaves: Pinnate compound leaves with serrated edges, ovate leaflets, shiny green on top, paler beneath.

Flower Type: Brilliant showy flowers; the wild species are typically pink, the cultivated species encourage staminate to petal genetic change that develop magnificent roses.

Habitat: Open areas, roadsides, fields, and forest borders.

Season of Availability: The rose petals can be picked in the summer. The rose flowers can be picked or cut during the summer. Rose hips are collected in the fall.

Medical Terminology: Rose oil is considered an antiseptic, antispasmodic, aphrodisiac, laxative, emmenagogue, sedative, tonic, and stomachic.[81]

Related Disease Symptoms: The oil is used to treat cholecystitis, nausea, constipation, conjunctivitis, depression, impotence, frigidity, headache, insomnia, leukorrhea, nervous tension, menorrhagia, ophthalmia, skin care, sterility, uterine disorders and vomiting.[81]

Poisonous Aspects: All plants in the rose family contain cyanide compounds within their seeds.

Biological and Edible: Rose petals are sweet and very good to eat; they make a great garnish in salads.[47] Rose oil has been found to increase the secretion of bile.[81] The petals are a rich source of vitamin C.[82] Bees utilize this plant for honey.[92,93]

Chemistry & Pharmacognosy: The evaporation rate of the oil is 99, the odor intensity is 7.[81] The oil is obtained from the flower petals.[81] Extracts from the oil include tannic and gallic acids, quercitin, vitamin C, geraniol, citronellol, l-linalool, and eugenol.[82]

Personal Experimentation: During the summer months I always find myself picking rose petals for snacks. The petals are very sweet and taste similar to their smell but much sweeter. I find they make colorful additions to salads and improve the flavor. Personally, I have eaten over one cupful at a sitting with no ill effects.

Rosa spp.
Rose, wild rose, rose hips

239

RUBUS SPP
Rosaceae
Raspberry, blackberry, thimbleberry, blackcap, dewberry

Stem: Reddish canes, brittle, thorns, erect to arching.

Leaves: Alternate, compound, palmate for blackberry, pinnate for raspberry, 3 to 5 leaflets, ovate to obovate, serrate, acuminate, petiolate, green.

Flower Type: 5 white petals, in a corymb, numerous stamens, spring.

Fruit: Red to black clustering droplets, succulent, juicy, edible, late summer, fall.

Roots: Running prostrate taproot.

General Information: Perennial deciduous shrubby herb.

Habitat: Open fields, meadows.

Season of Availability: Collect the roots and root bark during spring or fall. Collect the leaves and fruit in summer and fall.

Preparation: The roots and root bark are used fresh or dried in a decoction. The leaves are dried completely, then used in an infusion. The fruit is eaten fresh, dried or made into an infusion or syrup. Dried leaves dose 4-8 grams or by infusion, liquid extract 1:1 in 25% ethanol dose 4 to 8 ml, all t.i.d.[83]

Medical Terminology: Considered astringent[a] and tonic.[b]

Related Disease Symptoms: The root bark tea is used to cure diarrhea.[c] The same root bark tea has been utilized to control dysentery.[d] The root tea is thought to prevent vomiting.[40] Chewed in the mouth, the fruit is supposed to remove tartar deposits on the teeth.[27,52] Native Americans gave their children a root decoction for bowel trouble.[63] The Potawatomi washed sore eyes with the root bark tea.[63] A tea of the leaves has been gargled for sore and irritated throats.[e] An extract from the leaves has been used to alleviate pains from labor.[27,83] The leaf or root tea was used as a wash to heal wounds and sores.[22,68] Other indications include stomatitis, tonsillitis, and conjunctivitis.[83]

Biological and Edible: The berries are edible.[f] Bees utilize this plant for honey.[92,93]

Chemistry & Pharmacognosy: *Rubus* contains tannins and polypeptide.[83] Chromatography has been done.[83]

---

[a] 27,32,38,52,63,68,83

[b] 5,22,30,51

[c] 5,8,18,22,27,30,38,51,83

---

[d] 22,27,30,36,38,40,51,63

[e] 22,27,30,83

[f] 15,18,29,30,34,47

Commercial Products & Uses:
The fruit, squeezed and made into a syrup, is an official pharmaceutical preparation.[g] The roots can be sold to drug companies.[37]

Personal Experimentation:
Blackberries and raspberries are commonly eaten in pies, jams and jellies throughout the Great Lakes area. I have eaten *Rubus spp.* berries for as long as I can remember.

---

[g] 2,32,82

Rubus spp
Raspberry, blackberry, thimbleberry, blackcap, dewberry

RUMEX CRISPUS
Polygonaceae
Yellow dock, curly dock, dock

Stem: Smooth, erect, red to brown, up to 1.5 m.

Leaves: Whorled, strongly wavy, curled margins, lanceolate, acute, truncate to cordate at base, green, 15-30 cm long.

Flower Type: Green, terminal racemes, small flowers from 1 to 3 mm, summer.

Fruit: 3 angled grain-like achene, winged, 1 to 3 mm across, summer, fall.

Roots: Taproot, yellow.

General Information: Annual herb, be careful not to mistake with *Rumex obtusifolius*.

Habitat: Open fields, roadsides, wet areas.

Season of Availability: The roots and leaves are gathered in the summer and fall.

Preparation: The roots are used in a decoction, fresh or dried. The leaves are used fresh as a poultice or squeezed for their juice. The powdered roots have been utilized as an abrasive tooth powder.[40,55] The root tea is made from one half ounce of the root to one pint of boiling water.[19]

Dried root 2 to 4 grams or by decoction, liquid extract 1:1 in 25% ethanol dose 2 to 4 ml, in t.i.d. doses.[84]

Medical Terminology: The root is used as an astringent[a] in a wash or ointment for skin diseases.[b] The root tea is utilized as a laxative[c] for constipation.[d] The root tea is also used as a tonic[e] and alterative.[f]

Related Disease Symptoms: Natives put the crushed green leaves on boils to bring them to suppuration.[36,63] The Ojibwe and Chippewa used the dried and pounded root as a poultice to heal cuts.[10,63] The Chippewa wet the dried and powdered root on a cloth and applied it to itching and eruptive skin.[10] To reduce swelling, the Chippewa used the freshly mashed root in a poultice.[10] In Appalachia, a wash to treat ringworm was made by putting the root of dock in vinegar.[36,38] The Cheyenne used a decoction of the pulverized dried root for lung hemorrhages.[24] The decoction of the root has been used as a wash for many skin diseases.[g]

---

[a] 19,35,38,44,51,55,58

[b] 10,32,36,72

[c] 19,22,32,38,40,52,55,56,58,63,68

[d] 36,72,84

---

[e] 52,55,58

[f] 10,19,22,32,35,40,44,51,63,68

[g] 10,22,32,36,63,72,84

The decoction has been used for obstructive jaundice.[84] Years ago, the root tea was used as a blood purifier.[19,35]

Poisonous Aspects: The leaves are known to have caused dermatitis.[46] Don't mistake with the toxic *Rumex obtusifolius*.

Biological and Edible: The brown seeds can be pounded into an edible flour.[h] The young spring leaves can be eaten as a pot herb.[i]

Chemistry & Pharmacognosy: *Rumex crispus* contains hydroxyanthraquinone glycosides based on emodin and chrysophanol, and tannins.[84]

---

[h] 15,19,25
[i] 15,19,25,34,47

Commercial Products & Uses: The root is salable to drug companies.[37]

Personal Experimentation: In the spring, I have eaten the leaves as a pot herb for many years. Since the seeds are plentiful and easy to obtain, I once collected a large bag full and tried to use them as sprouts. The experiment was a disaster; I could only get a few seeds to sprout with each batch I experimented with.

Rumex crispus
Yellow dock, curly dock, dock

SALIX NIGRA, SALIX ALBA
Salicaceae
Black willow, white willow, swamp willow, willow

Stem: Flaky dark brown to black bark, young branches green, flexible, up to 20 m.

Leaves: Alternate, lanceolate, acute, serrate, stipulate, deep green, 5 to 15 cm long, 5 to 15 mm across.

Flower Type: All *Salix spp.* are dioecious, greenish with yellow bracts; staminate flowers have 2 basal glands, 3 to 5 free arching filaments; pistillate flowers with a basal gland, style nearly obsolete; spring. The flowers turn into catkin fruit.

Fruit: 3 to 7 cm catkins with smooth ovoid capsules, spring, summer.

Roots: Taproot.

General: Perennial deciduous shrubby tree, common.

Habitat: Streams, wet areas.

Season of Availability: The bark is collected in the spring.

Preparation: The bark can be used fresh or dried in a decoction or infusion, and is sometimes powdered. Dry bark dose 1 to 3 grams or by decoction, liquid extract 1:1 in 25% ethanol dose 1 to 3 ml, all in t.i.d.[83]

Medical Terminology: The bark tea has been used as a tonic[a] for dyspepsia,[22] convalescence, and debility.[32] The bark tea's main use is as a febrifuge.[b] To stop the return of malarial fever, the bark tea was used for its anti-periodic action.[c] As a wash, it was considered astringent[d] for healing psoriasis and other skin diseases.[5,83] The catkins have been thought to be aphrodisiac in action.[22,36] Salicin has anti-rheumatic properties.[82]

Related Disease Symptoms: It has been used beneficially for rheumatic pains.[e] To ease arthritic pain, ingest the bark tea.[f] The Chippewa used a tea of the inner bark for indigestion.[10] The root decoction was taken internally for dysentery.[g] Natives used the root tea to cure headache[40,63] and curb diarrhea.[h] The bark tea is used to reduce and break a fever[i] and relieve dyspepsia.[22,32] Other indications include gout, upper respiratory infections, rheumatism, ankylosing spondylitis, and other connective tissue disorders.[83]

---

[a] 5,32,38,39,50,51,58,68

[b] 5,27,32,36,38,39,40,51,63,80,83

[c] 22,32,39,44,50,58,68,80

[d] 1,22,38,44,51,63,68

[e] 32,50,58,68,83

[f] 27,50,83

[g] 10,22,68

[h] 22,36,68

[i] 5,27,32,36,38,39,40,51,63,80,83

Poisonous Aspects: Asapirin is lethal to an adult with an ingestion of 10 grams or more. Five grams of asapirin has killed children.

Biological and Edible: The inner bark of willow trees is edible and recommended for survival situations.[79] Bees utilize this plant for honey.[92,93]

Chemistry & Pharmacognosy: The bark contains salicin.[j] Until recently, aspirin was made from willow bark.[80] The plant also contains tannin.[83] Chromatography has been done.[83]

Commercial Products & Uses: The bark can be collected and sold to drug companies.[37]

---

[j] 1,27,32,40,50,58,63,82,83

Salix nigra, Salix alba
Black willow, white willow, swamp willow, willow

SANGUINARIA CANADENSIS
Papaveraceae
Bloodroot, red puccoon

Stem: Stemless.

Leaves: 1 palmate-lobed, crenate margins, red veins, green, 10 to 25 cm across.

Flower Type: White, 8 to 12 petals, 2 to 4 cm across, solitary on a 15 to 40 cm smooth scape, 2 sepals that are soon falling, early spring.

Fruit: Fusiform capsule, spring.

Roots: Red thick rhizome, with blood red sap.

General: Perennial herb, early spring plant, all signs of plant gone by late summer.

Habitat: Rich forest floors, such as the sugar maple forests along the Firesteel river.

Season of Availability: Collect the roots in the early spring during flowering.[13]

Preparation: The roots are used fresh or dried in a decoction or infusion. Dried rhizome dose .6 to 2 grams, liquid extract 1:1 in 60% ethanol dose .6 to 2. ml, give t.i.d.[84]

Medical Terminology: There are many actions attributed to bloodroot. Its main actions are emetic,[40] expectorant[a] and cathartic.[b] The seeds are thought to have narcotic properties.[c]

The powdered root, applied externally, is said to have well marked escharotic properties,[d] but experimentation proves it practically useless.[5] The dried rhizome is considered official with the dose of .125 grams.[2,82]

Related Disease Symptoms: The decoction is used to treat respiratory diseases[32] such as chronic bronchitis[e] and asthma.[f] The Meskwaki chewed the root and placed their saliva with the root excretions on burns to heal them.[36,63] The Ojibwe squeezed the root sap onto a small lump of maple sugar and held it in the mouth to cure sore throat.[36,63] The root tea has been used to treat rheumatism.[g] To cure skin fungus infections such as ringworm, the root was prepared in an ointment or the decoction was used topically.[h] The Chippewa made a root tea mixed with *Caulophyllum thalictroides* root for stomach pain.[10] Some references have commented on the use of the tea for dyspepsia.[i] Other uses include topical application to warts and nasal polyps.[84]

---

[a] 1,10,30,32,36,51,58,63,82

[b] 5,22,38,72,84   [c] 10,51,63

[d] 22,63,72,84   [g] 36,40,63

[e] 38,51,68   [h] 22,27,32,68

[f] 22,27,72,84   [i] 22,32,35

Poisonous Aspects: Overdoses of the root cause violent vomiting, severe thirst, a burning sensation, heaviness in the chest, difficult breathing, pupil dilation, muscular prostration and eventually death from cardiac paralysis.[46,91] The sap has caused contact dermatitis.[46] Treatment is emesis.[91]

Biological and Edible: Native Americans made an insect repellant out of the root.[63] Some tribes used the root to paint their faces.[9] In antibiotic experiments, bloodroot showed gram + and - bacteria inhibition.[57] Bees utilize this plant for honey.[92,93]

Chemistry & Pharmacognosy: For dyeing, the roots are used fresh[82] and make a red dye.[j] The root contains the alkaloid sanguinarine,[k] which belongs to the opium group having physiological activity midway between codeine and thebaine.[l] The root is collected in the spring, when the amount of sanguinarine is the greatest.[13,82] Other compounds include chelerythrine, and allocryptopine, and protopine.[82,84]

Commercial Products & Uses: The root is of commercial value.[37] Commercial products containing *Sanguinaria* include Sedatussin and Prunicodeine.[82]

---

[j] 22,30,38,63,82
[k] 13,40,51,58,82,84

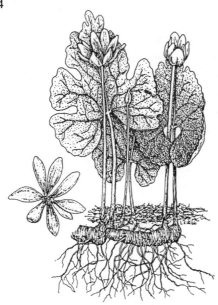

Sanguinaria canadensis
Bloodroot, red puccoon

SARRACENIA PURPUREA
Sarraceniaceae
Pitcher-plant, sidesaddle flower, huntsman's cup

Stem: Stemless.

Leaves: Rosette, green with purple veins, winged, recurved hairs at the apex, shaped like a pitcher, usually half filled with water and dead insects, 10 to 30 cm long, tubular, leathery.

Flower Type: Red to purple, on a 3 to 7 dm smooth tall scape, solitary, nodding, thick, leathery, 5 petals, 5 sepals, summer.

Fruit: Tiny seed capsule, summer, fall.

Roots: Fibrous.

General Information: Perennial herb, evergreen, leaves living more than one season.

Habitat: Bogs, wet acidic areas.

Season of Availability: Collect the roots in the spring, summer and fall.

Preparation: The roots are used fresh or dried in a decoction.

Medical Terminology: Therapeutically, the decoction is tonic[44,51] and stomachic in action.[a]

Related Disease Symptoms: The Canadian Indians used the root tea to treat smallpox.[b] It was used by Natives to sharpen their memory.[27] Another report says the tea was supposed to cause forgetfulness of sorrow.[22] The tea has been used with benefit in dyspepsia.[c] Ojibwe women drank a tea of the root to assist parturition.[75]

Poisonous Aspects: One report states that overdose can cause cerebral disturbances that were attributed to the presence of a narcotic principal.[32]

Biological and Edible: Native Americans used the leaves as drinking cups.[9]

Personal Experimentation: I heard one story about a man from the western Upper Peninsula of Michigan who lived to be 125 and attributed his old age to drinking the liquid in the leaves of the pitcher plant periodically. Whether it is true or false, I don't know. I have drank the liquid from the cuplike leaves and no harmful effects occurred, except that of ingesting a few rotten insects.

---

[a] 22,32,58,68

[b] 22,63,68,70

[c] 22,32,44,51,68

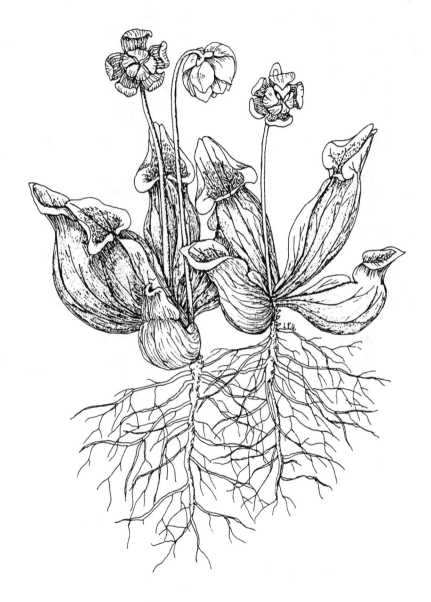

Sarracenia purpurea
Pitcher-plant, sidesaddle flower, huntsman's cup

SASSAFRAS ALBIDUM
Lauraceae
Sassafras

Stem: Black to brown furrowed bark, woody tree, up to 40 m, branching, pale green twigs.

Leaves: Alternate; 3 lobed, 2 lobed palm-shaped, or ovate; entire, smooth, green, spicy, 5 to 9 cm long, edible.

Flower Type: Green to yellow, peduncled corymb racemes, bracts, spring.

Fruit: Blue, ovoid, fleshy drupe, summer.

Roots: Lateral spreading roots, aromatic.

General: Perennial deciduous tree, in our lower area.

Habitat: Rich woods.

Season of Availability: The roots and root bark are dug up in the spring.

Preparation: The roots and root bark are made into a decoction. To make the tea, boil the root for 15 minutes and let it sit for 10 minutes. Dried bark dose 2 to 4 grams or by infusion, liquid extract 1:1 in 25% ethanol dose 2 to 4 ml, all t.i.d.[83]

Medical Terminology: Through experience I know the root bark tea is diaphoretic.[a] Other attributes are stimulant,[b] aromatic[c] and a flavoring agent.[32]

The root decoction is used as a carminative for stomach distress.[d] The pith is utilized in a topical application to inflamed eyes[e] because of its demulcent properties.[f] Large quantities of the tea are said to have narcotic properties.[18,40]

Related Disease Symptoms: Native Americans used the root bark tea as a wash for diseased eyes.[63] Reportedly a root bark poultice is used for sore and inflamed eyes.[36] Natives used the fresh or dried flowers for fevers.[63] The root bark decoction was used to reduce fever.[32,63] The boiled root tea was used to treat measles and scarlet fever.[63] The Seminole tribe used the tea for coughing, gallstones and pain in the bladder.[63] Others report the tea treated kidney disorders.[27,36] The tea has been used to slow down the milk flow in nursing mothers.[36] The root bark is placed on the tooth to relieve toothaches.[40] Topically, the oil has been used to rid pediculosis capitis.[83]

Poisonous Aspects: Although it was considered carcinogenic, it has been used to treat cancer.[40]

---

[a] 35,36,38,44,63,83   [c] 5,35,44,51

[b] 35,36,38,44,63

[d] 1,35,36,38,63,82,83

[e] 35,50,68   [f] 5,27,29,32,51

250

Biological and Edible: The dried leaves, ground into a powder, are used to thicken soup.[25,27] Bees use this plant for honey.[92,93]

Chemistry & Pharmacognosy: The oil contains safrole, pinene, isosafrole, and camphor.[g] Chromatography has been done.[83]

Commercial Products & Uses: The distilled oil of the root bark has been considered official.[2,59] Most of the commercial sassafras oil production is in the southern states.[53] The oil is used in the perfume industry.[82]

The wood is considered high quality and is used to make canoe paddles.

Personal Experimentation: I have drank over 2 quarts of the decoction at one sitting. I noticed a distinct diaphoretic and diuretic effect. I have drank at least one cup of the tea every day for over one month with no unusual effects.

---

[g] 31,82,83

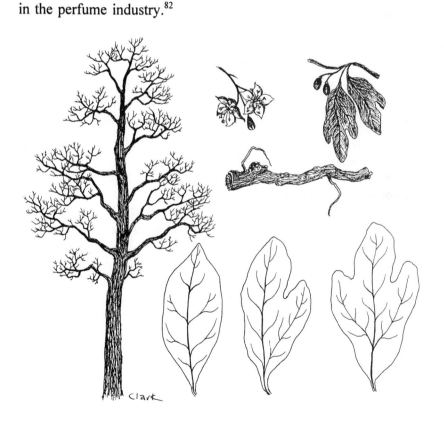

Sassafras albidum
Sassafras

SCROPHULARIA MARILANDICA
Scrophulariaceae
Maryland figwort, scrofula plant, carpenter's square, pilewort, figwort

Stem: Angled, grooved sides, smooth, green, 1 to 3 m.

Leaves: Opposite, petiolate, serrate, rounded to cordate at the base, acute, green, 8 to 20 cm.

Flower Type: Reddish-brown, tubular, two lipped, 5 to 8 mm; pyramid shaped panicle often 10 to 15 cm wide, spring, summer.

Fruit: Globose capsule, 4 to 7 mm long, shiny brown, summer.

Roots: Fibrous.

General Information: Perennial herb.

Habitat: Forest borders, open woods.

Season of Availability: Collect the herb and root in the spring and summer.

Preparation: The herb and roots are used fresh or dried in an infusion.

Medical Terminology: Therapeutically, *Scrophularia* is said to be diuretic, tonic, and diaphoretic.[36,38]

Related Disease Symptoms:
Years ago, the tea was thought to be effective for scrofula.[58] The root infusion was used to treat anxiety and sleeplessness in pregnant women.[36] In a poultice or ointment, it was used for skin diseases and scratches.[36,44] The tea has been used to increase menstrual flow.[36] It has also been used to reduce hemorrhoids.[36,38]

Chemistry & Pharmacognosy: It contains the compound scrophularin.[58]

Commercial Products & Uses:
The plant can be collected and sold to drug companies.[37]

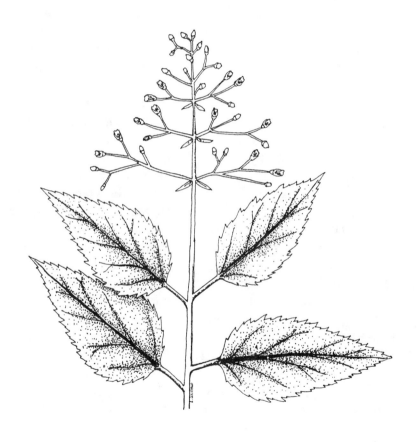

Scrophularia marilandica
Maryland figwort, scrofula plant, carpenter's square, pilewort, figwort

SCUTELLARIA LATERIFLORA
Labiatae
Mad-dog skullcap, mad-dog weed

Stem: Square, smooth, branching or simple, pilose on angles, green, 1 to 10 dm.

Leaves: Opposite, ovate, acute, petiolate, serrate, rounded at base, pinnately veined, 3 to 8 cm long, green.

Flower Type: Blue, tubular, lipped, 4 stamens, bract, 5 to 8 mm; axial erect racemes, summer, fall.

Fruit: Small nutlet, summer, fall.

Roots: Filiform rhizomes, stoloniferous.

General Information: Perennial herb, spreads mainly by roots.

Habitat: Wet fields, swampy woods.

Season of Availability: Collect the herb in spring and summer.

Preparation: The herb is dried and used in an infusion. Dried plant dose 1 to 2 grams or by infusion, liquid extract 1:1 in 25% ethanol dose 2 to 4 ml, both given t.i.d.[84]

Medical Terminology: The tea is used as a sedative[a] for neuralgia.[b] The infusion, considered antispasmodic,[c] was used for epilepsy and convulsions.[d]

The plant is also considered tonic in action.[e] The dried herb was once considered an official preparation with a one gram average dose.[2] Johnson feels it is very doubtful if *Scutellaria lateriflora* has any medicinal value at all.[32]

Related Disease Symptoms: The Cherokee made it into a tea with some other plants and used it to promote menstruation.[36,63] One or two cups of the tea supposedly cures nervous headaches.[f] Years ago, the tea was thought to cure hydrophobia.[g] The tea, taken internally, was also used to calm hysteria.[h] The British use it for grand mal seizures, chorea, and hysteria or nervous states.[84]

Poisonous Aspects: Overdoses are supposed to cause giddiness, stupor, confusion and twitching.[22]

Chemistry & Pharmacognosy: Skullcap contains scutellarin, a flavonoid glycoside.[84]

Commercial Products & Uses: The plant is periodically bought by drug companies.[37]

---

[a] 36,38,44,58,63   [d] 8,30,72,84

[b] 8,22,27,30,35,52,68,72,84

[c] 27,35,38,51,52,58

[e] 22,27,30,35,38,44,51,58,63,68

[f] 22,27,68   [h] 22,30,36,72

[g] 22,30,35,63

Scutellaria lateriflora
Mad-dog skullcap, mad-dog weed

SOLANUM DULCAMARA
Solanaceae
Bittersweet, nightshade

Stem: Woody vine, climbing, young growth green, old growth black to brown, branched.

Leaves: Alternate, acutinate, ovate, sometimes 2 to 4 small basal lobes, petiolate, smooth, entire, green, 5 to 7 cm long.

Flower Type: Purple corolla, anthers conspicuously yellow, 3 to 8 cm across, nodding, terminal cyme, summer, fall.

Fruit: Red ovoid berry, 8 to 11 mm in diameter, summer, fall.

Roots: Taproot.

General Information: Perennial woody vine, deciduous.

Habitat: Old fence rows, thickets, roadsides, forest borders.

Season of Availability: Collect the young branches in the fall.

Preparation: The twigs are dried and used in a decoction or made into an ointment.

Medical Terminology: *Solanum dulcamara* is mainly resolvent, mildly narcotic[68] and alterative in action.[a]

Related Disease Symptoms: The twigs are made into an ointment and used to treat rheumatism.[b] Allport notes that it has been used for rheumatism, but feels it is of doubtful value.[1]

The decoction treated pulmonary[5] and bronchial affections.[22,58] Native Americans mixed the crushed green leaves with grease and used the poultice on sores.[63] The ointment or decoction used topically was utilized in treating skin diseases like eczema and psoriasis.[c]

Poisonous Aspects: The plant is considered poisonous.[d]Poisoning may result if the berries are eaten in quantity.[46] In livestock, poisoning causes apathy, dyspepsia, salivation, drowsiness, trembling, paralysis, prostration and unconsciousness.[33] In humans, poisoning causes loss of sensation, stupefaction, and eventually death from paralysis.[33,91] Treatment is emesis.[91]

Chemistry & Pharmacognosy: *Solanum dulcamara* contains beta-scolarmarine.[40] It also contains the alkaloid solanine[46] and the saponine dulcamarine.[51,58]

Personal Experimentation: I have eaten small quantities of the berries; they are very bitter and I couldn't eat more than a few.

---

[a] 22,30,35,51   [b] 5,22,32,58,68   [c] 5,22,30,35,44,51,68   [d] 5,46,91

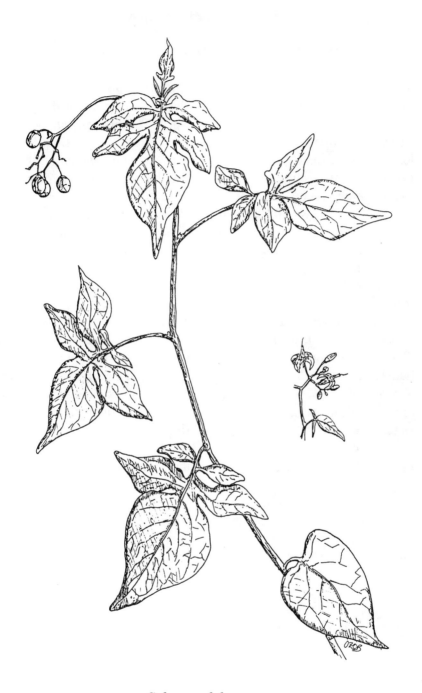

Solanum dulcamara
Bittersweet, nightshade

SORBUS AMERICANA
Rosaceae
Mountain ash, roundwood, missey-moosey

Stem: Woody, erect, lenticilate, up to 70 cm in diameter, up to 15 m tall, branching.

Leaves: Compound, 11 to 17 leaflets, lanceolate to oblong leaflets, serrate, acute.

Flower Type: White, flat topped cyme, many flowered, 20 cm across.

Fruit: Red, juicy pome, sour, edible and sweet after a couple of frosts.

Roots: Woody, lateral.

General Information: Pioneer species, perennial, deciduous.

Habitat: Old fields, meadows, burned areas.

Season of Availability: *Sorbus americana* berries should be collected in the late fall after one or two frosts.

Preparation: The berries are very tart raw, but sweeten after repeated frosts. The best preparation appears to be cooked into pies, jams or jellies.

Poisonous Aspects: Though there has been no experimentation of *Sorbus americana*, many members of the *Rosaceae* family are known to contain the deadly poisonous cyanide type compounds in their leaves and seeds.[33]

Biological and Edible: The berries are edible when thoroughly ripe.[a] The berries can be dried and ground into flour.[15] The fruit contains vitamin C[19] and can be made into a nutritious juice.[15]

Personal Experimentation: It is easiest to collect the berries in the fall before a snow, put them in a freezer, thaw and cook when needed. Because the berries are very tart and bitter until repeated freezing and thawing, many people add sweetener. My only experience with *Sorbus americana* has been eating the sweetened cooked mash. The flavor is similar to cherries. I find it difficult to determine when the bitter principle leaves the berries, it takes repeated frosts.

---

[a] 15,19,25,47

258

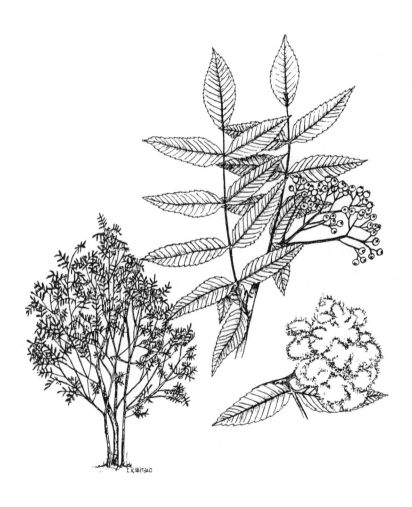

Sorbus americana
Mountain ash, roundwood, missey-moosey

SYMPHYTUM OFFICINALE
Boraginaceae
Comfrey

Stem: Up to 1 m, branching, upper stem densely pilose-hispid, recurved at the top.

Leaves: Alternate; lower leaves larger than the next succeeding ones, upper leaves broadly decurrent with wings along the stem, midvein, green.

Flower Type: 5 toothed corolla, white, yellow, or dull purple, 1.5 to 1.7 cm long, the lobes recurved at the top, summer.

Fruit: Nutlets around 4 to 5 mm long, not constricted above the base, brown, summer, fall.

Roots: Tap root, mucilaginous, bitter.

Habitat: Roadsides, fields, waste places.

Preparation: Dried leaf dose 2 to 8 grams or by infusion, liquid extract 1:1 in 25% ethanol dose 2 to 8 ml, all t.i.d.[83,84]

Medical Terminology: *Symphytum* is considered a vulnerary, demulcent, anti-inflammatory, antihemorrhagic, and antirheumatic.[83,84]

Related Disease Symptoms: Indications include rheumatic pain, gastric and duodenal ulcers, and arthritis.[83,84] Topically it is used on bruises, sprains, athlete's foot, crural ulcers, mastitis, and varicose ulcers.[83,84] The Cherokee used the root tea for cancer.

Biological and Edible: The tender young leaves, gathered in the early spring, can be prepared and eaten like spinach.

Chemistry & Pharmacognosy: The leaf contains tannin, mucilage, allantoin, symphytine, and echimidine.[83,84] Chromatography has been done.[83,84]

Poisonous Aspects: Do not confuse with Foxglove, which looks similar and could be fatal.

Symphytum officinale
Comfrey

SYMPLOCARPUS FOETIDUS
Araceae
Skunk cabbage, dracontium

Stem: Stemless.

Leaves: Basal rosette, large broad leaves, 3 to 6 dm long, similar to rhubarb leaves, smooth, entire, edible when young, green.

Flower Type: Purple spotted with green, 5-15 cm tall, ovoid shaped spathe, inrolled margins, conspicuous yellow stamens, late winter, early spring.

Fruit: Ovoid red fleshy mass of spherical seeds.

Roots: Fibrous, fleshy, thick.

General Information: Perennial herb, foul smelling, grows all over Isle Royale.

Habitat: Wet marsh, slow moving stream banks, swamps.

Season of Availability: The leaves and roots are collected in the spring, summer and fall.

Preparation: The roots are used dried in a powder, ointment or decoction. The roots and leaves are used fresh as a poultice. The leaves are also used fresh as an inhalant. The young curled leaf sprouts can be boiled in two waters and eaten as a pot herb. Powdered rhizome or root dose .5 to 1 gram in honey, infusion, or decoction, liquid extract 1:1 in 25% ethanol dose .5 to 1 ml, each given t.i.d.[84]

Medical Terminology: It is reputed to be antispasmodic,[a] slightly narcotic[22] and stimulant.[b] The dried ground root is taken internally as an expectorant for asthma, catarrh and bronchial affections.[c]

Related Disease Symptoms: The powdered root, mixed with grease, is used as an ointment to ally rheumatic pains.[d] To cure headaches, Native Americans picked the fresh leaves, rolled them into a ball and inhaled the vapors.[e] In a poultice, many Natives used the fresh roots or leaves for sores and swellings.[f] Some tribes used the fine rootlets and root hairs to stop the pain of toothaches.[63] The fine root hairs were used as a styptic to stop bleeding from cuts and scratches.[19,63] A decoction of the dried roots curbed coughing.[g] The plant has been employed in the treatment of hysteria[32,51] and epilepsy.[h] Its specific indication is bronchitis and asthma.[84]

---

[a] 32,35,58,63,84

[b] 19,30,44,51,52

[c] 19,22,27,30,32,35,36,40, 44,51,52,63,68,84

[d] 22,35,36,51,52

[e] 36,40,63,64

[f] 36,52,63

[g] 19,30,35,36,52,84

[h] 22,36,84

Poisonous Aspects: Overdoses are reported to cause nausea, vomiting and headache.[i] Death in humans and livestock is not known, probably because ingestion of more than one mouthful is rare.[33] Treatment is aluminum hydroxide for neutralizing and demulcent effects and symptomatic therapy.[91]

Biological and Edible: The young leaves can be eaten after boiling twice.[9,15]

Chemistry & Pharmacognosy: The whole plant contains calcium oxalate.[19,40]

---

[i] 19,22,51,91

Personal Experimentation: One spring, I gathered some young leaf sprouts. I steamed them in two waters and put margarine on them. They were great, no harmful effects at all. So I tried it again, this time with only one steaming. It felt like my mouth was on fire, fortunately the pain subsided in about 15 minutes. The leaves stink when bruised or crushed in any way. However, once cooked, they lose that characteristic.

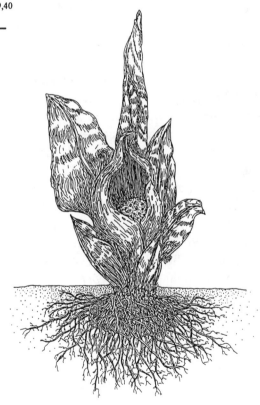

Symplocarpus foetidus
Skunk cabbage, dracontium

TANACETUM VULGARE
Compositae
Tansy, golden-buttons

Stem: Erect, slightly ribbed, smooth, branchless, green, up to 1.5 m.

Leaves: Alternate, pinnately compound, 1-3 times pinnately divided, segments are linear-oblong, toothed, aromatic, green, smooth, 10-30 cm long.

Flower Type: Yellow discoid heads of disk flowers, 5-10 mm across the head, 20-100 heads in the flat topped terminal corymb, aromatic, summer, fall.

Fruit: Tiny brown pappalate achenes, 1 mm long, sliver-like, fall.

Roots: Stout rhizome, spreading.

General: Perennial herb, grows in groups overtaking an area, aromatic, common along Lake Superior's south shore.

Habitat: Fields, waste areas.

Season of Availability: Collect the herb in the summer and fall.

Preparation: It is used in an infusion, fresh or dried. The oil is obtained by steam distillation. The tea is made from one ounce of the dried herb per one pint of boiling water. Dried herb dose 1 to 2 grams or by infusion, liquid extract 1:1 in 25% ethanol dose 1 to 2 ml, all t.i.d.[83]

Medical Terminology: Tansy has been used internally as an anthelmintic to expel worms.[a] The tea has been utilized for amenorrhea,[b] because of its emmenagogue action.[c] The oil has produced fatal results[40,66] when used as an abortifacient.[d] The herb is also considered stimulant in action.[e]

Related Disease Symptoms: Native Americans pounded the plant and bound it to the head to relieve headache.[63] The herb was used in a steam bath for sore and swollen feet and ankles.[36,63] Applied as a poultice, the bruised leaves were used to reduce swelling from sprains.[f] For sore throat, the root was chewed or gargled as a tea by the Chippewa.[10] The Chippewa used the leaves of tansy and *Nepeta cataria*, mixed equally, in a tea for fever.[10] To ease earache, the Chippewa made a root decoction and dropped the lukewarm tea into the ear.[10] The Cheyenne utilized the tea for weakness and dizziness.[24] An enema of the infusion was used for round and thread worms.[83] Topically, it has been used to

---

[a] 22,33,36,38,51,58,63,66,68,83

[b] 8,32,36   [f] 8,22,32,35,36

[c] 10,22,35,38,51,63,68

[d] 32,33,36,50,51,58,63

[e] 22,50,51,58,63,83

264

treat scabies and pruritus ani.[83]

Poisonous Aspects: Overdoses cause gastritis, convulsions and eventually death.[33,46] The oil is known to have caused contact dermatitis.[40] Pregnancy is a contraindication for its use.[83]

Biological and Edible: In antibiotic experiments, tansy showed gram + and - bacteria inhibition.[57]

Chemistry & Pharmacognosy: The plant contains malic acid, tanacetin, and tannin.[51] The volatile oil contains thujone.[g] Other volatile oils include umbellulone, monoterpene ester, camphor,. monoterpene, sesquiterpene, artemsia ketone, and chrysanthemum epoxide.[82] Chromatography has been done.[83]

Commercial Products & Uses: Most of the commercial tansy production occurs in lower Michigan.[53] Some drug companies still purchase the herb.[37]

Personal Experimentation: I drank one pint of the tea at one sitting and noticed no effects. The taste is agreeable.

---

[g] 31,58,82,83

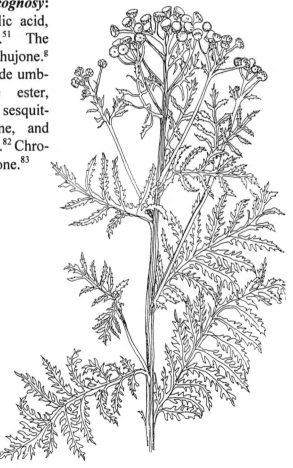

Tanacetum vulgare
Tansy, golden-buttons

TARAXACUM OFFICINALE
Compositae
Dandelion

Stem: Stemless.

Leaves: Rosette, oblanceolate, coarsely and irregularly toothed to pinnately cut, sometimes nearly entire, decurrent, 6 to 40 cm long, green, edible.

Flower Type: Yellow ray flowers in a head, solitary at the end of a 10 to 30 cm long purple to green scape, the scape is hollow and has milky sap, 150 to 200 heads per plant per summer, head is 2 to 5 cm across, spring, summer, fall, used in wine making.

Fruit: Small light brown achene on a parachute-like pappus, 1 to 2 mm long.

Roots: Deep black taproot, white center, used for tea.

General: Perennial herb.

Habitat: Open fields, waste places, roadsides, yards.

Season of Availability: The roots are collected in the fall and winter. The leaves and flowers are collected in the spring, summer and fall.

Preparation: Use the root fresh or dried in a decoction. The root can be roasted or ground and used in a decoction. Use the fresh leaves and flowers.

The leaves are eaten in salads or parboiled as a green vegetable. The flowers are used in wine making. Dried root dose 2 to 8 grams or by infusion or decoction, liquid extract dose 2 to 8 ml, both given t.i.d.[84] Dried leaf dose 4 to 10 grams or by infusion, liquid extract 1:1 in 25% ethanol dose 4 to 10 ml, given t.i.d.[84]

Medical Terminology: Therapeutically, the root is thought to be tonic,[a] diuretic[b] and aperient in action.[c] The root decoction is also used as a mild laxative.[d] Some consider it a cholagogue and antirheumatic.[84] The dried roots are considered official.[2]

Related Disease Symptoms: The root decoction has long been taken for liver diseases.[e] To cure heartburn, Natives drank the root tea.[f] The Meskwaki used the tea for chest pains.[63,73] A cup of the root decoction cures dyspepsia.[g] To promote appetite and aid digestion, the tea was taken before meals.[22,36] To remove warts, the milky sap was applied.[40,50] Specific indications include cholecystitis and dyspepsia.[84]

---

[a] 10,51,76   [c] 5,22,32,44,58,63,68,73

[b] 34,36,57,84   [d] 1,10,22,34,36,84

[e] 5,8,22,27,32,40,51,58,63,68,84

[f] 36,63,75   [g] 1,5,32,58,84

Biological and Edible: The roasted and ground roots are used as coffee substitute.[h] The spring leaves are edible and used as salad greens.[i] The plant has shown hypoglycemic activity.[40] Seeds can be sprouted and used as food.[86] Bees utilize this plant for honey.[92,93]

Chemistry & Pharmacognosy: Dandelion contains the compounds taraxacin, taraxacerin[l] and inulin.[j] Chromatography has been done.[84]

Personal Experimentation: I have eaten the leaves in salads for many years; if the leaves are bitter, boil or steam them, allow to cool, then use in a salad. I have roasted and ground the roots in hopes of finding a coffee substitute and sure enough, the decoction was almost identical to coffee in taste. It is common practice for Great Lakes people to gather dandelion flowers and use them to make wine.

---

[h] 5,15,18,22,25,34,47,50

[i] 5,15,18,34,41,47,68,74,76

[j] 51,58,84

Taraxacum officinale
Dandelion

THUJA OCCIDENTALIS
Pinaceae
White cedar, arbor-vitae

Stem: Erect, woody, reddish brown shreddy bark, light colored wood, up to 20 m.

Leaves: Small scale-like, appressed-imbricated in 4 rows, 1 to 2 mm, green.

Flower Type: Monoecious, scale-like, small, terminal, green, 1 to 3 mm, spring.

Fruit: Cone bearing, brown, winged nutlet like seeds, fall.

Roots: Lateral taproot.

General Information: Perennial evergreen tree or shrub.

Habitat: Swamps, cool rocky stream banks; the largest I've seen was on the Salmon Trout river near Big Valley creek.

Season of Availability: Collect the leaves and branches in every season. Collect the cones in the summer and fall.

Preparation: The leaves and twigs are used in an infusion or decoction, fresh or dried. The cones are ground into a powder. The Chippewa made a cough syrup from *Ostrya virginiana* wood and cedar leaves.[10] Dried herb dose 1 to 2 grams or by infusion, liquid extract 1:1 in 50% ethanol dose 2 ml, both in t.i.d. doses.[84]

Medical Terminology: The main actions of white cedar are emmenagogue[68] and diuretic.[a] It also appears to be stimulant in action.[b] Topically it is used as a counter irritant.[84]

Related Disease Symptoms: To sooth coughs[68] and reduce fever,[c] Native Americans made a decoction of the leaves. The oil or ground leaves mixed with grease was used as a topical ointment for rheumatism.[d] This ointment has also been used for skin fungus diseases and wart removal.[e] For muscular aches, some tribes used the branches in sweat baths.[63] The tea has also been used to treat scurvy.[f] The Chippewa combined the burned and charcoaled wood with bear grease, rubbed it on the temples and pricked it with needles as a remedy for convulsions.[10] For relief from rheumatism, the cones, ground into a powder and mixed with fern leaves, were rubbed on painful joints.[36] Catarrhal affections is another use for cedar tea.[g] The tea has been used to promote menstruation.[h]

Poisonous Aspects: Overdoses are thought to cause abortion.[i]

---

[a] 19,22,58,84 [c] 9,22,27,35,36,50,63 [e] 27,32,50,68,84 [g] 9,32,35,84

[b] 19,58,63,84 [d] 9,19,22,35,36,50,63 [f] 9,22,35,36 [h] 19,32,63,84

Convulsions are another symptom of overdose.[19,63] The oil has a toxic effect on the central nervous system.[84]

Biological and Edible: The dried leaves can be made into incense.[27,63]

Chemistry & Pharmacognosy: The volatile oil contains thujone,[58,82] cedrene and cedrol.[31]

Commercial Products & Uses: Cedar leaf oil is considered official.[59] Most of the commercial production of cedar oil is from wild plants in northern New England.[53]

Personal Experimentation: By steeping one ounce of the herb to one pint of boiling water, I made two quarts of the tea. I drank one quart of the tea within one hour, while I put the other in the icebox to cool. The next morning I drank the other quart. The only noticeable effects were that of a diuretic and clearing mucous from the mucous membranes, other than that, nothing.

---

[i] 22,27,63

Thuja occidentalis
White cedar, arbor-vitae

TRIFOLIUM PRATENSE
Leguminosae
Red clover, clover, cleavergrass

Stem: Slightly hairy, ascending or suberect, tends to bend over due to its own weight, green, from 5 to 40 cm tall, branching.

Leaves: Alternate, palmately 3 foliate compound, serrate, stipulate, lower leaves long petioled, upper leaves short petioled, distinct white striped arch across each leaflet, green.

Flower Type: Red, tubular, 10 to 20 mm long, in terminal heads that are 3 cm across, spring, summer, fall.

Fruit: Tiny round nutlet, brown, summer, fall.

Roots: Fibrous, nodule forming.

General Information: Short-lived perennial herb.

Habitat: Open fields, roadsides.

Season of Availability: Collect the flower heads during the summer and fall.

Preparation: The flowers are dried and used in an infusion or syrup. Dried inflorescence dose 4 grams or by infusion, liquid extract 1:1 in 25% ethanol, given t.i.d.[84]

Medical Terminology: Clover is said to be alterative[a] and antispasmodic in action.[b] Its main action, in a tea or syrup, is as a sedative[38,58] for whooping cough.[c] The dried flowers have been considered official in pharmaceutical preparations.[2] The British utilize clover as a dermatologic agent and an expectorant.[84]

Related Disease Symptoms: A cup of the infusion is supposed to improve the appetite.[36,38] The infusion, used as a wash or made into a salve, is used for skin ulcers and sores.[d] The tea has also been thought effective for liver ailments.[36,38] Specific diseases include eczema and psoriasis.[84]

Poisonous Aspects: There are some reported physiological problems occurring in cattle when too much clover was ingested, but nothing serious or recurring.[33]

Biological and Edible: The seeds and dried flowers are edible.[34] The herb can be cooked and eaten.[34] There have been reports of antineoplastic properties.[84] Bees utilize this plant for honey.[92,93]

Chemistry & Pharmacognosy: Coumarin is found in *Trifolium pratense*.[82] Another compound in *Trifolium* is trifoliin.[84]

---

[a] 30,35,50,51,58

[b] 22,38,50,68

[c] 22,35,36,44,47,51,68

[d] 8,30,36,84

Commercial Products & Uses: Drug companies still purchase the herb.[37]

Personal Experimentation: Using one ounce of the herb to one pint of boiling water I have made a tea and drank over a quart at one sitting with no unusual effects whatsoever.

Clover blossom tea was recommended to me by an Ojibwe woman from Baraga. She told me her mother and grandmother gave her the tea for persistent coughs.

Trifolium pratense
Red clover, clover, cleavergrass

TRILLIUM ERECTUM
Liliaceae
Stinking benjamin, purple trillium, trillium, squawroot

Stem: Stout, erect, 15 to 60 cm tall, green, smooth.

Leaves: Single whorl of 3 terminal leaves, rhombic-ovate, broad, prominently netted, 5-15 cm long, sessile, green, smooth.

Flower Type: Light crimson to purple, 3 petals, 3 green sepals, 3 to 7 cm across, standing on a terminal erect peduncle, early spring.

Fruit: Dark red 6 angled berry, summer.

Roots: Thick, stout, brown, up to 3 cm thick.

General Information: Perennial herb, small groups, rare.

Habitat: Rich forests.

Season of Availability: Dig the roots in the late summer or fall.

Preparation: The root is chewed fresh or used in an infusion, fresh or dried. Dried root and rhizome dose .5 to 2 grams or as a decoction, liquid extract 1:1 in 25% ethanol dose .5 to 2 ml, both given t.i.d.[84]

Medical Terminology: *Trillium* is considered astringent,[a] tonic[b] and alterative.[c] It has also been considered emmenagogue in action.[d] Natives put the root in food to be eaten by their special someone as an aphrodisiac.[36,38] The British consider it an antihemorrhagic.[84]

Related Disease Symptoms: Native Americans used the infusion for sore nipples.[63] To reduce eye swelling, the Menominee made a poultice of the grated raw root.[63] They also steeped the grated root and drank the infusion for menstrual irregularity and cramps.[63] The steeped ground root tea has been used to treat menorrhagia.[e] The root tea has been used for internal and external hemorrhaging.[f] To help promote childbirth, some tribes drank a root infusion.[g] The ground root has been applied as a local irritant in healing skin ulcers and sores.[h] The chewed root was used to slow heart palpitations.[36,63]

Biological and Edible: *Trillium* leaves are edible by boiling and serving with margarine.[88]

Chemistry & Pharmacognosy: The root contains the saponin trillin[31] and tannin.[58,84]

---

[a] 38,44,52,72,84
[b] 22,63,68
[c] 32,35,58
[d] 35,38,51
[e] 9,27,32,35,68,72,84
[f] 9,22,27,32,36,68,72,84
[g] 22,36,52,63,68
[h] 22,32,36,72,84

Personal Experimentation: I have made one pint of the tea using one half ounce of the root in boiling water. I drank the pint at one sitting. It was very bland and slightly bitter, and I noticed no effects.

Trillium erectum
Stinking benjamin, purple trillium, trillium, squawroot

TYPHA LATIFOLIA
Typhaceae
Cattail, bulrush, flag

Stem: Stout, stiff, erect, smooth, green, 1 to 3 m

Leaves: Alternate, mostly basal, sheathing, long linear, parallel veined, 1 to 1.5 m long, 6 to 23 mm wide, pale green.

Flower Type: Monoecious; staminate flowers, tiny green cylindric tubes that turn to yellow pollen, grouped in a cigar shape above the pistillate flowers; pistillate flowers, tiny green cylindric tubular, grouped in a cigar shape which turns brown and even looks like a cigar, spring, early summer, edible.

Fruit: Tiny nutlets connected to downy hairs, brown, fall.

Roots: Stout, rhizome, lateral root, thick, white.

General Information: Perennial, growing in great groups.

Habitat: Marsh, slow moving streams, ponds.

Season of Availability: Gather the roots in any season. Collect the immature flowers in the early summer (end of June) for eating. Collect the seeds and floss in the fall.

Preparation: The root is used fresh as a poultice or fresh or dried in a decoction. The immature male flowers are cooked and eaten like corn on the cob. The young leaf sprouts are eaten fresh. The yellow pollen is used as a flour.

Related Disease Symptoms: The Cheyenne used the dried and pulverized root in a decoction to relieve cramps in the abdomen.[24] For skin wounds and burns, a poultice of the freshly chopped root has been used.[36,76] The down has also been used in the treatment of burns.[36,54] The root has treated diarrhea.[36]

Poisonous Aspects: The pollen is a cause of hay fever.[40] There is one case of horse poisoning connected with cattails.[33,40]

Biological and Edible: The floss has been utilized for insulation and as a buoyancy material.[a] Great Lakes tribes used the leaves for mats and shingles.[b] The roots, young sprouts and underdeveloped flowers are edible.[c] The pollen can be used as a flour substitute.[d] The pollen is high in vitamin A.[18]

Personal Experimentation: I have eaten almost all the parts of cattail with no ill effects. My favorite meal is the immature flowers cooked like corn on the cob.

---

[a] 18,29,75   [c] 15,18,25,34,47,79
[b] 73,74,75,76   [d] 15,18,34,47,79

I have found the easiest way to procure the root flour is after collection, wash the roots thoroughly, cut them into 3 cm lengths, put them in an electric blender with 3 times the water, blend for 1 minute, pour the mixture in a bowl, wait 3 to 4 hours, scrape the floating fibers off the top, stir for an even mixture, pour through a sieve, and 2 to 3 hours later decant the excess water and the flour is ready for use. The young sprouts that emerge from the rhizomes can be put in pickle juice to make pickles.

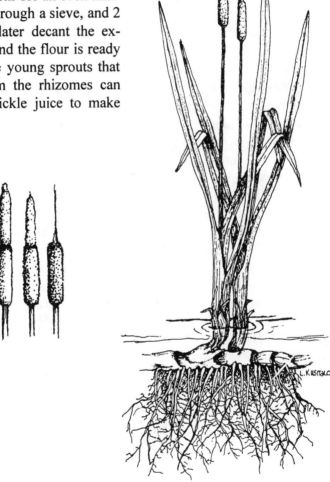

Typha latifolia
Cattail, bulrush, flag

URTICA DIOICA
Urticaceae
Stinging nettle, nettle

Stem: Up to 2 m, very bristly with stinging, (fluid filled) bristles (2 mm long), green, up to 2 m high.

Leaves: Lower and medium leaves cordate-ovate, coarsely toothed, upper leaves ovate to lanceolate, blades many times longer than petiole, edible when young, green.

Flower Type: Dioecious, clustered on branched racemes from leaf axils, green, summer.

Fruit: Brown achene, with straight embryo, summer, fall.

Roots: Tap root.

General Information: Very common plant, grows singly and in large groups.

Habitat: Fields, waste places, roadsides, common.

Season of Availability: The immature plant is gathered when less than 30 cm tall.

Preparation: The herb is boiled or steamed in water and eaten as a pot vegetable. Dried herb dose 2 to 4 grams or by infusion, liquid extract 1:1 in 25% ethanol dose 3 to 4 ml, both given t.i.d.[84]

Medical Terminology: Urtica actions include antihemorrhagic and hypoglycemic.[84]

Related Disease Symptoms: Urtica has been used to treat uterine hemorrhage, cutaneous eruptions, infantile and nervous eczema, epistaxis, and melena.[84] It has also treated dysentery and diarrhea, and the Germans use the root in prostrate cancer treatments.

Poisonous Aspects: Urtica causes a temporary dermatitis.

Biological and Edible: The young herb is edible as a pot herb. It is usually collected in the spring, boiled or steamed, and served with margarine or vinegar. The roots can be collected in the fall and winter and utilized as a starchy root vegetable.[85]

Chemistry & Pharmacognosy: It contains histamine, 5-hydroxytryptamine, and ascorbic acid.[84] Chromatography has been done.[84]

Personal Experimentation: To me, Urtica has been a friend and foe. At my first introduction I was stung by the brittle hairs. The sting feels like a severe burn, but goes away in minutes. My next introduction was with gloves. I picked a pot full of the young spring sprouts and steamed 'em up. To my surprise, they were great. They tasted a lot like spinach, but I guess most of these pot herbs taste like spinach. Since that time I've eaten *Urtica* many times and I've also been stung many times. Nevertheless, it is worth gathering because it's plentiful and good to eat.

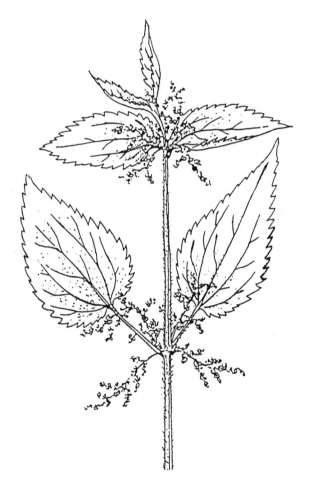

Urtica dioica
Stinging nettle, nettle

VACCINIUM ANGUSTIFOLIUM
Ericaceae
Blueberry, huckleberry, bilberry

Stem: Woody, bushy, intricate branching, stoloniferous, thin scaly bark, 2-3 cm in diameter, up to 1 m.

Leaves: Green, .7 to 2 cm long, narrowly lanceolate, glabrous, minutely spinulose-serrulate, alternate, used for tea.

Flower Type: White, bellshaped, 5 to 6 mm long, in racemes, aromatic, spring.

Fruit: Blue to black berry, 6 to 9 mm in diameter, edible, very sweet, late summer, fall.

Roots: Fibrous, off many stolons.

General Information: Bushy, perennial, deciduous, grows in groups, common.

Habitat: Boggy wet soils, dry sandy or rocky soils in boreal type forests.

Season of Availability: Collect the berries in the late summer.

Preparation: Blueberries can be eaten fresh, made into pies, syrup, or jam. The berries can be pressed and dried for future use.

Related Disease Symptoms: To treat 'craziness,' the Chippewa placed dried blueberry flowers on hot stones and inhaled the fumes.[10]

Poisonous Aspects: Though blueberries are thought to be harmless, the foliage of many members of the *Ericaceae* are highly toxic.[33]

Biological and Edible: The berries are edible raw or cooked.[a] Bees use this plant for honey.[92,93]

Personal Experimentation: Picking blueberries is a favorite pastime of many Great Lakes people. When I was 7 or 8, I remember spending all day in the woods picking blueberries, then bringing them back to town and selling them door to door for 50 cents a quart. Even with all that money to be made, I'd make sure and bring at least one quart home for my mother to make a blueberry pie.

---

[a] 10,15,18,47,78,79

Vaccinium angustifolium
Blueberry, huckleberry, bilberry

279

VACCINIUM MACROCARPON
Ericaceae
Cranberry, bog cranberry, american cranberry

Stem: Prostrate, dark red, intricate forking, 2 to 6 mm thick, up to 1 m long.

Leaves: Green, oblong-elliptic, blunt tip, 6 to 17 mm long, whitened beneath, slightly revolute, alternate.

Flower Type: Pink, bell-shaped with recurved petals, on a long pedicel, spring.

Fruit: Red, sometimes with mottled white spots, 2 to 4 cm long, round to ellipsoid, edible, late fall.

Roots: Fibrous.

General: Perennial, deciduous, grows in groups, berries look like marbles on the ground.

Habitat: Wet bog soils, usually in open areas, such as Big Traverse Bay in the Keweenaw Peninsula.

Season of Availability: Cranberries can be collected in late fall around the end of October and well into December.

Preparation: The tart cranberries can be eaten fresh or cooked into a sauce or jelly. The berries can be pulped into juice. The berries are also commonly prepared in muffins and pancakes.

Medical Terminology: People drinking cranberry juice are known to excrete hippuric acid in their urine.[96]

Hippuric acid is a known bacteriostatic agent.

Related Disease Symptoms: The juice is ingested as a folk remedy to cure bladder problems.

Poisonous Aspects: Though cranberries are thought to be harmless, the foliage of many members of the *Ericaceae* family are highly toxic.[33] Large quantities of cranberries have been known to cause diarrhea.[96]

Biological and Edible: Cranberries are edible raw or cooked.[a] Bees use this plant for honey.[92,93]

Chemistry & Pharmacognosy: The juice of the berries contains anthocyanins, catechin, triterpenoids, around 10% carbohydrates, and small amounts of protein, fiber and ascorbic acid.[96] Also citric, quinic, benzoic and glucuronic acids,[96] and anthocyanic dyes that are obtained from the cranberry pulp waste.[96]

Commercial Products & Uses: Anthocyanic dyes that are obtained from the cranberry pulp waste.[96]

Personal Experimentation: Picking cranberries off a sphagnum bog is like picking up marbles from a carpet. The process can be backbreaking.

---

[a] 15,18,47

Cranberry bogs are always wet, so plan on it. My favorite recipes are cranberry muffins and cranberry pancakes. Cranberry juice can be easily made by placing the berries in an electric blender.

Vaccinium macrocarpon
Cranberry, bog cranberry, american cranberry

VERBASCUM THAPSUS
Scrophulariaceae
Mullein, flannel-plant, aaron's rod, Indian tobacco

Stem: Stout, stiff, erect, branchless, densely woolly, grayish green, 1 to 2 m tall.

Leaves: Alternate, oblong, acute, densely woolly, decurrent to stem, entire to crenate, 20 to 40 cm long, first year plant only has a basal rosette.

Flower Type: Yellow, 5 petal-like lobed tubular corolla, 15 to 25 mm across, ephemeral, in a large terminal tightly packed spike, during summer and fall.

Fruit: Small, black, ellipsoid capsule.

Roots: Taproot.

General Information: Biennial, rosette first year keeping its leaves through the winter, flower stalk appears the second year, followed by death.

Habitat: Open fields, rocky soils, waste places.

Season of Availability: Collect the leaves and flowers in summer, fall; dig the root in fall.

Preparation: The leaves are used fresh or dried and smoked in an infusion.

The flowers are used for their volatile oil. The roots are dried. To make an ointment, soak the flowers in olive oil for 21 days in the sunlight.[19,36] Dried leaves dose 4-8 grams or by infusion, liquid extract 1:1 in 25% ethanol dose 4-8 ml, all t.i.d.[83]

Medical Terminology: Therapeutically, it is demulcent,[a] emollient,[b] and an expectorant.[83]

Related Disease Symptoms: To relieve asthma congestion, the leaves are dried and smoked.[c] The dried leaves are used in a tea or smoked to treat chest congestion catarrhal affections.[d] An infusion of the leaves has been beneficial to stop coughing.[e] The British use the leaves for upper respiratory infections.[83] The Choctaw smoked the leaves to relieve sore throats and asthma.[36,63] The Choctaw also put the leaves on their heads to cure headache.[63] The Menominee used the dried root for pulmonary diseases.[63,74] The flowers have remedied tuberculosis.[40,63] The soaked leaves have been used in a poultice to relieve hemorrhoids.[f] The leaf tea was used to curb diarrhea.[g] Dropped into the ear, the ointment cured earache.[h]

---

[a] 30,32,44,51,58,68 [g] 19,22,35,44
[b] 19,22,27,35,56,83 [h] 19,22,36
[c] 8,19,27,35,36,38,40,51,52,55,63,76
[d] 8,19,22,27,30,40,44,51,52,68
[e] 8,19,22,27,30,40,44,51,52,68
[f] 19,22,30,36

282

Biological and Edible: The leaves are smoked as a tobacco substitute.[39,74] In antibiotic experiments, mullein showed gram + and - bacteria inhibition.[57]

Chemistry & Pharmacognosy: A yellow dye is made from the flowers.[19] The leaves contain mucilage, a volatile oil, resin, and a saponin.[83]

Commercial Products & Uses: The plant can be collected and sold to drug companies.[37]

Personal Experimentation: I have drank over a pint of the infusion at one sitting with no ill effects. I made the infusion by using one ounce of the dried leaves to one pint of boiling water. It is bland but very soothing to the throat.

Verbascum thapsus
Mullein, flannel-plant, aaron's rod, Indian tobacco

VIBURNUM OPULUS
Caprifoliaceae
Nanny berry, geulder-rose, cramp bark

Stem: Woody, gray smooth bark, branching, up to 4 m.

Leaves: Opposite, 3 lobed, palmately veined, coarsely toothed, maple-like, stipulate, 7 to 10 cm long.

Flower Type: White, 5 lobed corolla, 5 stamens, pedunculate, in a concave topped cyme, 5 to 10 cm across, spring.

Fruit: Red, single seeded fleshy drupe, 10 to 15 mm in diameter, fall.

Roots: Taproot.

General Information: Perennial deciduous shrub, bushy.

Habitat: Moist woods, rocky slopes.

Season of Availability: Collect the bark in every season.

Preparation: The bark is made into an alcohol extract or decoction. Dried bark dose 2-4 grams or by decoction, liquid extract 1:1 in 25% ethanol base dose 2-4 ml, both given t.i.d.[84]

Medical Terminology: Therapeutically, it is antispasmodic[a] and sedative in action.[b] The bark is also considered a uterine sedative[c] because it acts specifically on the uterus.[32,84]

Related Disease Symptoms: The Ojibwe made a tea from the bark that was taken internally for stomach cramps.[d] The bark tea was also used for menstrual cramps and pains.[e] The tea has been used to relieve asthma and convulsions.[19,22] In cases of threatened abortion, the tea or extract was ingested.[f]

Poisonous Aspects: In his experiments, Johnson found use of cramp bark caused nausea and vomiting in his patients and considered it much overrated.[32]

Biological and Edible: The berries contain vitamin C and are considered edible.[19,36] Bees use this plant for honey.[92,93]

Chemistry & Pharmacognosy: *Viburnum* contains the glucoside viburnin and valeric acid.[71,84] It contains scopoletin and other coumarins.[82] Chromatography has been done.[84]

Commercial Products & Uses: There is some controversy in the validity of cramp bark's authenticity; the commercial cramp bark is *Acer spicatum*, a mistake made by unknowledgeable collectors years ago.[14]

---

[a] 19,44,51,82

[b] 22,30,32,63,68,84

[c] 19,27,71

---

[d] 19,22,63,68,73,74,75

[e] 19,27,30,32,71,84

[f] 32,71,84

Viburnum opulus
Nanny berry, geulder-rose, cramp bark

285

VIBURNUM TRILOBUM
Caprifoliaceae
Highbush-cranberry, cranberry, pimbina

Stem: Woody, gray bark, shrubby, branching at top, up to 4 m, 1 to 5 cm in diameter.

Leaves: Green, ovate, palmately 3 to 5 ribbed, rounded, rounded at base, 3 lobes long acuminate, entire in sinus.

Flower Type: White, terminal cymes, 4 to 15 cm across, summer.

Fruit: Red drupe, globose to ellipsoid, sour, edible, sweet and juicy after repeated frosts, late fall.

Roots: Woody, lateral.

General: Perennial, deciduous, bushy, grows in groups.

Habitat: Stream banks, lake shores.

Season of Availability: Highbush cranberries can be picked after a frost in the late fall and into winter. Before that time, the berries are too tart.

Preparation: The highbush cranberries can be made into jam, jelly, pies, or used as an addition to muffins or pancakes. The berries can be eaten raw.

Related Disease Symptoms: For cramps and colic, the Menominee drank a tea made from the inner bark.[63,70] The Chippewa made a decoction from the inner bark of tag alder and highbush-cranberry and ingested the tea as an emetic.[10]

Biological and Edible: The berries are edible raw or cooked.[a] Bees use this plant for honey.[92,93]

Personal Experimentation: In my search for highbush-cranberries, I have never gathered more than a quart at one time because I have never found a plentiful supply. I have met a few people who have not found any problem with collection. The berries are very tasty and make good jam.

---

[a] 15,19,25,47

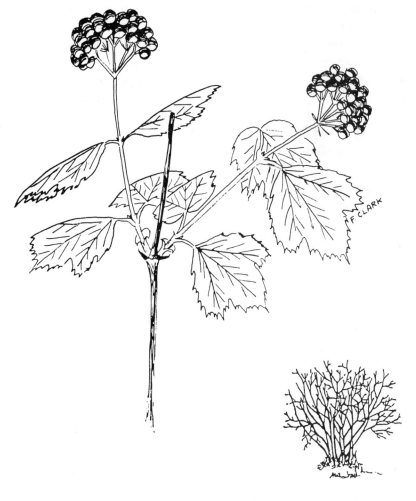

Viburnum trilobum
Highbush-cranberry, cranberry, pimbina

VIOLA PAPILIONACEAE
Violaceae
Blue violet, viola, violet

Stem: Stemless, has rhizomes.

Leaves: Broad cordate-ovate blades, 4-12 cm broad, green.

Flower Type: Rich violet, whitish center, petaliferous flowers, bluish veins, beard, on pedicels above leaves, 2-6 mm across, edible, spring.

Fruit: Ellipsoid capsule, green to purple, 1-2 cm long, contains brown or brown dotted seeds (2 mm long), summer.

Roots: Rhizomes with netted fibrous roots.

General Information: Grows in clumps about 2 feet in diameter, it sometimes lines artesian springs in the side of hills.

Habitat: Damp woods, sugar maple forests, meadows.

Season of Availablity: The flowers are collected in the spring.

Preparation: The fresh flowers can be eaten and/or made into a sweet preserves.

Biological and Edible: The flowers are good in salads, the young leaves should be cooked for 10-15 minutes and are best mixed with other greens.

Viola papilionaceae
Blue violet, viola, violet

Bryophytes

CONOCEPHALUM CONICUM
Bryophyta: Marchantiaceae
Great scented liverwort

Stem: None except on fruiting structure.

Leaves: Ribbon-like prostrate thallus with polygons; looks like snake skin; raised pores.

Fruit: Capsules in cone-shaped umbrella.

General Information: Very strong mushroom-like smell when crushed.

Habitat: Damp organic soil and rocks, light shade.

---

[a] 100,109,136

Season of Availability: All parts, any season.

Preparation: Dried

Medical Terminology: Mixed with vegetable oils as ointments for boils, eczema, cuts, bites, wounds, and burns;[a] inhibits growth of micro-organisms.[117]

Biological and Edible: Serves as food for slugs.[119]

Chemistry & Pharmacognosy: Growth-inhibitory substances: tulipinolide and zaluzanin.

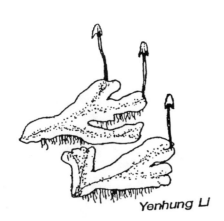

Yenhung LI

Zen Iwatsuki

Conocephalum conicum
Great scented liverwort

DICRANUM SPOPARIUM
Bryophyta: Dicranaceae
Broom moss

Stem: Upright

Leaves: Long, curved like a sickle; strong costa with 4 ridges on back; teeth at apex.

Fruit: Capsule

General Information: Dark green cushions.

Habitat: Soil of moist to dry forests.

Season of Availability: All parts, any season.

Preparation: Dried

Medical Terminology: Strongly inhibited all bacteria tested but gram negative *Escherichia coli*.[122]

Biological and Edible:
Between babies' thighs as diapers.[104]

Commercial Products & Uses:
Shop window displays; moss gardens; bedding, mattresses, cushions, pillows (alpine Himalayas).[120]

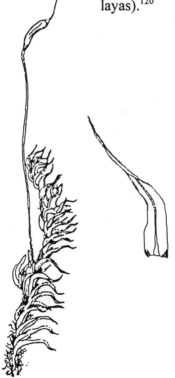

Dicranum spoparium
Broom moss

FONTINALIS
Bryophyta: Fontinalaceae
Brook Moss

Stem: Usually dark and stiff, sometimes wiry.

Leaves: In 3 rows around stem, ovate to lanceolate, keeled.

Fruit: Capsule with no stalk, somewhat rare.

General Information: Long, dangling.

Habitat: Attached in streams or lakes.

Season of Availability: All parts, any season.

Preparation: Dried

Biological: Roach (*Rutilus rutilus*), lays its eggs among the branches; survives 35 μg cadmium per liter of water without visible damage, whereas waterfleas and salmonid fish die at 1.2 μg per liter.

Chemistry & Pharmacognosy: Decomposes 32-43% of phenol at low concentrations (50 mg phenol/dm3);[125] intolerant of four weeks of exposure to 0.02 mg/l phenol;[111] used as bioindicators of excessive ethylene glycol in water.[126]

Commercial Products & Uses: Insulator between walls and chimney to prevent fires;[133] stabilizes weirs in streams; used as aquarium plants; foresters in Pennsylvania use *Fontinalis* to help stabilize weirs.

Yenhung Li

Fontinalis
Brook Moss

HYLOCOMIUM SPLENDENS
Bryophyta: Hylocomiaceae
Stairstep moss, mountain fern moss

Stem: Stiff; primary, secondary, and tertiary branches arranged like fern; new primary branch originating midway on primary branch, creating steps through subsequent years of growth; abundant branched paraphyllia (filamentous stem outgrowths resembling hairs at first glance).
Leaves: Costa (rib) short, double; stem leaves plicate.
Fruit: Capsule
General Information: Dull green or yellowish thick mats.
Habitat: Northern moist or wet forests on humus, soil, or rocks.

Season of Availability: All parts, any season.
Preparation: Dried
Biological and Edible: Moss bags to assess heavy metal concentrations (Finland); absorption of water and urine (55% absorption);[127] packing and stuffing.[127]
Commercial Products & Uses: In Alaska, used as chinking for log cabins;[116] cushion to carry water vessels on heads of women in Kumaun, India, absorbs splashing water;[120] moss gardens; carpets for floral exhibitions.

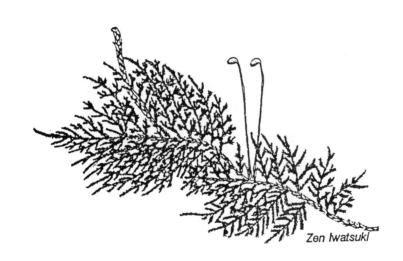

Zen Iwatsuki

Hylocomium splendens
Stairstep moss, mountain fern moss

HYPNUM CUPRESSIFORME
Bryophyta: Hypnaceae
Cypress-leaved feather moss

Leaves: Curved to one side, costa (midrib) very short and double, small, dense cells at leaf base.

Fruit: Capsule with two rings of teeth.

General Information: Pale green, yellowish, or brownish mats, shiny.

Habitat: Dry, exposed calcareous soil or rocks; on bark in Australia.

Season of Availability: All parts, any season.

Preparation: Dried

Medical Terminology: Marked antibacterial and antifungal effects.

Related Disease Symptoms: Supposed to induce sleep,[104] perhaps because commonly used for pillows.

Commercial Products & Uses: Decoration for shop window display (France);[99] sold as sheet moss for Christmas tree yards and nativity scenes;[106] bedding, mattresses, cushions, and pillows in alpine highlands of Himalayas because they are insect-repellent and resist rot; wrap apples and plums in Himalayas (lightweight and resist insects).[121]

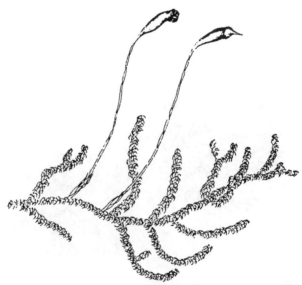

Hypnum cupressiforme
Cypress-leaved feather moss

MARCHANTIA POLYMORPHA
Bryophyta: Marchantiaceae
Common liverwort

Stem: None

Leaves: Broad thallus (ribbon-like plant body on surface of ground) with conspicuous pores; blackish midribs.

General Information: Gemmae (bits of plant tissue for asexual reproduction) in cups; stalks with umbrella tops for sexual reproduction.

Habitat: Bare soil after fire; greenhouse weed; wet places on soil, humus, and logs.

Season of Availability: All parts, any season.

---

[a] 136,109,100

Medical Terminology: Cytotoxicity against the KB cells;[101] antileukemic activity in several compounds from leafy liverworts.[101]

Related Disease Symptoms: In China, to treat jaundice, hepatitis and as an external cure to reduce inflammation[114] (no medical evidence); in Himalayas for boils and abscesses[121] (no medical evidence); mixed with vegetable oils as ointments for boils, eczema, cuts, bites, wounds, and burns.[a]

Chemistry & Pharmacognosy: Marchantin A

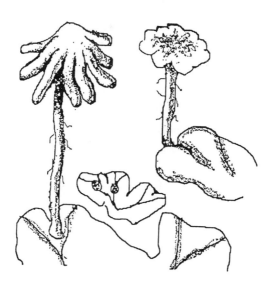

Marchantia polymorpha
Common liverwort

PHILONOTIS FONTANA
Bryophyta: Bartramiaceae
Aquatic apple moss

Stem: Upright
Leaves: Light green, cells slightly protruding at ends; ovate.
Fruit: Round capsules
Habitat: Wet soil in sun.
Season of Availability: All parts, any season.
Preparation: Dried
Medical Terminology: Used by Gasuite Indians of Utah to alleviate pain of burns; crushed into paste and applied as poultice;[110] covering for bruises and wounds or as padding under splints in setting broken bones. Indians in the Himalayas use burned ash of mosses mixed with fat and honey and prepared in ointment for cuts, burns, and wounds. This mixture provides both healing and soothing.[121]

Commercial Products & Uses: Chinking by shepherds in the Himalayan highlands for temporary summer homes.[120]

Yenhung Li

Philonotis fontana
Aquatic apple moss

296

POLYTRICHUM COMMUNE
Bryophyta: Polytrichaceae
Common hairy cap moss

Stem: Upright, stiff; male plants with cup at apex.

Leaves: Lamellae (rows of cells extending as upward flanges); spiraled; marginal teeth.

Fruit: Capsule with square cross section; apophysis (ring) at base.

General Information: Up to 60 cm tall in clumps.

Habitat: Soil of wet forest.

Season of Availability: Stem or stem & leaves, any season.

Preparation: Dried

Medical Terminology: Reduces inflammation, as an anti-fever agent, detergent, diuretic, laxative, and hemostatic agent;[114] *Polytrichum juniperinum* inhibitory to Sarcoma[37] in mice.

Related Disease Symptoms: Used as a tea for treating the common cold and to dissolve kidney and gall bladder stones (China).[112]

Biological and Edible: Aqueous extracts stimulate growth of larch (Larix) seedlings.

Commercial Products & Uses: Household—bedding material by Linnaeus, stuffing for beds by Laplanders;[103] brooms for dusting curtains, carpets, and beds,[106] stripped of leaves;[132] baskets in early Rome;[104] hassocks (Great Britain);[134] stuff upholstery (Great Britain).[104]

Horticulture—bowl gardens (Japan);[115] garden of Poet Laureate Wordsworth;[99] to simulate mountains in garden at Ryoanji Temple in Kyoto; for gardens, dried and pulverized, broadcast like grass seed, grow in flats; frequent watering and light shade needed; when plants form solid patches, harvested with 2 cm soil and stacked to dry; 20 x 20 squares sold to customers, planted in checkerboard, trampled, watered frequently.

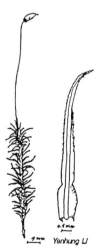

Polytrichum commune
Common hairy cap moss

RACOMITRIUM CANESCENS and RACOMITRIUM LANUGINOSUM

Bryophyta: Grimmiaceae

Finge moss; woolly moss

Leaves: Light green, tipped with white hair; margins revolute (rolled under); papillae (bumps) visible under microscope.
Fruit: Capsule on 1-2 cm stalk.
General Information: Branched, horizontal branches in tufts.
Habitat: Sand or gravel.

Season of Availability: All parts, any season.
Preparation: Dried
Commercial Products & Uses: Bowl cultivation; chinking;[116] lamp wicks by Labrador eskimos.[104]

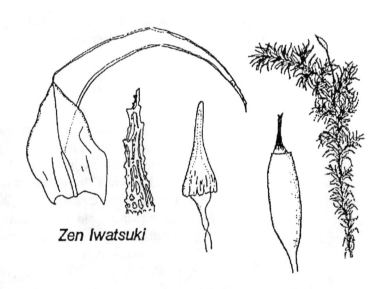

Zen Iwatsuki

Racomitrium canescens,
Racomitrium lanuginosum
Finge moss; woolly moss

RHODOBRYUM ONTARIENSE
Bryophyta: Bryaceae
Rose moss

Stem: Upright
Leaves: Ovate, possess rib, clustered at top of stem in rosette.
Fruit: Capsules
Habitat: Moist to somewhat dry soil in light shade.
Season of Availability: All parts, any season.
Preparation: Dried
Medical Terminology: Treatment of cardiovascular diseases and nervous prostration in China;[109] cures angina.[137]

Chemistry & Pharmacognosy: Ether extract contains volatile oils, lactones, and amino acids; extract actually did increase the rate of flow in aorta of white mice by over 30%, causing reduction in amount of oxygen resistance.

Commercial Products & Uses: Related species grown as overwintering host of a Chinese gallnut maker.

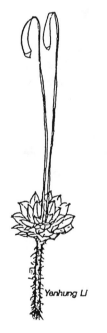
Yanhung LI

Diana LI

Rhodobryum ontariense
Rose moss

SPHAGNUM
Bryophyta: Sphagnaceae
Peat moss

Stem: Branches in clusters; dense branches at apex form "head."

Leaves: Hood-shaped; cells of two types, forming a network.

Fruit: Spherical capsule.

General Information: Upright, with dead and dying parts extending down many meters.

Habitat: Bogs and fens.

Season of Availability: All parts, spring melt until winter freeze.

Preparation: Fresh or dried.

Medical Terminology: Medical dressing, especially in World War I, because of antibacterial, antiviral action and water-holding capacity; amount of wound area covered by new epidermis doubled with Sphagnum dressing compared to no dressing.[135]

Related Disease Symptoms: Fungal-caused sporotrichosis is a hazard to nursery workers and harvesters of Sphagnum[108,130] and is a danger in bandage use; effective against certain human cancer tissue cultures.[98]

Poisonous Aspects: Fungal-caused sporotrichosis is hazardous to nursery workers and harvesters of Sphagnum[108,130] and is dangerous in bandage use; pulmonary sporotrichosis (infection of lung resulting from breathing Sphagnum fungi).[118]

Biological and Edible: Peat moss is listed as famine food in China; Laplanders have used sphagnum as ingredient in bread; not very palatable; fed to baby pigs as binder for iron and vitamins (piglets are born anemic).

Chemistry & Pharmacognosy: Cation exchange (using polyuronic acids) useful for cleaning up heavy metals and toxic wastes; absorbancy useful to clean oil spills and dyes[123] and for sewage disposal;[131] It is especially effective at removing nitrogen (96%) and phosphorus (97%) from eutrophic river water or sewage.[107]

Commercial Products & Uses: Household—good, cheap cloth prepared by mixing Sphagnum with wool and weaving together;[113] inner soles of hiking boots to cushion foot and absorb moisture and odors; between Chippewa Indian babies' thighs like diapers;[106] pillows; dried to keep milk warm or cool; footmats; line children's cradles to keep infant clean, dry, and warm.[128] Horticulture—extracts induce germination of Jack pine (*Pinus banksiana*)[105] and stimulate growth of larch (Larix) seedlings; good in plant propagation

300

for air-layering; hydroponic gardening; totem poles for climbing plants and moss-filled wreaths; shipping plants, fresh vegetables, flowers; storage of roots and bulbs; maintaining fishing worms.

Construction—binders for solidification and strengthening, sold as "peatcrete" and "peatwood";[124] insulation of domestic housing and refrigerators;[129,124] Indian pharki (door). Using hand methods makes crop renewable in about 10 years.

Yenhung Li

Sphagnum
Peat moss

Cross Index Tables

The following tables will enable the reader to easily locate a list of plants used to treat specific symptoms. The plants listed are not a sure cure for the symptoms, diseases, or properties described. At one time or another, the plants included have been used for the specified phenomena according to literature or first hand information.

If one wishes to experiment with plants, use the greatest caution and understand that many plants have lethal side effects. Extensive research on the specified plants and effects that one is working with is highly recommended.

Each table lists the common name, Latin name, habitat, season, and page number for the plants found in that category.

🌳	=	Plants found in forests
❁	=	Plants found in fields and open areas
≈	=	Plants found in streams and wet areas
■	=	Plants found in bogs
💧	=	Plants collected in the spring
☼	=	Plants collected in the summer
🍁	=	Plants collected in the fall
❄	=	Plants collected in the winter

Nervous System
Headache

Common name	Latin name	🌳	⊛	~	■	●	☼	🍁	❄	Page
Yarrow	*Achillea millefolium*		⊛				☼	🍁		10
Dogbane	*Apocynum androsaemifolium*	🌳	⊛				☼	🍁	❄	12
Columbine	*Aquilegia canadensis*	🌳		~			☼			40
Bearberry	*Arctostaphylos uva-ursi*	🌳	⊛					🍁		46
Case weed	*Capsella bursa-pastoris*		⊛			●	☼	🍁		74
Lady's slipper	*Cypripedium calceolus*	🌳		~	■	●		🍁		108
Pennyroyal	*Hedeoma pulegioides*	🌳					☼			140
Wild oregano	*Monarda fistulosa*	🌳	⊛				☼	🍁		196
Catnip	*Nepeta cataria*		⊛				☼			206
Ginseng	*Panax quinquefolius*	🌳						🍁		212
White pine	*Pinus strobus*	🌳				●	☼	🍁	❄	216
Rose	*Rosa spp*	🌳	⊛				☼	🍁		238
Black willow	*Salix nigra*			~		●				244
Mad-dog weed	*Scutellaria lateriflora*	🌳	⊛	~		●	☼			254
Skunk cabbage	*Symplocarpus foetidus*			~		●	☼	🍁		262
Tansy	*Tanacetum vulgare*		⊛				☼	🍁		264
Mullein	*Verbascum thapsus*		⊛				☼	🍁		282

Nervous Complaints

Common name	Latin name	🌳	⊛	~	■	●	☼	🍁	❄	Page
Hemp	*Cannabis sativa*		⊛					🍁		72
Lady's slipper	*Cypripedium calceolus*	🌳		~	■	●		🍁		108
Pennyroyal	*Hedeoma pulegioides*	🌳					☼			140
Cow parsnip	*Heracleum lanatum*	🌳		~		●	☼	🍁	❄	150
Motherwort	*Leonurus cardiaca*		⊛				☼	🍁		172
Catnip	*Nepeta cataria*		⊛				☼			206
Ginseng	*Panax quinquefolius*	🌳						🍁		212
Rose	*Rosa spp*	🌳	⊛				☼	🍁		238
Mad-dog weed	*Scutellaria lateriflora*	🌳	⊛	~		●	☼			254
Stinging nettle	*Urtica dioica*		⊛				☼	🍁		276
Rose moss	*Rhodobryum ontariense*		⊛			●	☼	🍁	❄	299

Circulatory System
Heart Problems

Common name	Scientific name	🌳	⊛	〰	💧	☼	🍁	❄	Page
Dogbane	*Apocynum androsaemifolium*	🌳	⊛			☼	🍁		38
Wild ginger	*Asarum canadense*	🌳		〰			🍁		54
Milkweed	*Asclepias syriaca*		⊛			☼	🍁		56
Marsh-marigold	*Caltha palustris*			〰	💧				70
Carrot	*Daucus carota*		⊛			☼	🍁		110
Trout lily	*Erythronium americanum*	🌳			💧		🍁		118
Joe-pye weed	*Eupatorium purpureum*			〰		☼	🍁		122
Avens	*Geum rivale*			〰	💧	☼	🍁	❄	136
Wild iris	*Iris versicolor*			〰			🍁		160
Motherwort	*Leonurus cardiaca*		⊛			☼	🍁		172
Watercress	*Nasturtium officinale*			〰	💧	☼	🍁	❄	204
Ginseng	*Panax quinquefolius*	🌳					🍁		212
Seneca-snakert	*Polygala senega*		⊛				🍁		222
Balsam poplar	*Populus balsamifera*	🌳		〰	💧	☼	🍁	❄	226
Dandelion	*Taraxacum officinale*		⊛		💧	☼	🍁	❄	266
Purple trillium	*Trillium erectum*	🌳				☼	🍁		272

Respiratory System
Bronchial

Common name	Scientific name	🌳	⊛	■	〰	💧	☼	🍁	❄	Page
Putty-root	*Aplectrum hymale*	🌳		■				🍁		36
Wake robin	*Arisaema triphyllum*	🌳			〰			🍁		48
Butterfly weed	*Asclepias tuberosa*		⊛					🍁		58
Hound's tongue	*Cynoglossum officinale*		⊛				☼	🍁		106
Wild oregano	*Monarda fistulosa*	🌳	⊛				☼	🍁		196
Seneca-snakert	*Polygala senega*		⊛					🍁		222
Black cherry	*Prunus serotina*	🌳	⊛			💧	☼	🍁	❄	230
Nightshade	*Solanum dulcamara*	🌳						🍁		256

Asthma

Common name	Latin name	🌲	⊛	≋	♦	☼	♣	❄	Page
Balsam fir	*Abies balsamea*	🌲			♦	☼	♣	❄	8
Wake robin	*Arisaema triphyllum*	🌲		≋			♣		48
Milkweed	*Asclepias syriaca*		⊛			☼	♣		56
Red root	*Ceanothus americanus*	🌲	⊛			☼	♣		78
Motherwort	*Leonurus cardiaca*		⊛			☼	♣		172
Indian tobacco	*Lobelia inflata*	🌲	⊛			☼			176
Horehound	*Marrubium vulgare*		⊛		♦				182
Watercress	*Nasturtium officinale*			≋	♦	☼	♣	❄	204
Seneca-snakert	*Polygala senega*		⊛				♣		222
Sumac	*Rhus glabra*		⊛		♦	☼	♣		234
Bloodroot	*Sanguinaria canadensis*	🌲			♦				246
Skunk cabbage	*Symplocarpus foetidus*			≋	♦	☼	♣		262
Mullein	*Verbascum thapsus*		⊛			☼	♣		282
Cramp bark	*Viburnum opulus*	🌲			♦	☼	♣	❄	284

Catarrh

Common name	Latin name	🌲	⊛	≋	♦	☼	♣	❄	Page
Yarrow	*Achillea millefolium*		⊛			☼	♣		10
Sweet flag	*Acorus calamus*			≋	♦		♣		12
Wake robin	*Arisaema triphyllum*	🌲		≋			♣		48
Hound's tongue	*Cynoglossum officinale*		⊛			☼	♣		106
Goldenseal	*Hydrastis canadensis*	🌲				☼	♣		154
Juniper	*Juniperus communis*		⊛		♦	☼	♣	❄	166
Wild oregano	*Monarda fistulosa*	🌲	⊛			☼	♣		196
Pokeweed	*Phytolacca americana*	🌲	⊛				♣		214
Seneca-snakert	*Polygala senega*		⊛				♣		222
Balsam poplar	*Populus balsamifera*	🌲		≋	♦	☼	♣	❄	226
Black cherry	*Prunus serotina*	🌲			♦	☼	♣	❄	230
Mullein	*Verbascum thapsus*		⊛			☼	♣		282

Colds

Common name	Latin name	Tree	⊗	≋	■	♦	☼	✿	❄	Page
Balsam fir	*Abies balsamea*	🌳				♦	☼	✿	❄	8
Yarrow	*Achillea millefolium*		⊗				☼	✿		10
Sweet flag	*Acorus calamus*			≋		♦		✿		12
Dogbane	*Apocynum androsaemifolium*	🌳	⊗				☼	✿		38
Hound's tongue	*Cynoglossum officinale*		⊗				☼	✿		106
Horseweed	*Erigeron canadensis*		⊗					✿		116
Boneset	*Eupatorium perfoliatum*			≋			☼	✿		120
Sunflower	*Helianthus annuus*		⊗				☼	✿		142
Juniper	*Juniperus communis*		⊗			♦	☼	✿	❄	166
Horehound	*Marrubium vulgare*		⊗			♦				182
Peppermint	*Mentha piperita*			≋		♦	☼	✿		190
Wild oregano	*Monarda fistulosa*	🌳	⊗				☼	✿		196
Watercress	*Nasturtium officinale*			≋		♦	☼	✿	❄	204
Catnip	*Nepeta cataria*		⊗				☼			206
White pine	*Pinus strobus*	🌳				♦	☼	✿	❄	216
Seneca-snakert	*Polygala senega*		⊗					✿		222
Balsam poplar	*Populus balsamifera*	🌳		≋		♦	☼	✿	❄	226
Black cherry	*Prunus serotina*	🌳				♦	☼	✿	❄	230
Hairy cap moss	*Polytrichum commune*	🌳			■	♦	☼	✿	❄	297

Cough

Common name	Latin name	Tree	⊗	≋	■	♦	☼	✿	❄	Page
Balsam fir	*Abies balsamea*	🌳				♦	☼	✿	❄	8
Sweet flag	*Acorus calamus*			≋		♦		✿		12
Sarsaprilla	*Aralia nudicaulis*	🌳	⊗				☼	✿		42
Burdock	*Arctium lappa*		⊗				☼	✿		44
Wake robin	*Arisaema triphyllum*	🌳		≋				✿		48
Marsh-marigold	*Caltha palustris*			≋		♦				70
Red root	*Ceanothus americanus*	🌳	⊗				☼	✿		78
Blazing star	*Chamaelirium luteum*	🌳			■			✿		82
Hound's tongue	*Cynoglossum officinale*		⊗				☼	✿		106
Trout lily	*Erythronium americanum*	🌳				♦		✿		118

Cough (cont.)

Common	Latin	🌳	⊛	≋	●	☼	🍁	❄	Page
Boneset	*Eupatorium perfoliatum*			≋		☼	🍁		120
Sunflower	*Helianthus annuus*		⊛			☼	🍁		142
Hepatica	*Hepatica acutiloba*	🌳			●				148
Lettuce	*Lactuca scariola*		⊛			☼	🍁		168
Indian tobacco	*Lobelia inflata*	🌳	⊛			☼			176
Bugleweed	*Lycopus virginicus*			≋		☼	🍁		178
Horehound	*Marrubium vulgare*		⊛		●				182
Spearmint	*Mentha spicata*			≋	●	☼	🍁		192
Seneca-snakert	*Polygala senega*		⊛				🍁		222
Black cherry	*Prunus serotina*	🌳			●	☼	🍁	❄	230
Sassafras	*Sassafras albidum*	🌳			●				250
Skunk cabbage	*Symplocarpus foetidus*			≋	●	☼	🍁		262
Arbor-vitae	*Thuja occidentalis*			≋	●	☼	🍁	❄	268
Mullein	*Verbascum thapsus*		⊛			☼	🍁		282

Pulmonary Problems

Common	Latin	🌳	⊛	≋	●	☼	🍁	❄	Page
Butterfly weed	*Asclepias tuberosa*		⊛				🍁		58
Red root	*Ceanothus americanus*	🌳	⊛			☼	🍁		78
Hound's tongue	*Cynoglossum officinale*		⊛			☼	🍁		106
Horseweed	*Erigeron canadensis*		⊛				🍁		116
Sunflower	*Helianthus annuus*		⊛			☼	🍁		142
St. John's wort	*Hypericum perforatum*		⊛			☼			156
Horehound	*Marrubium vulgare*		⊛		●				182
Seneca-snakert	*Polygala senega*		⊛				🍁		222
Solomon's seal	*Polygonatum biflorum*	🌳					🍁		224
Balsam poplar	*Populus balsamifera*	🌳		≋	●	☼	🍁	❄	226
Nightshade	*Solanum dulcamara*	🌳					🍁		256
Mullein	*Verbascum thapsus*		⊛			☼	🍁		282

Throat

Common name	Botanical name	🌳	⊛	≈	■	💧	✿	🍁	✳	Page
Yarrow	*Achillea millefolium*		⊛				✿	🍁		10
Anemone	*Anemone canadensis*	🌳		≈		💧				32
Columbine	*Aquilegia canadensis*	🌳		≈			✿			40
Wild ginger	*Asarum canadense*	🌳		≈				🍁		54
Wild indigo	*Baptisia tinctoria*		⊛					🍁		62
Gold thread	*Coptis groenlandica*	🌳			■	💧	✿	🍁		100
Horseweed	*Erigeron canadensis*		⊛					🍁		116
Strawberry	*Fragaria virginiana*		⊛			💧	✿	🍁		126
Wild geranium	*Geranium maculatum*	🌳				💧		🍁		134
Avens	*Geum rivale*			≈		💧	✿	🍁	✳	136
Cow parsnip	*Heracleum lanatum*	🌳		≈		💧	✿	🍁	✳	150
Black walnut	*Juglans nigra*	🌳				💧	✿	🍁		164
Wild oregano	*Monarda fistulosa*	🌳	⊛				✿	🍁		196
Watercress	*Nasturtium officinale*			≈		💧	✿	🍁	✳	204
Sweet cicely	*Osmorhiza longistylis*	🌳					✿	🍁		208
White pine	*Pinus strobus*	🌳				💧	✿	🍁	✳	216
Seneca-snakert	*Polygala senega*		⊛					🍁		222
Self-heal	*Prunella vulgaris*	🌳	⊛			💧	✿	🍁		228
Shinleaf	*Pyrola rotundifolia*	🌳			■	💧	✿	🍁		232
Sumac	*Rhus glabra*		⊛			💧	✿	🍁		234
Blackberry	*Rubus spp*		⊛			💧	✿	🍁		240
Bloodroot	*Sanguinaria canadensis*	🌳				💧				246
Tansy	*Tanacetum vulgare*		⊛				✿	🍁		264
Mullein	*Verbascum thapsus*		⊛				✿	🍁		282

Tuberculosis

Common name	Botanical name	🌳	⊛	≈	■	💧	✿	🍁	✳	Page
Balsam fir	*Abies balsamea*	🌳				💧	✿	🍁	✳	8
Turtle head	*Chelone glabra*			≈		💧	✿	🍁		84
Chicory	*Cichorium intybus*		⊛			💧		🍁		90
Boneset	*Eupatorium perfoliatum*			≈			✿	🍁		120
Bugleweed	*Lycopus virginicus*			≈			✿	🍁		178

Tuberculosis (cont.)

Horehound	*Marrubium vulgare*		⊛		💧				182
Ginseng	*Panax quinquefolius*	🌿					🍁		212
White pine	*Pinus strobus*	🌿			💧	☼	🍁	❋	216
Solomon's seal	*Polygonatum biflorum*	🌿					🍁		224
Black cherry	*Prunus serotina*	🌿			💧	☼	🍁	❋	230

Digestive System
Colic

Balsam fir	*Abies balsamea*	🌿			💧	☼	🍁	❋	8
Yarrow	*Achillea millefolium*		⊛			☼	🍁		10
Sweet flag	*Acorus calamus*			∿	💧		🍁		12
Star grass	*Aletris farinosa*	🌿					🍁		20
Angelica	*Angelica atropurpurea*	🌿		∿		☼	🍁		34
Wake robin	*Arisaema triphyllum*	🌿		∿			🍁		48
Blue cohosh	*Caulophyllum thalictroides*	🌿		∿			🍁		76
Turtle head	*Chelone glabra*			∿	💧	☼	🍁		84
Sweet fern	*Comptonia peregrina*		⊛			☼	🍁		96
Carrot	*Daucus carota*		⊛			☼	🍁		110
Wintergreen	*Gaultheria procumbens*	🌿			💧		🍁		132
Cow parsnip	*Heracleum lanatum*	🌿		∿	💧	☼	🍁	❋	150
Lettuce	*Lactuca scariola*		⊛			☼	🍁		168
Peppermint	*Mentha piperita*			∿	💧	☼	🍁		190
Spearmint	*Mentha spicata*			∿	💧	☼	🍁		192
Wild oregano	*Monarda fistulosa*	🌿	⊛			☼	🍁		196
Catnip	*Nepeta cataria*		⊛			☼			206
Cranberry	*Viburnum trilobum*			∿			🍁	❋	286

Dyspepsia

Sweet flag	*Acorus calamus*			≋	◆		✤		12
Star grass	*Aletris farinosa*	🌳					✤		20
Wormwood	*Artemisia absinthium*		✾			✿	✤		52
Barberry	*Berberis vulgaris*		✾				✤		66
Turtle head	*Chelone glabra*			≋	◆	✿	✤		84
Boneset	*Eupatorium perfoliatum*			≋		✿	✤		120
Avens	*Geum rivale*			≋	◆	✿	✤	❆	136
Horehound	*Marrubium vulgare*		✾		◆				182
Yellow parilla	*Menispermum canadense*	🌳					✤		188
Ginseng	*Panax quinquefolius*	🌳					✤		212
Bloodroot	*Sanguinaria canadensis*	🌳			◆				246
Pitcher-plant	*Sarracenia purpurea*			≋ ■	◆	✿	✤		248
Dandelion	*Taraxacum officinale*		✾		◆	✿	✤	❆	266

Indigestion

Wormwood	*Artemisia absinthium*		✾			✿	✤		52
Wild ginger	*Asarum canadense*	🌳		≋			✤		54
Blue cohosh	*Caulophyllum thalictroides*	🌳		≋			✤		76
Turtle head	*Chelone glabra*			≋	◆	✿	✤		84
Pennyroyal	*Hedeoma pulegioides*	🌳				✿			140
Hops	*Humulus lupulus*		✾				✤		152
Juniper	*Juniperus communis*		✾		◆	✿	✤	❆	166
Pineapple weed	*Matricaria matricarioides*		✾			✿	✤		184
Peppermint	*Mentha piperita*			≋	◆	✿	✤		190
Spearmint	*Mentha spicata*			≋	◆	✿	✤		192
Ginseng	*Panax quinquefolius*	🌳					✤		212
Black willow	*Salix nigra*			≋	◆				244

Stomach

Common name	Latin name	🌲	⊛	≈	■	💧	✿	🍁	❄	#
Yarrow	*Achillea millefolium*		⊛				✿	🍁		10
Doll's eyes	*Actaea alba*	🌲				💧	✿	🍁	❄	14
Angelica	*Angelica atropurpurea*	🌲		≈			✿	🍁		34
Burdock	*Arctium lappa*		⊛				✿	🍁		44
Wild ginger	*Asarum canadense*	🌲		≈				🍁		54
Birch	*Betula alleghaniensis*	🌲				💧	✿	🍁	❄	68
Case weed	*Capsella bursa-pastoris*		⊛			💧	✿	🍁		74
Wild spinach	*Chenopodium album*		⊛					🍁		86
Pipsissewa	*Chimaphila umbellata*	🌲				💧	✿	🍁		88
Chicory	*Cichorium intybus*		⊛			💧		🍁		90
Gold thread	*Coptis groenlandica*	🌲			■	💧	✿	🍁		100
Horseweed	*Erigeron canadensis*		⊛					🍁		116
Trout lily	*Erythronium americanum*	🌲				💧		🍁		118
Witch hazel	*Hamamelis virginiana*	🌲				💧		🍁		138
Pennyroyal	*Hedeoma pulegioides*	🌲					✿			140
Cow parsnip	*Heracleum lanatum*	🌲		≈		💧	✿	🍁	❄	150
Hops	*Humulus lupulus*		⊛					🍁		152
Goldenseal	*Hydrastis canadensis*	🌲					✿	🍁		154
Wild oregano	*Monarda fistulosa*	🌲	⊛				✿	🍁		196
Sweet cicely	*Osmorhiza longistylis*	🌲					✿	🍁		208
Ginseng	*Panax quinquefolius*	🌲						🍁		212
Bloodroot	*Sanguinaria canadensis*	🌲				💧				246
Cramp bark	*Viburnum opulus*	🌲				💧	✿	🍁	❄	284

Sore Mouth and Canker Sores

Common name	Latin name	🌲	⊛	≈	■	💧	✿	🍁	#
Columbine	*Aquilegia canadensis*	🌲		≈			✿		40
Wild indigo	*Baptisia tinctoria*		⊛					🍁	62
Red root	*Ceanothus americanus*	🌲	⊛				✿	🍁	78
Gold thread	*Coptis groenlandica*	🌲			■	💧	✿	🍁	100
Strawberry	*Fragaria virginiana*		⊛			💧	✿	🍁	126

311

Sore Mouth and Canker Sores (cont.)

Common Name	Scientific Name	🌳	❀	≈	■	💧	☼	🍁	❄	Page
Wild geranium	*Geranium maculatum*	🌳				💧		🍁		134
Avens	*Geum rivale*			≈		💧	☼	🍁	❄	136
Witch hazel	*Hamamelis virginiana*	🌳				💧		🍁		138
Goldenseal	*Hydrastis canadensis*	🌳					☼	🍁		154
Black walnut	*Juglans nigra*	🌳				💧	☼	🍁		164
Sweet cicely	*Osmorhiza longistylis*	🌳					☼	🍁		208
Self-heal	*Prunella vulgaris*	🌳	❀			💧	☼	🍁		228
Shinleaf	*Pyrola rotundifolia*	🌳	❀		■	💧	☼	🍁		232
Sumac	*Rhus glabra*		❀			💧	☼	🍁		234
Blackberry	*Rubus spp*		❀			💧	☼	🍁		240
Tansy	*Tanacetum vulgare*		❀				☼	🍁		264

Toothache

Common Name	Scientific Name	🌳	❀	≈	■	💧	☼	🍁	Page
Yarrow	*Achillea millefolium*		❀				☼	🍁	10
Sweet flag	*Acorus calamus*			≈		💧		🍁	12
Sweet fern	*Comptonia peregrina*		❀				☼	🍁	96
Lady's slipper	*Cypripedium calceolus*	🌳		≈	■	💧		🍁	108
Wintergreen	*Gaultheria procumbens*	🌳				💧		🍁	132
Hops	*Humulus lupulus*		❀					🍁	152
Catnip	*Nepeta cataria*		❀				☼		206
Sassafras	*Sassafras albidum*	🌳				💧			250
Skunk cabbage	*Symplocarpus foetidus*			≈		💧	☼	🍁	262

Ulcer

Common Name	Scientific Name	🌳	❀	≈	■	💧	☼	🍁	Page
Sweet flag	*Acorus calamus*			≈		💧		🍁	12
Wild indigo	*Baptisia tinctoria*		❀					🍁	62
Turtle head	*Chelone glabra*			≈		💧	☼	🍁	84
Gold thread	*Coptis groenlandica*	🌳			■	💧	☼	🍁	100
Horseweed	*Erigeron canadensis*		❀					🍁	116
Trout lily	*Erythronium americanum*	🌳				💧		🍁	118

Ulcer (cont.)

Common name	Latin name	🌳	⊛	≈	■	💧	☼	🍁	❄	Page
Wild geranium	*Geranium maculatum*	🌳				💧		🍁		134
Hops	*Humulus lupulus*		⊛					🍁		152
Goldenseal	*Hydrastis canadensis*	🌳					☼	🍁		154
Black cherry	*Prunus serotina*	🌳				💧	☼	🍁	❄	230
Comfrey	*Symphytum officinale*		⊛			💧				260
Red clover	*Trifolium pratense*		⊛				☼	🍁		270
Purple trillium	*Trillium erectum*	🌳					☼	🍁		272

Urinary System
Liver

Common name	Latin name	🌳	⊛	≈	■	💧	☼	🍁	❄	Page
Bittersweet	*Celastrus scandens*		⊛					🍁		80
Blazing star	*Chamaelirium luteum*	🌳			■			🍁		82
Turtle head	*Chelone glabra*			≈		💧	☼	🍁		84
Chicory	*Cichorium intybus*		⊛			💧		🍁		90
Carrot	*Daucus carota*		⊛				☼	🍁		110
Hepatica	*Hepatica acutiloba*	🌳				💧				148
Goldenseal	*Hydrastis canadensis*	🌳					☼	🍁		154
Dandelion	*Taraxacum officinale*		⊛			💧	☼	🍁	❄	266
Red clover	*Trifolium pratense*		⊛				☼	🍁		270
Liverwort	*Marchantia polymorpha*	🌳				💧	☼	🍁	❄	295
Hairy cap moss	*Polytrichum commune*	🌳			■	💧	☼	🍁	❄	297

Urinary

Common name	Latin name	🌳	⊛	≈	■	💧	☼	🍁	❄	Page
Balsam fir	*Abies balsamea*	🌳				💧	☼	🍁	❄	8
Bearberry	*Arctostaphylos uva-ursi*	🌳	⊛					🍁		46
Blazing star	*Chamaelirium luteum*	🌳			■			🍁		82
Chicory	*Cichorium intybus*		⊛			💧		🍁		90
Carrot	*Daucus carota*		⊛				☼	🍁		110
Arbutus	*Epigaea repens*	🌳			■	💧				114
Joe-pye weed	*Eupatorium purpureum*			≈			☼	🍁		122

Urinary (cont.)

Common	Latin	🌳	❁	~~~	💧	☼	🍁	❄	Page
Cleavers	*Galium aparine*			~~~	💧	☼			130
Juniper	*Juniperus communis*		❁		💧	☼	🍁	❄	166
White pine	*Pinus strobus*	🌳			💧	☼	🍁	❄	216

Gastrointestinal System
Constipation

Common	Latin	🌳	❁	~~~	💧	☼	🍁	❄	Page
Wake robin	*Arisaema triphyllum*	🌳		~~~			🍁		48
Goldenseal	*Hydrastis canadensis*	🌳				☼	🍁		154
Butternut	*Juglans cinerea*	🌳		~~~	💧	☼	🍁	❄	162
Rose	*Rosa spp*	🌳	❁			☼	🍁		238

Diarrhea

Common	Latin	🌳	❁	~~~	💧	☼	🍁	❄	Page
Star grass	*Aletris farinosa*	🌳					🍁		20
Swamp alder	*Alnus rugosa*			~~~	💧	☼	🍁	❄	24
Columbine	*Aquilegia canadensis*	🌳		~~~		☼			40
Bearberry	*Arctostaphylos uva-ursi*	🌳	❁				🍁		46
Barberry	*Berberis vulgaris*		❁				🍁		66
Sweet fern	*Comptonia peregrina*		❁			☼	🍁		96
Hound's tongue	*Cynoglossum officinale*		❁			☼	🍁		106
Horseweed	*Erigeron canadensis*		❁				🍁		116
Strawberry	*Fragaria virginiana*		❁		💧	☼	🍁		126
Wild geranium	*Geranium maculatum*	🌳			💧		🍁		134
Avens	*Geum rivale*			~~~	💧	☼	🍁	❄	136
Butternut	*Juglans cinerea*	🌳		~~~	💧	☼	🍁	❄	162
Lettuce	*Lactuca scariola*		❁			☼	🍁		168
Peppermint	*Mentha piperita*			~~~	💧	☼	🍁		190
Partridge berry	*Mitchella repens*	🌳					🍁		194
Self-heal	*Prunella vulgaris*	🌳	❁		💧	☼	🍁		228
Black cherry	*Prunus serotina*	🌳			💧	☼	🍁	❄	230

Diarrhea (cont.)

Common	Latin	Tree	Flower	Water	Drop	Sun	Leaf	Snow	Page
Sumac	*Rhus glabra*		⊛		💧	☼	🍁		234
Blackberry	*Rubus spp*		⊛		💧	☼	🍁		240
Black willow	*Salix nigra*			〰	💧				244
Cattail	*Typha latifolia*			〰	💧	☼	🍁	❄	274
Mullein	*Verbascum thapsus*		⊛			☼	🍁		282

Dysentery

Common	Latin	Tree	Flower	Water	Drop	Sun	Leaf	Snow	Page
Shadbush	*Amelanchier spp*	🌳	⊛			☼			28
Milkweed	*Asclepias syriaca*		⊛			☼	🍁		56
Barberry	*Berberis vulgaris*		⊛				🍁		66
Hound's tongue	*Cynoglossum officinale*		⊛			☼	🍁		106
Horseweed	*Erigeron canadensis*		⊛				🍁		116
Strawberry	*Fragaria virginiana*		⊛		💧	☼	🍁		126
Wild geranium	*Geranium maculatum*	🌳			💧		🍁		134
Butternut	*Juglans cinerea*	🌳		〰	💧	☼	🍁	❄	162
Blackberry	*Rubus spp*		⊛		💧	☼	🍁		240
Black willow	*Salix nigra*			〰	💧				244

Flatulence

Common	Latin	Tree	Flower	Water	Drop	Sun	Leaf	Page
Sweet flag	*Acorus calamus*			〰	💧		🍁	12
Carrot	*Daucus carota*		⊛			☼	🍁	110
Pennyroyal	*Hedeoma pulegioides*	🌳				☼		140
Peppermint	*Mentha piperita*			〰	💧	☼	🍁	190
Spearmint	*Mentha spicata*			〰	💧	☼	🍁	192
Catnip	*Nepeta cataria*		⊛			☼		206

Hemorrhoids

Common name	Scientific name	🌳	⊛	≈	■	◆	☼	✿	❄	Page
Horse chestnut	*Aesculus hippocastanum*	🌳				◆	☼	✿	❄	18
White ash	*Fraxinus americana*	🌳				◆	☼	✿		128
Wild geranium	*Geranium maculatum*	🌳				◆		✿		134
Witch hazel	*Hamamelis virginiana*	🌳				◆		✿		138
Goldenseal	*Hydrastis canadensis*	🌳					☼	✿		154
Spearmint	*Mentha spicata*			≈		◆	☼	✿		192
Solomon's seal	*Polygonatum biflorum*	🌳						✿		224
Sumac	*Rhus glabra*		⊛			◆	☼	✿		234
Figwort	*Scrophularia marilandica*	🌳				◆	☼			252
Mullein	*Verbascum thapsus*		⊛				☼	✿		282

Worms

Common name	Scientific name	🌳	⊛	≈	■	◆	☼	✿	❄	Page
Angelica	*Angelica atropurpurea*	🌳		≈			☼	✿		34
Dogbane	*Apocynum androsaemifolium*	🌳	⊛				☼	✿		38
Blazing star	*Chamaelirium luteum*	🌳			■			✿		82
Lady's slipper	*Cypripedium calceolus*	🌳		≈	■	◆		✿		108
Carrot	*Daucus carota*		⊛				☼	✿		110
Butternut	*Juglans cinerea*	🌳		≈		◆	☼	✿	❄	162
Black walnut	*Juglans nigra*	🌳				◆	☼	✿		164
Horehound	*Marrubium vulgare*		⊛			◆				182
Black cherry	*Prunus serotina*	🌳				◆	☼	✿	❄	230
Tansy	*Tanacetum vulgare*		⊛				☼	✿		264

Lymphatic System
Dropsy

Common name	Scientific name	🌳	⊛	≈	◆	☼	✿	Page
Dogbane	*Apocynum androsaemifolium*	🌳	⊛			☼	✿	38
Milkweed	*Asclepias syriaca*		⊛			☼	✿	56
Marsh-marigold	*Caltha palustris*			≈	◆			70
Carrot	*Daucus carota*		⊛			☼	✿	110
Trout lily	*Erythronium americanum*	🌳			◆		✿	118

316

Dropsy (cont.)

Common name	Scientific name	🌳	≋	✳	💧	☼	🍁	❄	Page
Joe-pye weed	*Eupatorium purpureum*		≋			☼	🍁		122
Wild iris	*Iris versicolor*		≋				🍁		160
Seneca-snakert	*Polygala senega*			✳			🍁		222

Fever

Common name	Scientific name	🌳	≋	✳	💧	☼	🍁	❄	Page
Horse chestnut	*Aesculus hippocastanum*	🌳			💧	☼	🍁	❄	18
Angelica	*Angelica atropurpurea*	🌳	≋			☼	🍁		34
Columbine	*Aquilegia canadensis*	🌳	≋			☼			40
Wild indigo	*Baptisia tinctoria*			✳			🍁		62
Barberry	*Berberis vulgaris*			✳			🍁		66
Coral root	*Corallorhiza maculata*	🌳			💧	☼	🍁		102
Horseweed	*Erigeron canadensis*			✳			🍁		116
Boneset	*Eupatorium perfoliatum*		≋			☼	🍁		120
Wintergreen	*Gaultheria procumbens*	🌳			💧		🍁		132
Hops	*Humulus lupulus*			✳			🍁		152
Bugleweed	*Lycopus virginicus*		≋			☼	🍁		178
Wild oregano	*Monarda fistulosa*	🌳		✳		☼	🍁		196
Catnip	*Nepeta cataria*			✳		☼			206
Ginseng	*Panax quinquefolius*	🌳					🍁		212
Plantain	*Plantago major*			✳		☼	🍁		218
Black cherry	*Prunus serotina*	🌳			💧	☼	🍁	❄	230
Sumac	*Rhus glabra*			✳	💧	☼	🍁		234
Black willow	*Salix nigra*		≋		💧				244
Sassafras	*Sassafras albidum*	🌳			💧				250
Tansy	*Tanacetum vulgare*			✳		☼	🍁		264
Arbor-vitae	*Thuja occidentalis*		≋		💧	☼	🍁	❄	268

Infection

Common	Latin	🌳	✲	≈	■	●	☼	❦	❄	Page
Swamp alder	*Alnus rugosa*			≈		●	☼	❦	❄	24
Anemone	*Anemone canadensis*	🌳		≈		●				32
Bearberry	*Arctostaphylos uva-ursi*	🌳	✲					❦		46
Wild ginger	*Asarum canadense*	🌳		≈				❦		54
Joe-pye weed	*Eupatorium purpureum*			≈			☼	❦		122
Goldenseal	*Hydrastis canadensis*	🌳					☼	❦		154
Wild iris	*Iris versicolor*			≈				❦		160
Butternut	*Juglans cinerea*	🌳		≈		●	☼	❦	❄	162
Balsam poplar	*Populus balsamifera*	🌳		≈		●	☼	❦	❄	226
Black willow	*Salix nigra*			≈		●				244
Bloodroot	*Sanguinaria canadensis*	🌳				●				246
Mullein	*Verbascum thapsus*		✲				☼	❦		282

Gynecology
Diseases of Women

Common	Latin	🌳	✲	≈	■	●	☼	❦	❄	Page
Doll's eyes	*Actaea alba*	🌳				●	☼	❦	❄	14
Burdock	*Arctium lappa*		✲				☼	❦		44
Blazing star	*Chamaelirium luteum*	🌳			■			❦		82
Lady's slipper	*Cypripedium calceolus*	🌳		≈	■	●		❦		108
Boneset	*Eupatorium perfoliatum*			≈			☼	❦		120
Lettuce	*Lactuca scariola*		✲				☼	❦		168
Motherwort	*Leonurus cardiaca*		✲				☼	❦		172
Partridge berry	*Mitchella repens*	🌳						❦		194
Indian pipe	*Monotropa uniflora*	🌳					☼			198
Sweet cicely	*Osmorhiza longistylis*	🌳					☼	❦		208
Ginseng	*Panax quinquefolius*	🌳						❦		212
Plantain	*Plantago major*		✲				☼	❦		218
Black cherry	*Prunus serotina*	🌳				●	☼	❦	❄	230
Sumac	*Rhus glabra*		✲			●	☼	❦		234
Pitcher-plant	*Sarracenia purpurea*			≈	■	●	☼	❦		248
Figwort	*Scrophularia marilandica*	🌳				●	☼			252
Purple trillium	*Trillium erectum*	🌳					☼	❦		272

Leukorrhea

Common	Latin	🌳	⊛	■	💧	☼	🍁	❄	Page
Bearberry	*Arctostaphylos uva-ursi*	🌳	⊛				🍁		46
Bittersweet	*Celastrus scandens*		⊛				🍁		80
Blazing star	*Chamaelirium luteum*	🌳		■			🍁		82
Wild geranium	*Geranium maculatum*	🌳			💧		🍁		134
Hepatica	*Hepatica acutiloba*	🌳			💧				148
Goldenseal	*Hydrastis canadensis*	🌳				☼	🍁		154
Juniper	*Juniperus communis*		⊛		💧	☼	🍁	❄	166

Menstruation

Common	Latin	🌳	⊛	〜	💧	☼	🍁	❄	Page
Yarrow	*Achillea millefolium*		⊛			☼	🍁		10
Doll's eyes	*Actaea alba*	🌳			💧	☼	🍁	❄	14
Maiden hair frn	*Adiantum capillus-veneris*	🌳			💧	☼	🍁		16
Angelica	*Angelica atropurpurea*	🌳		〜		☼	🍁		34
Bittersweet	*Celastrus scandens*		⊛				🍁		80
Horseweed	*Erigeron canadensis*		⊛				🍁		116
Motherwort	*Leonurus cardiaca*		⊛			☼	🍁		172
Horehound	*Marrubium vulgare*		⊛		💧				182
Ginseng	*Panax quinquefolius*	🌳					🍁		212
Balsam poplar	*Populus balsamifera*	🌳		〜	💧	☼	🍁	❄	226
Figwort	*Scrophularia marilandica*	🌳			💧	☼			252
Purple trillium	*Trillium erectum*	🌳				☼	🍁		272
Cramp bark	*Viburnum opulus*	🌳			💧	☼	🍁	❄	284

Dermatologic System
Diseases of the Skin

Common name	Latin name	🌲	⊛	≋	♦	☼	✿	❄	Page
Balsam fir	*Abies balsamea*	🌲			♦	☼	✿	❄	8
Yarrow	*Achillea millefolium*		⊛			☼	✿		10
Maiden hair frn	*Adiantum capillus-veneris*	🌲			♦	☼	✿		16
Horse chestnut	*Aesculus hippocastanum*	🌲			♦	☼	✿	❄	18
Leek	*Allium tricoccum*	🌲			♦				22
Swamp alder	*Alnus rugosa*			≋	♦	☼	✿	❄	24
Sarsaprilla	*Aralia nudicaulis*	🌲	⊛			☼	✿		42
Burdock	*Arctium lappa*		⊛			☼	✿		44
Wild indigo	*Baptisia tinctoria*		⊛				✿		62
Bittersweet	*Celastrus scandens*		⊛				✿		80
Turtle head	*Chelone glabra*			≋	♦	☼	✿		84
Pipsissewa	*Chimaphila umbellata*	🌲			♦	☼	✿		88
Coral root	*Corallorhiza maculata*	🌲			♦	☼	✿		102
Squirrel corn	*Dicentra canadensis*	🌲			♦		✿		112
Joe-pye weed	*Eupatorium purpureum*			≋		☼	✿		122
White ash	*Fraxinus americana*	🌲			♦	☼	✿		128
Cleavers	*Galium aparine*			≋	♦	☼			130
Goldenseal	*Hydrastis canadensis*	🌲				☼	✿		154
St. John's wort	*Hypericum perforatum*		⊛			☼			156
Wild iris	*Iris versicolor*			≋			✿		160
Butternut	*Juglans cinerea*	🌲		≋	♦	☼	✿	❄	162
Black walnut	*Juglans nigra*	🌲			♦	☼	✿		164
Lettuce	*Lactuca scariola*		⊛			☼	✿		168
Yellow parilla	*Menispermum canadense*	🌲					✿		188
Spearmint	*Mentha spicata*			≋	♦	☼	✿		192
Watercress	*Nasturtium officinale*			≋	♦	☼	✿	❄	204
White pine	*Pinus strobus*	🌲			♦	☼	✿	❄	216
Plantain	*Plantago major*		⊛			☼	✿		218
Solomon's seal	*Polygonatum biflorum*	🌲					✿		224
Balsam poplar	*Populus balsamifera*	🌲		≋	♦	☼	✿	❄	226

Diseases of the Skin (cont.)

Common name	Scientific name	🌳	✻	〰	◼	💧	☼	🍁	❄	Page
Black cherry	*Prunus serotina*	🌳				💧	☼	🍁	❄	230
Shinleaf	*Pyrola rotundifolia*	🌳			◼	💧	☼	🍁		232
Rose	*Rosa spp*	🌳	✻				☼	🍁		238
Curly dock	*Rumex crispus*		✻	〰			☼	🍁		242
Bloodroot	*Sanguinaria canadensis*	🌳				💧				246
Figwort	*Scrophularia marilandica*	🌳				💧	☼			252
Nightshade	*Solanum dulcamara*	🌳						🍁		256
Arbor-vitae	*Thuja occidentalis*			〰		💧	☼	🍁	❄	268
Red clover	*Trifolium pratense*		✻				☼	🍁		270
Purple trillium	*Trillium erectum*	🌳					☼	🍁		272
Cattail	*Typha latifolia*			〰		💧	☼	🍁	❄	274

Bruises

Common name	Scientific name	🌳	✻	〰	◼	💧	☼	🍁	❄	Page
Leek	*Allium tricoccum*	🌳				💧				22
Butterfly weed	*Asclepias tuberosa*		✻					🍁		58
Chicory	*Cichorium intybus*		✻			💧		🍁		90
Carrot	*Daucus carota*		✻				☼	🍁		110
Witch hazel	*Hamamelis virginiana*	🌳				💧		🍁		138
Pennyroyal	*Hedeoma pulegioides*	🌳					☼			140
St. John's wort	*Hypericum perforatum*		✻				☼			156
Wild iris	*Iris versicolor*			〰				🍁		160
Indian tobacco	*Lobelia inflata*	🌳	✻				☼			176
Plantain	*Plantago major*		✻				☼	🍁		218
Solomon's seal	*Polygonatum biflorum*	🌳						🍁		224
Self-heal	*Prunella vulgaris*	🌳	✻			💧	☼	🍁		228
Black cherry	*Prunus serotina*	🌳				💧	☼	🍁	❄	230
Comfrey	*Symphytum officinale*		✻			💧				260
Tansy	*Tanacetum vulgare*		✻				☼	🍁		264
Liverwort	*Marchantia polymorpha*	🌳				💧	☼	🍁	❄	295
Aq. apple moss	*Philonotis fontana*				◼	💧	☼	🍁	❄	296

Burns

Common	Scientific	🌳	⊛	≈	■	●	☼	✤	❄	Page
Sarsaprilla	*Aralia nudicaulis*	🌳	⊛				☼	✤		42
Burdock	*Arctium lappa*		⊛				☼	✤		44
Bittersweet	*Celastrus scandens*		⊛					✤		80
Hound's tongue	*Cynoglossum officinale*		⊛				☼	✤		106
Joe-pye weed	*Eupatorium purpureum*			≈			☼	✤		122
Beechnut	*Fagus grandifolia*	🌳				●	☼	✤	❄	124
White ash	*Fraxinus americana*	🌳				●	☼	✤		128
Cleavers	*Galium aparine*			≈		●	☼			130
Witch hazel	*Hamamelis virginiana*	🌳				●		✤		138
Pennyroyal	*Hedeoma pulegioides*	🌳					☼			140
White pine	*Pinus strobus*	🌳				●	☼	✤	❄	216
Sumac	*Rhus glabra*		⊛			●	☼	✤		234
Bloodroot	*Sanguinaria canadensis*	🌳				●				246
Dandelion	*Taraxacum officinale*		⊛			●	☼	✤	❄	266
Arbor-vitae	*Thuja occidentalis*			≈		●	☼	✤	❄	268
Cattail	*Typha latifolia*			≈		●	☼	✤	❄	274
Scent liverwort	*Conocephalum conicum*		⊛			●	☼	✤	❄	290
Liverwort	*Marchantia polymorpha*	🌳				●	☼	✤	❄	295
Aq. apple moss	*Philonotis fontana*				■	●	☼	✤	❄	296

Cuts

Common	Scientific	🌳	⊛	≈	●	☼	✤	❄	Page
Balsam fir	*Abies balsamea*	🌳			●	☼	✤	❄	8
Swamp alder	*Alnus rugosa*			≈	●	☼	✤	❄	24
Wild indigo	*Baptisia tinctoria*		⊛				✤		62
Carrot	*Daucus carota*		⊛			☼	✤		110
Wild geranium	*Geranium maculatum*	🌳			●		✤		134
Witch hazel	*Hamamelis virginiana*	🌳			●		✤		138
Goldenseal	*Hydrastis canadensis*	🌳				☼	✤		154
St. John's wort	*Hypericum perforatum*		⊛			☼			156
White pine	*Pinus strobus*	🌳			●	☼	✤	❄	216
Plantain	*Plantago major*		⊛			☼	✤		218

322

Cuts (cont.)

		🌳	✽	〰	■	💧	☼	🍁	❄	
Black cherry	*Prunus serotina*	🌳				💧	☼	🍁	❄	230
Sumac	*Rhus glabra*		✽			💧	☼	🍁		234
Curly dock	*Rumex crispus*		✽	〰			☼	🍁		242
Skunk cabbage	*Symplocarpus foetidus*			〰		💧	☼	🍁		262
Scent liverwort	*Conocephalum conicum*		✽			💧	☼	🍁	❄	290
Liverwort	*Marchantia polymorpha*	🌳				💧	☼	🍁	❄	295
Aq. apple moss	*Philonotis fontana*				■	💧	☼	🍁	❄	296

Inflammation

		🌳	✽	〰	■	💧	☼	🍁	❄	
Swamp alder	*Alnus rugosa*			〰		💧	☼	🍁	❄	24
Wild ginger	*Asarum canadense*	🌳		〰				🍁		54
Turtle head	*Chelone glabra*			〰		💧	☼	🍁		84
Chicory	*Cichorium intybus*		✽			💧		🍁		90
Gold thread	*Coptis groenlandica*	🌳			■	💧	☼	🍁		100
Joe-pye weed	*Eupatorium purpureum*			〰			☼	🍁		122
Cleavers	*Galium aparine*			〰		💧	☼			130
Witch hazel	*Hamamelis virginiana*	🌳				💧		🍁		138
Hops	*Humulus lupulus*		✽					🍁		152
Goldenseal	*Hydrastis canadensis*	🌳					☼	🍁		154
Plantain	*Plantago major*		✽				☼	🍁		218

Insect Bite

		🌳	✽	〰	💧	☼	🍁	❄	
St. John's wort	*Hypericum perforatum*		✽			☼			156
Jewelweed	*Impatiens capensis*			〰		☼			158
Plantain	*Plantago major*		✽			☼	🍁		218
Liverwort	*Marchantia polymorpha*	🌳			💧	☼	🍁	❄	295

Wounds

		Tree	⊛	≈	■	●	○	✿	❄	
Swamp alder	*Alnus rugosa*			≈		●	○	✿	❄	24
Anemone	*Anemone canadensis*	🌳		≈		●				32
Burdock	*Arctium lappa*		⊛				○	✿		44
Wild ginger	*Asarum canadense*	🌳		≈				✿		54
Butterfly weed	*Asclepias tuberosa*		⊛					✿		58
Goldenseal	*Hydrastis canadensis*	🌳					○	✿		154
St. John's wort	*Hypericum perforatum*		⊛				○			156
Juniper	*Juniperus communis*		⊛			●	○	✿	❄	166
White pine	*Pinus strobus*	🌳				●	○	✿	❄	216
Plantain	*Plantago major*		⊛				○	✿		218
Shinleaf	*Pyrola rotundifolia*	🌳			■	●	○	✿		232
Blackberry	*Rubus spp*		⊛			●	○	✿		240
Cattail	*Typha latifolia*			≈		●	○	✿	❄	274
Scent liverwort	*Conocephalum conicum*		⊛			●	○	✿	❄	290
Liverwort	*Marchantia polymorpha*	🌳				●	○	✿	❄	295
Aq. apple moss	*Philonotis fontana*				■	●	○	✿	❄	296

Diseases of the Ear
Ear

		Tree	⊛	≈	●	○	✿	❄	
Pearly everlast	*Anaphalis margaritacea*		⊛			○			30
Anemone	*Anemone canadensis*	🌳		≈	●				32
Dogbane	*Apocynum androsaemifolium*	🌳	⊛			○	✿		38
Bearberry	*Arctostaphylos uva-ursi*	🌳	⊛				✿		46
Wild ginger	*Asarum canadense*	🌳		≈			✿		54
Milkweed	*Asclepias syriaca*		⊛			○	✿		56
Marsh-marigold	*Caltha palustris*			≈	●				70
Case weed	*Capsella bursa-pastoris*		⊛		●	○	✿		74
Carrot	*Daucus carota*		⊛			○	✿		110
Trout lily	*Erythronium americanum*	🌳			●		✿		118
Joe-pye weed	*Eupatorium purpureum*			≈		○	✿		122
Avens	*Geum rivale*			≈	●	○	✿	❄	136

Ear (cont.)

Common name	Scientific name	🌳	⊛	∿	■	💧	☼	🍁	❄	Page
Hops	*Humulus lupulus*		⊛					🍁		152
Wild iris	*Iris versicolor*			∿				🍁		160
Motherwort	*Leonurus cardiaca*		⊛				☼	🍁		172
Bugleweed	*Lycopus virginicus*			∿			☼	🍁		178
Watercress	*Nasturtium officinale*			∿		💧	☼	🍁	❄	204
Catnip	*Nepeta cataria*		⊛				☼			206
Ginseng	*Panax quinquefolius*	🌳						🍁		212
Seneca-snakert	*Polygala senega*		⊛					🍁		222
Balsam poplar	*Populus balsamifera*	🌳		∿		💧	☼	🍁	❄	226
Curly dock	*Rumex crispus*		⊛	∿			☼	🍁		242
Figwort	*Scrophularia marilandica*	🌳				💧	☼			252
Mad-dog weed	*Scutellaria lateriflora*	🌳	⊛	∿		💧	☼			254
Tansy	*Tanacetum vulgare*		⊛				☼	🍁		264
Dandelion	*Taraxacum officinale*		⊛			💧	☼	🍁	❄	266
Arbor-vitae	*Thuja occidentalis*			∿		💧	☼	🍁	❄	268
Purple trillium	*Trillium erectum*	🌳					☼	🍁		272
Mullein	*Verbascum thapsus*		⊛				☼	🍁		282

Diseases of the Eye
Eye

Common name	Scientific name	🌳	⊛	∿	■	💧	☼	🍁	❄	Page
Doll's eyes	*Actaea alba*	🌳				💧	☼	🍁	❄	14
Swamp alder	*Alnus rugosa*			∿		💧	☼	🍁	❄	24
Shadbush	*Amelanchier spp*	🌳	⊛				☼			28
Anemone	*Anemone canadensis*	🌳		∿		💧				32
Wake robin	*Arisaema triphyllum*	🌳		∿				🍁		48
Wild ginger	*Asarum canadense*	🌳		∿				🍁		54
Case weed	*Capsella bursa-pastoris*		⊛			💧	☼	🍁		74
Pipsissewa	*Chimaphila umbellata*	🌳				💧	☼	🍁		88
Chicory	*Cichorium intybus*		⊛			💧		🍁		90
Gold thread	*Coptis groenlandica*	🌳			■	💧	☼	🍁		100

Eye (cont.)

Witch hazel	*Hamamelis virginiana*	🌳			💧		🍁		138
Hepatica	*Hepatica acutiloba*	🌳			💧				148
Goldenseal	*Hydrastis canadensis*	🌳				☼	🍁		154
Indian tobacco	*Lobelia inflata*	🌳	❀			☼			176
Peppermint	*Mentha piperita*			≈	💧	☼	🍁		190
Indian pipe	*Monotropa uniflora*	🌳				☼			198
Sweet cicely	*Osmorhiza longistylis*	🌳				☼	🍁		208
Solomon's seal	*Polygonatum biflorum*	🌳					🍁		224
Shinleaf	*Pyrola rotundifolia*	🌳		■	💧	☼	🍁		232
Blackberry	*Rubus spp*		❀		💧	☼	🍁		240
Curly dock	*Rumex crispus*		❀	≈		☼	🍁		242
Sassafras	*Sassafras albidum*	🌳			💧				250
Tansy	*Tanacetum vulgare*		❀			☼	🍁		264
Purple trillium	*Trillium erectum*	🌳				☼	🍁		272
Cattail	*Typha latifolia*			≈	💧	☼	🍁	❄	274

Diseases of the Joints
Back Pain

Balsam fir	*Abies balsamea*	🌳			💧	☼	🍁	❄	8
Sarsaprilla	*Aralia nudicaulis*	🌳	❀			☼	🍁		42
Bearberry	*Arctostaphylos uva-ursi*	🌳	❀				🍁		46
Balsam poplar	*Populus balsamifera*	🌳		≈	💧	☼	🍁	❄	226
White pine	*Pinus strobus*	🌳			💧	☼	🍁	❄	216

326

Gout

Common name	Scientific name							
Angelica	*Angelica atropurpurea*	🌲	♒			☼	🍁	34
Chicory	*Cichorium intybus*	✳			💧		🍁	90
Carrot	*Daucus carota*	✳				☼	🍁	110
Boneset	*Eupatorium perfoliatum*		♒			☼	🍁	120
Strawberry	*Fragaria virginiana*	✳			💧	☼	🍁	126
Yellow parilla	*Menispermum canadense*	🌲					🍁	188
Seneca-snakert	*Polygala senega*	✳					🍁	222
Solomon's seal	*Polygonatum biflorum*	🌲					🍁	224
Balsam poplar	*Populus balsamifera*	🌲	♒		💧	☼	🍁 ❄	226
Black willow	*Salix nigra*		♒		💧			244

Poultice

Common name	Scientific name							
Yarrow	*Achillea millefolium*	✳				☼	🍁	10
Maiden hair frn	*Adiantum capillus-veneris*	🌲			💧	☼	🍁	16
Star grass	*Aletris farinosa*	🌲					🍁	20
Leek	*Allium tricoccum*	🌲			💧			22
Swamp alder	*Alnus rugosa*		♒		💧	☼	🍁 ❄	24
Anemone	*Anemone canadensis*	🌲	♒		💧			32
Angelica	*Angelica atropurpurea*	🌲	♒			☼	🍁	34
Sarsaprilla	*Aralia nudicaulis*	🌲 ✳				☼	🍁	42
Wild ginger	*Asarum canadense*	🌲	♒				🍁	54
Butterfly weed	*Asclepias tuberosa*	✳					🍁	58
Wild indigo	*Baptisia tinctoria*	✳					🍁	62
Turtle head	*Chelone glabra*		♒		💧	☼	🍁	84
Chicory	*Cichorium intybus*	✳			💧		🍁	90
Carrot	*Daucus carota*	✳				☼	🍁	110
Squirrel corn	*Dicentra canadensis*	🌲			💧		🍁	112
Trout lily	*Erythronium americanum*	🌲			💧		🍁	118
Joe-pye weed	*Eupatorium purpureum*		♒			☼	🍁	122
Beechnut	*Fagus grandifolia*	🌲			💧	☼	🍁 ❄	124
Wild geranium	*Geranium maculatum*	🌲			💧		🍁	134

Poultice (cont.)

Common name	Latin name	🌲	⊛	≈	●	☼	❀	✳	Page
Cow parsnip	*Heracleum lanatum*	🌲		≈	●	☼	❀	✳	150
Wild iris	*Iris versicolor*			≈			❀		160
Black walnut	*Juglans nigra*	🌲			●	☼	❀		164
Juniper	*Juniperus communis*		⊛		●	☼	❀	✳	166
Hoary puccoon	*Lithospermum canescens*	🌲	⊛		●	☼			174
Indian tobacco	*Lobelia inflata*	🌲	⊛			☼			176
Catnip	*Nepeta cataria*		⊛			☼			206
White pine	*Pinus strobus*	🌲			●	☼	❀	✳	216
Plantain	*Plantago major*		⊛			☼	❀		218
Solomon's seal	*Polygonatum biflorum*	🌲					❀		224
Black cherry	*Prunus serotina*	🌲			●	☼	❀	✳	230
Sumac	*Rhus glabra*		⊛		●	☼	❀		234
Curly dock	*Rumex crispus*		⊛	≈		☼	❀		242
Sassafras	*Sassafras albidum*	🌲			●				250
Figwort	*Scrophularia marilandica*	🌲			●	☼			252
Nightshade	*Solanum dulcamara*	🌲					❀		256
Skunk cabbage	*Symplocarpus foetidus*			≈	●	☼	❀		262
Tansy	*Tanacetum vulgare*		⊛			☼	❀		264
Purple trillium	*Trillium erectum*	🌲				☼	❀		272
Cattail	*Typha latifolia*			≈	●	☼	❀	✳	274
Mullein	*Verbascum thapsus*		⊛			☼	❀		282

Sprains

Common name	Latin name	🌲	⊛	≈	●	☼	❀	Page
Wormwood	*Artemisia absinthium*		⊛			☼	❀	52
Witch hazel	*Hamamelis virginiana*	🌲			●		❀	138
Jewelweed	*Impatiens capensis*			≈		☼		158
Indian tobacco	*Lobelia inflata*	🌲	⊛			☼		176
Comfrey	*Symphytum officinale*		⊛		●			260
Tansy	*Tanacetum vulgare*		⊛			☼	❀	264

Rheumatism

Common name	Latin name	🌳	✤	〰	💧	☼	🍁	❉	
Doll's eyes	*Actaea alba*	🌳			💧	☼	🍁	❉	14
Maiden hair frn	*Adiantum capillus-veneris*	🌳			💧	☼	🍁		16
Star grass	*Aletris farinosa*	🌳					🍁		20
Angelica	*Angelica atropurpurea*	🌳		〰		☼	🍁		34
Dogbane	*Apocynum androsaemifolium*	🌳	✤			☼	🍁		38
Wake robin	*Arisaema triphyllum*	🌳		〰			🍁		48
Milkweed	*Asclepias syriaca*		✤			☼	🍁		56
Butterfly weed	*Asclepias tuberosa*		✤				🍁		58
Blue cohosh	*Caulophyllum thalictroides*	🌳		〰			🍁		76
Bittersweet	*Celastrus scandens*		✤				🍁		80
Boneset	*Eupatorium perfoliatum*			〰		☼	🍁		120
Joe-pye weed	*Eupatorium purpureum*			〰		☼	🍁		122
Hops	*Humulus lupulus*		✤				🍁		152
Lettuce	*Lactuca scariola*		✤			☼	🍁		168
Hoary puccoon	*Lithospermum canescens*	🌳	✤		💧	☼			174
Pokeweed	*Phytolacca americana*	🌳	✤				🍁		214
White pine	*Pinus strobus*	🌳			💧	☼	🍁	❉	216
Seneca-snakert	*Polygala senega*		✤				🍁		222
Solomon's seal	*Polygonatum biflorum*	🌳					🍁		224
Balsam poplar	*Populus balsamifera*	🌳		〰	💧	☼	🍁	❉	226
Black willow	*Salix nigra*			〰	💧				244
Bloodroot	*Sanguinaria canadensis*	🌳			💧				246
Nightshade	*Solanum dulcamara*	🌳					🍁		256
Arbor-vitae	*Thuja occidentalis*			〰	💧	☼	🍁	❉	268

Related Medical Terminology
Alterative

Common name	Latin name	🌳	✾	∿	⬤	☼	🍁	❋	No.
Swamp alder	*Alnus rugosa*			∿	⬤	☼	🍁	❋	24
Sarsaprilla	*Aralia nudicaulis*	🌳	✾			☼	🍁		42
Burdock	*Arctium lappa*		✾			☼	🍁		44
Bittersweet	*Celastrus scandens*		✾				🍁		80
Squirrel corn	*Dicentra canadensis*	🌳			⬤		🍁		112
Cleavers	*Galium aparine*			∿	⬤	☼			130
Wild iris	*Iris versicolor*			∿			🍁		160
Yellow parilla	*Menispermum canadense*	🌳					🍁		188
Curly dock	*Rumex crispus*		✾	∿		☼	🍁		242
Nightshade	*Solanum dulcamara*	🌳					🍁		256
Red clover	*Trifolium pratense*		✾			☼	🍁		270
Purple trillium	*Trillium erectum*	🌳				☼	🍁		272

Antibiotic

Common name	Latin name	🌳	✾	∿	⬤	☼	🍁	No.
Yarrow	*Achillea millefolium*		✾			☼	🍁	10
Sweet flag	*Acorus calamus*			∿	⬤		🍁	12
Leek	*Allium tricoccum*	🌳			⬤			22
Dogbane	*Apocynum androsaemifolium*	🌳	✾			☼	🍁	38
Burdock	*Arctium lappa*		✾			☼	🍁	44
Bearberry	*Arctostaphylos uva-ursi*	🌳	✾				🍁	46
Wild ginger	*Asarum canadense*	🌳		∿			🍁	54
Hemp	*Cannabis sativa*		✾				🍁	72
Wild geranium	*Geranium maculatum*	🌳			⬤		🍁	134
Hops	*Humulus lupulus*		✾				🍁	152
St. John's wort	*Hypericum perforatum*		✾			☼		156
Partridge berry	*Mitchella repens*	🌳					🍁	194
Bloodroot	*Sanguinaria canadensis*	🌳			⬤			246
Tansy	*Tanacetum vulgare*		✾			☼	🍁	264
Mullein	*Verbascum thapsus*		✾			☼	🍁	282
Peat moss	*Sphagnum*				■ ⬤	☼	🍁	300

Antiseptic

		🌲	⊛	∿	■	💧	☼	🍁	❄	
Bearberry	*Arctostaphylos uva-ursi*	🌲	⊛					🍁		46
Wild indigo	*Baptisia tinctoria*		⊛					🍁		62
Barberry	*Berberis vulgaris*		⊛					🍁		66
Birch	*Betula alleghaniensis*	🌲				💧	☼	🍁	❄	68
Case weed	*Capsella bursa-pastoris*		⊛			💧	☼	🍁		74
Beechnut	*Fagus grandifolia*	🌲				💧	☼	🍁	❄	124
Wintergreen	*Gaultheria procumbens*	🌲				💧		🍁		132
St. John's wort	*Hypericum perforatum*		⊛				☼			156
Juniper	*Juniperus communis*		⊛			💧	☼	🍁	❄	166
Peppermint	*Mentha piperita*			∿		💧	☼	🍁		190
Rose	*Rosa spp*	🌲	⊛				☼	🍁		238
Peat moss	*Sphagnum*				■	💧	☼	🍁		300

Antispasmodic

		🌲	⊛	∿	■	💧	☼	🍁	❄	
Hemp	*Cannabis sativa*		⊛					🍁		72
Red root	*Ceanothus americanus*	🌲	⊛				☼	🍁		78
Poison hemlock	*Conium maculatum*									98
Lady's slipper	*Cypripedium calceolus*	🌲		∿	■	💧		🍁		108
Cow parsnip	*Heracleum lanatum*	🌲		∿		💧	☼	🍁	❄	150
Motherwort	*Leonurus cardiaca*		⊛				☼	🍁		172
Indian tobacco	*Lobelia inflata*	🌲	⊛				☼			176
Spearmint	*Mentha spicata*			∿		💧	☼	🍁		192
Catnip	*Nepeta cataria*		⊛				☼			206
Rose	*Rosa spp*	🌲	⊛				☼	🍁		238
Mad-dog weed	*Scutellaria lateriflora*	🌲	⊛	∿		💧	☼			254
Skunk cabbage	*Symplocarpus foetidus*			∿		💧	☼	🍁		262
Red clover	*Trifolium pratense*		⊛				☼	🍁		270
Cramp bark	*Viburnum opulus*	🌲				💧	☼	🍁	❄	284

Aphrodisiac

		🌳	⊛	≋	●	☼	🍁	❄	
Burdock	*Arctium lappa*		⊛			☼	🍁		44
Hemp	*Cannabis sativa*		⊛				🍁		72
Joe-pye weed	*Eupatorium purpureum*			≋		☼	🍁		122
White ash	*Fraxinus americana*	🌳			●	☼	🍁		128
Watercress	*Nasturtium officinale*			≋	●	☼	🍁	❄	204
Ginseng	*Panax quinquefolius*	🌳					🍁		212
Rose	*Rosa spp*	🌳	⊛			☼	🍁		238
Black willow	*Salix nigra*			≋	●				244
Purple trillium	*Trillium erectum*	🌳				☼	🍁		272

Aromatic

		🌳	⊛	≋	●	☼	🍁	❄	
Sweet flag	*Acorus calamus*			≋	●		🍁		12
Angelica	*Angelica atropurpurea*	🌳		≋		☼	🍁		34
Sarsaprilla	*Aralia nudicaulis*	🌳	⊛			☼	🍁		42
Wild ginger	*Asarum canadense*	🌳		≋			🍁		54
Spearmint	*Mentha spicata*			≋	●	☼	🍁		192
Sweet cicely	*Osmorhiza longistylis*	🌳				☼	🍁		208
Ginger	*Panax quinquefolius*	🌳					🍁		212
Sassafras	*Sassafras albidum*	🌳			●				250

Astringent

		🌳	⊛	≋	●	☼	🍁	❄	
Yarrow	*Achillea millefolium*		⊛			☼	🍁		10
Horse chestnut	*Aesculus hippocastanum*	🌳			●	☼	🍁	❄	18
Swamp alder	*Alnus rugosa*			≋	●	☼	🍁	❄	24
Pearly everlast	*Anaphalis margaritacea*		⊛			☼			30
Bearberry	*Arctostaphylos uva-ursi*	🌳	⊛				🍁		46
Birch	*Betula alleghaniensis*	🌳			●	☼	🍁	❄	68
Case weed	*Capsella bursa-pastoris*		⊛		●	☼	🍁		74
Red root	*Ceanothus americanus*	🌳	⊛			☼	🍁		78

Astringent (cont.)

Common Name	Latin Name	🌳	✽	≋	■	💧	☼	🍁	❄	Page
Pipsissewa	*Chimaphila umbellata*	🌳				💧	☼	🍁		88
Sweet fern	*Comptonia peregrina*		✽				☼	🍁		96
Hound's tongue	*Cynoglossum officinale*		✽				☼	🍁		106
Arbutus	*Epigaea repens*	🌳			■	💧				114
Horseweed	*Erigeron canadensis*		✽					🍁		116
Joe-pye weed	*Eupatorium purpureum*			≋			☼	🍁		122
Beechnut	*Fagus grandifolia*	🌳				💧	☼	🍁	❄	124
Strawberry	*Fragaria virginiana*		✽			💧	☼	🍁		126
Wintergreen	*Gaultheria procumbens*	🌳				💧		🍁		132
Wild geranium	*Geranium maculatum*	🌳				💧		🍁		134
Avens	*Geum rivale*			≋		💧	☼	🍁	❄	136
Witch hazel	*Hamamelis virginiana*	🌳				💧		🍁		138
Hepatica	*Hepatica acutiloba*	🌳				💧				148
Goldenseal	*Hydrastis canadensis*	🌳					☼	🍁		154
St. John's wort	*Hypericum perforatum*		✽				☼			156
Black walnut	*Juglans nigra*	🌳				💧	☼	🍁		164
Bugleweed	*Lycopus virginicus*			≋			☼	🍁		178
Partridge berry	*Mitchella repens*	🌳						🍁		194
Solomon's seal	*Polygonatum biflorum*	🌳						🍁		224
Self-heal	*Prunella vulgaris*	🌳	✽			💧	☼	🍁		228
Black cherry	*Prunus serotina*	🌳				💧	☼	🍁	❄	230
Shinleaf	*Pyrola rotundifolia*	🌳			■	💧	☼	🍁		232
Sumac	*Rhus glabra*		✽			💧	☼	🍁		234
Blackberry	*Rubus spp*		✽			💧	☼	🍁		240
Curly dock	*Rumex crispus*		✽	≋			☼	🍁		242
Black willow	*Salix nigra*			≋		💧				244
Purple trillium	*Trillium erectum*	🌳					☼	🍁		272

Carminative

Common name	Scientific name	🌳	⊛	≈	◆	☼	❀	❄	Page
Sweet flag	*Acorus calamus*			≈	◆		❀		12
Wild ginger	*Asarum canadense*	🌳		≈			❀		54
Pennyroyal	*Hedeoma pulegioides*	🌳				☼			140
Cow parsnip	*Heracleum lanatum*	🌳		≈	◆	☼	❀	❄	150
Juniper	*Juniperus communis*		⊛		◆	☼	❀	❄	166
Peppermint	*Mentha piperita*			≈	◆	☼	❀		190
Spearmint	*Mentha spicata*			≈	◆	☼	❀		192
Wild oregano	*Monarda fistulosa*	🌳	⊛			☼	❀		196
Catnip	*Nepeta cataria*		⊛			☼			206
Sweet cicely	*Osmorhiza longistylis*	🌳				☼	❀		208
Self-heal	*Prunella vulgaris*	🌳	⊛		◆	☼	❀		228
Sassafras	*Sassafras albidum*	🌳			◆				250

Cathartic

Common name	Scientific name	🌳	⊛	≈	◆	☼	❀	❄	Page
Dogbane	*Apocynum androsaemifolium*	🌳	⊛			☼	❀		38
Milkweed	*Asclepias syriaca*		⊛			☼	❀		56
Wild indigo	*Baptisia tinctoria*		⊛				❀		62
Boneset	*Eupatorium perfoliatum*			≈		☼	❀		120
White ash	*Fraxinus americana*	🌳			◆	☼	❀		128
Wild iris	*Iris versicolor*			≈			❀		160
Butternut	*Juglans cinerea*	🌳		≈	◆	☼	❀	❄	162
Black walnut	*Juglans nigra*	🌳			◆	☼	❀		164
Indian tobacco	*Lobelia inflata*	🌳	⊛			☼			176
Seneca-snakert	*Polygala senega*		⊛				❀		222
Bloodroot	*Sanguinaria canadensis*	🌳			◆				246

Demulcent

Common name	Latin name	🌲	✾	∿	💧	☼	🍁	Page
Maiden hair frn	*Adiantum capillus-veneris*	🌲			💧	☼	🍁	16
Putty-root	*Aplectrum hymale*	🌲			■		🍁	36
Hound's tongue	*Cynoglossum officinale*		✾			☼	🍁	106
Hepatica	*Hepatica acutiloba*	🌲			💧			148
Solomon's seal	*Polygonatum biflorum*	🌲					🍁	224
Sassafras	*Sassafras albidum*	🌲			💧			250
Comfrey	*Symphytum officinale*		✾		💧			260
Mullein	*Verbascum thapsus*		✾			☼	🍁	282

Diaphoretic

Common name	Latin name	🌲	✾	∿	💧	☼	🍁	Page
Yarrow	*Achillea millefolium*		✾			☼	🍁	10
Angelica	*Angelica atropurpurea*	🌲		∿		☼	🍁	34
Dogbane	*Apocynum androsaemifolium*	🌲	✾			☼	🍁	38
Columbine	*Aquilegia canadensis*	🌲		∿		☼		40
Sarsaprilla	*Aralia nudicaulis*	🌲	✾			☼	🍁	42
Burdock	*Arctium lappa*		✾			☼	🍁	44
Wake robin	*Arisaema triphyllum*	🌲		∿			🍁	48
Wild ginger	*Asarum canadense*	🌲		∿			🍁	54
Milkweed	*Asclepias syriaca*		✾			☼	🍁	56
Butterfly weed	*Asclepias tuberosa*		✾				🍁	58
Bittersweet	*Celastrus scandens*		✾				🍁	80
Coral root	*Corallorhiza maculata*	🌲			💧	☼	🍁	102
Boneset	*Eupatorium perfoliatum*			∿		☼	🍁	120
Joe-pye weed	*Eupatorium purpureum*			∿		☼	🍁	122
Pennyroyal	*Hedeoma pulegioides*	🌲				☼		140
Motherwort	*Leonurus cardiaca*		✾			☼	🍁	172
Indian tobacco	*Lobelia inflata*	🌲	✾			☼		176
Horehound	*Marrubium vulgare*		✾		💧			182
Wild oregano	*Monarda fistulosa*	🌲	✾			☼	🍁	196
Catnip	*Nepeta cataria*		✾			☼		206

335

Diaphoretic (cont.)

Common name	Scientific name	🌳	⊛	〰	■	●	☼	✿	❋	Page
Seneca-snakert	*Polygala senega*		⊛					✿		222
Sassafras	*Sassafras albidum*	🌳				●				250
Figwort	*Scrophularia marilandica*	🌳				●	☼			252

Diuretic

Common name	Scientific name	🌳	⊛	〰	■	●	☼	✿	❋	Page
Balsam fir	*Abies balsamea*	🌳				●	☼	✿	❋	8
Star grass	*Aletris farinosa*	🌳						✿		20
Dogbane	*Apocynum androsaemifolium*	🌳	⊛				☼	✿		38
Columbine	*Aquilegia canadensis*	🌳		〰			☼			40
Burdock	*Arctium lappa*		⊛				☼	✿		44
Bearberry	*Arctostaphylos uva-ursi*	🌳	⊛					✿		46
Milkweed	*Asclepias syriaca*		⊛				☼	✿		56
Case weed	*Capsella bursa-pastoris*		⊛			●	☼	✿		74
Blue cohosh	*Caulophyllum thalictroides*	🌳		〰				✿		76
Bittersweet	*Celastrus scandens*		⊛					✿		80
Blazing star	*Chamaelirium luteum*	🌳			■			✿		82
Pipsissewa	*Chimaphila umbellata*	🌳				●	☼	✿		88
Chicory	*Cichorium intybus*		⊛			●		✿		90
Carrot	*Daucus carota*		⊛				☼	✿		110
Squirrel corn	*Dicentra canadensis*	🌳				●		✿		112
Arbutus	*Epigaea repens*	🌳			■	●				114
Horseweed	*Erigeron canadensis*		⊛					✿		116
Joe-pye weed	*Eupatorium purpureum*			〰			☼	✿		122
Strawberry	*Fragaria virginiana*		⊛			●	☼	✿		126
White ash	*Fraxinus americana*	🌳				●	☼	✿		128
Cleavers	*Galium aparine*			〰		●	☼			130
Wintergreen	*Gaultheria procumbens*	🌳				●		✿		132
Sunflower	*Helianthus annuus*		⊛				☼	✿		142
Hops	*Humulus lupulus*		⊛					✿		152
Goldenseal	*Hydrastis canadensis*	🌳					☼	✿		154

Diuretic (cont.)

Common	Latin	🌳	⊛	≋	■	💧	☼	🍁	❄	Page
St. John's wort	*Hypericum perforatum*		⊛				☼			156
Wild iris	*Iris versicolor*			≋				🍁		160
Juniper	*Juniperus communis*		⊛			💧	☼	🍁	❄	166
Lettuce	*Lactuca scariola*		⊛				☼	🍁		168
Yellow parilla	*Menispermum canadense*	🌳						🍁		188
Partridge berry	*Mitchella repens*	🌳						🍁		194
Wild oregano	*Monarda fistulosa*	🌳	⊛				☼	🍁		196
Plantain	*Plantago major*		⊛				☼	🍁		218
Seneca-snakert	*Polygala senega*		⊛					🍁		222
Figwort	*Scrophularia marilandica*	🌳				💧	☼			252
Dandelion	*Taraxacum officinale*		⊛			💧	☼	🍁	❄	266
Arbor-vitae	*Thuja occidentalis*			≋		💧	☼	🍁	❄	268
Hairy cap moss	*Polytrichum commune*	🌳		≋	■	💧	☼	🍁	❄	297

Emetic

Common	Latin	🌳	⊛	≋	■	💧	☼	🍁	❄	Page
Doll's eyes	*Actaea alba*	🌳				💧	☼	🍁	❄	14
Leek	*Allium tricoccum*	🌳				💧				22
Angelica	*Angelica atropurpurea*	🌳		≋			☼	🍁		34
Dogbane	*Apocynum androsaemifolium*	🌳	⊛				☼	🍁		38
Milkweed	*Asclepias syriaca*		⊛				☼	🍁		56
Butterfly weed	*Asclepias tuberosa*		⊛					🍁		58
Wild indigo	*Baptisia tinctoria*		⊛					🍁		62
Barberry	*Berberis vulgaris*		⊛					🍁		66
Turtle head	*Chelone glabra*			≋		💧	☼	🍁		84
Trout lily	*Erythronium americanum*	🌳				💧		🍁		118
Boneset	*Eupatorium perfoliatum*			≋			☼	🍁		120
Wild iris	*Iris versicolor*			≋				🍁		160
Indian tobacco	*Lobelia inflata*	🌳	⊛				☼			176
Pokeweed	*Phytolacca americana*	🌳	⊛					🍁		214
Seneca-snakert	*Polygala senega*		⊛					🍁		222
Bloodroot	*Sanguinaria canadensis*	🌳				💧				246

Emmenagogue

Common name	Latin name	Tree	Wheel	Wave	Drop	Sun	Leaf	Snow	Page
Blue cohosh	*Caulophyllum thalictroides*	🌳		≈			🍁		76
White ash	*Fraxinus americana*	🌳			●	☼	🍁		128
Wintergreen	*Gaultheria procumbens*	🌳			●		🍁		132
Pennyroyal	*Hedeoma pulegioides*	🌳				☼			140
Juniper	*Juniperus communis*		⊛		●	☼	🍁	❄	166
Motherwort	*Leonurus cardiaca*		⊛			☼	🍁		172
Catnip	*Nepeta cataria*		⊛			☼			206
Seneca-snakert	*Polygala senega*		⊛				🍁		222
Rose	*Rosa spp*	🌳	⊛			☼	🍁		238
Tansy	*Tanacetum vulgare*		⊛			☼	🍁		264
Arbor-vitae	*Thuja occidentalis*			≈	●	☼	🍁	❄	268
Purple trillium	*Trillium erectum*	🌳				☼	🍁		272

Expectorant

Common name	Latin name	Tree	Wheel	Wave	Drop	Sun	Leaf	Snow	Page
Maiden hair frn	*Adiantum capillus-veneris*	🌳			●	☼	🍁		16
Dogbane	*Apocynum androsaemifolium*	🌳	⊛			☼	🍁		38
Wake robin	*Arisaema triphyllum*	🌳		≈			🍁		48
Milkweed	*Asclepias syriaca*		⊛			☼	🍁		56
Butterfly weed	*Asclepias tuberosa*		⊛				🍁		58
Red root	*Ceanothus americanus*	🌳	⊛			☼	🍁		78
Sunflower	*Helianthus annuus*		⊛			☼	🍁		142
Indian tobacco	*Lobelia inflata*	🌳	⊛			☼			176
White pine	*Pinus strobus*	🌳			●	☼	🍁	❄	216
Seneca-snakert	*Polygala senega*		⊛				🍁		222
Balsam poplar	*Populus balsamifera*	🌳		≈	●	☼	🍁	❄	226
Black cherry	*Prunus serotina*	🌳			●	☼	🍁	❄	230
Bloodroot	*Sanguinaria canadensis*	🌳			●				246
Skunk cabbage	*Symplocarpus foetidus*			≈	●	☼	🍁		262
Red clover	*Trifolium pratense*		⊛			☼	🍁		270
Mullein	*Verbascum thapsus*		⊛			☼	🍁		282

Febrifuge

Common Name	Latin Name								Page
Barberry	*Berberis vulgaris*		✹					🍁	66
Coral root	*Corallorhiza maculata*	🌳				♦	☼	🍁	102
Black willow	*Salix nigra*			≈		♦			244
Hairy cap moss	*Polytrichum commune*	🌳			■	♦	☼	🍁 ❅	297

Laxative

Common Name	Latin Name								Page
Barberry	*Berberis vulgaris*		✹					🍁	66
Turtle head	*Chelone glabra*			≈		♦	☼	🍁	84
Wild spinach	*Chenopodium album*		✹					🍁	86
Chicory	*Cichorium intybus*		✹			♦		🍁	90
Boneset	*Eupatorium perfoliatum*			≈			☼	🍁	120
Goldenseal	*Hydrastis canadensis*	🌳					☼	🍁	154
Horehound	*Marrubium vulgare*		✹			♦			182
Plantain	*Plantago major*		✹				☼	🍁	218
Rose	*Rosa spp*	🌳	✹				☼	🍁	238
Curly dock	*Rumex crispus*		✹	≈			☼	🍁	242
Dandelion	*Taraxacum officinale*		✹			♦	☼	🍁 ❅	266
Hairy cap moss	*Polytrichum commune*	🌳			■	♦	☼	🍁 ❅	297

Narcotic

Common Name	Latin Name								Page
Horse chestnut	*Aesculus hippocastanum*	🌳				♦	☼	🍁 ❅	18
Bittersweet	*Celastrus scandens*		✹					🍁	80
Hops	*Humulus lupulus*		✹					🍁	152
Bugleweed	*Lycopus virginicus*			≈			☼	🍁	178
Bloodroot	*Sanguinaria canadensis*	🌳				♦			246
Sassafras	*Sassafras albidum*	🌳				♦			250
Nightshade	*Solanum dulcamara*	🌳						🍁	256
Skunk cabbage	*Symplocarpus foetidus*			≈		♦	☼	🍁	262

Official

Common name	Scientific name	🌳	⊛	≋	●	○	✽	❈	Page
Sweet flag	*Acorus calamus*			≋	●		✽		12
Star grass	*Aletris farinosa*	🌳					✽		20
Dogbane	*Apocynum androsaemifolium*	🌳	⊛			○	✽		38
Burdock	*Arctium lappa*		⊛			○	✽		44
Wild ginger	*Asarum canadense*	🌳		≋			✽		54
Blue cohosh	*Caulophyllum thalictroides*	🌳		≋			✽		76
Pipsissewa	*Chimaphila umbellata*	🌳			●	○	✽		88
Squirrel corn	*Dicentra canadensis*	🌳			●		✽		112
Trout lily	*Erythronium americanum*	🌳			●		✽		118
Boneset	*Eupatorium perfoliatum*			≋		○	✽		120
Witch hazel	*Hamamelis virginiana*	🌳			●		✽		138
Hops	*Humulus lupulus*		⊛				✽		152
Goldenseal	*Hydrastis canadensis*	🌳				○	✽		154
Wild iris	*Iris versicolor*			≋			✽		160
Juniper	*Juniperus communis*		⊛		●	○	✽	❈	166
Indian tobacco	*Lobelia inflata*	🌳	⊛			○			176
Peppermint	*Mentha piperita*			≋	●	○	✽		190
Spearmint	*Mentha spicata*			≋	●	○	✽		192
Partridge berry	*Mitchella repens*	🌳					✽		194
Catnip	*Nepeta cataria*		⊛			○			206
Seneca-snakert	*Polygala senega*		⊛				✽		222
Balsam poplar	*Populus balsamifera*	🌳		≋	●	○	✽	❈	226
Bloodroot	*Sanguinaria canadensis*	🌳			●				246
Mad-dog weed	*Scutellaria lateriflora*	🌳	⊛	≋	●	○			254
Dandelion	*Taraxacum officinale*		⊛		●	○	✽	❈	266
Red clover	*Trifolium pratense*		⊛			○	✽		270

Sedative

Common name	Latin name	🌲	❀	≈	■	💧	☼	🍁	❄	Page
Star grass	*Aletris farinosa*	🌲						🍁		20
Blue cohosh	*Caulophyllum thalictroides*	🌲		≈				🍁		76
Red root	*Ceanothus americanus*	🌲	❀				☼	🍁		78
Poison hemlock	*Conium maculatum*		❀				☼			98
Coral root	*Corallorhiza maculata*	🌲				💧	☼	🍁		102
Lady's slipper	*Cypripedium calceolus*	🌲		≈	■	💧		🍁		108
Witch hazel	*Hamamelis virginiana*	🌲				💧		🍁		138
Hops	*Humulus lupulus*		❀					🍁		152
St. John's wort	*Hypericum perforatum*		❀				☼			156
Lettuce	*Lactuca scariola*		❀				☼	🍁		168
Motherwort	*Leonurus cardiaca*		❀				☼	🍁		172
Bugleweed	*Lycopus virginicus*			≈			☼	🍁		178
Black cherry	*Prunus serotina*	🌲				💧	☼	🍁	❄	230
Rose	*Rosa spp*	🌲	❀				☼	🍁		238
Mad-dog weed	*Scutellaria lateriflora*	🌲	❀	≈		💧	☼			254
Red clover	*Trifolium pratense*		❀				☼	🍁		270
Cramp bark	*Viburnum opulus*	🌲				💧	☼	🍁	❄	284

Stimulant

Common name	Latin name	🌲	❀	≈	■	💧	☼	🍁	❄	Page
Balsam fir	*Abies balsamea*	🌲				💧	☼	🍁	❄	8
Yarrow	*Achillea millefolium*		❀				☼	🍁		10
Sweet flag	*Acorus calamus*			≈		💧		🍁		12
Angelica	*Angelica atropurpurea*	🌲		≈			☼	🍁		34
Sarsaprilla	*Aralia nudicaulis*	🌲	❀				☼	🍁		42
Wormwood	*Artemisia absinthium*		❀				☼	🍁		52
Wild ginger	*Asarum canadense*	🌲		≈				🍁		54
Barberry	*Berberis vulgaris*		❀					🍁		66
Birch	*Betula alleghaniensis*	🌲				💧	☼	🍁	❄	68
Red root	*Ceanothus americanus*	🌲	❀				☼	🍁		78
Carrot	*Daucus carota*		❀				☼	🍁		110
Wintergreen	*Gaultheria procumbens*	🌲				💧		🍁		132

Stimulant (cont.)

		🌳	❀	≋	■	●	☼	✿	❄	
Pennyroyal	*Hedeoma pulegioides*	🌳					☼			140
Cow parsnip	*Heracleum lanatum*	🌳		≋		●	☼	✿	❄	150
Goldenseal	*Hydrastis canadensis*	🌳					☼	✿		154
St. John's wort	*Hypericum perforatum*		❀				☼			156
Juniper	*Juniperus communis*		❀			●	☼	✿	❄	166
Motherwort	*Leonurus cardiaca*		❀				☼	✿		172
Peppermint	*Mentha piperita*			≋		●	☼	✿		190
Catnip	*Nepeta cataria*		❀				☼			206
Ginseng	*Panax quinquefolius*	🌳						✿		212
Balsam poplar	*Populus balsamifera*	🌳		≋		●	☼	✿	❄	226
Sassafras	*Sassafras albidum*	🌳				●				250
Skunk cabbage	*Symplocarpus foetidus*			≋		●	☼	✿		262
Tansy	*Tanacetum vulgare*		❀				☼	✿		264
Arbor-vitae	*Thuja occidentalis*			≋		●	☼	✿	❄	268

Stomachic

		🌳	❀	≋	■	●	☼	✿	
Wormwood	*Artemisia absinthium*		❀				☼	✿	52
Pipsissewa	*Chimaphila umbellata*	🌳				●	☼	✿	88
Gold thread	*Coptis groenlandica*	🌳			■	●	☼	✿	100
Hops	*Humulus lupulus*		❀					✿	152
Peppermint	*Mentha piperita*			≋		●	☼	✿	190
Sweet cicely	*Osmorhiza longistylis*	🌳					☼	✿	208
Ginseng	*Panax quinquefolius*	🌳						✿	212
Rose	*Rosa spp*	🌳	❀				☼	✿	238
Pitcher-plant	*Sarracenia purpurea*			≋	■	●	☼	✿	248

Tonic

Common name	Latin name	🌳	⊛	≈	■	💧	☼	♣	❄	Page
Yarrow	*Achillea millefolium*		⊛				☼	♣		10
Sweet flag	*Acorus calamus*			≈		💧		♣		12
Horse chestnut	*Aesculus hippocastanum*	🌳				💧	☼	♣	❄	18
Star grass	*Aletris farinosa*	🌳						♣		20
Dogbane	*Apocynum androsaemifolium*	🌳	⊛				☼	♣		38
Bearberry	*Arctostaphylos uva-ursi*	🌳	⊛					♣		46
Wormwood	*Artemisia absinthium*		⊛				☼	♣		52
Wild ginger	*Asarum canadense*	🌳		≈				♣		54
Barberry	*Berberis vulgaris*		⊛					♣		66
Case weed	*Capsella bursa-pastoris*		⊛			💧	☼	♣		74
Blue cohosh	*Caulophyllum thalictroides*	🌳		≈				♣		76
Blazing star	*Chamaelirium luteum*	🌳			■			♣		82
Turtle head	*Chelone glabra*			≈		💧	☼	♣		84
Pipsissewa	*Chimaphila umbellata*	🌳				💧	☼	♣		88
Chicory	*Cichorium intybus*		⊛			💧		♣		90
Sweet fern	*Comptonia peregrina*		⊛				☼	♣		96
Gold thread	*Coptis groenlandica*	🌳			■	💧	☼	♣		100
Squirrel corn	*Dicentra canadensis*	🌳				💧		♣		112
Horseweed	*Erigeron canadensis*		⊛					♣		116
Boneset	*Eupatorium perfoliatum*			≈			☼	♣		120
Joe-pye weed	*Eupatorium purpureum*			≈			☼	♣		122
Beechnut	*Fagus grandifolia*	🌳				💧	☼	♣	❄	124
White ash	*Fraxinus americana*	🌳				💧	☼	♣		128
Avens	*Geum rivale*			≈		💧	☼	♣	❄	136
Witch hazel	*Hamamelis virginiana*	🌳				💧		♣		138
Hepatica	*Hepatica acutiloba*	🌳				💧				148
Hops	*Humulus lupulus*		⊛					♣		152
Goldenseal	*Hydrastis canadensis*	🌳					☼	♣		154
Motherwort	*Leonurus cardiaca*		⊛				☼	♣		172
Bugleweed	*Lycopus virginicus*			≈			☼	♣		178
Horehound	*Marrubium vulgare*		⊛			💧				182
Yellow parilla	*Menispermum canadense*	🌳						♣		188

Tonic (cont.)

Common name	Latin name	🌳	⊛	≈	■	●	☼	♣	❆	Page
Partridge berry	*Mitchella repens*	🌳						♣		194
Catnip	*Nepeta cataria*		⊛				☼			206
Ginseng	*Panax quinquefolius*	🌳						♣		212
Plantain	*Plantago major*		⊛				☼	♣		218
Solomon's seal	*Polygonatum biflorum*	🌳						♣		224
Balsam poplar	*Populus balsamifera*	🌳		≈		●	☼	♣	❆	226
Black cherry	*Prunus serotina*	🌳				●	☼	♣	❆	230
Rose	*Rosa spp*	🌳	⊛				☼	♣		238
Blackberry	*Rubus spp*		⊛			●	☼	♣		240
Curly dock	*Rumex crispus*		⊛	≈			☼	♣		242
Black willow	*Salix nigra*			≈		●				244
Pitcher-plant	*Sarracenia purpurea*			≈	■	●	☼	♣		248
Figwort	*Scrophularia marilandica*	🌳				●	☼			252
Mad-dog weed	*Scutellaria lateriflora*	🌳	⊛	≈		●	☼			254
Dandelion	*Taraxacum officinale*		⊛			●	☼	♣	❆	266
Purple trillium	*Trillium erectum*	🌳					☼	♣		272

Biological and Edible Aspects
Edible

Common name	Scientific name	🌲	✹	≋	◗	■	☼	🍁	❊	Page
Sweet flag	*Acorus calamus*			≋	◗			🍁		12
Leek	*Allium tricoccum*	🌲			◗					22
Shadbush	*Amelanchier spp*	🌲	✹				☼			28
Burdock	*Arctium lappa*		✹				☼	🍁		44
Bearberry	*Arctostaphylos uva-ursi*	🌲	✹					🍁		46
Wake robin	*Arisaema triphyllum*	🌲		≋				🍁		48
Milkweed	*Asclepias syriaca*		✹				☼	🍁		56
Barberry	*Berberis vulgaris*		✹					🍁		66
Birch	*Betula alleghaniensis*	🌲			◗		☼	🍁	❊	68
Marsh-marigold	*Caltha palustris*			≋	◗					70
Wild spinach	*Chenopodium album*		✹					🍁		86
Pipsissewa	*Chimaphila umbellata*	🌲			◗		☼	🍁		88
Spring beauty	*Claytonia virginica*	🌲			◗					94
Sweet fern	*Comptonia peregrina*		✹				☼	🍁		96
Hazelnut	*Corylus cornuta*	🌲						🍁		104
Carrot	*Daucus carota*		✹				☼	🍁		110
Arbutus	*Epigaea repens*	🌲			◗	■				114
Beechnut	*Fagus grandifolia*	🌲			◗		☼	🍁	❊	124
Strawberry	*Fragaria virginiana*		✹		◗		☼	🍁		126
Cleavers	*Galium aparine*			≋	◗		☼			130
Wintergreen	*Gaultheria procumbens*	🌲			◗			🍁		132
Sunflower	*Helianthus annuus*		✹				☼	🍁		142
Jerusalem artck	*Helianthus tuberosus*		✹					🍁		144
Cow parsnip	*Heracleum lanatum*	🌲		≋	◗		☼	🍁	❊	150
Hops	*Humulus lupulus*		✹					🍁		152
Butternut	*Juglans cinerea*	🌲		≋	◗		☼	🍁	❊	162
Black walnut	*Juglans nigra*	🌲			◗		☼	🍁		164
Lettuce	*Lactuca scariola*		✹				☼	🍁		168
Apple	*Malus spp*		✹					🍁	❊	180
Peppermint	*Mentha piperita*			≋	◗		☼	🍁		190
Spearmint	*Mentha spicata*			≋	◗		☼	🍁		192

Edible (cont.)

Common name	Scientific name	🌲	✳	≋	■	💧	☼	🍁	❄	Page
Partridge berry	*Mitchella repens*	🌲						🍁		194
Indian pipe	*Monotropa uniflora*	🌲					☼			198
Morel	*Morchella semilibera*	🌲				💧				200
Watercress	*Nasturtium officinale*			≋		💧	☼	🍁	❄	204
Fiddlehead	*Osmunda cinnamonea*	🌲		≋		💧				210
Pokeweed	*Phytolacca americana*	🌲	✳					🍁		214
White pine	*Pinus strobus*	🌲				💧	☼	🍁	❄	216
Solomon's seal	*Polygonatum biflorum*	🌲						🍁		224
Black cherry	*Prunus serotina*	🌲				💧	☼	🍁	❄	230
Black currant	*Ribes americanum*	🌲					☼			236
Blackberry	*Rubus spp*		✳			💧	☼	🍁		240
Curly dock	*Rumex crispus*		✳	≋			☼	🍁		242
Black willow	*Salix nigra*			≋		💧				244
Mountain ash	*Sorbus americana*		✳					🍁		258
Dandelion	*Taraxacum officinale*		✳			💧	☼	🍁	❄	266
Red clover	*Trifolium pratense*		✳				☼	🍁		270
Purple trillium	*Trillium erectum*	🌲					☼	🍁		272
Cattail	*Typha latifolia*			≋		💧	☼	🍁	❄	274
Stinging nettle	*Urtica dioica*		✳				☼	🍁		276
Bilberry	*Vaccinium angustifolium*	🌲		≋	■		☼			278
Cranberry	*Vaccinium macrocarpon*			≋	■			🍁		280
Cramp bark	*Viburnum opulus*	🌲				💧	☼	🍁	❄	284
Cranberry	*Viburnum trilobum*			≋				🍁	❄	286

Flour

Common name	Scientific name	🌲	✳	≋	■	💧	☼	🍁	❄	Page
Wake robin	*Arisaema triphyllum*	🌲		≋				🍁		48
Birch	*Betula alleghaniensis*	🌲				💧	☼	🍁	❄	68
Wild spinach	*Chenopodium album*		✳					🍁		86
Curly dock	*Rumex crispus*		✳	≋			☼	🍁		242
Mountain ash	*Sorbus americana*		✳					🍁		258
Cattail	*Typha latifolia*			≋		💧	☼	🍁	❄	274

Honey

Common name	Latin name	🌳	❋	〰	■	🌢	☼	🍁	❆	
Balsam fir	*Abies balsamea*	🌳				🌢	☼	🍁	❆	8
Horse chestnut	*Aesculus hippocastanum*	🌳				🌢	☼	🍁	❆	18
Swamp alder	*Alnus rugosa*			〰		🌢	☼	🍁	❆	24
Green amaranth	*Amaranthus retroflexus*		❋				☼			26
Shadbush	*Amelanchier spp*	🌳	❋				☼			28
Burdock	*Arctium lappa*		❋				☼	🍁		44
Bearberry	*Arctostaphylos uva-ursi*	🌳	❋					🍁		46
Milkweed	*Asclepias syriaca*		❋				☼	🍁		56
Butterfly weed	*Asclepias tuberosa*		❋					🍁		58
Asparagus	*Asparagus officinale*		❋			🌢				60
Wild indigo	*Baptisia tinctoria*		❋					🍁		62
Winter-cress	*Barbarea vulgaris*	🌳	❋	〰		🌢	☼			64
Red root	*Ceanothus americanus*	🌳	❋				☼	🍁		78
Chicory	*Cichorium intybus*		❋			🌢		🍁		90
Hound's tongue	*Cynoglossum officinale*		❋				☼	🍁		106
Carrot	*Daucus carota*		❋				☼	🍁		110
Arbutus	*Epigaea repens*	🌳			■	🌢				114
Boneset	*Eupatorium perfoliatum*			〰			☼	🍁		120
Joe-pye weed	*Eupatorium purpureum*			〰			☼	🍁		122
Wintergreen	*Gaultheria procumbens*	🌳				🌢		🍁		132
Sunflower	*Helianthus annuus*		❋				☼	🍁		142
Hops	*Humulus lupulus*		❋					🍁		152
Butternut	*Juglans cinerea*	🌳		〰		🌢	☼	🍁	❆	162
Black walnut	*Juglans nigra*	🌳				🌢	☼	🍁		164
Apple	*Malus spp*		❋					🍁	❆	180
Horehound	*Marrubium vulgare*		❋			🌢				182
Alfalfa	*Medicago sativa*		❋				☼	🍁		186
Peppermint	*Mentha piperita*			〰		🌢	☼	🍁		190
Spearmint	*Mentha spicata*			〰		🌢	☼	🍁		192
Wild oregano	*Monarda fistulosa*	🌳	❋				☼	🍁		196
Catnip	*Nepeta cataria*		❋				☼			206
Black cherry	*Prunus serotina*	🌳				🌢	☼	🍁	❆	230

Honey (cont.)

Black currant	*Ribes americanum*	🌳				☼			236
Rose	*Rosa spp*	🌳 ⊛				☼	♣		238
Blackberry	*Rubus spp*	⊛			💧	☼	♣		240
Black willow	*Salix nigra*		≋		💧				244
Bloodroot	*Sanguinaria canadensis*	🌳			💧				246
Sassafras	*Sassafras albidum*	🌳			💧				250
Dandelion	*Taraxacum officinale*	⊛			💧	☼	♣	❋	266
Red clover	*Trifolium pratense*	⊛				☼	♣		270
Bilberry	*Vaccinium angustifolium*	🌳	≋ ■			☼			278
Cranberry	*Vaccinium macrocarpon*		≋ ■				♣		280
Cramp bark	*Viburnum opulus*	🌳			💧	☼	♣	❋	284
Cranberry	*Viburnum trilobum*		≋				♣	❋	286

Poisonous Aspects
Death

Doll's eyes	*Actaea alba*	🌳			💧	☼	♣	❋	14
Horse chestnut	*Aesculus hippocastanum*	🌳			💧	☼	♣	❋	18
Dogbane	*Apocynum androsaemifolium*	🌳 ⊛				☼	♣		38
Wake robin	*Arisaema triphyllum*	🌳	≋				♣		48
Wormwood	*Artemisia absinthium*	⊛				☼	♣		52
Pennyroyal	*Hedeoma pulegioides*	🌳				☼			140
St. John's wort	*Hypericum perforatum*	⊛				☼			156
Indian tobacco	*Lobelia inflata*	🌳 ⊛				☼			176
Apple	*Malus spp*	⊛					♣	❋	180
Alfalfa	*Medicago sativa*	⊛				☼	♣		186
Black cherry	*Prunus serotina*	🌳			💧	☼	♣	❋	230
Bloodroot	*Sanguinaria canadensis*	🌳			💧				246
Nightshade	*Solanum dulcamara*	🌳					♣		256
Tansy	*Tanacetum vulgare*	⊛				☼	♣		264

Dermatitis

Common name	Latin name	🌳	⊛	〰	■	💧	☼	♣	❄	Page
Balsam fir	*Abies balsamea*	🌳				💧	☼	♣	❄	8
Dogbane	*Apocynum androsaemifolium*	🌳	⊛				☼	♣		38
Burdock	*Arctium lappa*		⊛				☼	♣		44
Wake robin	*Arisaema triphyllum*	🌳		〰				♣		48
Wormwood	*Artemisia absinthium*		⊛				☼	♣		52
Wild ginger	*Asarum canadense*	🌳		〰				♣		54
Hemp	*Cannabis sativa*		⊛					♣		72
Blue cohosh	*Caulophyllum thalictroides*	🌳		〰				♣		76
Lady's slipper	*Cypripedium calceolus*	🌳		〰	■	💧		♣		108
Carrot	*Daucus carota*		⊛				☼	♣		110
Horseweed	*Erigeron canadensis*		⊛					♣		116
Boneset	*Eupatorium perfoliatum*			〰			☼	♣		120
White ash	*Fraxinus americana*	🌳				💧	☼	♣		128
Pennyroyal	*Hedeoma pulegioides*	🌳					☼			140
Cow parsnip	*Heracleum lanatum*	🌳		〰		💧	☼	♣	❄	150
Hops	*Humulus lupulus*		⊛					♣		152
St. John's wort	*Hypericum perforatum*		⊛				☼			156
Wild iris	*Iris versicolor*			〰				♣		160
Motherwort	*Leonurus cardiaca*		⊛				☼	♣		172
Indian tobacco	*Lobelia inflata*	🌳	⊛				☼			176
Spearmint	*Mentha spicata*			〰		💧	☼	♣		192
May apple	*Podophyllum peltatum*	🌳	⊛					♣		220
Balsam poplar	*Populus balsamifera*	🌳		〰		💧	☼	♣	❄	226
Curly dock	*Rumex crispus*		⊛	〰			☼	♣		242
Bloodroot	*Sanguinaria canadensis*	🌳				💧				246
Tansy	*Tanacetum vulgare*		⊛				☼	♣		264
Stinging nettle	*Urtica dioica*		⊛				☼	♣		276
Peat moss	*Sphagnum*				■	💧	☼	♣		300

Hayfever

Common	Latin	🌳	⊛	≋	■	💧	☼	♣	❄	Page
Wormwood	*Artemisia absinthium*		⊛				☼	♣		52
Hemp	*Cannabis sativa*		⊛					♣		72
Beechnut	*Fagus grandifolia*	🌳				💧	☼	♣	❄	124
White ash	*Fraxinus americana*	🌳				💧	☼	♣		128
Hops	*Humulus lupulus*		⊛					♣		152
Butternut	*Juglans cinerea*	🌳		≋		💧	☼	♣	❄	162
Black walnut	*Juglans nigra*	🌳				💧	☼	♣		164

Overdose

Common	Latin	🌳	⊛	≋	■	💧	☼	♣	❄	Page
Horse chestnut	*Aesculus hippocastanum*	🌳				💧	☼	♣	❄	18
Juniper	*Juniperus communis*		⊛			💧	☼	♣	❄	166
Indian tobacco	*Lobelia inflata*	🌳	⊛				☼			176
Pitcher-plant	*Sarracenia purpurea*			≋	■	💧	☼	♣		248
Skunk cabbage	*Symplocarpus foetidus*			≋		💧	☼	♣		262
Arbor-vitae	*Thuja occidentalis*			≋		💧	☼	♣	❄	268

Poison

Common	Latin	🌳	⊛	≋	■	💧	☼	♣	❄	Page
Yarrow	*Achillea millefolium*		⊛				☼	♣		10
Doll's eyes	*Actaea alba*	🌳				💧	☼	♣	❄	14
Horse chestnut	*Aesculus hippocastanum*	🌳				💧	☼	♣	❄	18
Shadbush	*Amelanchier spp*	🌳	⊛				☼			28
Anemone	*Anemone canadensis*	🌳		≋		💧				32
Columbine	*Aquilegia canadensis*	🌳		≋			☼			40
Sarsaprilla	*Aralia nudicaulis*	🌳	⊛				☼	♣		42
Hemp	*Cannabis sativa*		⊛					♣		72
Case weed	*Capsella bursa-pastoris*		⊛			💧	☼	♣		74
Blue cohosh	*Caulophyllum thalictroides*	🌳		≋				♣		76
Bittersweet	*Celastrus scandens*		⊛					♣		80

Poison (cont.)

Common name	Scientific name	🌲	❀	∿	■	●	✿	🍁	❆	Page
Blazing star	*Chamaelirium luteum*	🌲			■			🍁		82
Wild spinach	*Chenopodium album*		❀					🍁		86
Squirrel corn	*Dicentra canadensis*	🌲				●		🍁		112
Indian tobacco	*Lobelia inflata*	🌲	❀				✿			176
Apple	*Malus spp*		❀					🍁	❆	180
Pokeweed	*Phytolacca americana*	🌲	❀					🍁		214
May apple	*Podophyllum peltatum*	🌲	❀					🍁		220
Seneca-snakert	*Polygala senega*		❀					🍁		222
Nightshade	*Solanum dulcamara*	🌲						🍁		256
Mountain ash	*Sorbus americana*		❀					🍁		258
Cattail	*Typha latifolia*			∿		●	✿	🍁	❆	274

Toxic

Common name	Scientific name	🌲	❀	∿	■	●	✿	🍁	❆	Page
Leek	*Allium tricoccum*	🌲				●				22
Wormwood	*Artemisia absinthium*		❀				✿	🍁		52
Wild ginger	*Asarum canadense*	🌲		∿				🍁		54
Milkweed	*Asclepias syriaca*		❀				✿	🍁		56
Wild indigo	*Baptisia tinctoria*		❀					🍁		62
Marsh-marigold	*Caltha palustris*			∿		●				70
Lettuce	*Lactuca scariola*		❀				✿	🍁		168
Labrador tea	*Ledum groenlandicum*									171
May apple	*Podophyllum peltatum*	🌲	❀					🍁		220
Black currant	*Ribes americanum*	🌲					✿			236
Curly dock	*Rumex crispus*		❀	∿			✿	🍁		242
Arbor-vitae	*Thuja occidentalis*			∿		●	✿	🍁	❆	268
Bilberry	*Vaccinium angustifolium*	🌲		∿	■		✿			278
Cranberry	*Vaccinium macrocarpon*			∿	■			🍁		280

Vomiting

Common name	Scientific name	🌳	⊛	≈	💧	☼	🍁	❄	Page
Horse chestnut	*Aesculus hippocastanum*	🌳			💧	☼	🍁	❄	18
Wake robin	*Arisaema triphyllum*	🌳		≈			🍁		48
Marsh-marigold	*Caltha palustris*			≈	💧				70
Hemp	*Cannabis sativa*		⊛				🍁		72
Blazing star	*Chamaelirium luteum*	🌳			■		🍁		82
Squirrel corn	*Dicentra canadensis*	🌳			💧		🍁		112
Goldenseal	*Hydrastis canadensis*	🌳				☼	🍁		154
Wild iris	*Iris versicolor*			≈			🍁		160
Indian tobacco	*Lobelia inflata*	🌳	⊛			☼			176
Pokeweed	*Phytolacca americana*	🌳	⊛				🍁		214
Seneca-snakert	*Polygala senega*		⊛				🍁		222
Solomon's seal	*Polygonatum biflorum*	🌳					🍁		224
Bloodroot	*Sanguinaria canadensis*	🌳			💧				246
Skunk cabbage	*Symplocarpus foetidus*			≈	💧	☼	🍁		262
Cramp bark	*Viburnum opulus*	🌳			💧	☼	🍁	❄	284

Commercial Utilization
Commercial

Common name	Scientific name	🌳	⊛	≈	💧	☼	🍁	❄	Page
Balsam fir	*Abies balsamea*	🌳			💧	☼	🍁	❄	8
Shadbush	*Amelanchier spp*	🌳	⊛			☼			28
Bearberry	*Arctostaphylos uva-ursi*	🌳	⊛				🍁		46
Wild ginger	*Asarum canadense*	🌳		≈			🍁		54
Birch	*Betula alleghaniensis*	🌳			💧	☼	🍁	❄	68
Hemp	*Cannabis sativa*		⊛				🍁		72
Blue cohosh	*Caulophyllum thalictroides*	🌳		≈			🍁		76
Wild spinach	*Chenopodium album*		⊛				🍁		86
Spring beauty	*Claytonia virginica*	🌳			💧				94
Coral root	*Corallorhiza maculata*	🌳			💧	☼	🍁		102
Hazelnut	*Corylus cornuta*	🌳					🍁		104

Commercial (cont.)

Common name	Scientific name	🌲	✾	〜	■	◆	○	🍁	❄	Page
Lady's slipper	*Cypripedium calceolus*	🌲		〜	■	◆		🍁		108
Horseweed	*Erigeron canadensis*		✾					🍁		116
Wintergreen	*Gaultheria procumbens*	🌲				◆		🍁		132
Witch hazel	*Hamamelis virginiana*	🌲				◆		🍁		138
Pennyroyal	*Hedeoma pulegioides*	🌲					○			140
Jerusalem artck	*Helianthus tuberosus*		✾					🍁		144
Goldenseal	*Hydrastis canadensis*	🌲					○	🍁		154
Wild iris	*Iris versicolor*			〜				🍁		160
Butternut	*Juglans cinerea*	🌲		〜		◆	○	🍁	❄	162
Black walnut	*Juglans nigra*	🌲				◆	○	🍁		164
Juniper	*Juniperus communis*		✾			◆	○	🍁	❄	166
Lettuce	*Lactuca scariola*		✾				○	🍁		168
Indian tobacco	*Lobelia inflata*	🌲	✾				○			176
Catnip	*Nepeta cataria*		✾				○			206
White pine	*Pinus strobus*	🌲				◆	○	🍁	❄	216
Plantain	*Plantago major*		✾				○	🍁		218
Sumac	*Rhus glabra*		✾			◆	○	🍁		234
Bloodroot	*Sanguinaria canadensis*	🌲				◆				246
Sassafras	*Sassafras albidum*	🌲				◆				250
Tansy	*Tanacetum vulgare*		✾				○	🍁		264
Arbor-vitae	*Thuja occidentalis*			〜		◆	○	🍁	❄	268
Cramp bark	*Viburnum opulus*	🌲				◆	○	🍁	❄	284
Broom moss	*Dicranum spoparium*	🌲				◆	○	🍁	❄	291
Brook moss	*Fontinalis*			〜		◆	○	🍁	❄	292
Stairstep moss	*Hylocomium splendens*	🌲				◆	○	🍁	❄	293
Feather moss	*Hypnum cupressiforme*		✾			◆	○	🍁	❄	294
Hairy cap moss	*Polytrichum commune*	🌲			■	◆	○	🍁	❄	297
Finge moss	*Racomitrium canescens*		✾			◆	○	🍁	❄	298
Peat moss	*Sphagnum*				■	◆	○	🍁		300

Commercial Drugs

Common Name	Scientific Name	🌳	⊛	≈	■	💧	✿	🍁	❋	Page
Yarrow	*Achillea millefolium*		⊛				✿	🍁		10
Maiden hair frn	*Adiantum capillus-veneris*	🌳				💧	✿	🍁		16
Star grass	*Aletris farinosa*	🌳						🍁		20
Angelica	*Angelica atropurpurea*	🌳		≈			✿	🍁		34
Putty-root	*Aplectrum hymale*	🌳			■			🍁		36
Dogbane	*Apocynum androsaemifolium*	🌳	⊛				✿	🍁		38
Sarsaprilla	*Aralia nudicaulis*	🌳	⊛				✿	🍁		42
Burdock	*Arctium lappa*		⊛				✿	🍁		44
Wild ginger	*Asarum canadense*	🌳		≈				🍁		54
Butterfly weed	*Asclepias tuberosa*		⊛					🍁		56
Hemp	*Cannabis sativa*		⊛					🍁		72
Strawberry	*Fragaria virginiana*		⊛			💧	✿	🍁		126
White ash	*Fraxinus americana*	🌳				💧	✿	🍁		128
Wintergreen	*Gaultheria procumbens*	🌳				💧		🍁		132
Hepatica	*Hepatica acutiloba*	🌳				💧				148
Goldenseal	*Hydrastis canadensis*	🌳					✿	🍁		154
Indian tobacco	*Lobelia inflata*	🌳	⊛				✿			176
Yellow parilla	*Menispermum canadense*	🌳						🍁		188
Peppermint	*Mentha piperita*			≈		💧	✿	🍁		190
Ginseng	*Panax quinquefolius*	🌳						🍁		212
White pine	*Pinus strobus*	🌳				💧	✿	🍁	❋	216
Black cherry	*Prunus serotina*	🌳				💧	✿	🍁	❋	230
Blackberry	*Rubus spp*		⊛			💧	✿	🍁		240
Curly dock	*Rumex crispus*		⊛	≈			✿	🍁		242
Black willow	*Salix nigra*			≈		💧				244
Figwort	*Scrophularia marilandica*	🌳				💧	✿			252
Mad-dog weed	*Scutellaria lateriflora*	🌳	⊛	≈		💧	✿			254
Mullein	*Verbascum thapsus*		⊛				✿	🍁		282

Glossary of Botanical Terms

Achene: A small, dry, hard, 1-seeded fruit.

Acuminate: Tapering at the end to a gradual point.

Acute: Terminating in a sharp or well defined angle.

Acutinate: Being acute.

Alternate: Leaves borne singly at a node.

Angled: Having distinct edges.

Annual: Living a single season.

alternate

Anther: The pollen producing portion of the stamen.

Apex: Upper end or tip (of leaf, petal, etc).

Appressed: Lying flat and close against another structure.

anther

Aril: A fleshy structure that forms around a seed, such as, seed covering on yew.

Aromatic: Having a distinct aroma, usually from a volatile oil.

Auricle: Ear-shaped appendage or lobe.

Awn: Slender, usually stiff, terminal bristle.

Axil: Angle formed between the leaf and the stem, or branch and stem.

Axillary: In an axil.

Barb: Ridged points or short bristles usually reflexed like a fish hook.

Basal: Pertaining to the bottom, or the starting point.

Base: The bottom, the originating spot.

basal

Beak: A projection ending in an elongated tip.

Bearded: Bearing long or stiff hairs.

Berry: A fleshy fruit having a thin skin with the seeds surrounded by the pulp, such as the tomato.

Biennial: Living only two years and flowering the second year.

Bisexual: Having both stamens (male organs) and pistils (female organs) on the same plant, such as in perfect flowers.

Blade: Flattened, green portion of a leaf.

Bract: A small leaf, often scalelike and usually subtending a flower or inflorescence.

Bracted: Having bracts.

Bristle: A stiff hair.

Bristly: Having bristles.

Bulb: Underground bud surrounded by modified fleshy leaves, such as onions.

Bulbous: Having the character of a bulb.

Calyx: The outer, usually green, portion of the flower.

Canes: Usually branchless stems that live for a few years then are replaced by new ones, such as blackberry stems.

capitate

Capitate: Arranged in a head, or dense cluster.

Capsule: A dry fruit composed of several units, which separate and open at maturity.

Carpel: A simple pistil, or one unit of a compound pistil.

Catkin: A dry scaly spike of flowers, usually unisexual, such as flowers of willow, alders, and birches.

Cauline: Belonging to the stem.

Chaff: The scales or bracts on the receptacle of many composite flowers.

Chlorophyll: The green coloring compound responsible for converting sunlight into chemical energy and the plant's green color.

Ciliate: Fringed with hairs.

Clasping: Partly surrounding another structure at the base, such as mullein's leaves clasp the stem.

clasping

Clavate: Club shaped, gradually thickening upward.

Cleft: Deeply cut.

Coarse: Rough surface.

Compound: Composed of 2 or more similar parts united into one whole.

compound

Compound leaf: A leaf divided into separate parts called leaflets.

Cones: Seed producing structures of conifers.

Conic: Cone shaped.

Connate: United, used especially of like structures, such as leaves, joined from the start.

Connective: The portion of a stamen that joins the two anther cavities.

Conspicuous: Easily noticed.

Cordate: Heart-shaped, the broadest part at the base.

cordate

Corm: The enlarged, solid, bulblike base of some stems.

Corolla: The second or inner set of floral parts, composed of separate or united petals, usually conspicuous by its size and/or color.

Corona: A crownlike structure on inner side of the corolla, as in milkweed.

Corymb: A flat-topped or convex flower cluster, the outer flowers opening first. *Achillea millifolium* is an example.

corymb

Crease: A fold or the appearance of a fold.

Crenate: Having rounded teeth.

Crenulate: Finely crenate.

Crested: Bearing elevated ridges on projections, especially on petals.

crenate

Cuneate: Shaped like a wedge.

Cuspidate: Tipped with a cusp or sharp and firm point.

Cyanthium: Cuplike involucre around the flowers, such as in the spurges.

Cylindric: Shaped like a cylinder.

Cyme: A convex or flat flower cluster, the central flowers unfolding first. *Tanacetum vulgare* is an example.

Deciduous: Not persistent, such as trees that drop their leaves every year are deciduous.

Decompound: More than once compound or divided.

Decumbent: Stems in a reclining position, but the end is ascending.

Decurrent: Extending downward, applied to leaves in which the blade is extended as wings along the petiole.

Deltoid: Shaped like a triangle.

dentate

Dentate: With sharp teeth.

Denticulate: Minutely dentate.

Diadelphous: Stamens which are combined in two, often unequal sets.

357

Dicotyledon (dicot): Plant with 2 seed-leaves or cotyledons. In practice usually recognized by net veined leaves, the parts of the flower in 4's or 5's, the fibers of the stem in a ring.

Dioecious: Unisexual, with two kinds of flowers on separate parts of the inflorescence.

Discoid: Resembling a disk.

Disk: Central part of the head of many compositae flowers.

Disk-flower: In compositae flowers, the tubular flowers in the center of the head, or comprising the head. *Tanacetum vulgare* has only disk flowers.

disk-flower

Dissected: Cut or divided into narrow segments. *Artemesia absinthium* has highly dissected leaves.

dissected

Downy: Covered with fine and soft hairs.

Drupe: A fleshy fruit with a single hard stone (seed) in the center, such as peach, plum, and cherry.

Druplets: A diminutive drupe, each unit of a raspberry or blackberry fruit.

Ellipsoid: Elliptic, oval; in outline, widest at the middle and narrow about equally at the ends.

Elliptic: In the form of an ellipse, rounded about equally at both ends.

Entire: With a continuous, unbroken margin; without teeth, scallops, or lobes.

Ephemeral: Lasting for one day or less.

Erect: Standing straight up.

entire

Evergreen: Persistent leaves throughout the year, not deciduous.

Fertile: Capable of normal reproductive functions.

Fiberous: Having long tough stringy fibers.

Filament: The stalk of the stamen.

Filamentous: Threadlike.

Filiform: Thread shaped, long, slender and terete.

Flexous: Curved alternately in opposite directions.

Foliate: Having leaves.

Foliolate: Having leaflets.

Follicle: A dry fruit developed from a single ovary, opening by a slit along one side, such as a milkweed pod.

Fruit: The seed-bearing part of a plant; the ripened ovary with attachments.

Fusiform: Spindle shaped, swollen in the middle and narrowing gradually toward each end.

Gelatinous: Having a mucous-like gelatin layer.

Glabrous: Smooth, especially not pubescent nor hairy.

Gland: A secreting structure or surface.

Globose: Round or nearly round.

Glutinous: Covered with a sticky exudation.

Herb: The part of the plant above the ground, a plant with no perennial parts above the ground.

Hirsute: Covered with rather coarse or stiff hairs.

Hirsutulous: Slightly hirsute.

Hispid: With rigid or bristly hairs or with bristles.

Imbricate: Overlapping, either vertically or spirally, where the lower piece covers the base of the next higher; or laterally as in the aestivation of a calyx or corolla, where at least one piece must be wholly external and one internal.

Imbricated: Being imbricate.

Indehiscent: Not opening at maturity.

Indusia: The covering of the fruiting structure on the underside of a fern leaf.

Inflated: Blown up, bladdery.

Inflorescence: Arrangement of flowers on a stem.

Intolerant: Needing sunlight; a plant that needs an open area or lots of sun.

Introduced: Brought intentionally from another region, as for the purpose of cultivation.

Involucre: A circle or collection of bracts surrounding a flower cluster, head or single flower.

involucre

Irregular: Showing inequality in the size, form or union of its similar parts.

Laciniate: Slashed, cut into narrow pointed lobes.

Lanceolate: Shaped like a lance, several times longer than wide, broadest toward the base and narrowed to the apex.

lanceolate

Lateral: Belonging to or borne near the sides.

Leaflet: A single unit of a compound leaf.

Leathery: Having the texture of leather.

Lenticel: A type of gas exchange pore found in the bark of many trees, such as the elongated brown spots in birch bark.

Lenticilate: Having lenticels.

Linear: Long and narrow with parallel margins.

Lip: Each of the upper and lower divisions of a bilabiate corolla.

lip

Lipped: Having lips.

Lobed: Having lobes.

Lobeless: Not having lobes.

Lobes: Any rounded portion of an organ.

Locular: Having locules.

Locule: A cavity.

Lustrous: A dull shine.

Margin: The edge.

Membranaceous: Thin, rather soft, more or less translucent and pliable.

Midrib: The central or main rib of a leaf or similar structure.

Midvein: The middle most vein, the most prominent vein.

Minute: Very small.

Monoecious: With stamens (male) and pistils (female) in separate flowers on the same plant.

Mottled: Splotchy, different colors in splotches.

Nerve: A simple or unbranched vein or slender rib.

Node: The place upon a stem which normally bears a leaf or whorl of leaves.

Nodule: Diminutive of node.

Nut: A hard one-seeded fruit, which has no natural lines for opening.

Nutlet: A diminutive nut.

Obcordate: Inverted heart-shaped, with the point basal.

obcordate

Oblanceolate: Lanceolate with the broadest part toward the apex.

Oblong: Two to three times longer than broad and with nearly parallel sides.

Obovate: Inverated ovate.

Obsolete: Not evident, extinct.

Obtuse: Blunt or rounded at the end.

obovate

Opposite leaves: Two leaves at a node.

Oval: Broadly elliptical.

Ovary: The part of the pistil which contains the ovules.

opposite

Ovate: Having an egg-shaped outline.

Ovoid: A solid with an ovate outline.

Ovule: Embryonic seed.

Palmate: Radiately lobed or divided, palm shaped.

palmate

Palmately: In a palmate manner.

Panicle: A loose irregularly compound
inflorescence with pedicellate flowers,
such as a branched raceme or corymb.

panicle

Paniculate: Flowers borne in a panicle-like structure.

Papillose: Bearing minute nipple-shaped projections.

Pappalate: Having a pappus.

Pappus: The modified calyx in compositae, forming a crown of hairs at
the summit of an achene.

Parasitic: Growing on and deriving nourishment from another living
organism.

Pedate: Palmately divided or parted, with the lateral segments 2 cleft.

Pedicel: The supporting stem of a single flower or leaf.

Peduncle: A primary flower stalk, supporting either a cluster or a
solitary flower.

Pedunculate: Born on a peduncle.

Perennial: Lasting year after year.

Perfect: (Flower) Having both functional
pistil and stamens.

perfoliate

Perfoliate: Having the stem apparently passing through the leaf.

Perianth: The floral envelope, consisting of the calyx and corolla.

Persistent: Enduring, as a calyx upon the fruit, leaves through the
winter.

Petal: A unit of the corolla.

Petiolate: Having a petiole

Petiole: The support stem of a leaf stalk.

Petiolulate: Having a petiolule.

Petiolule: The foot stalk of a leaflet.

Pilose: Hairy, especially with soft hairs.

Pinnate: Compound with the leaflets arranged on each side of a common axis.

pinnate

Pinnately: Being pinnate.

Pinnule: One of the smallest units of a several compound leaf.

Pistil: The seed bearing organ of the flower, consisting of the ovary, stigma and style.

Pistilate: Provided with pistils.

pistil

Polygamodioeous: Polygamous but chiefly dioecious.

Polygamous: With hermaphrodite and unisexual flowers on the same or on different individuals of the same species.

Prickly: Having sharp outgrowths from the epidermis.

Prostrate: Lying flat on the ground.

Pubescence: Having the property of being pubescent.

Pubescent: Covered with hairs, especially short and soft or down-like.

Raceme: A simple inflorescence of pedicelled flowers upon a common axis.

raceme

Ray flower: The ligule or strap-like marginal flower of many compositae, when differentiated from the disk flowers.

ray flower

Receptacle: The more or less expanded portion of a stem that bears flower organs or the collected flowers of a head.

Recurved: Curved downward or backward.

Reflexed: Abruptly bent or turned downward.

Resin: Sticky clear amber sap of pines or similar substances in other plants.

Resinous: Containing resin.

Retrorsely: Directed back or downwards.

Rhizome: Any prostrate or subterranean stem, usually rooting at the nodes and becoming upcurved at the apex.

rhizome

Rhombic: With the outline of an equilateral oblique-angled figure.

Ribbed: With prominent vein formations.

Ridged: The outer surface angled prominently with acute bumps.

Root: The descending axis of the plant, usually growing in the opposite direction from the stem, without nodes and internodes; mostly develops underground and absorbs moisture from the soil.

rootstock

Rootlets: Small branch-like offshoots from the root.

Rootstock: A rhizome or the elongate, unmodified subterranean offshoots of roots.

Rosette: A cluster of leaves or other organs in a circular formation, usually hugging the ground.

rosette

Runners: A filaform or very slender stolon.

Sagitate: Shaped like an arrow-head, the basal lobes directed downward or backward.

Samara: An indehiscent winged fruit.

Sap: The fluid material that flows from the roots, through certain conducting cells and into the leaves, it is usually clear but can be colored.

Scabrous: Rough to the touch.

Scale: Any thin scarious body, usually a degenerate leaf, sometimes of epidermal origin, a trichome, if disc-like or flattened.

Scape: A naked flowering stem rising from the ground.

Seed: The ripened ovule, consisting of the embryo, stored food, and a seed coat.

Sepals: A unit of the calyx, the outer most set of floral leaves.

Serrate: Having sharp teeth pointing forward.

serrate

Serrulate: Finely serrate.

Sessile: Without stalk of any kind, leaves with no petioles are sessile.

Sheathing: Inclosing or surrounding.

Shrub: A woody perennial usually with several stems.

Silicle: A short silique.

sessile

Silique: A specialized fruit or capsule in which a thin membrane separates the valves, notably in the cruciferae family.

Smooth: Without roughness, rather inaccurately used to signify without pubescence.

Spadix: A spike with a fleshy axis, as in the araceae family.

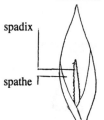

spadix

spathe

Spathe: A large bract inclosing an inflorescence, usually inclosing a spadix.

Spatulate: Oblong, with the basal end attenuated like a druggist's spatula.

spatulate

Speckled: Having spots or small splotches.

Spherical: Round or global.

Spicy: Flavorful, aromatic.

Spike: A form of simple inflorescence with the flowers sessile or nearly so upon a more or less elongated common axis.

spike

Spines: Sharp woody or rigid outgrowths from the stem.

Spiny: Having spines.

Spinulose: Having tiny spines.

Spiral: In a twisted circular manner, like a spring.

Spur: A hollow sac-like or tubular extension of some part of a flower.

spur

Spurred: Having spurs.

Stamen: One of the pollen-bearing organs of the flower.

Staminate: Having stamens.

stamen

Stem: The main ridged growth of which the branches and leaves originate.

Stigma: That part of a pistil which receives the pollen, fertilization of the ovules follows.

Stipe: The leaf-stalk of a fern frond.

Stipulate: Having stipules.

Stipule: An appendage at the base of a petiole or leaf.

Stoloniferous: Producing stolons.

stipule

Stolon: A runner, or any basal branch that is inclined to root.

Stout: Broad, large.

Strobile: An inflorescence marked by imbricated bracts or scales, as in the hop plant or pine cone.

Style: The usually attenuated portion of the pistil connecting the stigma and ovary.

Subcordate: Slightly cordate in shape.

Subcylindric: Slightly cylindric, tending to be cylindric in shape.

Suberect: Tending to be erect.

Subglobose: Tending to be globose in shape.

Suborbicular: Tending to be obicular in shape.

Subrotound: Tending to be rotound in shape.

Subspherical: Tending to be spherical in shape.

Succulent: Fleshy, juicy.

Taproot: A primary descending root.

Terminal: At the end of the growing points, such as at the branch and stem tips.

Ternate: In threes, trimerous.

Thorn: Same as spine, a woody sharp appendage.

Toothed: Having sharp lobes, like serrate but larger.

Trailing: With runners or stolons.

Truncate: Ending abruptly, as if cut off transversely.

Tubular: Small cylindric in shape, like a tube.

Twining: Wrapping itself around, like vines wrapping around trees.

umbel

Umbel: An inflorescence in which the peduncles or pedicels spring from the same level, shaped like an upside down umbrella.

Undulate: With a wavy surface or margin, repand.

Unisexual: Of one sex, either staminate or pistillate.

United: Joined together.

Valve: One of the pieces into which a capsule splits, or the partially detached lid of an anther.

Valved: Having valves.

Vein: Threads of conducting tissue in a leaf or other organ, especially those which branch.

Villious: Bearing long and soft hairs that are not interwoven.

Vine: A long trailing stem that is prostrate or uses other structures or plants as supporting structures.

Whorl: An arrangement of leaves, branches or flowers in a circle around the stem.

Whorled: Having leaves or branches arranged in a whorl.

whorl

Wing: Any membranous or thin expansion bordering or surrounding an organ, such as elm seeds and maple seeds are winged.

Winged: Having a wing.

Wooley: With long and tortuous or matted hairs.

Glossary of Medical Terms

Abortifacient: An agent that causes abortion.

Acne: An affection of the skin with eruption of the papules or pustules.

Adulterant: Foreign material mixed in with the drug plant.

Alkaloid: Any principle of organic origin containing a nitrogen atom.

Alterative: To change gradually the nutritive process and bodily habits to a normal state.

Amenorrhea: Absence of menstruation.

Analgesic: To allay pain by depressing the sensory nerve centers.

Anesthesia: Absence of sensitivity to stimuli, narcosis produced by a drug for surgery.

Anodyne: To produce relief from pain by action on the sensory nervous system.

Anthelmintic: To expel or kill intestinal worms.

Antibiotic: A drug that destroys bacteria or inhibits the growth of.

Antiperiodic: To modify or prevent return of malarial fever.

Antiscorbutic: Counter acting scurvy.

Antiseptic: To inhibit, check the growth of, or kill microorganisms on living tissue.

Antispasmodic: Preventing or relieving spasms.

Aperient: Mildly cathartic.

Aphrodisiac: A substance that produces sexual stimulation.

Aromatic: Having a spicy fragrance.

Arrhythmia: Variation from the normal rhythm, especially of the heart beat.

Arthritis: Inflammation of the joints.

Ascorbutic: Containing ascorbic acid.

Asphyxia: Apparent or actual cessation of life due to interruption of effective gaseous exchange in the lungs.

Asthma: A term applied loosely to a condition of difficult breathing; used specifically to designate a condition of allergic bronchospasm.

Astringent: To shrink, blanche, wrinkle or harden tissue, diminish secretions and exudates, and coagulate blood.

Bitters: A bitter tasting substance usually used to aid digestion.

Boils: Furuncle, a cutaneous localized pus containing infection.

Bronchitis: Inflammation of the bronchi, usually with profuse mucous discharge.

Cancer: A malignant tumor.

Canker: An ulceration, especially of the lip or oral mucosa.

Carbuncle: A deeply situated staphylococcal infection producing multiple adjacent draining skin openings.

Carcinogenic: An agent that causes cancer.

Cardiac: Pertaining to the heart.

Carminative: To expel gas and relieve colic.

Catarrh: Inflammation of a mucous membrane with free discharge.

Cathartic: An agent that promotes defecation.

Cholagogue: To stimulate emptying of the gall bladder and flow of bile into the duodenum.

Cholera: An acute infectious condition marked by severe diarrhea, vomiting, and dehydration.

Cold: A condition of suspected viral causation, with inflammation of the nasopharynx and variable degrees of malaise.

Condiment: Something used to season or give relish to food.

Congestion: Abnormal accumulation of blood or fluid in a part.

Constipation: A condition of abnormally infrequent and difficult evacuation of feces.

Consumption: Wasting of the body, pulmonary tuberculosis.

Convalescence: The stage of recovering from an illness, operation or accidental injury.

Convulsions: Involuntary spasm or contraction of muscles.

Corrective: To correct or render more pleasant the action of other remedies, especially purgatives.

Coryza: Profuse discharge from the mucous membrane of the nose.

Counterirritant: Substance or method to cause irritation of the part to which it is applied.

Cramps: A painful spasmodic muscular contraction.

Cutaneous: Pertaining to the skin.

Debility: Weakness, a run-down state.

Demulcent: To sooth and protect mucous membranes.

Dentifrice: A preparation for cleansing and polishing teeth.

Deobstruent: A medicine which removes obstructions.

Depressant: To lessen functional activity.

Dermatitis: Inflammation of the skin.

Dermatomycosis: A skin disease due to parasitic fungi.

Detergent: To cleanse abnormal areas, as granulating wounds and ulcers.

Diabetes: A condition characterized by inability of the tissues to utilize sugar.

Diaphoretic: To increase perspiration.

Diarrhea: Frequent evacuation of watery feces.

Diphtheria: An infectious disease characterized by the formation of false membranes in the throat and nose.

Discutient: To scatter swellings.

Diuretic: To increase urine flow.

Douche: A stream of water directed against a part or into a cavity, usually associated with a vaginal wash.

Dropsy: Accumulation of serous fluid in a cavity or in the tissues.

Dysentery: Inflammation of the large intestine, with cramping pain and the evacuation of liquid and bloody stools.

Dysmenorrhea: Painful menstruation.

Dyspepsia: Indigestion, difficulty of digestion.

Dysuria: Painful urination.

Eczema: A skin disease with itching, redness and infiltration.

Emetic: An agent that causes vomiting.

Emmenagogue: To reestablish or increase menstrual flow.

Emollient: To soften and protect the skin.

Emphysema: Abnormal volume and pressure of air in the lungs.

Enema: Introduction of fluid into the rectum.

Epilepsy: A disorder characterized by convulsive seizures or disturbances of consciousness, or both, and associated with disturbance of electrical activity of the brain.

Erysipelas: A febrile disease characterized by inflammation and redness of the skin, mucous membranes, etc and due to streptococcus pyogenes.

Escharotic: Causing lesions, i.e. due to a bite of an infected mite, resulting in scrub typhus, or by application of a caustic agent, a necrotic mass ultimately separating from healthy tissue and being cast off.

Ester: The coproduct, within water, resulting from reaction of an alcohol with an acid.

Expectorant: An agent that liquefies secretions and aid the removal of mucous from the respiratory tract.

Febrifuge: A remedy that dispels fever.

Flatulence: Excessive formation of gases in the stomach or intestines.

Flux: An abnormal discharge from the body.

Fomentation: A warm, moist application.

Galactagogue: Substance used to increase secretion of breast milk.

Gastritis: Inflammation of the stomach.

Glaucoma: A condition of the eye characterized by increased intraocular pressure.

Glycoside: A vegetable principle decomposable into a carbohydrate and another substance.

Gout: Painful constitutional disease with joint inflammation and chalky deposits, due to disturbance of the purine metabolism of the body.

Hayfever: An allergy from pollen causing stuffed up nose and head.

Heartburn: A burning sensation in the epigastrium.

Hemorrhage: The escape of blood from a ruptured vessel.

Hemorrhoid: A varicose dilatation of a vein or veins in the rectal area.

Hemostatic: An agent used to check or stop the escape of blood.

Hydrophobia: Rabies.

Hypnotic: An agent that induces sleep.

Hypochondriac: A person with a morbid anxiety about one's own health, with complaint of imaginary disorders.

Hypoglycemic: Deficiency of sugar in the blood.

Hysteria: A psychoneurosis with symptoms based on conversion and characterized by lack of control over acts and emotions by morbid self-consciousness, by anxiety, by exaggeration of the effect of sensory impressions and by simulation of various disorders.

Impotence: Partial or complete inability of the male to perform the sexual act or to achieve orgasm.

Indigestion: Failure of digestive function, usually accompanied by stomach pains.

Indolent: Chronic, changing very slowly.

Insomnia: Inability to sleep.

Intoxicant: A substance that creates another state of consciousness, usually combined with difficult coordination and muscular control.

Jaundice: Yellowness of the skin and eyes from retention of bile pigments.

Lactone: An aromatic liquid from lactic acid; a cyclic ester.

Laryngitis: Inflammation of the larynx, sometimes causing inability to talk.

Laxative: An agent that promotes evacuation of the bowels.

Lectinic: An agent that causes hemagglutination.

Leukorrhea: A whitish discharge from the vagina.

Malignant: Progressing in virulence.

Menorrhagia: Excessive menstruation.

Menstruation: The cyclic, physiologic discharge of blood from the nonpregnant uterus, occurring approximately every 28 days in humans.

Miscarriage: Loss of products of conception from the uterus before the fetus is viable.

Mucilage: An aqueous solution of a gummy substance, used as a demulcent.

Narcotic: To relieve distress and induce sleep.

Nausea: Tendency to vomit.

Nephritis: Inflammation of the kidney.

Neuralgia: Pain in the nerve.

Nutritive: Aiding in nutrition.

Ophthalmia: Inflammation or affection of the eye.

Panacea: A supposed remedy for all diseases.

Paralysis: Loss of power of voluntary motion.

Parturifacient: A medicine which facilitates childbirth.

Pectoral: Pertaining to the chest area.

Phlegm: Mucous.

Physic: A medicine, especially a cathartic.

Piles: Hemorrhoids.

Pleurisy: Inflammation of the pleura, a lung disease.

Pneumonia: An acute inflammation of the lung marked by formation of an exudate in the interstitial and cellular portions of the lung.

Poultice: A soft, pultaceous mass to be placed hot upon the skin.

Priapism: A prolonged erection, may last days, many times painful.

Pruritus: Intense itching.

Psoriasis: A chronic, patchy, scaly dermatitis.

Purgative: A cathartic.

Pyorrhea: A purulent inflammation of the dental periosteum, with progressive necrosis of the alveoli and looseness of the teeth; a gum disease.

Quinsy: Acute suppurative inflammation of the tonsil and the surrounding tissue.

Refrigerant: To allay thirst and give a sensation of coolness.

Resolvent: Promoting the subsidence of a pathologic state.

Rheumatism: A disease marked by pain in the joints or muscles, usually recurrent and progressive.

Rubefacient: To produce mild irritation accompanied by reddening when applied to the skin.

Salivation: The secretion of saliva.

Saponin: A glycosidal principle from various plants that characteristically foams when shaken in water.

Scrofula: Tuberculosis disease of lymphatic nodes and of bone, with slowly suppurating abscesses.

Scurvy: A disease due to deficiency of ascorbic acid, marked by weakness, anemia, spongy gums and mucocutaneous hemorrhages.

Sedative: Substance used to allay excitement and soothe the nervous system.

Sialagogue: An agent that stimulates the flow of saliva.

Smallpox: An acute, highly communicable, febrile viral disease, characterized by sustained high fever and appearance first of macules and later of papules on the skin and mucous membranes.

Spasmodic: Of the nature of spasms, an agent that causes spasms.

Spermatorrhea: Involuntary escape of semen.

Sternutatory: An agent that causes sneezing.

Stimulant: To increase functional activity.

Stomachic: To stimulate appetite and gastric secretion.

Strangury: Dysuria, difficult urination, may be painful.

Styptic: Arresting hemorrhage by the means of an astringent quality.

Sudorific: An agent that causes perspiration.

Syphilis: A venereal disease caused by treponema pallidum, leading to many structural and cutaneous lesions.

Taeniafuge: To expel tapeworms.

Thrush: Fungus or yeast like infection of the oral mucous membrane characterized by superficial, confluent white patches on a red, moist, inflammatory surface.

Tonic: To stimulate restoration of tone to muscle tissue.

Tremor: Involuntary movement due to alternating contractions of opposing muscles, occurring physiologically or pathologically.

Tuberculosis: An infectious disease caused by mycobacterium tuberculosis, and characterized by the formation of tubercles in the tissues.

Ulcer: A local defect, or excavation of the surface of an organ, produced by sloughing of necrotic inflammatory tissue.

Vaginitis: Inflammation of the vagina.

Vasopressor: An agent that stimulants contraction of the muscular tissue of capillaries and arteries.

Vermifuge: An agent that expels worms.

Vesicant: An agent that produces blisters.

Vulnerary: An agent that promotes the healing of cuts and skin wounds.

Common Names—Latin Names

Aaron's rod . . . . *Verbascum thapsus*
Absinthe . . . . *Artemisia absinthium*
Adam-and-eve root . . . . *Aplectrum hymale*
Adder's tongue . . . . *Erythronium americanum*
Alder . . . . *Alnus rugosa*
Alfalfa . . . . *Medicago sativa*
Alum root . . . . *Geranium maculatum*
American cranberry . . . . *Vaccinium macrocarpon*
American pennyroyal . . . . *Hedeoma pulegioides*
Anemone . . . . *Anemone canadensis*
Angelica . . . . *Angelica atropurpurea*
Anise-root . . . . *Osmorhiza longistylis*
Apple . . . . *Malus spp*
Aquatic apple moss . . . . *Philonotis fontana*
Arbor-vitae . . . . *Thuja occidentalis*
Arbutus . . . . *Epigaea repens*
Ash . . . . *Fraxinus americana*
Asparagus . . . . *Asparagus officinale*
Avens . . . . *Geum rivale*
Balmony . . . . *Chelone glabra*
Balsam fir . . . . *Abies balsamea*
Balsam poplar . . . . *Populus balsamifera*
Balsam . . . . *Abies balsamea*
Baneberry . . . . *Actaea alba*
Baneberry . . . . *Actaea rubra*
Baneberry . . . . *Actaea arguta*
Barberry . . . . *Berberis vulgaris*
Beach pea . . . . *Lathyrus japonicus*
Beaked hazel . . . . *Corylus cornuta*
Bearberry . . . . *Arctostaphylos uva-ursi*
Bedstraw . . . . *Galium aparine*
Beech . . . . *Fagus grandifolia*
Beech . . . . *Fagus americana*
Beechnut . . . . *Fagus grandifolia*
Beechnut . . . . *Fagus americana*
Bilberry . . . . *Vaccinium angustifolium*
Birch . . . . *Betula alleghaniensis*
Bittersweet . . . . *Celastrus scandens*

Bittersweet	Solanum dulcamara
Black cherry	Prunus serotina
Black morel	Morchella semilibera
Black morel	Morchella angusticeps
Black morel	Morchella esculenta
Black morel	Morchella deliciosa
Black snakeroot	Asarum canadense
Black walnut	Juglans nigra
Black willow	Salix nigra
Black willow	Salix alba
Blackberry	Rubus spp
Blackcap	Rubus spp
Blazing star	Chamaelirium luteum
Bloodroot	Sanguinaria canadensis
Blue cohosh	Caulophyllum thalictroides
Blue flag	Iris versicolor
Blue violet	Viola papilionaceae
Blueberry	Caulophyllum thalictroides
Blueberry	Vaccinium angustifolium
Bog cranberry	Vaccinium macrocarpon
Bog gale	Myrica gale
Bog onion	Arisaema triphyllum
Boneset	Eupatorium perfoliatum
Bristly sarsaprilla	Aralia nudicaulis
Bristly sarsaprilla	Aralia hispida
Bristly sarsaprilla	Aralia racemosa
Broad-leaved sarabacca	Asarum canadense
Bronze birch	Betula alleghaniensis
Brook moss	Fontinalis
Broom moss	Dicranum spoparium
Buckeye	Aesculus hippocastanum
Buckhorn	Osmunda cinnamonea
Bugleweed	Lycopus virginicus
Bulrush	Typha latifolia
Burdock	Arctium lappa
Burdock	Arctium minus
Burrseed	Arctium lappa
Burrseed	Arctium minus
Butterfly weed	Asclepias tuberosa
Butternut	Juglans cinerea

Butterweed . . . . *Erigeron canadensis*
Calamus . . . . *Acorus calamus*
Canada anemone . . . . *Anemone canadensis*
Canada moonseed . . . . *Menispermum canadense*
Canadian sweet gale . . . . *Comptonia peregrina*
Canker root . . . . *Coptis groenlandica*
Canne . . . . *Amaranthus retroflexus*
Carpenter's square . . . . *Scrophularia marilandica*
Carpenter-weed . . . . *Prunella vulgaris*
Carrot . . . . *Daucus carota*
Case weed . . . . *Capsella bursa-pastoris*
Catmint . . . . *Nepeta cataria*
Catnip . . . . *Nepeta cataria*
Cattail . . . . *Typha latifolia*
Celandine . . . . *Impatiens capensis*
Checkerberry . . . . *Gaultheria procumbens*
Chicory . . . . *Cichorium intybus*
Chocolate root . . . . *Geum rivale*
Cinnamon-fern . . . . *Osmunda cinnamonea*
Cleavergrass . . . . *Trifolium pratense*
Cleavers . . . . *Galium aparine*
Climbing bittersweet . . . . *Celastrus scandens*
Climbing orange root . . . . *Celastrus scandens*
Clivers . . . . *Galium aparine*
Clotbur . . . . *Arctium lappa*
Clotbur . . . . *Arctium minus*
Clover bloom . . . . *Baptisia tinctoria*
Clover . . . . *Trifolium pratense*
Cohosh . . . . *Caulophyllum thalictroides*
Colic root . . . . *Aletris farinosa*
Colicroot . . . . *Apocynum androsaemifolium*
Colicroot . . . . *Apocynum cannabinum*
Coltsfoot . . . . *Asarum canadense*
Columbine . . . . *Aquilegia canadensis*
Comfrey . . . . *Symphytum officinale*
Common hairy cap moss . . . . *Polytrichum commune*
Common liverwort . . . . *Marchantia polymorpha*
Common sunflower . . . . *Helianthus annuus*
Convulsion-root . . . . *Monotropa uniflora*
Coral root . . . . *Corallorhiza maculata*

Coral root	Corallorhiza odontorhiza
Corpse-plant	Monotropa uniflora
Cow parsnip	Heracleum lanatum
Cowbane	Cicuta maculata
Cowbane	Cicuta bulbifera
Cowslip	Caltha palustris
Cramp bark	Viburnum opulus
Cranberry	Viburnum trilobum
Cranberry	Vaccinium macrocarpon
Crane's bill	Geranium maculatum
Crawley	Corallorhiza maculata
Crawley	Corallorhiza odontorhiza
Curly dock	Rumex crispus
Cypress-leaved feather moss	Hypnum cupressiforme
Dandelion	Taraxacum officinale
Day lily	Hemerocallis fulva
Devil's bit	Chamaelirium luteum
Devil's ear	Arisaema triphyllum
Dewberry	Rubus spp
Dock	Rumex crispus
Dog toothed violet	Erythronium americanum
Dogbane	Apocynum androsaemifolium
Dogbane	Apocynum cannabinum
Doll's eyes	Actaea alba
Doll's eyes	Actaea rubra
Doll's eyes	Actaea arguta
Dracontium	Symplocarpus foetidus
Dragon root	Arisaema triphyllum
Dutchman's breeches	Dicentra canadensis
Dutchman's breeches	Dicentra cucullaria
False unicorn	Chamaelirium luteum
Ferngale	Comptonia peregrina
Fiddle-heads	Osmunda cinnamonea
Figwort	Scrophularia marilandica
Filbert	Corylus cornuta
Fits-root	Monotropa uniflora
Flag	Typha latifolia
Flannel-plant	Verbascum thapsus
Fleabane	Erigeron canadensis
Fleur-de-lys	Iris versicolor

Fringe moss	Racomitrium canescens
Gale	Myrica gale
Garget	Phytolacca americana
Geranium	Geranium maculatum
Geulder-rose	Viburnum opulus
Ginger	Asarum canadense
Ginseng	Panax quinquefolius
Gobo	Arctium lappa
Gobo	Arctium minus
Gold thread	Coptis groenlandica
Golden seal	Hydrastis canadensis
Golden-buttons	Tanacetum vulgare
Goose grass	Galium aparine
Great scented liverwort	Conocephalum conicum
Green amaranth	Amaranthus retroflexus
Ground laurel	Epigaea repens
Hackmatack	Populus balsamifera
Harebur	Arctium lappa
Harebur	Arctium minus
Hazelnut	Corylus cornuta
Heal-all	Prunella vulgaris
Helonias	Chamaelirium luteum
Hemlock	Cicuta maculata
Hemlock	Cicuta bulbifera
Hemlock	Conium maculatum
Hemp	Apocynum androsaemifolium
Hemp	Apocynum cannabinum
Hemp	Cannabis sativa
Hepatica	Hepatica acutiloba
Highbush-cranberry	Viburnum trilobum
Hoary puccoon	Lithospermum canescens
Honey mushroom	Armillariella mella
Hops	Humulus lupulus
Horehound	Marrubium vulgare
Horse chesnut	Aesculus hippocastanum
Horsetail fleabane	Erigeron canadensis
Horseweed	Erigeron canadensis
Hound's tongue	Cynoglossum officinale
Huckleberry	Vaccinium angustifolium
Huntsman's cup	Sarracenia purpurea

378

Indian hemp . . . . *Apocynum androsaemifolium*
Indian hemp . . . . *Apocynum cannabinum*
Indian paint . . . . *Lithospermum canescens*
Indian pipe . . . . *Monotropa uniflora*
Indian root . . . . *Aralia nudicaulis*
Indian root . . . . *Aralia hispida*
Indian root . . . . *Aralia racemosa*
Indian tobacco . . . . *Lobelia inflata*
Indian tobacco . . . . *Verbascum thapsus*
Indian turnip . . . . *Arisaema triphyllum*
Indigo . . . . *Baptisia tinctoria*
Jack-in-the-pulpit . . . . *Arisaema triphyllum*
Jalap . . . . *Podophyllum peltatum*
Japanese beach pea . . . . *Lathyrus japonicus*
Jerusalem artichoke . . . . *Helianthus tuberosus*
Jewelweed . . . . *Impatiens capensis*
Joe-pye weed . . . . *Eupatorium purpureum*
Juneberry . . . . *Amelanchier spp*
Juniper . . . . *Juniperus communis*
Kinnikinick . . . . *Arctostaphylos uva-ursi*
Labrador tea . . . . *Ledum groenlandicum*
Lady's earrings . . . . *Impatiens capensis*
Lady's slipper . . . . *Cypripedium calceolus*
Lamb's-quarters . . . . *Chenopodium album*
Leek . . . . *Allium tricoccum*
Lettuce . . . . *Lactuca scariola*
Lettuce . . . . *Lactuca serriola*
Liverleaf . . . . *Hepatica acutiloba*
Liverwort . . . . *Hepatica acutiloba*
Lobelia . . . . *Lobelia inflata*
Lucerne . . . . *Medicago sativa*
Mad-dog skullcap . . . . *Scutellaria lateriflora*
Mad-dog weed . . . . *Scutellaria lateriflora*
Maiden hair fern . . . . *Adiantum capillus-veneris*
Maiden hair fern . . . . *Adiantum pedatum*
Mandrake . . . . *Podophyllum peltatum*
Marijuana . . . . *Cannabis sativa*
Marsh-marigold . . . . *Caltha palustris*
Maryland figwort . . . . *Scrophularia marilandica*
Masterwort . . . . *Angelica atropurpurea*

Masterwort . . . . *Heracleum lanatum*
May apple . . . . *Podophyllum peltatum*
May-blob . . . . *Caltha palustris*
Mayflower . . . . *Epigaea repens*
Mayflower . . . . *Claytonia virginica*
Meetinghouses . . . . *Aquilegia canadensis*
Milfoil . . . . *Achillea millefolium*
Milfoil . . . . *Achillea lanulosa*
Milkweed . . . . *Apocynum androsaemifolium*
Milkweed . . . . *Apocynum cannabinum*
Milkweed . . . . *Asclepias syriaca*
Milkweed . . . . *Lactuca scariola*
Milkweed . . . . *Lactuca serriola*
Missey-moosey . . . . *Sorbus americana*
Moccasin flower . . . . *Cypripedium calceolus*
Mock pennyroyal . . . . *Hedeoma pulegioides*
Morels . . . . *Morchella semilibera*
Morels . . . . *Morchella angusticeps*
Morels . . . . *Morchella esculenta*
Morels . . . . *Morchella deliciosa*
Motherwort . . . . *Leonurus cardiaca*
Mountain ash . . . . *Sorbus americana*
Mountain fern moss . . . . *Hylocomium splendens*
Mulberry . . . . *Morus rubra*
Mullein . . . . *Verbascum thapsus*
Nanny berry . . . . *Viburnum opulus*
Nerve root . . . . *Cypripedium calceolus*
Nettle . . . . *Urtica dioica*
New Jersey tea . . . . *Ceanothus americanus*
Nightshade . . . . *Solanum dulcamara*
Orange day lily . . . . *Hemerocallis fulva*
Orangeroot . . . . *Hydrastis canadensis*
Papoose root . . . . *Caulophyllum thalictroides*
Partridge berry . . . . *Mitchella repens*
Pearly everlasting . . . . *Anaphalis margaritacea*
Peat moss . . . . *Sphagnum*
Pennyroyal . . . . *Hedeoma pulegioides*
Peppermint . . . . *Mentha piperita*
Pigeonberry . . . . *Phytolacca americana*
Pigweed . . . . *Amaranthus retroflexus*

Pigweed . . . . *Chenopodium album*
Pilewort . . . . *Scrophularia marilandica*
Pimbina . . . . *Viburnum trilobum*
Pineapple weed . . . . *Matricaria matricarioides*
Pipsissewa . . . . *Chimaphila umbellata*
Pitcher-plant . . . . *Sarracenia purpurea*
Plantain . . . . *Plantago major*
Pleurisy root . . . . *Asclepias tuberosa*
Poison hemlock . . . . *Conium maculatum*
Poke salad . . . . *Phytolacca americana*
Poke . . . . *Phytolacca americana*
Pokeweed . . . . *Phytolacca americana*
Pot . . . . *Cannabis sativa*
Prickly lettuce . . . . *Lactuca scariola*
Prickly lettuce . . . . *Lactuca serriola*
Prince's pine . . . . *Chimaphila umbellata*
Pulioll-royall . . . . *Hedeoma pulegioides*
Purple trillium . . . . *Trillium erectum*
Purple water avens . . . . *Geum rivale*
Purplestem angelica . . . . *Angelica atropurpurea*
Putty-root . . . . *Aplectrum hymale*
Queen anne's lace . . . . *Daucus carota*
Raspberry . . . . *Rubus spp*
Rattleweed . . . . *Baptisia tinctoria*
Red clover . . . . *Trifolium pratense*
Red mulberry . . . . *Morus rubra*
Red puccoon . . . . *Sanguinaria canadensis*
Red root . . . . *Ceanothus americanus*
Reefer . . . . *Cannabis sativa*
Rockbells . . . . *Aquilegia canadensis*
Rose hips . . . . *Rosa spp*
Rose . . . . *Rosa spp*
Rose moss . . . . *Rhodobryum ontariense*
Round-leaved pyrola . . . . *Pyrola rotundifolia*
Roundwood . . . . *Sorbus americana*
Rum cherry . . . . *Prunus serotina*
Saint John's wort . . . . *Hypericum perforatum*
Sang . . . . *Panax quinquefolius*
Sarsaprilla . . . . *Aralia nudicaulis*
Sarsaprilla . . . . *Aralia hispida*

Sarsaprilla . . . . *Aralia racemosa*
Sassafras . . . . *Sassafras albidum*
Scoke . . . . *Phytolacca americana*
Scrofula plant . . . . *Scrophularia marilandica*
Self-heal . . . . *Prunella vulgaris*
Seneca-snakeroot . . . . *Polygala senega*
Serviceberry . . . . *Amelanchier spp*
Shadbush . . . . *Amelanchier spp*
Shaggymane . . . . *Coprinus comatus*
Sharp-lobed hepatica . . . . *Hepatica acutiloba*
Shepard's purse . . . . *Capsella bursa-pastoris*
Shinleaf . . . . *Pyrola rotundifolia*
Shovel weed . . . . *Capsella bursa-pastoris*
Sidesaddle flower . . . . *Sarracenia purpurea*
Silkweed . . . . *Asclepias syriaca*
Skunk cabbage . . . . *Symplocarpus foetidus*
Smooth sumac . . . . *Rhus glabra*
Smooth sumac . . . . *Rhus typhina*
Snakehead . . . . *Chelone glabra*
Snapweed . . . . *Impatiens capensis*
Solomon's seal . . . . *Polygonatum biflorum*
Spearmint . . . . *Mentha spicata*
Speckled alder . . . . *Alnus rugosa*
Spignet . . . . *Aralia nudicaulis*
Spignet . . . . *Aralia hispida*
Spignet . . . . *Aralia racemosa*
Spikenard . . . . *Aralia nudicaulis*
Spikenard . . . . *Aralia hispida*
Spikenard . . . . *Aralia racemosa*
Spotted coral root . . . . *Corallorhiza maculata*
Spotted coral root . . . . *Corallorhiza odontorhiza*
Spotted cowbane . . . . *Cicuta maculata*
Spotted cowbane . . . . *Cicuta bulbifera*
Spotted hemlock . . . . *Conium maculatum*
Spring beauty . . . . *Claytonia virginica*
Squaw berry . . . . *Mitchella repens*
Squaw plum . . . . *Mitchella repens*
Squaw vine . . . . *Mitchella repens*
Squawroot . . . . *Trillium erectum*
Squirrel corn . . . . *Dicentra canadensis*

Squirrel corn . . . . *Dicentra cucullaria*
Staghorn sumac . . . . *Rhus glabra*
Staghorn sumac . . . . *Rhus typhina*
Stairstep moss . . . . *Hylocomium splendens*
Star grass . . . . *Aletris farinosa*
Star root . . . . *Chamaelirium luteum*
Stickers . . . . *Cynoglossum officinale*
Stickers . . . . *Arctium lappa*
Stickers . . . . *Arctium minus*
Stickers . . . . *Galium aparine*
Stinging nettle . . . . *Urtica dioica*
Stinking benjamin . . . . *Trillium erectum*
Strawberry . . . . *Fragaria virginiana*
Succory . . . . *Cichorium intybus*
Sugarplum . . . . *Amelanchier spp*
Sumac . . . . *Rhus glabra*
Sumac . . . . *Rhus typhina*
Sunflower . . . . *Helianthus annuus*
Sunflower . . . . *Helianthus tuberosus*
Swamp alder . . . . *Alnus rugosa*
Swamp willow . . . . *Salix nigra*
Swamp willow . . . . *Salix alba*
Sweet cicely . . . . *Osmorhiza longistylis*
Sweet fern . . . . *Comptonia peregrina*
Sweet flag . . . . *Acorus calamus*
Sweet gale . . . . *Myrica gale*
Tag alder . . . . *Alnus rugosa*
Tansy . . . . *Tanacetum vulgare*
Teaberry . . . . *Gaultheria procumbens*
Thimbleberry . . . . *Rubus spp*
Thoroughwort . . . . *Eupatorium perfoliatum*
Touch-me-not . . . . *Impatiens capensis*
Trailing arbutus . . . . *Epigaea repens*
Trillium . . . . *Trillium erectum*
Trout lily . . . . *Erythronium americanum*
Turtle head . . . . *Chelone glabra*
Unicorn plant . . . . *Aletris farinosa*
Uva-ursi . . . . *Arctostaphylos uva-ursi*
Viola . . . . *Viola papilionaceae*
Violet . . . . *Viola papilionaceae*

Wake robin . . . . *Arisaema triphyllum*
Water hemlock . . . . *Cicuta maculata*
Water hemlock . . . . *Cicuta bulbifera*
Water-horehound . . . . *Lycopus virginicus*
Watercress . . . . *Nasturtium officinale*
Waxwork . . . . *Celastrus scandens*
White ash . . . . *Fraxinus americana*
White cedar . . . . *Thuja occidentalis*
White morel . . . . *Morchella semilibera*
White morel . . . . *Morchella angusticeps*
White morel . . . . *Morchella esculenta*
White morel . . . . *Morchella deliciosa*
White pine . . . . *Pinus strobus*
White walnut . . . . *Juglans cinerea*
White willow . . . . *Salix nigra*
White willow . . . . *Salix alba*
Whiteman's foot . . . . *Plantago major*
Wild asparagus . . . . *Asparagus officinale*
Wild beet . . . . *Amaranthus retroflexus*
Wild bergamont . . . . *Monarda fistulosa*
Wild black currant . . . . *Ribes americanum*
Wild carrot . . . . *Daucus carota*
Wild chamomile . . . . *Matricaria matricarioides*
Wild cherry . . . . *Prunus serotina*
Wild garlic . . . . *Allium tricoccum*
Wild geranium . . . . *Geranium maculatum*
Wild ginger . . . . *Asarum canadense*
Wild indigo . . . . *Baptisia tinctoria*
Wild iris . . . . *Iris versicolor*
Wild jalap . . . . *Podophyllum peltatum*
Wild onion . . . . *Allium tricoccum*
Wild oregano . . . . *Monarda fistulosa*
Wild pea . . . . *Lathyrus japonicus*
Wild rose . . . . *Rosa spp*
Wild sarsaprilla . . . . *Aralia nudicaulis*
Wild sarsaprilla . . . . *Aralia hispida*
Wild sarsaprilla . . . . *Aralia racemosa*
Wild spinach . . . . *Chenopodium album*
Wild tobacco . . . . *Lobelia inflata*
Willow . . . . *Salix nigra*

Willow . . . . *Salix alba*
Winter-cress . . . . *Barbarea vulgaris*
Wintergreen . . . . *Gaultheria procumbens*
Wintergreen . . . . *Pyrola rotundifolia*
Witch hazel . . . . *Hamamelis virginiana*
Woolly moss . . . . *Racomitrium lanuginosum*
Wormwood . . . . *Artemisia absinthium*
Yarrow . . . . *Achillea millefolium*
Yarrow . . . . *Achillea lanulosa*
Yarroway . . . . *Achillea millefolium*
Yarroway . . . . *Achillea lanulosa*
Yellow birch . . . . *Betula alleghaniensis*
Yellow broom . . . . *Baptisia tinctoria*
Yellow dock . . . . *Rumex crispus*
Yellow lady's slipper . . . . *Cypripedium calceolus*
Yellow parilla . . . . *Menispermum canadense*
Yellow puccoon . . . . *Hydrastis canadensis*
Yellow rocket . . . . *Barbarea vulgaris*
Yellowroot . . . . *Hydrastis canadensis*

Latin Names—Common Names

Abies balsamea	*Balsam fir*
Abies balsamea	*Balsam*
Achillea lanulosa	*Milfoil*
Achillea lanulosa	*Yarrow*
Achillea lanulosa	*Yarroway*
Achillea millefolium	*Milfoil*
Achillea millefolium	*Yarrow*
Achillea millefolium	*Yarroway*
Acorus calamus	*Calamus*
Acorus calamus	*Sweet flag*
Actaea alba	*Baneberry*
Actaea alba	*Doll's eyes*
Actaea arguta	*Baneberry*
Actaea arguta	*Doll's eyes*
Actaea rubra	*Baneberry*
Actaea rubra	*Doll's eyes*
Adiantum capillus-veneris	*Maiden hair fern*
Adiantum pedatum	*Maiden hair fern*
Aesculus hippocastanum	*Buckeye*
Aesculus hippocastanum	*Horse chesnut*
Aletris farinosa	*Colic root*
Aletris farinosa	*Star grass*
Aletris farinosa	*Unicorn plant*
Allium tricoccum	*Leek*
Allium tricoccum	*Wild garlic*
Allium tricoccum	*Wild onion*
Alnus rugosa	*Alder*
Alnus rugosa	*Speckled alder*
Alnus rugosa	*Swamp alder*
Alnus rugosa	*Tag alder*
Amaranthus retroflexus	*Canne*
Amaranthus retroflexus	*Green amaranth*
Amaranthus retroflexus	*Pigweed*
Amaranthus retroflexus	*Wild beet*
Amelanchier spp	*Juneberry*
Amelanchier spp	*Serviceberry*
Amelanchier spp	*Shadbush*
Amelanchier spp	*Sugarplum*

Anaphalis margaritacea .... Pearly everlasting
Anemone canadensis .... Anemone
Anemone canadensis .... Canada anemone
Angelica atropurpurea .... Angelica
Angelica atropurpurea .... Masterwort
Angelica atropurpurea .... Purplestem angelica
Aplectrum hymale .... Adam-and-eve root
Aplectrum hymale .... Putty-root
Apocynum androsaemifolium .... Colicroot
Apocynum androsaemifolium .... Dogbane
Apocynum androsaemifolium .... Hemp
Apocynum androsaemifolium .... Indian hemp
Apocynum androsaemifolium .... Milkweed
Apocynum cannabinum .... Colicroot
Apocynum cannabinum .... Dogbane
Apocynum cannabinum .... Hemp
Apocynum cannabinum .... Indian hemp
Apocynum cannabinum .... Milkweed
Aquilegia canadensis .... Columbine
Aquilegia canadensis .... Meetinghouses
Aquilegia canadensis .... Rockbells
Aralia hispida .... Bristly sarsaprilla
Aralia hispida .... Indian root
Aralia hispida .... Sarsaprilla
Aralia hispida .... Spignet
Aralia hispida .... Spikenard
Aralia hispida .... Wild sarsaprilla
Aralia nudicaulis .... Bristly sarsaprilla
Aralia nudicaulis .... Indian root
Aralia nudicaulis .... Sarsaprilla
Aralia nudicaulis .... Spignet
Aralia nudicaulis .... Spikenard
Aralia nudicaulis .... Wild sarsaprilla
Aralia racemosa .... Bristly sarsaprilla
Aralia racemosa .... Indian root
Aralia racemosa .... Sarsaprilla
Aralia racemosa .... Spignet
Aralia racemosa .... Spikenard
Aralia racemosa .... Wild sarsaprilla
Arctium lappa .... Burdock

Arctium lappa . . . . *Burrseed*
Arctium lappa . . . . *Clotbur*
Arctium lappa . . . . *Gobo*
Arctium lappa . . . . *Harebur*
Arctium lappa . . . . *Stickers*
Arctium minus . . . . *Burdock*
Arctium minus . . . . *Burrseed*
Arctium minus . . . . *Clotbur*
Arctium minus . . . . *Gobo*
Arctium minus . . . . *Harebur*
Arctium minus . . . . *Stickers*
Arctostaphylos uva-ursi . . . . *Bearberry*
Arctostaphylos uva-ursi . . . . *Kinnikinick*
Arctostaphylos uva-ursi . . . . *Uva-ursi*
Arisaema triphyllum . . . . *Bog onion*
Arisaema triphyllum . . . . *Devil's ear*
Arisaema triphyllum . . . . *Dragon root*
Arisaema triphyllum . . . . *Indian turnip*
Arisaema triphyllum . . . . *Jack-in-the-pulpit*
Arisaema triphyllum . . . . *Wake robin*
Armillariella mella . . . . *Honey mushroom*
Artemisia absinthium . . . . *Absinthe*
Artemisia absinthium . . . . *Wormwood*
Asarum canadense . . . . *Black snakeroot*
Asarum canadense . . . . *Broad-leaved sarabacca*
Asarum canadense . . . . *Coltsfoot*
Asarum canadense . . . . *Ginger*
Asarum canadense . . . . *Wild ginger*
Asclepias syriaca . . . . *Milkweed*
Asclepias syriaca . . . . *Silkweed*
Asclepias tuberosa . . . . *Butterfly weed*
Asclepias tuberosa . . . . *Pleurisy root*
Asparagus officinale . . . . *Asparagus*
Asparagus officinale . . . . *Wild asparagus*
Baptisia tinctoria . . . . *Clover bloom*
Baptisia tinctoria . . . . *Indigo*
Baptisia tinctoria . . . . *Rattleweed*
Baptisia tinctoria . . . . *Wild indigo*
Baptisia tinctoria . . . . *Yellow broom*
Barbarea vulgaris . . . . *Winter-cress*

Barbarea vulgaris . . . . *Yellow rocket*
Berberis vulgaris . . . . *Barberry*
Betula alleghaniensis . . . . *Birch*
Betula alleghaniensis . . . . *Bronze birch*
Betula alleghaniensis . . . . *Yellow birch*
Caltha palustris . . . . *Cowslip*
Caltha palustris . . . . *Marsh-marigold*
Caltha palustris . . . . *May-blob*
Cannabis sativa . . . . *Hemp*
Cannabis sativa . . . . *Marijuana*
Cannabis sativa . . . . *Pot*
Cannabis sativa . . . . *Reefer*
Capsella bursa-pastoris . . . . *Case weed*
Capsella bursa-pastoris . . . . *Shepard's purse*
Capsella bursa-pastoris . . . . *Shovel weed*
Caulophyllum thalictroides . . . . *Blue cohosh*
Caulophyllum thalictroides . . . . *Blueberry*
Caulophyllum thalictroides . . . . *Cohosh*
Caulophyllum thalictroides . . . . *Papoose root*
Ceanothus americanus . . . . *New Jersey tea*
Ceanothus americanus . . . . *Red root*
Celastrus scandens . . . . *Bittersweet*
Celastrus scandens . . . . *Climbing bittersweet*
Celastrus scandens . . . . *Climbing orange root*
Celastrus scandens . . . . *Waxwork*
Chamaelirium luteum . . . . *Blazing star*
Chamaelirium luteum . . . . *Devil's bit*
Chamaelirium luteum . . . . *False unicorn*
Chamaelirium luteum . . . . *Helonias*
Chamaelirium luteum . . . . *Star root*
Chelone glabra . . . . *Balmony*
Chelone glabra . . . . *Snakehead*
Chelone glabra . . . . *Turtle head*
Chenopodium album . . . . *Lamb's-quarters*
Chenopodium album . . . . *Pigweed*
Chenopodium album . . . . *Wild spinach*
Chimaphila umbellata . . . . *Pipsissewa*
Chimaphila umbellata . . . . *Prince's pine*
Cichorium intybus . . . . *Chicory*
Cichorium intybus . . . . *Succory*

Cicuta bulbifera	Cowbane
Cicuta bulbifera	Hemlock
Cicuta bulbifera	Spotted cowbane
Cicuta bulbifera	Water hemlock
Cicuta maculata	Cowbane
Cicuta maculata	Hemlock
Cicuta maculata	Spotted cowbane
Cicuta maculata	Water hemlock
Claytonia virginica	Mayflower
Claytonia virginica	Spring beauty
Comptonia peregrina	Canadian sweet gale
Comptonia peregrina	Ferngale
Comptonia peregrina	Sweet fern
Conium maculatum	Hemlock
Conium maculatum	Poison hemlock
Conium maculatum	Spotted hemlock
Conocephalum conicum	Great scented liverwort
Coprinus comatus	Shaggymane
Coptis groenlandica	Canker root
Coptis groenlandica	Gold thread
Corallorhiza maculata	Coral root
Corallorhiza maculata	Crawley
Corallorhiza maculata	Spotted coral root
Corallorhiza odontorhiza	Coral root
Corallorhiza odontorhiza	Crawley
Corallorhiza odontorhiza	Spotted coral root
Corylus cornuta	Beaked hazel
Corylus cornuta	Filbert
Corylus cornuta	Hazelnut
Cynoglossum officinale	Hound's tongue
Cynoglossum officinale	Stickers
Cypripedium calceolus	Lady's slipper
Cypripedium calceolus	Moccasin flower
Cypripedium calceolus	Nerve root
Cypripedium calceolus	Yellow lady's slipper
Daucus carota	Carrot
Daucus carota	Queen anne's lace
Daucus carota	Wild carrot
Dicentra canadensis	Dutchman's breeches
Dicentra canadensis	Squirrel corn

Dicentra cucullaria . . . . *Dutchman's breeches*
Dicentra cucullaria . . . . *Squirrel corn*
Dicranium spoparium . . . . *Broom moss*
Epigaea repens . . . . *Arbutus*
Epigaea repens . . . . *Ground laurel*
Epigaea repens . . . . *Mayflowere*
Epigaea repens . . . . *Trailing arbutus*
Erigeron canadensis . . . . *Butterweed*
Erigeron canadensis . . . . *Fleabane*
Erigeron canadensis . . . . *Horsetail fleabane*
Erigeron canadensis . . . . *Horseweed*
Erythronium americanum . . . . *Adder's tongue*
Erythronium americanum . . . . *Dog toothed violet*
Erythronium americanum . . . . *Trout lily*
Eupatorium perfoliatum . . . . *Boneset*
Eupatorium perfoliatum . . . . *Thoroughwort*
Eupatorium purpureum . . . . *Joe-pye weed*
Fagus americana . . . . *Beech*
Fagus americana . . . . *Beechnut*
Fagus grandifolia . . . . *Beech*
Fagus grandifolia . . . . *Beechnut*
Fontinalis . . . . *Brook moss*
Fragaria virginiana . . . . *Strawberry*
Fraxinus americana . . . . *Ash*
Fraxinus americana . . . . *White ash*
Galium aparine . . . . *Bedstraw*
Galium aparine . . . . *Cleavers*
Galium aparine . . . . *Clivers*
Galium aparine . . . . *Goose grass*
Galium aparine . . . . *Stickers*
Gaultheria procumbens . . . . *Checkerberry*
Gaultheria procumbens . . . . *Teaberry*
Gaultheria procumbens . . . . *Wintergreen*
Geranium maculatum . . . . *Alum root*
Geranium maculatum . . . . *Crane's bill*
Geranium maculatum . . . . *Geranium*
Geranium maculatum . . . . *Wild geranium*
Geum rivale . . . . *Avens*
Geum rivale . . . . *Chocolate root*
Geum rivale . . . . *Purple water avens*

Hamamelis virginiana . . . . *Witch hazel*
Hedeoma pulegioides . . . . *American pennyroyal*
Hedeoma pulegioides . . . . *Mock pennyroyal*
Hedeoma pulegioides . . . . *Pennyroyal*
Hedeoma pulegioides . . . . *Pulioll-royall*
Helianthus annuus . . . . *Common sunflower*
Helianthus annuus . . . . *Sunflower*
Helianthus tuberosus . . . . *Jerusalem artichoke*
Helianthus tuberosus . . . . *Sunflower*
Hemerocallis fulva . . . . *Day lily*
Hemerocallis fulva . . . . *Orange day lily*
Hepatica acutiloba . . . . *Hepatica*
Hepatica acutiloba . . . . *Liverleaf*
Hepatica acutiloba . . . . *Liverwort*
Hepatica acutiloba . . . . *Sharp-lobed hepatica*
Heracleum lanatum . . . . *Cow parsnip*
Heracleum lanatum . . . . *Masterwort*
Humulus lupulus . . . . *Hops*
Hydrastis canadensis . . . . *Golden seal*
Hydrastis canadensis . . . . *Orangeroot*
Hydrastis canadensis . . . . *Yellow puccoon*
Hydrastis canadensis . . . . *Yellowroot*
Hypericum perforatum . . . . *Saint John's wort*
Hylocomium splendens . . . . *Mountain fern moss*
Hylocomium splendens . . . . *Stairstep moss*
Hypnum cupressiforme . . . . *Cypress-leaved feather moss*
Impatiens capensis . . . . *Celandine*
Impatiens capensis . . . . *Jewelweed*
Impatiens capensis . . . . *Lady's earrings*
Impatiens capensis . . . . *Snapweed*
Impatiens capensis . . . . *Touch-me-not*
Iris versicolor . . . . *Blue flag*
Iris versicolor . . . . *Fleur-de-lys*
Iris versicolor . . . . *Wild iris*
Juglans cinerea . . . . *Butternut*
Juglans cinerea . . . . *White walnut*
Juglans nigra . . . . *Black walnut*
Juniperus communis . . . . *Juniper*
Lactuca scariola . . . . *Lettuce*
Lactuca scariola . . . . *Milkweed*

Lactuca scariola . . . . *Prickly lettuce*
Lactuca serriola . . . . *Lettuce*
Lactuca serriola . . . . *Milkweed*
Lactuca serriola . . . . *Prickly lettuce*
Lathyrus japonicus . . . . *Beach pea*
Lathyrus japonicus . . . . *Japanese beach pea*
Lathyrus japonicus . . . . *Wild pea*
Ledum groenlandicum . . . . *Labrador tea*
Leonurus cardiaca . . . . *Motherwort*
Lithospermum canescens . . . . *Hoary puccoon*
Lithospermum canescens . . . . *Indian paint*
Lobelia inflata . . . . *Indian tobacco*
Lobelia inflata . . . . *Lobelia*
Lobelia inflata . . . . *Wild tobacco*
Lycopus virginicus . . . . *Bugleweed*
Lycopus virginicus . . . . *Water-horehound*
Malus spp . . . . *Apple*
Marchantia polymorpha . . . . *Common liverwort*
Marrubium vulgare . . . . *Horehound*
Matricaria matricarioides . . . . *Pineapple weed*
Matricaria matricarioides . . . . *Wild chamomile*
Medicago sativa . . . . *Alfalfa*
Medicago sativa . . . . *Lucerne*
Menispermum canadense . . . . *Canada moonseed*
Menispermum canadense . . . . *Yellow parilla*
Mentha piperita . . . . *Peppermint*
Mentha spicata . . . . *Spearmint*
Mitchella repens . . . . *Partridge berry*
Mitchella repens . . . . *Squaw berry*
Mitchella repens . . . . *Squaw plum*
Mitchella repens . . . . *Squaw vine*
Monarda fistulosa . . . . *Wild bergamont*
Monarda fistulosa . . . . *Wild oregano*
Monotropa uniflora . . . . *Convulsion-root*
Monotropa uniflora . . . . *Corpse-plant*
Monotropa uniflora . . . . *Fits-root*
Monotropa uniflora . . . . *Indian pipe*
Morchella angusticeps . . . . *Black morel*
Morchella angusticeps . . . . *Morels*
Morchella angusticeps . . . . *White morel*

Morchella deliciosa . . . . Black morel
Morchella deliciosa . . . . Morels
Morchella deliciosa . . . . White morel
Morchella esculenta . . . . Black morel
Morchella esculenta . . . . Morels
Morchella esculenta . . . . White morel
Morchella semilibera . . . . Black morel
Morchella semilibera . . . . Morels
Morchella semilibera . . . . White morel
Morus rubra . . . . Mulberry
Morus rubra . . . . Red mulberry
Myrica gale . . . . Bog gale
Myrica gale . . . . Gale
Myrica gale . . . . Sweet gale
Nasturtium officinale . . . . Watercress
Nepeta cataria . . . . Catmint
Nepeta cataria . . . . Catnip
Osmorhiza longistylis . . . . Anise-root
Osmorhiza longistylis . . . . Sweet cicely
Osmunda cinnamonea . . . . Buckhorn
Osmunda cinnamonea . . . . Cinnamon-fern
Osmunda cinnamonea . . . . Fiddle-heads
Panax quinquefolius . . . . Ginseng
Panax quinquefolius . . . . Sang
Philonotis fontana . . . . Aquatic apple moss
Phytolacca americana . . . . Garget
Phytolacca americana . . . . Pigeonberry
Phytolacca americana . . . . Poke salad
Phytolacca americana . . . . Poke
Phytolacca americana . . . . Pokeweed
Phytolacca americana . . . . Scoke
Pinus strobus . . . . White pine
Plantago major . . . . Plantain
Plantago major . . . . Whiteman's foot
Podophyllum peltatum . . . . Jalap
Podophyllum peltatum . . . . Mandrake
Podophyllum peltatum . . . . May apple
Podophyllum peltatum . . . . Wild jalap
Polygala senega . . . . Seneca-snakeroot
Polygonatum biflorum . . . . Solomon's seal

Polytrichum commune . . . . *Common hairy cap moss*
Populus balsamifera . . . . *Balsam poplar*
Populus balsamifera . . . . *Hackmatack*
Prunella vulgaris . . . . *Carpenter-weed*
Prunella vulgaris . . . . *Heal-all*
Prunella vulgaris . . . . *Self-heal*
Prunus serotina . . . . *Black cherry*
Prunus serotina . . . . *Rum cherry*
Prunus serotina . . . . *Wild cherry*
Pyrola rotundifolia . . . . *Round-leaved pyrola*
Pyrola rotundifolia . . . . *Shinleaf*
Pyrola rotundifolia . . . . *Wintergreen*
Racomitrium canescens . . . . *Woolly moss*
Racomitrium lanuginosum . . . . *Woolly moss*
Rhodobryum ontariense . . . . *Rose moss*
Rhus glabra . . . . *Smooth sumac*
Rhus glabra . . . . *Staghorn sumac*
Rhus glabra . . . . *Sumac*
Rhus typhina . . . . *Smooth sumac*
Rhus typhina . . . . *Staghorn sumac*
Rhus typhina . . . . *Sumac*
Ribes americanum . . . . *Wild black currant*
Rosa spp . . . . *Rose hips*
Rosa spp . . . . *Rose*
Rosa spp . . . . *Wild rose*
Rubus spp . . . . *Blackberry*
Rubus spp . . . . *Blackcap*
Rubus spp . . . . *Dewberry*
Rubus spp . . . . *Raspberry*
Rubus spp . . . . *Thimbleberry*
Rumex crispus . . . . *Curly dock*
Rumex crispus . . . . *Dock*
Rumex crispus . . . . *Yellow dock*
Salix alba . . . . *Black willow*
Salix alba . . . . *Swamp willow*
Salix alba . . . . *White willow*
Salix alba . . . . *Willow*
Salix nigra . . . . *Black willow*
Salix nigra . . . . *Swamp willow*
Salix nigra . . . . *White willow*

395

Salix nigra	*Willow*
Sanguinaria canadensis	*Bloodroot*
Sanguinaria canadensis	*Red puccoon*
Sarracenia purpurea	*Huntsman's cup*
Sarracenia purpurea	*Pitcher-plant*
Sarracenia purpurea	*Sidesaddle flower*
Sassafras albidum	*Sassafras*
Scrophularia marilandica	*Carpenter's square*
Scrophularia marilandica	*Figwort*
Scrophularia marilandica	*Maryland figwort*
Scrophularia marilandica	*Pilewort*
Scrophularia marilandica	*Scrofula plant*
Scutellaria lateriflora	*Mad-dog skullcap*
Scutellaria lateriflora	*Mad-dog weed*
Solanum dulcamara	*Bittersweet*
Solanum dulcamara	*Nightshade*
Sorbus americana	*Missey-moosey*
Sorbus americana	*Mountain ash*
Sorbus americana	*Roundwood*
Sphagnum	*Peat moss*
Symphytum officinale	*Comfrey*
Symplocarpus foetidus	*Dracontium*
Symplocarpus foetidus	*Skunk cabbage*
Tanacetum vulgare	*Golden-buttons*
Tanacetum vulgare	*Tansy*
Taraxacum officinale	*Dandelion*
Thuja occidentalis	*Arbor-vitae*
Thuja occidentalis	*White cedar*
Trifolium pratense	*Cleavergrass*
Trifolium pratense	*Clover*
Trifolium pratense	*Red clover*
Trillium erectum	*Purple trillium*
Trillium erectum	*Squawroot*
Trillium erectum	*Stinking benjamin*
Trillium erectum	*Trillium*
Typha latifolia	*Bulrush*
Typha latifolia	*Cattail*
Typha latifolia	*Flag*
Urtica dioica	*Nettle*
Urtica dioica	*Stinging nettle*

Vaccinium angustifolium . . . . *Bilberry*
Vaccinium angustifolium . . . . *Blueberry*
Vaccinium angustifolium . . . . *Huckleberry*
Vaccinium macrocarpon . . . . *American cranberry*
Vaccinium macrocarpon . . . . *Bog cranberry*
Vaccinium macrocarpon . . . . *Cranberry*
Verbascum thapsus . . . . *Aaron's rod*
Verbascum thapsus . . . . *Flannel-plant*
Verbascum thapsus . . . . *Indian tobacco*
Verbascum thapsus . . . . *Mullein*
Viburnum opulus . . . . *Cramp bark*
Viburnum opulus . . . . *Geulder-rose*
Viburnum opulus . . . . *Nanny berry*
Viburnum trilobum . . . . *Cranberry*
Viburnum trilobum . . . . *Highbush-cranberry*
Viburnum trilobum . . . . *Pimbina*
Viola papilionaceae . . . . *Blue violet*
Viola papilionaceae . . . . *Viola*
Viola papilionaceae . . . . *Violet*

Family Names—Latin Names

Agaricaceae . . . . *Armillariella mella*
Agaricaceae . . . . *Coprinus comatus*
Amaranthaceae . . . . *Amaranthus retroflexus*
Anacardiaceae . . . . *Rhus glabra*
Anacardiaceae . . . . *Rhus typhina*
Apocynaceae . . . . *Apocynum androsaemifolium*
Apocynaceae . . . . *Apocynum cannabinum*
Araceae . . . . *Acorus calamus*
Araceae . . . . *Arisaema triphyllum*
Araceae . . . . *Symplocarpus foetidus*
Araliaceae . . . . *Aralia hispida*
Araliaceae . . . . *Aralia nudicaulis*
Araliaceae . . . . *Aralia racemosa*
Araliaceae . . . . *Panax quinquefolius*
Aristolochiaceae . . . . *Asarum canadense*
Asclepiadaceae . . . . *Asclepias syriaca*
Asclepiadaceae . . . . *Asclepias tuberosa*
Ascomycetes . . . . *Morchella angusticeps*
Ascomycetes . . . . *Morchella deliciosa*
Ascomycetes . . . . *Morchella esculenta*
Ascomycetes . . . . *Morchella semilibera*
Bartramiaceae . . . . *Philonotis fontana*
Berberidaceae . . . . *Berberis vulgaris*
Berberidaceae . . . . *Caulophyllum thalictroides*
Balsaminaceae . . . . *Impatiens capensis*
Berberidaceae . . . . *Podophyllum peltatum*
Betulaceae . . . . *Alnus rugosa*
Betulaceae . . . . *Betula alleghaniensis*
Betulaceae . . . . *Corylus cornuta*
Boraginaceae . . . . *Cynoglossum officinale*
Boraginaceae . . . . *Lithospermum canescens*
Boraginaceae . . . . *Symphytum officinale*
Bryaceae . . . . *Rhodobryum ontariense*
Campanulaceae . . . . *Lobelia inflata*
Cannabinaceae . . . . *Cannabis sativa*
Cannabinaceae . . . . *Humulus lupulus*
Caprifoliaceae . . . . *Viburnum opulus*
Caprifoliaceae . . . . *Viburnum trilobum*

398

Celastraceae . . . . *Celastrus scandens*
Chenopodiaceae . . . . *Chenopodium album*
Compositae . . . . *Achillea lanulosa*
Compositae . . . . *Achillea millefolium*
Compositae . . . . *Anaphalis margaritacea*
Compositae . . . . *Arctium lappa*
Compositae . . . . *Arctium minus*
Compositae . . . . *Artemisia absinthium*
Compositae . . . . *Cichorium intybus*
Compositae . . . . *Erigeron canadensis*
Compositae . . . . *Eupatorium perfoliatum*
Compositae . . . . *Helianthus annuus*
Compositae . . . . *Helianthus tuberosus*
Compositae . . . . *Lactuca scariola*
Compositae . . . . *Lactuca serriola*
Compositae . . . . *Matricaria matricarioides*
Compositae . . . . *Tanacetum vulgare*
Compositae . . . . *Taraxacum officinale*
Cruciferae . . . . *Barbarea vulgaris*
Cruciferae . . . . *Capsella bursa-pastoris*
Cruciferae . . . . *Nasturtium officinale*
Dicranaceae . . . . *Dicranum spoparium*
Ericaceae . . . . *Arctostaphylos uva-ursi*
Ericaceae . . . . *Epigaea repens*
Ericaceae . . . . *Gaultheria procumbens*
Ericaceae . . . . *Ledum groenlandicum*
Ericaceae . . . . *Vaccinium angustifolium*
Ericaceae . . . . *Vaccinium macrocarpon*
Fagaceae . . . . *Fagus americana*
Fagaceae . . . . *Fagus grandifolia*
Fontinalaceae . . . . *Fontinalis*
Fumariaceae . . . . *Dicentra canadensis*
Fumariaceae . . . . *Dicentra cucullaria*
Geraniaceae . . . . *Geranium maculatum*
Grimmiaceae . . . . *Racomitrium canescens*
Grimmiaceae . . . . *Racomitrium lanuginosum*
Hamamelidaceae . . . . *Hamamelis virginiana*
Hippocastanaceae . . . . *Aesculus hippocastanum*
Hylocomiaceae . . . . *Hylocomium splendens*
Hypericaceae . . . . *Hypericum perforatum*

Hypnaceae .... *Hypnum cupressiforme*
Iridaceae .... *Iris versicolor*
Juglandaceae .... *Juglans cinerea*
Juglandaceae .... *Juglans nigra*
Labiatae .... *Hedeoma pulegioides*
Labiatae .... *Leonurus cardiaca*
Labiatae .... *Lycopus virginicus*
Labiatae .... *Marrubium vulgare*
Labiatae .... *Mentha piperita*
Labiatae .... *Mentha spicata*
Labiatae .... *Monarda fistulosa*
Labiatae .... *Nepeta cataria*
Labiatae .... *Prunella vulgaris*
Labiatae .... *Scutellaria lateriflora*
Lauraceae .... *Sassafras albidum*
Leguminosae .... *Baptisia tinctoria*
Leguminosae .... *Lathyrus japonicus*
Leguminosae .... *Medicago sativa*
Leguminosae .... *Trifolium pratense*
Liliaceae .... *Aletris farinosa*
Liliaceae .... *Allium tricoccum*
Liliaceae .... *Asparagus officinale*
Liliaceae .... *Chamaelirium luteum*
Liliaceae .... *Erythronium americanum*
Liliaceae .... *Hemerocallis fulva*
Liliaceae .... *Polygonatum biflorum*
Liliaceae .... *Trillium erectum*
Marchantiaceae .... *Conocephalum conicum*
Marchantiaceae .... *Marchantia polymorpha*
Menispermaceae .... *Menispermum canadense*
Moraceae .... *Morus rubra*
Myricaceae .... *Myrica gale*
Myricaceae .... *Comptonia peregrina*
Oleaceae .... *Fraxinus americana*
Orchidaceae .... *Aplectrum hymale*
Orchidaceae .... *Corallorhiza maculata*
Orchidaceae .... *Corallorhiza odontorhiza*
Orchidaceae .... *Cypripedium calceolus*
Osmundaceae .... *Osmunda cinnamonea*
Papaveraceae .... *Sanguinaria canadensis*

Phytolaccaceae	*Phytolacca americana*
Pinaceae	*Abies balsamea*
Pinaceae	*Pinus strobus*
Pinaceae	*Thuja occidentalis*
Pinaceae (Cupressaceae)	*Juniperus communis*
Plantaginaceae	*Plantago major*
Polygalaceae	*Polygala senega*
Polygalaceae	*Rumex crispus*
Polypodiaceae	*Adiantum capillus-veneris*
Polypodiaceae	*Adiantum pedatum*
Polytrichaeae	*Polytrichum commune*
Portulacaceae	*Claytonia virginica*
Pyrolaceae	*Chimaphila umbellata*
Pyrolaceae	*Pyrola rotundifolia*
Pyrolaceae (Ericaceae)	*Monotropa uniflora*
Ranunculaceae	*Actaea alba*
Ranunculaceae	*Actaea arguta*
Ranunculaceae	*Anemone canadensis*
Ranunculaceae	*Aquilegia canadensis*
Ranunculaceae	*Caltha palustris*
Ranunculaceae	*Coptis groenlandica*
Ranunculaceae	*Hepatica acutiloba*
Ranunculaceae	*Hydrastis canadensis*
Rhamnaceae	*Ceanothus americanus*
Rosaceae	*Amelanchier spp*
Rosaceae	*Fragaria virginiana*
Rosaceae	*Geum rivale*
Rosaceae	*Malus spp*
Rosaceae	*Prunus serotina*
Rosaceae	*Rosa spp*
Rosaceae	*Rubus spp*
Rosaceae	*Sorbus americana*
Rubiaceae	*Galium aparine*
Rubiaceae	*Mitchella repens*
Salicaceae	*Populus balsamifera*
Salicaceae	*Salix alba*
Salicaceae	*Salix nigra*
Sarraceniaceae	*Sarracenia purpurea*
Saxifragaceae	*Ribes americanum*
Scrophulariaceae	*Chelone glabra*

Scrophulariaceae	*Scrophularia marilandica*
Scrophulariaceae	*Verbascum thapsus*
Solanaceae	*Solanum dulcamara*
Sphagnaceae	*Sphagnum*
Typhaceae	*Typha latifolia*
Umbelliferae	*Angelica atropurpurea*
Umbelliferae	*Cicuta bulbifera*
Umbelliferae	*Cicuta maculata*
Umbelliferae	*Conium maculatum*
Umbelliferae	*Daucus carota*
Umbelliferae	*Heracleum lanatum*
Umbelliferae	*Osmorhiza longistylis*
Urticaceae	*Urtica dioica*
Violaceae	*Viola papilionaceae*

Bibliography

1. Allport, N. L. 1944. *The Chemistry and Pharmacy of Vegetable Drugs*. Chemical Publishing Company, Inc. Brooklyn, NY.

2. American Pharmaceutical Association. 1942. *The National Formulary Seventh Edition*. American Pharmaceutical Assocn. Washington, DC.

3. Ash, A. L. 1948. Hemp—production and utilization. *Economic Botany*. 2:158-169.

4. Baker, H. G. 1970. *Plants and Civilization*. Wadsworth Publishing Company, Inc. Belmont, CA.

5. Bentley, R. and H. Trimen. 1880. *Medicinal Plants*, Four Volumes. J. and A. Churchill, New Burlington Street, London, England.

6. Berkman, B. 1949. Milkweed—a war strategic material and a potential industrial crop for submarginal lands in the U. S., *Economic Botany* 3:223-239.

7. Boruttan and Cappenberg. 1921. *Capsella bursa-pastoris*. Arch. Pharm. 259:33. In *Year Book of the American Pharmaceutical Association* Vol. 10:219.

8. Conway, D. 1976. *The Magic Herbs*. E. P. Dutton & Co. Inc. New York, NY.

9. Core, E. L. 1967. Ethnobotany of the southern Appalachian aborigines. *Economic Botany*, 21:199-214.

10. Densmore, F. 1928. *How Indians Use Wild Plants for Food, Medicine, and Crafts*. Dover Publishing Co, Inc. New York, NY.

11. Edwardson, J. R. 1952. Hops—their botany, history, production and utilization. *Economic Botany* 6:160-175.

12. Ellis, N. K. and Stevenson, E. C. 1950. Domestic production of the essential oils of peppermint and spearmint. *Economic Botany* 4:139-149.

13. Farwell, O. A. 1916. *The proper time to collect Sanguinaria*. Papers From Research Lab: Parke, Davis and Co. Detroit, MI. 4:467-468.

14. Farwell, O. A. 1919. Cramp bark, highbush cranberry. *The Northwestern Druggist*. In Collected Papers From the Medical Research Laboratories, Parke, Davis and Company. 8:277-278

15. Fernald, M. L., A. C. Kinsey, and R. C. Rollins. 1961. *Edible Wild Plants of Eastern North America*. Harper and Row Publishers, NY.

16. Fernald, M. L. 1950. *Gray's Manual of Botany*. American Book Co. New York, NY.

17. Fulling, E. H. 1953. American witch hazel—history, nomenclature and modern utilization. *Economic Botany* 7:359-381.

18. Gibbons, E. 1962. *Stalking the Wild Asparagus*. David Mckay Company, Inc. NY.

19. Gibbons, E. 1966. *Stalking the Healthful Herbs*. David Mckay and Company, Inc. NY.

20. Gleason, H. A. and Cronquist, A. 1963. *Manual of Vascular Plants of the Northeastern United States and Adjacent Canada*. D. Van Nostrand Company, Princeton, NJ.

21. Gleason, H. A. 1963. *The New Britton and Brown Illustrated Flora of the Northeastern United States and Adjacent Canada*. 3 Volumes., Hafner Publishing Company, Inc. NY.

22. Grieve, M. 1931. *A Modern Herbal*. 2 volumes. Harcourt, Brace and Company, NY.

23. Grinell, G. B. 1905. Cheyenne plant medicine. *American Anthropologist*. 7:37-45.

24. Grinell, G. B. 1923. *The Cheyenne Indians: Their History and Ways of Life*. 2 volumes. Yale University Press.

25. Hall, A. 1973. *The Wild Food Trail Guide*. Holt, Rinehart, and Winston. NY.

26. Hamilton, H. C., Lescohier, A. W. and Perkins, R. A. 1913. *The physiological activity of Cannabis sativa. Journal of the American Pharmaceutical Association*. 2:22-30. In Collected Papers From the Research Labratory Parke, Davis and Co. Detroit, MI. 2:311.

27. Harris, B. C. 1972. *The Compleat Herbal*. Barre Pub., Barre, MA.

28. Herz, W., Kalyanaraman, P. S., Ramakrishnan, G., and Blout, J. F. 1977. Sesquiterpene lactones of *Eupatorium perfoliatum*. *Journal of Organic Chemistry* 42:2264-2771.

29. Hill, A. F. 1952. *Economic Botany*. McGraw-Hill Book Company, Inc. NY.

30. Hutchens, A. R. 1969. *Indian Herbology of North America*. Homeo Hous Press, Kumbakonam S. India.

31. Jenkins, G. L. and W. H. Hartung 1941. *The Chemistry of Organic Medicinal Products*. John Wiley and Sons, Inc. New York, NY.

32. Johnson, L. 1884. *Medicinal Botany of North America*. William Wood and Company NY.

33. Kingsbury, J. M. 1964. *Poisonous Plants of the United States and Canada*. Prentice Hall, Inc., Englewood Cliffs, NJ.

34. Kirk, D. R. 1970. *Wild Edible Plants of the Western United States*. Naturegraph Publishers, Healdsburg, CA.

35. Kloss, J. 1971. *Back To Eden*. Lancer Books, Inc. NY.

36. Krochmal, A. and C. Krochmal. 1973. *A Guide To Medicinal Plants of the United States*. Quadrangle/New York Times Book Co. NY.

37. Krochmal, A. 1968. Medicinal plants and Appalachia. *Economic Botany*, 22:332-337.

38. Krochmal, A., R. S. Walters, R. M. Doughty. 1971. *A Guide To Medicinal Plants of Appalachia*. Agriculture Hndbk No. 400 USDA.

39. Krochmal, A., S. Paur, and P. Duisberg. 1954. Useful native plants in the American southwestern deserts. *Economic Botany* 8:3-20.

40. Lewis, W. H. and Elvin-Lewis, M. P. F. 1977. *Medical Botany Plants Affecting Man's Health*. John Wiley & Sons, New York, NY.

41. Lust, B. 1961. *About Herbs: Medicines From the Meadows*. Benedict Lust Publications. London, England.

42. Massey, J. S. 1976. Ginseng, folkelore, cure all, is being regarded seriously. *Smithsonian* 6:105-111.

43. McMurray, R. L. 1933. *Achillea millefolium, linne. constituents of the petroleum ether extract of the blossoms*. Am J. Pharm. 105:573-582.

44. Meyer, C. 1960. *The Herbalist*. Clarence Meyer Publishing.

45. Moldenke, H. N. 1954. The economic plants of the Bible. *Economic Botany* 8:152-163.

46. Muenscher, W. C. 1951. *Poisonous Plants of the United States*. The Macmillan Company, New York, NY.

47. Naegele, Thomas A. 1974. *Edible Wild Plants of the Copper Country*. Greenlee Printing, Calumet, MI.

48. Nagata, K. M. 1971. Hawaiian medicinal plants. *Economic Botany* 25:245-262.

49. Porterfield, B. 1977. *Our Michigan herbal*. The Michigan Natural Resources Magazine 46:17-32.

50. Rose, J. 1972. *Herbs and Things*. Grosset and Dunlap. NY.

51. Sayer, L. U. 1905. *A Manual of Organic Materia Medica and Pharmacognosy*. P. Blakiston's Son and Co. Philadelphia, PA.

52. Scully, V. 1970. *A Treasury of American Indian Herbs, Their Lore and Their Use For Food, Drugs, and Medicine*. Bonanza, NY.

53. Sievers, A. F. 1947. The production of minor essential oils in the United States. *Economic Botany* 1:148-160.

54. Smith, H. V. 1966. *Michigan Wild Flowers*. The Cranbrook Press. Bloomfield Hills, MI.

55. Spencer, E. R. 1940. *All About Weeds*. Dover Publications NY.

56. Stuhr, E. T. 1948. The distribution, abundance and uses of wild drug plants in Oregon and southern California. *Economic Botany* 1:57-68.

57. Suter, C. M.: Editor-In-Chief. 1951. *Medicinal Chemistry*. 3 volumes. John Wiley and Sons, Inc. London.

58. Tehon, L. R. 1951. *The Drug Plants of Illinois*. Illinois Natural History Survey Circular 44.

59. The Pharmacopoeia of the United States of America. 1947. *The Pharmacopoeia of the United States of America*. Mack Printing Company, Easton, PA.

60. Turner, N. C. and Bell, M. A. M. 1971. The ethnobotany of the coast Salish Indians of Vancover Island. *Economic Botany* 25:63-99.

61. Van Urk, H. W. 1921. Over de werkzame bestanddeelen van *Capsella bursa-pastoris*. J. Soc. Chem. Ind. 40:409a In *Year Book of the American Pharmaceutical Association*. 10:219.

62. Verrill, A. H. 1937. *Foods America Gave the World*. L. C. Page and Company, Clinton, MA.

63. Vogel, V. J. 1970. *American Indian Medicine*. University of Okalahoma Press, NY.

64. Wallis, W. D. 1922. *Medicines used by the Micmac Indians*. American Anthropologist. 24:24-30.

65. Williams, L. O. 1957. Ginseng. *Economic Botany* 11:344-348.

66. Williams, L. O. 1960. *Drug and Condiment Plants*, Agriculture Handbook No. 172 USDA.

67. Woodward, E. F. 1947. Botanical drugs—a brief review of the industry with comments on recent development. *Economic Botany* 1:402-414.

68. Wren, R. C. 1972. *Potter's New Cyclopaedia of Medicinal Herbs and Preparations*. Harper & Row, Publishers. NY.

69. Youngken, H. W. 1924. *The drugs of the North American Indian*. American Journal of Pharmacy, 96:485-502.

70. Youngken, H. W. 1925. *The drugs of the North American Indians (II)*. American Journal of Pharmacy. 97:158-185.

71. Youngken, H. W. 1932. *The pharmacognosy, chemistry and pharmacology of Viburnam*. III. history, botany and pharmacognosy of *Viburnam opulus* 1. var. americanum (miller) ait. Journal of American Pharmaceutical Association. 21:444-462.

72. Zaricor, B. R. and L. Veninga. 1976. *Golden Seal/Etc. A Pharmacognosy of Wild Herbs*. Ruka Publications, Santa Cruz, CA.

73. Smith, H. H. 1928. *Ethnobotany of the Meskwaki Indians*. Bulletin of the Public Museum of City of Milwaukee 4:175-326.

74. Smith, H. H. 1923. *Ethnobotany of the Menomini Indians*. Bulletin of the Public Museum of City of Milwaukee 4:1-174

75. Smith, H. H. 1932. *Ethnobotany of the Ojibwe Indians*. Bulletin of the Public Museum of the City of Milwaukee 4:330-522.

76. Smith, H. H. 1933. *Ethnobotany of the Forest Potawatomi Indians*. Bulletin of the Public Museum of the City of Milwaukee 7:1-230.

77. Center for Disease Control. 1978. *Fatality and illness associated with consumption of pennyroyal oil-Colorado*. Morbidity and Mortality Weekly Report. 27:511-513.

78. Harrington, H.D. 1972. *Western Edible Wild Plants*. The New Mexico Press, Alburquerque, NM.

79. U. S. Army 1969. *Survival, Evasion, and Escape*. FM21-76. U. S. Government Printing Office. Washington, DC.

80. Goodman, L.S. and A. Gilman. 1975. *The Pharmacological Basis of Therapeutics (fifth ed.)*. MacMillan Publishing Co., Inc. New York, NY.

81. Tisserand, Robert. 1977. *The Art of Aromatherapy*. The C. W. Daniel Company Ltd., London, England.

82. Tyler, V.E., Brady, L.R., and Robbers, J.E. *Pharmacognosy*. 1976 Leigh and Febiger, Philadelphia, PA.

83. British Herbal Medicine Association. 1976. *British Herbal Pharmacopoeia. Part One*. British Herbal Medicine Association, London.

84. British Herbal Medicine Association. 1979. *British Herbal Pharmacopoeia. Part Two*. British Herbal Medicine Association, W Yorks.

85. Roody, William. 1981. *Nettle Roots*. Coltsfoot. volume 2, number 6. Shipman, VA.

86. Champman, William. 1981. *Wild Sprouts*. Coltsfoot. volume 2, number 5. Shipman, VA.

87. Roody, William. 1982. *Wintergreen*. Coltsfoot. volume 3, number 1. Shipman, VA.

88. Chapman, William 1982. *Wild Foods Calendar*. Coltsfoot. volume 3, number 1. Shipman, VA.

89. Roody, William. 1982. *Marsh Marigold*. Coltsfoot. volume 3, number 2. Shipman, VA.

90. Maze, Sara. 1982. *Balm of Gilead Salve*. Coltsfoot. volume 3, number 2. Shipman, VA.

91. Arena, Jay M. 1981. Plants That Poison. *Emergency Medicine*. June 15, 1981.

92. Pellet, Frank C. 1976. *American Honey Plants*. Dandant and Sons, Inc., Carthage, IL.

93. Lovell, Harvey B. 1966. *Honey Plants Manual*. A. I. Root Company, Louisville, KY.

94. Davis, Patricia. 1988. *Aromatherapy an A-Z Saffron Walden*. The C.W. Daniel Company Limited, Essex, England.

95. Stafford, Peter 1978, 1983, 1992. *Psychedelics Encyclopedia*. Ronin Publishing, Inc. Berkeley, CA.

96. Der Marderosian, Ara and Liberti, Lawrence. 1988. *Natural Product Medicine. A scientific guide to foods, drugs, cosmetics*. George F. Stickley, Co. Philadelphia, PA.

97. Liebes, L, Mazur, Y, Freeman, D, Lavie, D and others. *Annals of Biochemistry* 1991, May 15:195 A method for the quantitation of hypericin, an antiviral agent, in biological fluids by high-performance liquid chromatography.

98. Adamek, W. 1976. *Introductory report on oncostatic and therapeutic nature of the peat preparation in human neoplastic disease*. In Proc. 5th Internat. Peat Congr., Poznabn, Poland, Vol. 1 (Peat & Peatlands in the Natural Environment Protection.), Pp. 417-429.

99. Ando, H. 1972. *Uses of bryophytes seen in Europe*. Proc. Bryol. soc. Jap. 1: 25.

100. Ando, H. 1983. *Use of bryophytes in China 2. Mosses indispensable to the production of Chinese gallnuts*. Proc. Bryol. Soc. Jap. 3: 124-125.

101. Asakawa, Y. 1981. *Biologically active substances obtained from bryophytes*. J. Hattori Bot. Lab. 50: 123-142.

102. Asakawa, Y. 1982. *Chemical constituents of the Hepaticae*. Prog. Chem. Org. Natur. Prod. 42: 1-285.

103. Black, D. (ed.). 1979. *Carl Linnaeus, Travels*. NY.

104. Bland, J. 1971. *Forests of Lilliput*. Prentice-Hall, Englewood, NJ.

105. Cox, R. L. and A. H. Westing. 1963. *The effect of peat-moss extract on seed germination*. Proc. Indiana Acad. Sci. 73: 113-115.

106. Crum, H. 1973. *Mosses of the Great Lakes Forest*. Contributions from the University of Michigan Herbarium. Vol 10.

107. Crum, H. 1988. *A focus on Peatlands and Peat mosses*. University of Michigan Press, Ann Arbor.

108. D'Alessio, D. J., L. J. Leavens, G. B. Strumpf, and C. D. Smith. 1965. *An outbreak of sporotrichosis in Vermont associated with Sphagnum moss as the source of infection*. New England J. Med. 272: 1054-1058.

109. Ding, H. 1982. *Medicinal spore-bearing plants of China*. Shanghai.

110. Flowers, S. 1957. *Ethnobryology of the Gosuite Indians of Utah*. Bryologist 60: 11-14.

111. Frahm, J.-P. 1976. *Weitere Toxitoleranzversuche an Wassermoosen*. Gewässer und Abwässer 60/61: 113-123.

112. Gulabani, A. 1974. *Bryophytes as economic plants*. Botanica 14: 73-75.

113. Hotson, J. W. 1921. *Sphagnum used as a surgical dressing in Germany during the world war*. Bryologist 24: 74-78, 89-96.

114. Hu, R. 1987. *Bryology*. Higher Education Press, Beijing, China.

115. Inoue, H. (ed.). 1980. *Koke engei no subete (All about the moss horticulture)*. Tokyo.

116. Lewis, M. 1981. *Human uses of bryophytes I. Use of mosses for chinking log structures in Alaska*. Bryologist: 571-572.

117. Madsen, G. C. and A. L. Pates. 1952. *Occurrence of antimicrobial substances in chlorophyllose plants growing in Florida*. Bot. Gaz. 113: 293-300.

118. McCain, W. H. and W. F. Buell. 1968. *Primary pulmonary sporotrichosis in Illinois*. Illinois Med. J. 131:255-258.

119. Ochi, H. 1960. *Conocephalum conicum, as a food for a slug*. Hikobia 2(2): 154-155.

120. Pant, G., and S. D. Tewari. 1989. *Various human uses of bryophytes in the Kumaun region of Northwest Himalaya*. Bryologist 92: 120-122.

121. Pant, G., S. D. Tewari, M. C. Pargaien, and L. S. Bisht. 1986. *Bryological activities in North-West Himalaya -- II. A bryophyte foray in the Askot region of district Pithoragarh* (Kumaun Himala-yas). Bryological Times 39: 2,3.

122. Pavletic, Z. and B. Stilinovic. 1963. *Untersuchungen ueber die antibiotische Wirkung von Moosextrakten auf einige Bakterien*. Acta Bot. Croat. 22: 133-139.

123. Poots, V. J. P., G. Mckay and J. J. Healy. 1976. *The removal of acid dye from effluent using natural absorbents I*. Peat Water Res. 10: 1061-1066.

124. Ruel, M., S. Chornet, B. Coupal, P. Aitcin and M. Cossette. 1977. *Industrial utilization of peat moss*. In N. W. Radforth and C. O. Brawner (eds.): Muskeg and the Northern Environment of Canada. Pp. 221-246. Toronto.

125. Samecka-Cymerman, A. 1983. *The effect of phenol on aquatic mosses Fontinalis antipyretica* L. and Platyhypnidium ruscifome Fleisch. in cultures. Polskie Archiwum Hydrobiologii 30: 141-147.

126. Sarosiek, J. and A. Samecka-Cymerman. 1987. *The bioindication of ethylene glycol in water by the mosses Fontinalis antipyretica L. and Platyhypnidium rusciforme* (Neck.) Fleisch. Symposia Biologica Hungarica 35: 835-841.

127. Seaward, M. R. D. and D. Williams. 1976. *An interpretation of mosses found in recent archaeological excavations*. J. Archaeol. Sci. 3: 173-177.

128. Stark, R. M. 1860. *A popular history of British mosses, 2nd edition*. Routledge, Warne, & Routledge, London (Wheldon & Wesley).

129. Sukhanov, M. A. 1972. *The use of peat as a thermal-insulating material in large panel building*. Proc. 4th Int. Peat Congr., Otaniemi, Finland.

130. Tamblyn, S. E. 1981. *Sporotrichosis and Sphagnum moss*. Alberta Social Services & Community Health Newsletter 4(2): 1-3.

131. Taylor, J. A. and R. T. Smith. 1980. *Peat -- a resource reassessed*. Nature 288: 319-320.

132. Thieret, J. W. 1954. *Mosses and liverworts: Old and new uses*. Chicago Nat. Hist. Mus. Bull., Pp. 4, 8.

133. Thieret, J. W. 1956. *Bryophytes as economic plants*. Economic Botany. 10: 75-91.

134. Tripp, F. 1888. *British mosses. Their homes, aspects, structure, and uses*. George Bell & Sons, Covent Garden, London (Wheldon & Wesley), 2 Vols.

135. Varley, S. J. and S. E. Barnett. 1987. *Sphagnum moss and wound healing II*. Clinical Rehabilitation 1: 153-160.

136. Wu, P. C. 1977. *Rhodobryum giganteum (Schwaegr.) Par can be used for curing cardiovascular disease*. Acta Phytotax. Sin. 15: 93.

137. Wu, P. C. 1982. *Some uses of mosses in China*. Bryol. Times 13: 5.

138. Angier, Bradford. *Field Guide to Medicinal Wild Plants*. 1978. Stackpole Books, Harrisburg, PA.

Index